THE GREAT JUDGMENT OF OSIRIS—THE WEIGHING OF THE HEART IN THE BALANCE.

The deceased Hunefer kneeling in prayer before Ra, Tem, Shu, Tefnut, Keb, Nut, Horus, Isis, Nephthys, Hu, Sa, Uat-rest, Uat-meht, Uat Ament.

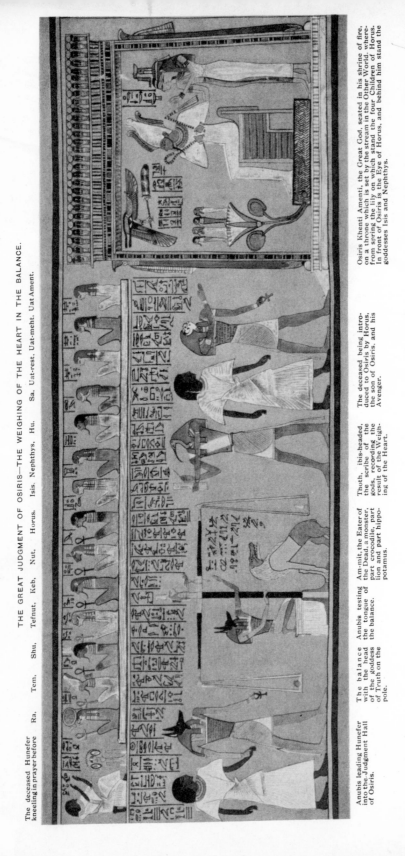

Anubis leading Hunefer into the Judgment Hall of Osiris.

The balance with the head of the goddess of Truth on the pole.

Anubis testing the tongue of the balance.

Am-mit, the Eater of the Dead, a monster, part crocodile, part lion and part hippopotamus.

Thoth, ibis-headed, the scribe of the gods, recording the result of the Weighing of the Heart.

The deceased being introduced to Osiris by Horus, the son of Osiris, and his Avenger.

Osiris Khenti Amenti, the Great God, seated in his shrine of fire, on a throne which is set by the stream in the Other World, wherefrom spring the lily on which stand the four Children of Horus. In front of Osiris is the Eye of Horus, and behind him stand the goddesses Isis and Nephthys.

Texts: A. A prayer recited by the deceased whilst his heart is being weighed before Osiris. Chap. XXXB of the Book of the Dead.

B. The Address of Thoth to the gods announcing the innocence of the deceased, and the result of the weighing.

C. Address of Horus, the Avenger of his father Osiris, who introduces Hunefer to Osiris, and informs him that the tongue of the Balance has remained unmoved, i.e., that the heart of the deceased counterbalances the symbol of Truth exactly.

From the Papyrus of Hunefer in the British Museum, (No. 9901).

OSIRIS AND THE EGYPTIAN RESURRECTION

BY E. A. WALLIS BUDGE
M.A. LITT.D. D.LITT. D.LIT. F.S.A. KEEPER OF THE EGYPTIAN AND ASSYRIAN ANTIQUITIES IN THE BRITISH MUSEUM.
ILLUSTRATED AFTER DRAWINGS FROM EGYPTIAN PAPYRI AND MONUMENTS

In Two Volumes

VOLUME II

DOVER PUBLICATIONS, INC., NEW YORK

This Dover edition, first published in 1973, is an unabridged republication of the work originally published in 1911 by The Medici Society, Ltd.

International Standard Book Number: 0-486-22781-2
Library of Congress Catalog Card Number: 72-81534

Manufactured in the United States of America
Dover Publications, Inc.
180 Varick Street
New York, N. Y. 10014

CONTENTS OF VOLUME II

Contents

ILLUSTRATIONS TO VOLUME II

The Weighing of the Heart of Hunefer in the Judgment
Hall of Osiris.   From the Papyrus of Hunefer in
the British Museum ...   .   *Frontispiece*

OSIRIS AND THE EGYPTIAN RESURRECTION

CHAPTER XIV.

THE SHRINES, MIRACLE PLAY, AND "MYSTERIES" OF OSIRIS.

IT is impossible to state when and where the first shrines in honour of Osiris were built in Egypt, but it is tolerably certain that his most ancient shrine in the South was at Abydos, and his most ancient shrine in the North at Busiris, and that the cult of the god was firmly established in these places at the beginning of, if not before, the Dynastic Period. Of these the older is probably Ȧbṭu (Abydos), for every tradition about the worship of Osiris asserts his head to have been buried there, and the importance of Abydos, even in the earliest times, appears to have been due to the fact that the town contained his head, the most important part of the god's body. Abydos was, moreover, quite near to Neṭȧt, or Neṭit,[1] the town on the Nile, or great canal of the district, near which Osiris was murdered by Set, and it was more natural for Isis when she found her husband's dead body there to take it to Abydos than to some more remote town. And as the symbol of the city and its name was the coffer, or basket, which contained the head of Osiris, with plumes above the coffer and a serpent passing through it, , we may assume that the connection of the city with the cult of Osiris was exceedingly ancient. Ṭaṭṭu (Busiris), in the Delta, which contained the backbone of Osiris , was undoubtedly the most important of all the shrines of Osiris in the North, but it never enjoyed the reputation and fame of Abydos.

1 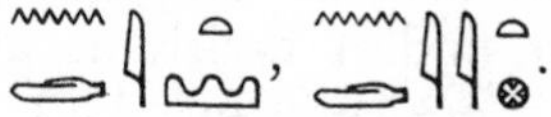

It is idle to speculate on the form of the shrine of Osiris under the first three dynasties, but it was probably a small building made of mud strengthened with reeds, and covered over with a wooden roof. Inside it was probably a figure of the god seated on a throne with steps, and near it was his characteristic symbol, either laid upon the ground, or supported on a stand. The cleaning and preservation of his shrine were, no doubt, committed to the care of a special body of men, who thus became his priests, and received the offerings made to him, and made arrangements for his festivals and for the performance of the annual play, in which his sufferings, death, and resurrection were acted. No details of these matters are found in the earliest texts, but we know from the evidence of the inscriptions that such a play was performed at Abydos once a year under the Middle and New Empires, and it is only reasonable to assume that it reproduced all the essential features of the great annual festival of the god which was celebrated under the Ancient Empire. In religious matters at least the conservatism of the ancient Egyptians was absolute.

When the worship of Osiris was first established at Abydos the inhabitants of the district worshipped Seker, the god of Death, the two Åp-uati gods, Anubis, Ån-ḥer, Khenti Åmenti, etc., but by the close of the VIth dynasty Osiris had become the chief god of the district, and all the local forms of the above-mentioned gods had become subordinate to him. The fame of the god who rose from the dead himself, and could make his followers to rise from death to life immortal, had spread to all parts of Egypt, and the bodies of the wealthy who died in other parts of Egypt were taken there and buried. It was believed that the dead who were buried at Abydos would be joined by the god to his company of followers in the Other World, that they would enjoy his protection, and that they would share in his offerings on festival days, and become partakers with him in immortality and everlasting happiness. The aim of every good man was to become an Osiris, and even in the Pyramid Texts we find it tacitly assumed that the kings for whom they were written had each become an

Osiris, and the name of Osiris is actually prefixed to the names of some of them. Osiris had become the god of the dead, *par excellence*, and Abydos was the earthly centre of his kingdom. Very few Egyptians who were not natives of the neighbourhood could afford to buy tombs there and be buried in them, and the transport of mummified bodies from a great distance was both difficult and costly. Nevertheless, many men were so eager that their dead bodies should rest on the sacred soil of Abydos, and be near Osiris, if only for a short time, that it became the custom among the well-to-do classes to transport the mummies of their kinsfolk to Abydos so that they might absorb the beneficent emanations from the shrine of the god, and be blessed by the influence of the place and its holy associations. These mummies were then taken back by river to the places whence they came, and buried in the tombs which had been provided for them. The popularity of Osiris could not fail to be of material benefit, not only to his priesthood, but also to the town of Abydos in general. The old mud shrine of the god would disappear, and a building made of wood or stone take its place, and his festivals would be celebrated with greater pomp and more lavish display. His priesthood would become wealthy, and every servant of his would benefit in every way by the great fame of his god. During the great festival of Osiris at the end of the year the plain round about Abydos would be thronged with pilgrims from all parts of the country, and at this time the inhabitants would gain enough to last them for the remainder of the year.

The great festival of Shêkh Sayyid al-Badawi at Ṭanṭa offers many parallels to the great festival of Osiris at Abydos. At Ṭanṭa I have seen dead bodies brought in and laid for a few moments by the tomb of the saint, or simply carried round his tomb-chamber, in order to obtain his blessing, and men and women stand motionless and silent by the iron gates of the tomb, merely to be blessed by its presence, and to gain a share in the spiritual benefits which are believed to emanate from it. A large iron box for offerings stands near the tomb gates, and though nine-tenths of the people are very poor, their humble contributions are said to amount to

£E.40,000 a year. Similarly the revenue of Osiris, though all the offerings were in kind, there being no money in Egypt before the reign of Darius, must have been very great, and his landed property large.

Of the history of Abydos and its god Osiris from the end of the VIth to the beginning of the XIIth dynasty we know nothing, but under the kings of the XIIth dynasty the worship of Osiris developed to an extraordinary degree, and his sanctuary attained to a position of importance hitherto unknown. Thus in an inscription published by Daressy,[1] we read that a king, probably Usertsen I, gave to Khenti-Åmenti [Osiris] three metal vases and an ebony censer-holder. From the stele of Khent-em-semti,[2] an official of Åmen-em-ḥāt at Abydos, we learn that Osiris was at that time called the "lord of life," "governor of eternity," and "Ruler of Åmenti," *i.e.*, the Other World, and that Abydos was the place to which all souls flocked to obtain blessing, to eat bread with the god, and to "come forth by day." This official had lived a righteous life, he says, so that Osiris might be gracious to him in judgment, and permit him to enter his holy boat. On the stele of I-kher-nefert we are told that Usertsen III ordered this official to go to Abydos and build a sanctuary for Osiris, and to adorn his shrine with some of the gold which the god had enabled him to bring from Nubia after his victorious campaign in that country. I-kher-nefert carried out his lord's commands, and built a shrine for Osiris made from sweet-smelling woods, and inlaid with gold, silver, and lapis-lazuli, and he made new shrines for the other gods of Abydos. He drew up regulations for the service of the priests, and defined the duties of each of them, and made careful arrangements for the celebration of festivals throughout the year. He provided a new Neshmet Boat for Osiris, *i.e.*, a new copy of the famous boat in which Osiris set sail on the expedition against Set in which he lost his life, and added to it a suitable shrine wherein the figure or statue of the god was to be placed. He made a new statue of the god and decorated it with lapis-lazuli, turquoise, silver-gold, and precious stones of all kinds,

[1] *Annales du Service*, tom. IV. [2] British Museum, No. 146 (574).

and it was as beautiful as the body of the god should be, and he provided apparel and ornaments for the festal attire of Osiris.[1] In addition to the ordinary priests, I-kher-nefert appointed a priest to the sanctuary at Abydos whose title was "Sa-mer-f,"[2] *i.e.*, "his (the god's) beloved son." This priest ministered in the "golden house," and directed all ceremonies which were performed in connection with the "mystery of the Lord of Abydos."[3] He had charge of all the sacred dresses and ornaments of the god, and of all the furniture of the shrine, which no hands but his might touch, and he dressed the statue of Osiris for the festivals of the new moon and full moon each month, and directed the moving of it when it was necessary to do so. No one might assist him in his sacred office except the Sem priest, who also had to be a man of "clean fingers."[4]

The second portion of the inscription on the stele of I-kher-nefert is of very great importance, for it describes briefly the principal scenes in the Osiris play which was performed at Abydos annually. I-kher-nefert himself played a prominent part in this "Mystery play," and he describes his own acts as follows :—

"I performed the coming forth of Ȧp-uat when he set out to defend his father."

From this it is clear that in the XIIth dynasty Ȧp-uat was regarded as the son of Osiris, and that he acted the part of leader of Osiris's expedition, which was represented by a procession formed of priests and the ordinary people. Ȧp-uat walked in front, next came the boat containing the figure of the god and a company of priests or "followers" of the god, and the rear was brought up by a crowd of people.

"I drove back the enemy from the Neshmet Boat,[5] I overthrew the foes of Osiris."

The boat of the god was then attacked by a crowd

[1] For the text see Lepsius, *Denkmäler*, Band II, Plate 135, and Schäfer's monograph in Sethe, *Untersuchungen*, Band IV, No. 2, Leipzig, 1904. The stele is preserved in Berlin (No. 1024).

[2] 

[3] 

[4] 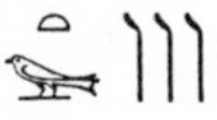

[5] 

of men who represented the foes of Osiris, and, as the god was defenceless, Åp-uat engaged them in combat, and beat them off, and the procession then continued on its way in the temple.

"I performed the 'Great Coming-forth,'[1] I followed the god in his footsteps."

This act was the greatest in the Osiris play, for it represented the "coming forth" of Osiris from the temple after his death, and the departure of his body to his tomb. A solemn service was performed in the temple before the body was carried from it, and offerings were eaten sacramentally, and then the procession set out for the tomb. When it reached the door of the temple it was received by a mighty crowd of men and women who raised the death-wail, and uttered piercing shrieks and lamentations, and the women beat their breasts.[2] Many of the men in the crowd were armed with sticks and staves, and some of them pressed forward towards the procession with the view of helping the god, whilst others strove to prevent them. Thus a sham fight took place, which, owing to the excitement of the combatants, often degenerated into a serious one. And, if Herodotus was correctly informed,[3] this combat with clubs was waged with great obstinacy, and heads were broken, and he says, though this the Egyptians denied, many men died of the wounds which they received on this occasion. This fight was, of course, intended to represent the great battle which took place in prehistoric times between Set and Osiris, when Osiris was killed. This battle, as has been already said, took place near Neṭit. Whether Osiris was killed outright whilst fighting, or whether he was wounded and taken prisoner by Set and slain afterwards, is not stated, but it is quite clear that for a time no one knew what had become of the body of Osiris, and that his followers went about on the battlefield searching for it. This search is referred to in the words, "I followed the god in his footsteps," *i.e.*, I traced the god by his footsteps. I-kher-nefert played the

1 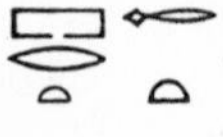.

2 Herodotus, II, 61.

3 II, 63.

part of leader of the search party, and their wanderings probably occupied three days, during which the sham fight between the followers of Osiris and the followers of Set was repeated at intervals, and great lamentations were made. All these events were represented by the words "great coming-forth," which to every Egyptian bore the most solemn significance.

At length the body of Osiris was found, but by whom is not said here.

[A passage in the text of Pepi I supplies the information, and shows that the finders of the body of Osiris were Isis and Nephthys, and that they made known their sad discovery to the gods of Pe by their cries of grief.[1] In answer to the appeal of Isis the god Thoth was sent in his boat to convey the body from the dyke (?) of Neṭȧt, or Neṭit, to its tomb. When Thoth arrived he saw Isis with the body, and the text says that when she found it it was lying on one side, and that she caressed the flesh, and fondled the hands, and embraced the body of her husband.][2]

The stele of I-kher-nefert goes on to say :—

"I made the boat of the god to move, and Thoth . . . ."

What exactly Thoth did is not certain, for the text is broken, but it is clear that I-kher-nefert acted the part of a ferryman for Thoth, and that he went in a boat containing a figure of Thoth to bring the body of Osiris from Neṭit to his tomb. The text continues :—

"I provided the Boat of the Lord of Abydos called "'Khā-em-Maāt' (*i.e.*, 'appearing in truth') with a cabin "shrine, and I put on him his splendid apparel and "ornaments when he set out to go to the region (?) of "Peqer" .

1 . Pepi I, l. 204 = Mer-en-Rā, l. 339 = Pepi II, l. 865.

2 Pepi I, l. 204.

From this passage it is certain that Osiris did not go to his grave in the Neshmet Boat, but in another boat called Khā-em-Maāt. Nothing is said here about the mummification of the body of Osiris which took place after it was brought from Neṭit, or of the elaborate ceremonies which were performed in connection with it by Horus and his Four Sons. These are mentioned in several places in this book, and are, therefore, not described here.

From an inscription quoted by Schäfer[1] we know that the two feathers of Maāti were fastened on the coffin, or coffer, of Osiris, , and that a bandlet was tied about the god's head, and that a model of his enemy Set was placed at his feet. These things having been done, I-kher-nefert continues:—

"I directed the ways of the god to his tomb in Peqer."

Here we have a definite statement that the body of Osiris was buried, and that his tomb was situated in Peqer. But where was Peqer? This question has been satisfactorily answered by the extensive excavations of M. Amélineau at Abydos,[2] who proved that Peqer is a portion of the great plain of Abydos which lies about a mile and a half from the temple of Osiris, and which is known to-day by the Arabic name of Umm al-Ka'âb, *i.e.*, "mother of pots," because of the large quantity of pottery which has been found there. In this portion of the plain are found the tombs of the kings of the First dynasty, and among them is one, that of King Khent, which the Egyptians identified as the tomb of Osiris. There is not the least doubt about the fact of the identification, for numerous proofs have been obtained from the excavations that the place was called Peqer, and that under the New Empire the Egyptians were firmly convinced that the tomb of Khent was the tomb of Osiris. Moreover, the famous cenotaph of Osiris, which was made probably

[1] *Op. cit.*, p. 27.

[2] Amélineau, *Le Tombeau d'Osiris*, Paris, 1899, and the other publications of the Mission Amélineau, *Les Nouvelles Fouilles d'Abydos*, Angers, 1893, etc.

under the XXIInd dynasty and which is described elsewhere, was found here by M. Amélineau. It has been argued by some[1] that the identification of the tomb of Khent as the tomb of Osiris is not older than the XVIIIth dynasty, because the oldest objects found round about it are of the time of Åmen-ḥetep III, about 1500 B.C. But the stele of I-kher-nefert of the XIIth dynasty says that the tomb of Osiris was in Peqer, and as the cult of Osiris developed greatly from the XIIth dynasty onwards, it seems to me wholly impossible for the Egyptians to have forgotten between the XIIth and the XVIIIth dynasties the whereabouts of the tomb of the god on whom their hopes of resurrection and immortality centred. When the Egyptians of the XVIIIth dynasty asserted that the tomb which we now know to be that of King Khent was the tomb of Osiris, they were undoubtedly asserting their belief in a tradition which was even at that time many centuries old. Similarly the Egyptians of the XXIInd dynasty asserted their acceptance of the traditional belief of the XVIIIth dynasty by making the famous cenotaph of Osiris, and placing it at Peqer, or Umm al-Ka'âb. Whether the identification of the tomb of Khent as that of Osiris is correct is a wholly different matter, which it is useless to argue, for the evidence which is necessary for deciding the question is not available, even if it exists. It is unlikely that there were two tombs in Peqer, each claiming to be the tomb of Osiris, but even if there were it is only reasonable to assume that the priestly authorities of the day would weigh the evidence in such an important

Seti I addressing Osiris in his shrine.
Mariette, *Abydos*, Vol. I, p. 43.

[1] Petrie, *Royal Tombs*, Vol. I.

matter carefully, and would decide in accordance with ancient tradition. If we assume that the identification of the tomb of Khent as the tomb of Osiris is not older than the reign of Ȧmen-ḥetep III we ignore the vital importance of the grave of the god to every Egyptian, and the great antiquity of the cult of Osiris at Ȧbydos. It is unlikely that Ȧbydos was the original home of the worship of Osiris, indeed there is good reason for thinking that it was not; but abundant evidence exists to show that the town was one of the principal centres of his cult from the beginning to the end of the Dynastic Period.

The official I-kher-nefert, having directed the ceremonies connected with the burial of Osiris, then proceeded to carry out those which were performed in connection with the avenging of the death of Osiris, and says:—

"I avenged Un-Nefer on the day of the Great Battle, I overthrew all his enemies on the dyke (?) of Neṭit."

The scene in the Osiris play here referred to represented the great battle which was waged by Horus, the "avenger of his father," against Set and his confederates, and is often mentioned in the religious texts. In it I-kher-nefert played the part of Horus, and led the victorious army in the sham fight, which probably took place at dawn, for it is the African custom to attack the enemy at that time. The foes of the god were supposed to be routed with great slaughter. The Book of the Dead (Chapter XVIII) makes it quite clear that in the original battle between Horus and Set large numbers of the followers of Set were slain on the field, and large numbers were taken prisoners. The prisoners were brought to the tomb of Osiris, where they were beheaded and, perhaps, hacked to pieces, and their blood was used in watering the sanctuary of Osiris in his tomb, and the ground round about it. This is, clearly, what is meant by the words, "On the night of the carrying out of the sentence upon these who are to die," and "the night of breaking and turning up the earth in their blood," and the "Tchatcha (chiefs), on the festival of the "breaking and turning up of the earth in Ṭaṭṭu (Busiris), "slay the fiends of Set in the presence of the gods who "are therein, and their blood runneth about among them "as they are smitten." Whether I-kher-nefert offered up human sacrifices or not is not known, but it is tolerably certain that so careful a traditionalist as he shows himself to have been would not have omitted to see that the grave of Osiris was properly "watered" with human blood. The victims would be prisoners of war and criminals, who by the laws of Egyptian society were bound to die. They would be sacrificed so that their blood might gratify the great ancestral spirit Osiris, just as the criminals and prisoners of war are sacrificed in Dahomey at the Annual Customs to gratify and renew the life of the spirits of the king's ancestors. The text of I-kher-nefert continues:—

"I caused him (*i.e.*, Osiris) to set out in the Boat, "which bore his Beauty. I made the hearts of the "dwellers in the East to expand with joy, and I caused "gladness to be in the dwellers in Åmentet (the West), "when they saw the Beauty as it landed at Abydos, "bringing Osiris Khenti-Åmenti, the Lord of Abydos, "to his palace."

This was the most glorious scene in the Osiris play, for the god appears once more in the Neshmet Boat, and he returns to his palace once more a living god. Thanks to his own divine power, and to the ceremonies which Horus and his Four Sons had performed between the transport of the body of Osiris to his tomb and his re-appearance in the Neshmet Boat, and, thanks to the eating of the Eye, which Horus had plucked from his own face and given to him, and to the vengeance which had been wreaked on Set and his fiends, and to the "watering" of the tomb of Osiris with their blood, Osiris became once more a living being. The crowds who had flocked to Abydos from the East and the West rejoiced greatly, for their god had come once more to live among them, and in him they saw the symbol of their own resurrection and immortality. In describing the Osiris play at Abydos, I-kher-nefert dwells chiefly upon the ceremonies in which he played the prominent part, for he assumed that those who read his inscription were thoroughly conversant with all the details of the Mysteries. It is quite clear from his narrative that the performance of the Mystery play of Osiris occupied many days, probably from first to last three or four weeks. The play was acted at Ṭaṭṭu (Busiris) with elaborate ceremonies, and a considerable number of human sacrifices must have been offered up at that place. Other towns in which special regard was paid to the festival of Osiris and its Mysteries were Ȧnu (Heliopolis), Sekhem (Letopolis), Pe-Ṭep (Buto), Taui-rekhti (?), Ȧn-ruṭ-f, and Re-stau.

In connection with the offerings to Osiris mention must be made of the belief, which was common among the Egyptians, that there existed at Abydos a means by which they might be despatched direct to the Other World for the use of the god. This means took the form of a well, or cistern, which was fed in some way by the Abydos canal, and was called "Ha ḥetepet," 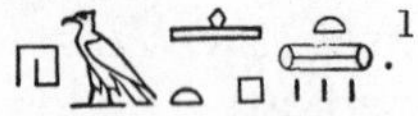.[1] Its waters[2] were mighty and most terrible, and the well was full of "great roarings"; the god who guarded it was Qa-ha-ḥetep,[3] and he allowed none to approach it. The ground about it was called the "region of offerings, the holy land, the mountain of Ȧmentet."[4] The roarings or noises which were heard in the well were caused by the fall of the offerings into it. The well is mentioned in the Stele of Menthu-ḥetep[5] (XIth dynasty), who says that he built it[6] by the order of Horus, *i.e.*, the king, but it is far more likely that he only cleared it out, and lined it

[1] 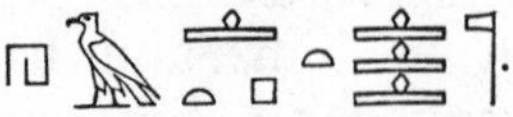. Pepi I, l. 708, and *see* Aat VIII, Chapter CXLVIII of the Book of the Dead.

[2] .

[3] 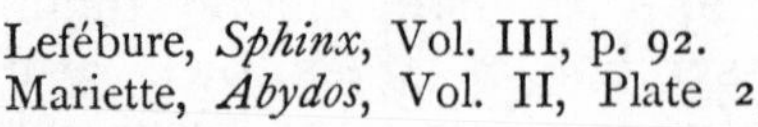.

[4] Lefébure, *Sphinx*, Vol. III, p. 92.

[5] Mariette, *Abydos*, Vol. II, Plate 23; Daressy, *Recueil*, Vol. X, pp. 144–149.

[6] .

with stone. Close to this well was the chamber which contained the relic of Osiris, and this is, as M. Lefébure pointed out, probably the tomb chamber of King Khent, which the Egyptians identified as the tomb of Osiris. It is about 28 feet square, and was surrounded by cells, which increased its size to 43 feet by 38 feet. At the north-west corner of this chamber M. Amélineau found a staircase of fourteen steps, and the cenotaph of Osiris, to which reference has already been made. The well, or cistern, was either built or repaired under the XIth dynasty, and it was certainly in existence in the time of Strabo, who seems to connect it with the "palace of Memnon." He says that there was a descent to the water, which was situated at a great depth, through an arched passage built of single stones, of remarkable size and workmanship. A canal led to the place from the Nile, and near it was a grove of Egyptian acanthus trees dedicated to Apollo.[1]

The building which Strabo calls the "palace of Memnon" cannot have been the temple of Seti I, as Mariette thought, but must have been the temple of Osiris; every large temple had its well, and the general plan of the temple well, or cisterns, is known. Mariette devoted much time and attention during his excavations at Abydos in searching for the well described by Strabo, but he failed to find it, and his successors have been equally unsuccessful in this respect. Professor Naville in the course of his excavations at Abydos (1909–11) discovered a large well, but it can hardly have been the well described by Strabo. M. Lefébure thought[2] that it might have been situated in the tomb of Osiris, and that its mouth was under the cenotaph of the god, but none of the excavators of the tomb mentions any trace of it. Still, it must be somewhere in the plain of Peqer, or Umm al-Ḳa'âb, though it is probably filled with sand. The Uārt 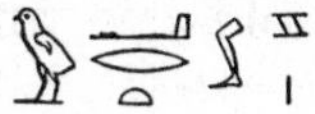, or passage to the well, the Ta tchesert 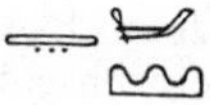, or "holy ground," Peqer, or Peḳa,

[1] Strabo, XVII, i, 41.
[2] *Sphinx*, Vol. III, p. 96.

the tomb region, and the "staircase" of the god[1] must all be near together, and it is to be hoped that in the near future the well may be brought to light.

Notwithstanding all the great works which the kings of the XIIth dynasty caused to be done for Osiris at Abydos, we find that under the XIIIth dynasty his sanctuary needed many repairs. King Nefer-ḥetep was a loyal worshipper of Osiris, and hearing that his temple was in ruins, and that a new statue of the god was required, he went to the temple of Temu at Heliopolis, and consulted the books in the library there, so that he might learn how to make a statue of Osiris which should be like that which had existed in the beginning of the world. Having obtained the information required, he set out for Abydos, and sent word to the priests there that the statue of Osiris should be brought out to meet him at the place where he was going to land on the river bank. When he arrived he found Osiris and his priests waiting for him, and the king journeyed from the Nile to the temple of Osiris at Abydos, under the escort of the god and his priests. As the king was going to the temple a number of the principal scenes in the Mystery play of Osiris were performed, no doubt to the great satisfaction of the actors and spectators. When Abydos was reached the king caused all the necessary works to be taken in hand at once, and he superintended personally their execution, in order that he might be certain that the directions which he had obtained from the books in the Library at Heliopolis were correctly carried out. In the making of the new statue of Osiris the king assisted with his own hands.[2]

Whether the sanctuary of Osiris at Abydos prospered or not under the XIVth, XVth, XVIth, and XVIIth dynasties, is not known, but with the rise to power of the kings of the XVIIIth dynasty it certainly began a new period of glory. Thothmes I made a new statue of the god, or repaired the old one, and a shrine-

[1] See the Stele of Sebek-khu, who built his tomb by the staircase of the god, at the Uārt, so that he might smell the incense burnt there.—Garstang, *El Arabah*, Plate 4, l. 8.

[2] See Mariette, *Abydos*, tom. II, Plates 28–30, and Breasted, *Egypt*, Vol. I, p. 333 ff.

boat of silver, gold, lapis-lazuli, copper, and precious stones, tables for offerings, sistra of various kinds, censers and bowls, a new barge in which the god might journey from the temple to Peqer during the Miracle play, and statues of all the gods of Abydos, each with his silver-gold standard.[1] Thothmes III caused a great many restorations to be carried out in the temple of Osiris,[2] and the results of the excavations made during recent years at Abydos prove that, in the reigns of Åmen-ḥetep III and the other kings of the XVIIIth dynasty, the income derived by Osiris from his worshippers must have been considerable.

The Soul of Osiris, incarnate in a Ram, as worshipped at Busiris, Philae, etc.

Hitherto reference has been made only to the two chief shrines of Osiris, viz., Abydos in the South, and Busiris in the North, but since the legend of the scattering of the parts of the body of Osiris all over Egypt was generally accepted, even in early times, it follows that many shrines of the god existed in the country at an early period, although of such shrines there is no list older than the XVIIIth dynasty. Of this period, however, we have several copies of a List of the Forms and Shrines of Osiris, and from this it seems that there must have been a shrine of Osiris in every nome in Egypt. The List forms part of the CXLIInd Chapter of the Book of the Dead,[3] and the oldest form of it is probably that given in the Papyrus of Nu. It follows a list[4] of all the gods whose names are to be commemorated by a man for his

[1] See Mariette, *Abydos*, tom. II, Plate 31.

[2] *Ibid.*, Plate 33.

[3] See the Papyrus of Nu, Sheet 15, and the Papyrus of Iuåu, Plate IX.

[4] This list begins with the name of Åsår-Khenti-Amenti.

father or for his son during the Festival of Åmentet, and contains the following:—

1. Åsår Un-nefer. Un-nefer was an ancient god of Abydos.

2. Åsår Ānkhti.

3. Åsår neb-ānkh, *i.e.*, Osiris, Lord of life.

4. Åsår neb-er-tcher, *i.e.*, Osiris, lord to the limit, or the universal Lord.

5. Åsår Khenti-Peḳu (?).

6. Åsår-Saḥ, *i.e.*, Osiris Orion. The constellation of Orion was one of the abodes of Osiris.

7. Åsår-Saa, *i.e.*, Osiris the Protector, or Shepherd.

8. Åsår Khenti peru, *i.e.*, Osiris, Chief of the Temples.[1]

9. Åsår in Resenet, *i.e.*, Osiris in the House of the South.

10. Åsår in Meḥenet, *i.e.*, Osiris in the House of the North.

11. Åsår nub-ḥeḥ, *i.e.*, Osiris, golden one of millions of years.

12. Åsår bati-Erpit, *i.e.*, Osiris, double soul of Isis and Nephthys.

13. Åsår Ptaḥ-neb-ānkh, *i.e.*, Osiris plus Ptaḥ, Lord of life.

14. Åsår Khenti Re-stau, *i.e.*, Osiris, Chief of the Door of the Funeral Passages, or, Osiris, Chief of the domain of Seker (Ṣaḳkârah), an ancient god of Death.

15. Åsår ḥer-åb-set, *i.e.*, Osiris, Dweller in the funeral mountain.[2]

16. Åsår in Ati (?).[3]

17. Åsår in Seḥtet.[4]

18. Åsår in Netchefet.[5]

[1] The Papyrus of Iuåu gives Åsår Khenti Un.

[2] Iuåu gives Åsår in Seḥnen, 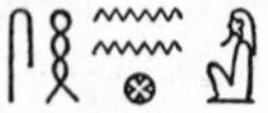.

[3] Iuåu gives Asår in Busiris, .

[4] Iuåu gives Åsår in Sekri, 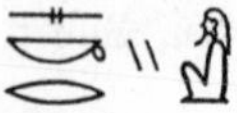.

[5] Iuåu gives Åsår in Sau (Saïs).

19. Ȧsȧr in Resu (Southlands?).
20. Ȧsȧr in Pe (Buto).
21. Ȧsȧr in Netru, *i.e.*, Osiris in the Divine Lake.[1]
22. Ȧsȧr in Lower Sau (Saïs).
23. Ȧsȧr in Bȧket, *i.e.*, Osiris in the City of the hawk.
24. Ȧsȧr in Sunnu.
25. Ȧsȧr in Reḥnent.
26. Ȧsȧr in Āper.
27. Ȧsȧr in Ḳefṭenu.
28. Ȧsȧr-Sekri in Pet-she.[2]
29. Ȧsȧr Khenti-nut-f, *i.e.*, Osiris, Chief in his city.
30. Ȧsȧr in Pesḳ-re.[3]
31. Ȧsȧr in his shrines (or, seats) in the Land of the North.
32. Ȧsȧr in heaven.[4]
33. Ȧsȧr in his shrines in Re-stau.
34. Ȧsȧr Netchesti.
35. Ȧsȧr Atef-ur.
36. Ȧsȧr-Sekri.[5]
37. Ȧsȧr, Governor of eternity.
38. Ȧsȧr Tua, *i.e.*, the Begetter.
39. Ȧsȧr in Ȧter.[6]
40. Ȧsȧr in his tiara and plumes (?).
41. Ȧsȧr, Lord of everlastingness.
42. Ȧsȧr Ȧti, *i.e.*, the Prince.
43. Ȧsȧr Taiti.
44. Ȧsȧr in Re-stau.
45. Ȧsȧr on his sand.[7]
46. Ȧsȧr, Chief of the Chamber of the Cow (*i.e.*, Lord of Isis).
47. Ȧsȧr in Tanent.
48. Ȧsȧr in Neṭbit.[8]

[1] Iuȧu gives Ȧsȧr in Reḥnent, 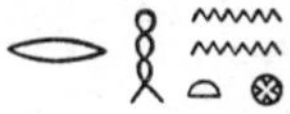.

[2] Iuȧu, in Pesṭ of his city.

[3] Iuȧu, Pesu-re.

[4] Iuȧu adds, Ȧsȧr in the earth.

[5] Iuȧu omits.

[6] Iuȧu, Ȧsȧr Lord of Ȧn (?).

[7] Iuȧu, within his sand.

[8] Iuȧu, Ṭenit, .

49. Åsår in Sati.
50. Åsår in Beshu.[1]
51. Åsår in Ṭepu.
52. Åsår in Upper Saïs.
53. Åsår in Nepert.
54. Åsår in Shennu.
55. Åsår in Ḥenket.
56. Åsår in the Land of Sekri.
57. Åsår in Shau.
58. Åsår in Fat-Ḥeru.
59. Åsår in Maāti.
60. Åsår in Henȧ.[2]

In the Saïte Period the Forms and Shrines of Osiris were 112 in number; they will be found tabulated in the *Todtenbuch* of Lepsius, Bl. 59.

Under the XIXth dynasty the temple of Osiris was restored, or rebuilt, and a large number of repairs were carried out at Abydos in connection with the property of the god. Seti I regarded Osiris with great awe, and spoke of him as the god who would destroy those who declined to obey his commands.[3] The reverence which Seti I personally showed to Osiris is well illustrated by the sections of the Book of Gates which specially deal with the kingdom of Osiris, appearing on his alabaster coffin. On this we have the remarkable vignette of Osiris seated in judgment on the top of his staircase, with the Scales set before him, and the boat containing the black pig of Set, which an ape is beating. The further scenes which illustrate the kingdom of Osiris prove that Seti was a believer in the doctrine of rewards for the blessed and punishments for the wicked, and in the existence of a place where the beatified lived with Osiris. The famous well of Osiris at Abydos appears in funerary literature copied during his reign, for we see Osiris seated by the side of it, or over it, in the Papyrus

[1] Iuȧu, in Beṭshet.

[2] Iuȧu, Nehnȧ, 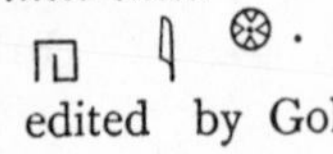.

[3] See the text edited by Golenischeff, in *Recueil*, tom. XIII, Plate II.

of Hu-nefer, and pictures of it appear in some of the Books of the Other World.

Rameses II was a loyal servant of Osiris, and repaired his shrines and erected fine buildings in his honour. Rameses says in the great inscription at Abydos[1] that he did for Osiris what Horus did for his father, that he set up monuments to him, and doubled the offerings to his KA, and his piety caused him to restore some of the royal tombs at Abydos which were in ruins. He finished the temple begun by his father, and built close to it a temple to Osiris. Rameses III restored Abydos and endowed the temples with great possessions, and made a great barge for the god.[2] Under the rule of the later kings of the XXth dynasty the cult of Osiris does not seem to have been specially considered, and the priest-kings of the XXIst dynasty devoted most of their attention and their possessions to the glorification of Åmen-Rā, the "king of the gods," at Thebes. Exact data are wanting, but it seems clear that with the end of the XXIst dynasty the importance of Abydos began to decline, and with it the cult of Osiris in this place. The first great revival of the glory of Osiris at Abydos after about 900 B.C., happened in the reign of Amasis (XXVIth dynasty), and it was entirely due to his chief physician Pef-ā-nef-Net, or Pef-ṭā-nef-Net. He interested the king in Abydos, and ultimately obtained from him the funds necessary for the restoration of the temple and the divine service. Much of the work of restoration he superintended personally. He built the god's temple, provided a silver-gold shrine, and implements for service made of gold, silver, etc. He built U-Peḳ and set up its altars, and cleaned out the famous well or cistern, and planted trees about it. He established a regular supply of food for the temple, he settled there slaves, male and female, he endowed the temple with 1000 *stat* of land with its flocks and herds and peasant dwellers. He re-established the offerings, planted date groves and vineyards, restored the library, and built a sacred barge. He revived the Miracle play of Osiris, and took the leading part in the great scene

[1] Mariette, *Abydos*, tom. I, Plates 5–9.

[2] Birch, *Papyrus of Rameses III*, Plate 58, l. 11.

in which the representative of Horus beats back the foes of his father Osiris. He made provision for burying the people of Abydos by confiscating certain dues, which the lord of the district had been in the habit of exacting from the desert tribes, and the earnings of a certain ferry[1] which the owner had assumed to be his private possession. Whatever may have happened to the shrine of Osiris at Abydos we may be quite certain that it did not in any way affect the general progress of the cult of Osiris in Egypt. It is probable that there was a small temple of Osiris attached to every great temple in Egypt, and there is good reason to think that such temples of Osiris were better and more regularly served by the priests than the larger temples. Little by little the Egyptians seem to have dropped the active cult of the other gods, Osiris and Isis, or Hathor, being in the eyes of the purely indigenous section of the population of more importance than all the other gods put together, for they gave resurrection and immortality to those who were dead, and protected the lives, property, and fortunes of those who were living.

[1] Breasted, *Egypt*, IV, p. 517.

CHAPTER XV.

THE MYSTERIES OF OSIRIS AT DENDERAH.

THE walls of one of the two courts which form part of the temple of Osiris at Denderah contain a long inscription[1] describing the bas-reliefs which illustrate the

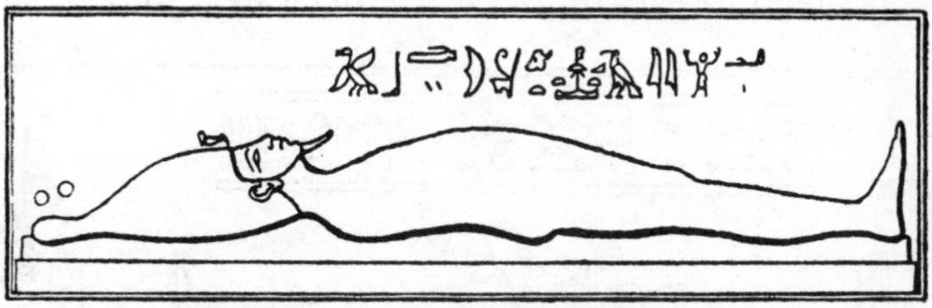

The model of Osiris which was used in the ceremonies performed during the celebration of his festival at Denderah.
Mariette, *Dendérah*, IV, 38.

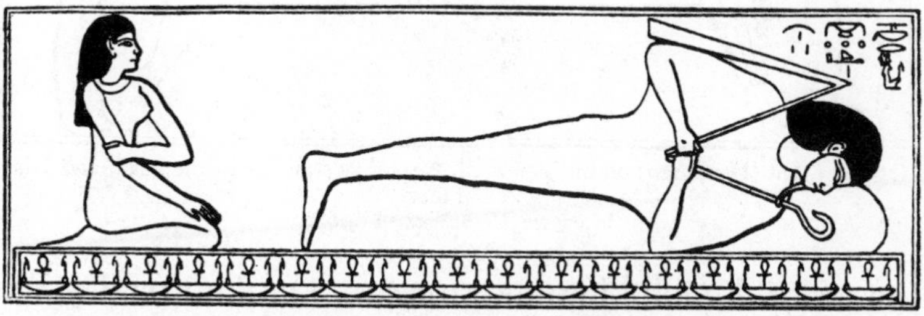

The model of Seker which was used in the ceremonies performed during the celebration of his festival at Denderah.
Mariette, *Dendérah*, IV, 39.

mysteries and ceremonies that were performed annually in honour of Osiris in that city. The First Section of this text deals with the making of sixteen models of the sixteen pieces into which the body of Osiris was hacked by Set. Each model was made of wheat mixed with some specially prepared paste, and was sent to the town

[1] See Brugsch and Dümichen, *Recueil*, I, 15, 16, and IV, 1–27; Dümichen, *Résultats*; Mariette, *Dendérah*, tom. IV, Plates 35–39; Lauth, *A.Z.*, 1866, p. 64 ff.; Loret, *Recueil*, tom. III, p. 43 ff.; tom. IV, p. 21 ff.; tom. V, p. 85 ff.

in which that member of the body of Osiris was believed to have been found, and it was there put in a specially prepared vessel in the "house of Osiris," and placed under the protection of the gods.

The Second Section of the inscription deals with the making of the figure of Khenti-Åmenti, and is of peculiar interest. At Mendes, a town closely connected with Busiris and the cult of Osiris, one *hin* of wheat and three *hin* of paste were placed in a large stone trough resting on four legs, and each day, from the 12th to the 21st day of Khoiak, three parts of a *hin* of water were poured

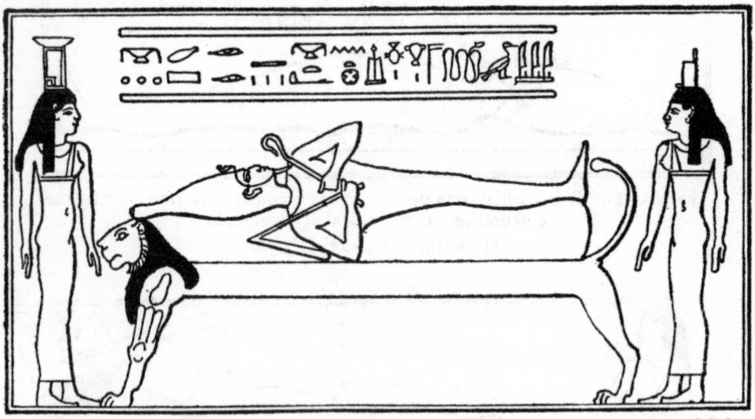

Osiris of Ånt (Denderah) on his bier, with Nephthys standing at the head, and Isis at the foot.
Mariette, *Dendérah*, IV, 68.

from a gold goblet into the trough. On the 21st day the contents of the trough were taken out, and a measure of incense having been added to it, the whole was kneaded into the two halves of a gold mould for making the figure of Khenti-Åmenti wearing the White Crown. The contents of the moulds were then taken out and tied together with four papyrus bands, and dried in the sun. At the eighth hour of the 22nd day of the month, the figure, and figures of gods and many lamps, were placed in boats, and taken by water to the tomb of the god, and there the figure of Khenti-Åmenti was covered with a cloth, and afterwards buried.

At Abydos, one *hin* of wheat and four *hin* of paste were placed in the two halves of a mould of Khenti-

Amenti on the 12th day of Khoiak, and the moulds were set in a large stone trough, with reeds laid above and below them ; each mould was covered with a cloth. Water was poured on each half of the figure of the god, morning and evening, and other ceremonies were performed in connection with them until the 21st of Khoiak. On that day the halves of the figure were removed from the moulds, dry incense was sprinkled over them, and they were then tied together with four bands of

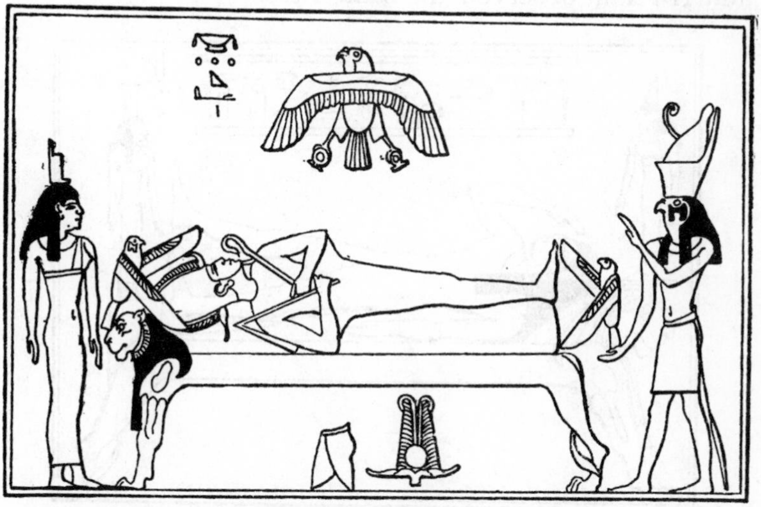

Osiris of Coptos. Isis stands at the head, and Horus, son of Isis, son of Osiris, at the foot. A crown and the tunic of the god are under the bier. Mariette, *Dendérah*, IV, 68.

papyrus, and set in the sun to dry until the 25th day of the month. On that day the figure was taken to the temple of Seker and laid there, and the ceremonies of embalmment continued from the 25th to the last day of the month, when the figure was buried. The ceremonial of Abydos was repeated at all the other sanctuaries of Osiris in Egypt.

The Third Section gives directions for making a figure of Seker in a mould, with his crook, whip, beard, and uraeus. The mould was of gold, and a cast made from it was one cubit in height. The paste of which the figure was made was composed of earth from the town of Neter, dates, incense, fresh myrrh, spices, precious stones, and water. The paste was made in the form of an egg, and set in a silver vase with sycamore leaves round it, and then pressed into the mould, and anointed with oil, and finally laid on the bed in the interior of the chamber. At Mendes this paste was made on the 14th day of Khoiak, and put in the mould on the 16th; on the 19th the figure was removed from the mould, embalmed on the 24th, and buried on the last day of the month. Memphis, Sma-Beḥuṭet, Kes, and Ka-kam observed the same rites.

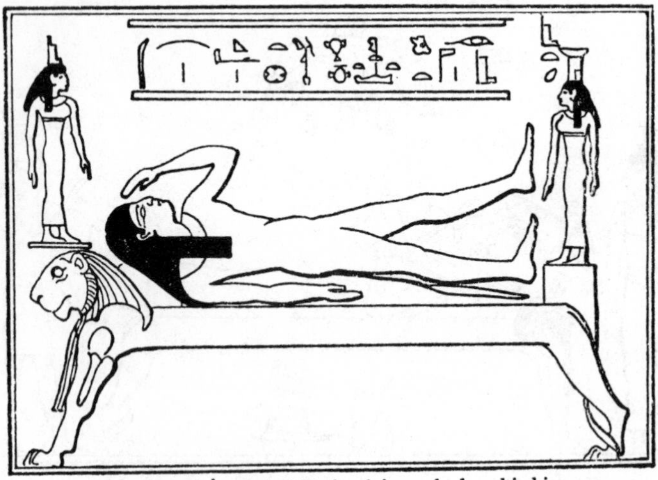

Osiris Khenti-Åmenti of Thebes lying naked on his bier.
Mariette, *Dendérah*, IV, 68.

The Fourth Section gives the names of the gods who were enshrined in the temple of the goddess Shent.

The Fifth Section supplies the legends which were cut on the fronts of the moulds of Seker, Khenti-Åmenti, and on the two vessels of Sep. The coffin of Osiris was made of sycamore wood and bore a long inscription; it was one cubit and two palms long, and three palms and three fingers broad. The coffin of Khenti-Åmenti and the coffer of the vessels of Sep were also made of sycamore. The moulds for the "divine bread" were made of the wood of a red tree, and cakes were made from them in the forms of the sixteen members of Osiris, viz., his head, feet, bones, arms, heart, intestines, tongue.

eye, fist, fingers, body, back, ears, backbone, ram's head, and hair. These cakes were put in a box, which was placed in a silver chest, and then set under the head of the god for protection. The other paragraphs of this Section deal minutely with the spices, precious stones, bandlets, knot, the fourteen amulets of Un-Nefer,[1] and the fourteen *tebēḥ* of the mould of Seker, which were in the forms of the fourteen divine members. The Field of Osiris in which the sacred grain was to be sown was

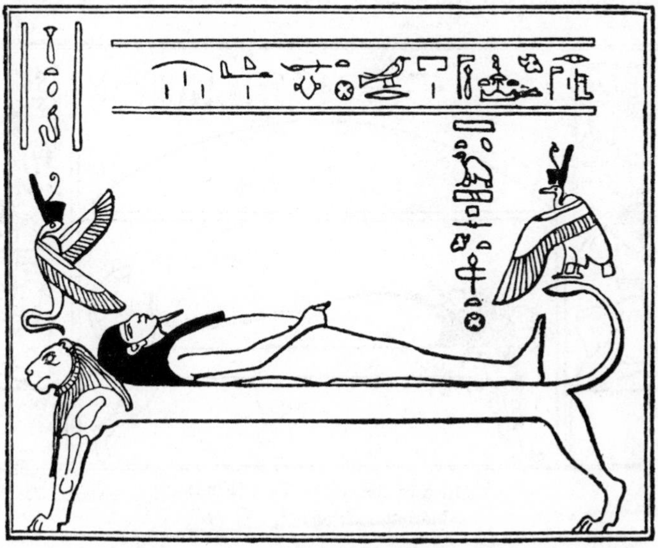

Osiris Khenti-Åmenti of Per-urt (Eileithyias). At the foot is the goddess Neith, and at the head the goddess Uatchit.
Mariette, *Dendérah*, IV, 69.

from 210 to 223 feet long ; one end of it was sown with barley, its centre with dhura, and the other end with flax. The plough frame was made of two kinds of wood, and the ploughshare of black bronze ; the cows which pulled it were black. The barley which grew in the Field was cut on the 20th day of Tobe, and was made into sacred cakes, the dhura was also made into cakes, and the linen made from the flax was used at the festival. Descriptions then follow of the sacred casket made of reeds, the cow

[1] The Four Sons of Horus, 4 ṭeṭs 𓊽, 2 lions, 1 Horus, 1 Thoth, 2 utchats.

Rement, the chamber which holds the mummy of Seker, the sacred linen chest, and the holy oil and its components.

The thirty-four boats with their 365 lamps and deities are next mentioned, and the names of the gods of the twenty-nine other boats are also given. The objects next spoken of are the sacred bier with silver wheels; the peace chamber, in which a man who represents the "lord of silence" is seated, with one hand on his mouth, and the other on his legs; the shrine of stone, 16 cubits

Osiris of the city of Ṭebt (Edfu).
Mariette, *Dendérah*, IV, 69.

long and 12 cubits broad, with seven doors, and containing a raised mound on which the god in his sarcophagus rests; and the gilded wooden coffer, with its jackal on its cover, and its sledge beneath it. The festival Un-per was celebrated on the 16th and 24th of the month of Khoiak, and on these days the god with his jackal appeared in the courtyard. The yoking of the two pairs of heifers to draw the funerary furniture took place on the 23rd day. The furniture consisted of two obelisks, four coffers, one for each of the Four Sons of Horus, with their four veils, one blue, one red, one green, one white, sixteen vulture plumes, four affixed to each coffer, and behind came a figure of the serpent Āpep, holding a knife with which to sever the cordage.

On the 12th day of Khoiak the festival of Tenȧ was

celebrated, and on the 14th the most solemn festival of Pert was observed. On the 16th the festival of Osiris Khenti-Åmenti was celebrated, and on that day the transformation of the god took place. On the 19th the figure of Seker was taken from its mould, and on that day Horus saw his father. On the 21st the figure of Osiris was taken from its mould; on the 24th Osiris was embalmed, and on the last day of the month the Ṭeṭ, 𓊽, was raised up, and Osiris was buried. For seven days, from the 24th to the last day of the month, Osiris remained unburied, and during these days he rested in

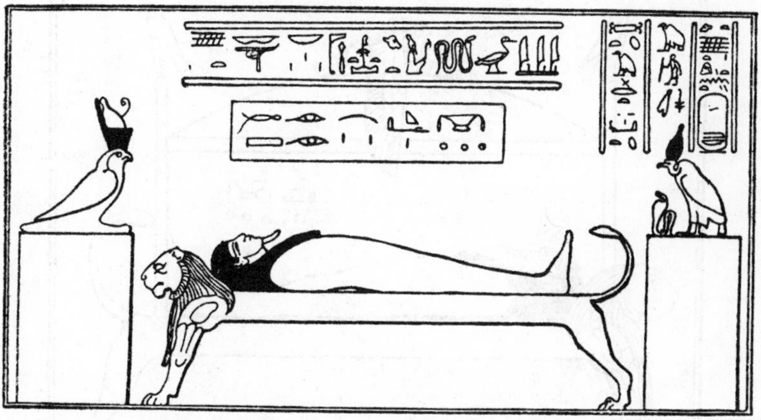

Osiris Khenti-Åmenti of Nubia. Horus sits at the head and Neith at the foot. Mariette, *Dendérah*, IV, 69.

the branches of the sycamores of Mendes. The seven days symbolize the seven months which he passed in the womb of his mother Nut, and the branches symbolize the goddess.

The Sixth Section states that the object used at the Tenȧ festival was made at each of the sixteen shrines of Osiris in Egypt. On the 12th of Khoiak the Festival of Ploughing the Earth was celebrated in the temple of the goddess Shentit in Mendes. The goddess appeared in the temple, and she was stripped naked. Some grain was strewn on a bed in the chamber of the goddess's dwelling, and then some of it was placed on a cloth and moistened with water, and at the sixth hour of the day this wet grain was placed in four gold vases in four equal parts. Two parts were intended for the mould of Khent-Ȧmenti, and two parts for the trough of Sep. A number of cakes (?) were then brought and treated in the same way. Next a piece of linen was laid in each half of the mould of Khent-Ȧmenti, and it was filled with the wet wheat and the cake-paste; both parts were then laid in the large trough and covered with reeds. The trough of Sep was then filled with the rest of the wheat and cake-

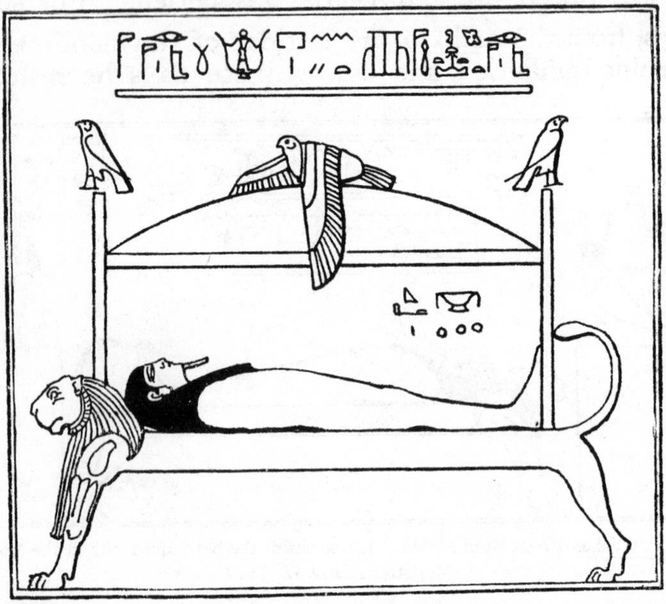

Osiris of Per-Kes (Cusae).
Mariette, *Dendérah*, IV, 69.

paste, and laid in the larger trough, and water was poured on them. On the 21st day of Khoiak the reeds which were about the halves of the mould were removed, and on the following day the superfluous water was drained off. The figures were then removed from the moulds, and tied together with four papyrus bands, and the two figures from the trough of Sep were joined in a similar manner, and then they were escorted along the water to the tomb by 34 boats decorated with 365 lamps. The figure of Khent-Ȧmenti and the figure from the trough of Sep, which had been made the previous year, were then brought from the place where they had been kept, and oiled, and embalmed on the 24th day of the month of Khoiak, and put each in a sycamore-wood coffin, and buried in Re-stau on the last day of the month.

The remaining paragraphs describe the details of the final ceremonies which were performed for "Osiris, Lord "of Ṭaṭṭu, Un-nefer, triumphant, Khent-Ȧmenti, Great "God, Lord of Abydos." The twelve magic spices and the twenty-four precious stones are enumerated; the weaving and the dyeing of the sacred linen are described,

Osiris Mer-ȧt-f of the town of Hep (Apis). Under the bier are the seven crowns of the god.
Mariette, *Dendérah*, IV, 70.

and the painting and decoration of the figure of the god, and the fixing of the fourteen amulets on it, and when this and much else had been carefully performed, the priests went, on the 25th day of Khoiak, and "expelled "from the tomb of the god all the words which had been "spoken there during the ceremonies the year before."

The reader will have noted that none of the ceremonies described in the text at Denderah are mentioned by the loyal official I-kher-Nefert in his account of the ceremonies at which he assisted. This is not to be wondered at, for he only took the lead in the great scenes of the Mystery play of Osiris which were always performed before the people. The ceremonies described above were all performed in secret by the priests, partly in the most sacred parts of the temple, and partly in the tomb, and the object of them all was to make three figures of the different forms of Osiris. From the first mould was made a figure of Khent-Åmenti, and from the trough of Sep, a figure of Sep, which was formed of sixteen distinct limbs of Osiris, and from the mould of Seker, a figure of the finished, reconstituted god. Every act was symbolic in character, and represented some ancient belief or tradition. The paste, the mixture of

Osiris of Libya (?) lying naked on his bier which is supported by the Four Sons of Horus. At the head stands Isis, and at the foot Horus.
Mariette, *Dendêrah*, IV, 70.

wheat and water, the egg, the naked goddess Shentit, *i.e.*, Isis in her chamber, the placing of the paste on her bed, the kneading of the paste into the moulds, etc., represented the great processes of Nature which are set in motion when human beings are begotten and conceived, as well as the inscrutable powers which preside over growth and development. The Egyptians believed that the original Osiris was re-made in the earth, and that the pieces of his body were woven together a second time through the words and ceremonies of the gods whose effigies were carried in the thirty-four boats during the procession on the water. And there was not the smallest action on the part of any member of the band who acted the

Miracle play of Osiris, and not a sentence in the Liturgy, which did not possess importance or vital significance to the followers of Osiris. The ceremonies performed at Denderah were not new, on the contrary, they were very old, and there is good reason to think the priests of the Ptolemaïc Period accepted with absolute faith the observances which the Osirian traditions imposed upon them, and carried them out with the most scrupulous care, even in the smallest detail.

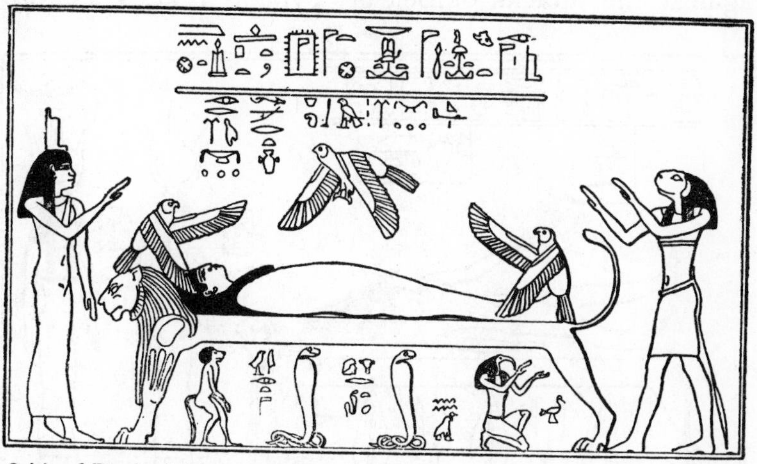

Osiris of Denderah lying on his bier which is supported by Thoth, two goddesses, and an Ape-god. The three hawks are Isis, Nephthys, and Hathor. At the head stands Isis, and at the foot Ḥeqet.

Mariette, *Dendérah*, IV, 70.

We may now consider the bas-reliefs at Denderah which illustrate the Festival and Mysteries of Osiris.[1] In the First Chamber North we see the figures of the priests of the shrines of Osiris from Lower Egypt marching with the king at their head; each holds in his hands the symbol of his nome, and above his head is his official title or designation (Plates 31, 32). In the First Chamber South we also see the figures of the priests of the shrines of Osiris in the South, or Upper Egypt (Plates 33, 34). In the same chamber is the long inscription which has already been summarized. It is illustrated by a figure of Osiris Khent-Ȧmenti (Plate 35),

[1] See Mariette, *Dendérah*, tom. IV, Plate XXXI ff.

and a representation of the mould of Khent-Åmenti (Plate 38), and the mould of Seker (Plate 39). On the walls of the Second Chamber (Plates 40–43) is sculptured a series of birds, each with its characteristic head, which represent the deities of the various nomes wherein shrines of Osiris were situated. These are followed by figures of the Eight Goddesses, Isis, Nephthys, etc. (Plate 44), and of the deities who accompany Osiris during the twenty-four hours of the day and night to protect him against the attacks of Set, or Typhon (Plates 45–56).

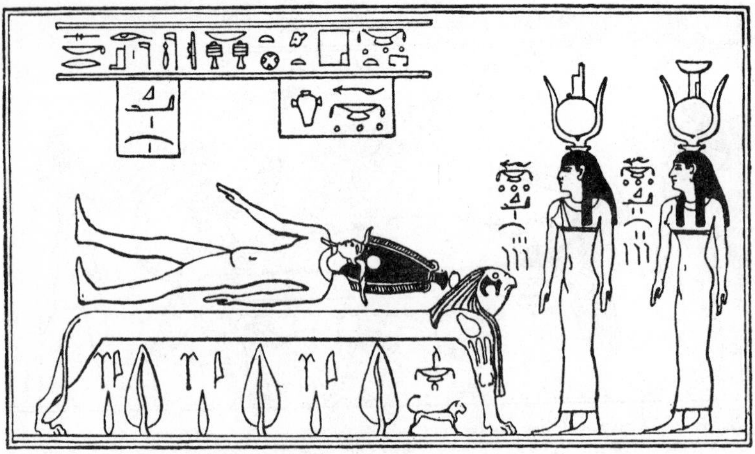

Seker-Osiris, Lord of Ṭaṭṭu (Busiris).
Mariette, *Dendérah*, IV, 71.

Then come a representation of the passage of the sun through the twelve hours of the day (Plate 57), and two scenes which illustrate ceremonies performed in connection with the renewal of the life of Osiris under the fostering influences of the goddesses Isis and Nephthys. The resurrection of Osiris is closely connected with the germination of wheat; the grain which is put into the ground is the dead Osiris, and the grain which has germinated is the Osiris who has once again renewed his life (Plate 58). The remaining reliefs in this chamber represent the gods who are charged with the protection of the tomb of Osiris (Plates 59–63).

In the Third Chamber we have representations of the Seven Boats of Osiris, the Ḥennu, Sektet, Māāt, etc., which took part in the procession of Osiris (Plates 64, 65), of Osiris as Harmakhis in a boat, and of a form of Osiris as the Lord of Life. The god lies on a bier under which are placed his diadems (Plate 65). The next relief (Third Chamber North), represents the adoration or protection of Osiris of the South and Osiris of the North by Isis and Nephthys (the two Shenti-goddesses), and the two Merti, *i.e.*, the goddesses of the Inundation of the South and North. In a

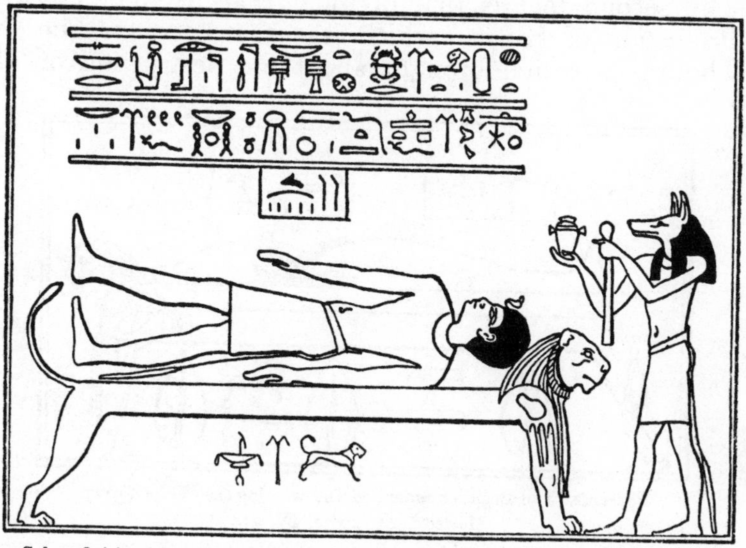

Seker-Osiris of Busiris. Anubis is bringing unguent and linen to embalm him.
Mariette, *Dendérah*, IV, 71.

lower scene we have a figure of Osiris of the North lying on his bier in his tomb which is placed close to a tamarisk tree (Plate 66). Then come the Seven Boats of Osiris (Plates 67, 68), and these are followed by representations of the funeral chests of Osiris in different localities. Thus we have the biers of Osiris of Denderah, Osiris of Coptos, Osiris Khent-Åmenti of Abydos (Plate 68), Osiris of Eileithyias, Osiris of Edfu, Osiris of Ta-sti (Nubia), Osiris of Cusae (Plate 69), Osiris of the town of Apis, Osiris revivified, Osiris of Libya (?), Osiris of Abydos, Osiris under a form worshipped at Denderah (Plate 70), Osiris of Busiris, in three forms, Osiris of Memphis, Osiris of Heliopolis

(Plate 71), Osiris of the East, Osiris of Behbêt, Osiris of Abydos, venerated in the town of Peḥu of the North, Osiris of Hermopolis in Lower Egypt, and Osiris of Bubastis (Plate 72).

Southern Group. First Chamber. Here the first text contains invocations to Osiris, in all his forms of Upper and Lower Egypt, and the bas-relief represents Osiris Un-Nefer of Denderah lying on his bier, with Isis at the head and Nephthys at the foot (Plate 74). The second text is that of the "Book of the Magical Protection of Horus," which was composed for him by Thoth; its recital brought about the destruction of all

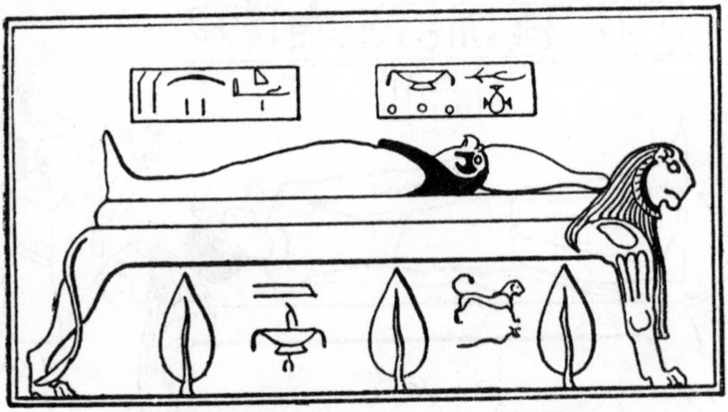

Seker-Osiris of Busiris mummified and wearing the White Crown.
Mariette, *Dendérah*, IV, 71.

the enemies of Osiris, and gave to the soul of the god the strength of a bull in the Other World. The bas-reliefs show us Osiris, followed by the four Meskhenit goddesses, and a figure of Thoth (Plate 74). The third text contains invocations to Osiris, and the bas-relief represents Osiris Un-Nefer, Lord of Busiris, lying on his bier (Plate 75).

Second Chamber. The fourth text contains directions for the covering of the biers of Osiris, and the placing of the proper amulets on them on the 25th day of Khoiak (Plate 77). The next group of bas-reliefs contains a series of figures of the gods of the Dekans, and Planets, and days of the week, which stand ready to guard the Sepulchre of Osiris (Plates 78–83). Following these we have the Twelve Hour-gods of the day, and their names (Plate 84), the Ḥennu Boat, and a scene of sacrifice (Plate 85), and a list of the nomes of Egypt, which the king presents to Hathor.

Third Chamber. Here on a tablet is given a list of the One Hundred and Four Amulets made of gold and precious stones of all kinds which were taken to the House of Gold, *i.e.*, the sarcophagus chamber, to protect this holy god and the burial

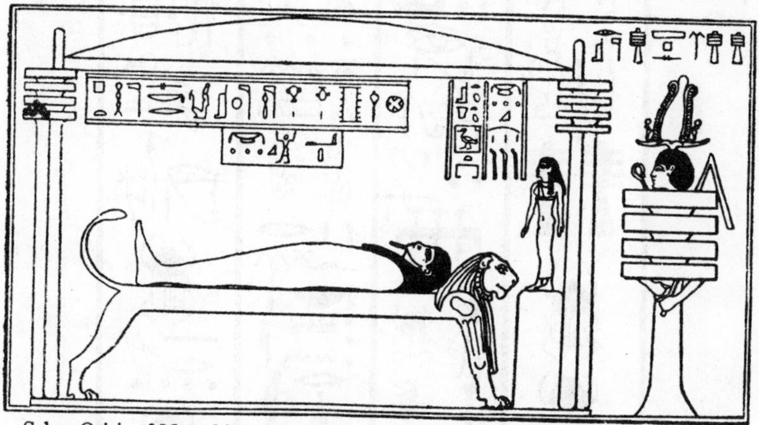

Seker-Osiris of Memphis ; the goddess at the head is Isis. Osiris-Ṭeṭ in Busiris.
Mariette, *Dendérah*, IV, 71.

furniture, or wrappings of his mummy (Plate 87). These amulets were :—

1. A breast plate, with figures of Osiris wearing the Atef Crown, Isis, and Nephthys.
2. A pectoral, with straps for fastening over the shoulders.
3. A figure of Thoth, in the form of a man with the head of an ibis.
4. The ibis, sacred to Thoth, resting on his stand .
5. The goddess Maāt, wearing the feather of Truth and holding the symbol of "life."
6. An Utchat, or Eye of Horus or Rā.
7. [Broken.]
8. A beetle, emblem of Kheperȧ.

All the above were made of *uḥer* stone.

9. A beetle, emblem of Kheperȧ.
10. A beetle, emblem of Kheperȧ.
11. An Utchat, or Eye of Horus or Rā.

These three were made of *Ṭeb* stone (read 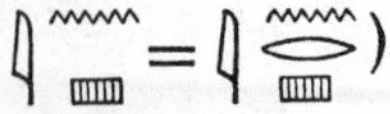).

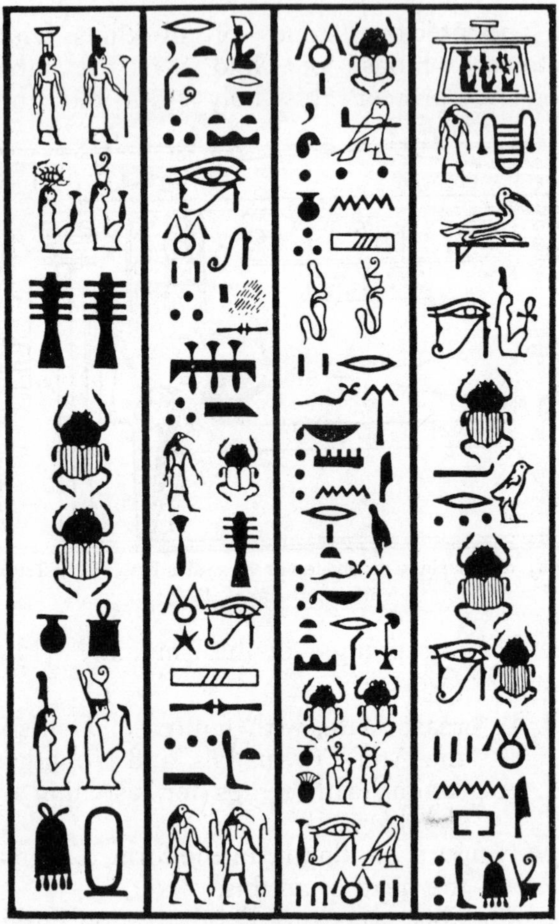

The 104 amulets of Osiris.
Mariette, *Dendérah*, IV, 87.

12. A beetle, emblem of Kheperȧ.

This was made of turquoise or green feldspar.

13. Uraeus wearing the Crown of the North.
14. Uraeus wearing the Crown of the South.

These were made of Ȧmen turquoise (?) stone.

15. A White Crown.

This was made of Syrian turquoise (?).

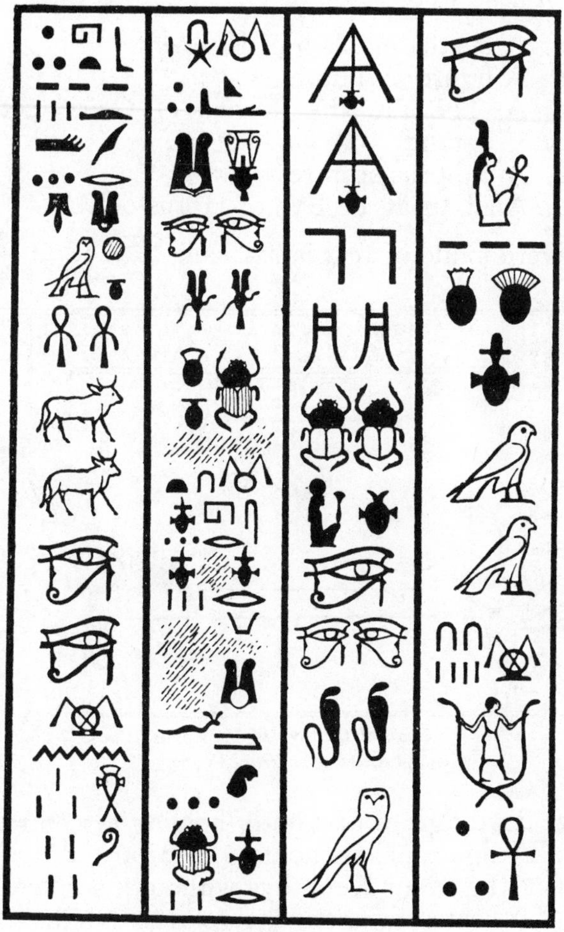

The 104 amulets of Osiris.
Mariette, *Dendérah*, IV, 87.

16, 17. Two beetles.
18. A seated figure of Isis.
19. A seated figure of Ȧmen.
20, 21. Two hawks, symbols of Horus.
22. An Utchat, or Eye of Horus or Rā.
23. A papyrus sceptre.

These were made of *Fert* stone of Rutenu.

24. An Utchat, or Eye of Horus or Rā.
25. A tear drop of the Utchat.

These were made of . . . . . or crystal.

26. A beetle, emblem of Kheperȧ.
27. A figure of Thoth.
28. A Ṭeṭ, *i.e.*, the sacrum of Osiris set on a stand.
29. A papyrus sceptre.
30. An Utchat, or Eye of Horus or Rā.

These were made of real lapis-lazuli

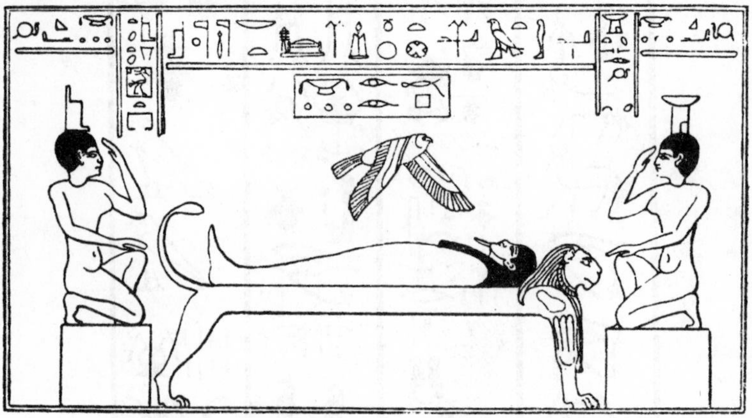

Osiris of the town of Heliopolis.
Mariette, *Dendérah*, IV, 71.

31, 32. Two figures of Thoth, holding a sceptre.
33. A figure of Isis holding a sceptre.
34. A figure of Nephthys without a sceptre.
35. A seated figure of the goddess Neith.
36. A seated figure of the goddess Serqet.
37, 38. Two Ṭeṭs.
39, 40. Two beetles.
41. A breastplate, with ring.
42. A vessel, with cover.
43. A seated figure of Osiris wearing the White and Red Crowns.
44. A seated figure of the goddess Maāt.
45. A cartouche.
46. An article of apparel.

47. An Utchat, or Eye of Horus, or Rā.
48. A seated figure of the goddess Maāt.
49. Three plaques (?).
50. A pomegranate.
51. A vessel (?).
52. A heart.
53, 54. Two hawks, symbols of Horus.

These were made in fine white "living" alabaster.

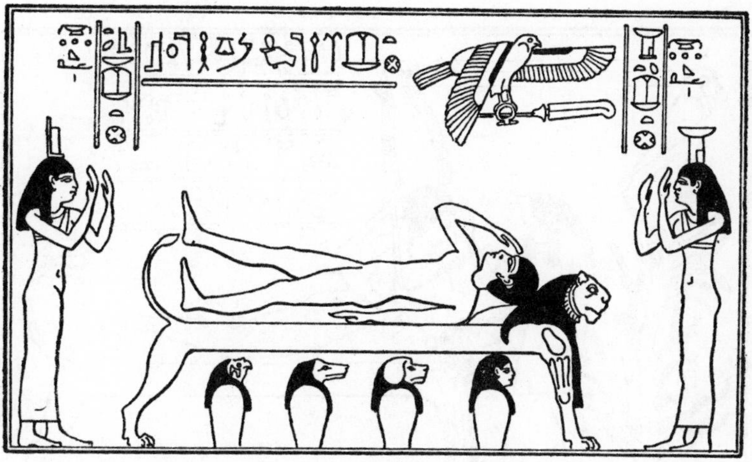

Osiris, Isis, and Nephthys of the town of Ḥebit (Beḥbît). Above is a hawk bringing air.
Mariette, *Dendérah*, IV, 72.

55. A pair of plumbing instruments.
56. A pair of angles.
57. A pair of stands (?).
58. A pair of beetles.
59. A fruit (?).
60. A seated figure of a goddess, with a disk on her head.
61. An Utchat, or Eye of Horus or Rā.
62. A pair of Utchats, the Eyes of the Sun and Moon.
63, 64. Two uraei.
65. A hawk, symbol of Horus.

These were made of *qā* stone.

66. A sistrum.
67. A pair of plumes.
68. Right Utchat.
69. Left Utchat.
70, 71. Two instruments with plumes and uraei.
72. A beetle, symbol of Kheperȧ.
73. A pomegranate.
74. A vessel, with cover (?).
75. . . . .

These were made of carnelian.

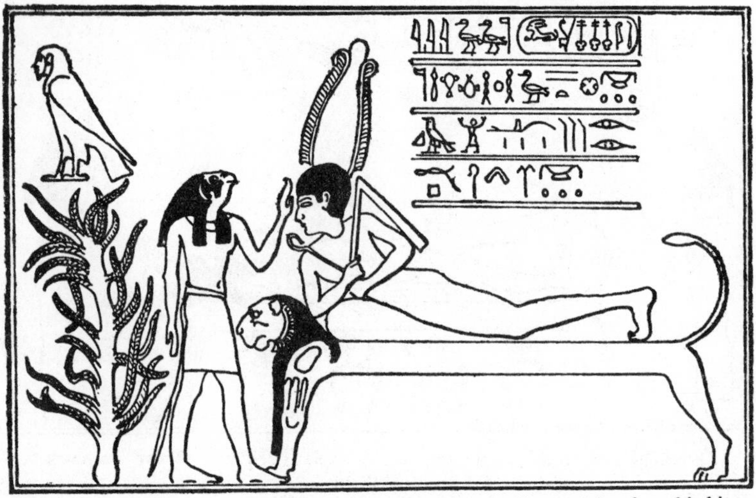

The soul of Osiris on the Erica tree. Osiris of Hermopolis of Lower Egypt rising from his bier at the command of Horus.
Mariette, *Dendérah*, IV, 72.

76–87 (?) {Vases for milk, or unguents (?). Perfume vases.}
88. A pair of plumes.

These were made of turquoise.

89. A milk vessel (?).
90. A beetle, emblem of Kheperȧ.

These were made of *behet* stone.

91–93. Three plaques (?).
94–96. Three knives made of black stone.
97. A pair of plumes.
98. An object.

These were made of *khenem* stone.

99, 100. Two amulets of Isis (?).
101, 102. Two bulls.
103, 104. Two Utchats.

Following these we have a group of the Sepulchres of Osiris, which may be briefly described :—

1. Osiris of Busiris, or Osiris Ṭeṭ, 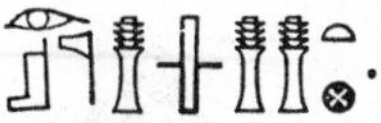.

The god standing upright, with Horus, son of Isis, holding his right arm. Isis and Nephthys stand before

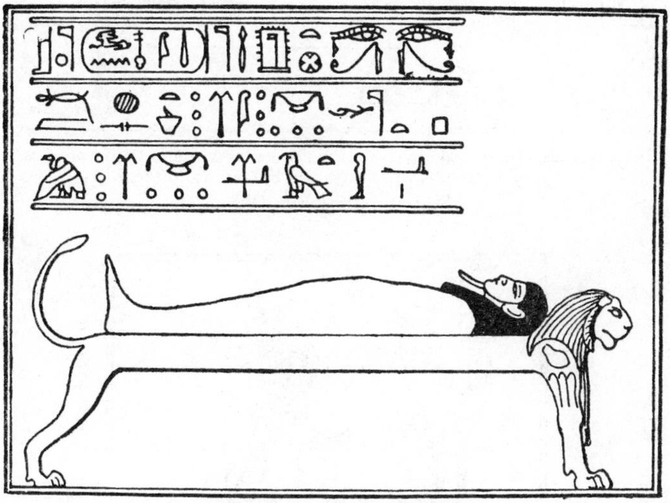

Osiris Un-nefer of Neter-ḥet (Bubastis).
Mariette, *Dendĕrah*, IV, 72.

him. Outside, at one end, is an ape, symbolic of the Four Sons of Horus, and at the other the goddess Shentit is seated.

2. An Osiris unnamed.

The god lying on his stomach on his bier. Horus his son driving a spear into his face, to open his mouth and his two eyes. Isis at the head, Nephthys at the foot. Beneath the bier is a row of diadems.

3. Osiris Khenti-Ȧmenti.

Osiris, lying on his bier in the act of begetting Horus by Isis, who is in the form of a hawk ; behind comes Nephthys in a similar form. At the head kneels Hathor, and at the foot the Frog-goddess Ḥeqet is seated.

Beneath the bier are Thoth, two uraei, and Bes. Behind Hathor stand four forms of Osiris.

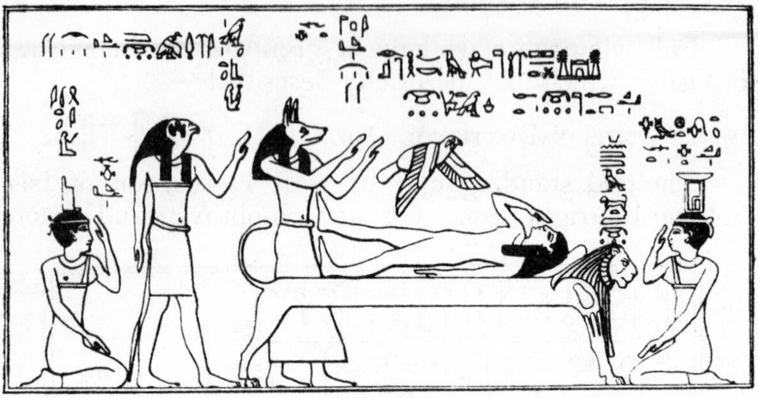

Osiris Ḥemka begetting a son by Isis, who hovers over him in the form of a hawk. Anubis, Horus, Nephthys and Shentit are present.
Mariette, *Dendérah*, IV, 90.

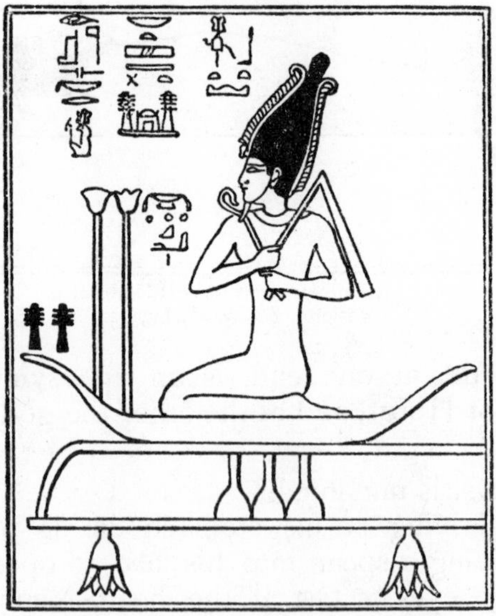

Osiris-Seker, Lord of the Shrine of Abydos.
Mariette, *Dendérah*, IV, 90.

4. Seker Osiris in Ṭaṭṭu (Busiris), 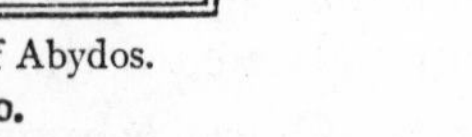

The god lying on his bier. At the head stands Nephthys and at the foot Isis.

5. Osiris in the embalmment chamber being operated upon by Anubis and Ḥeqet, according to instructions given by Thoth. Isis and Nephthys sit on the ground weeping.

6. Ptaḥ-Seker-Åsår lying on his bier.

7. Seker-Åsår lying on his bier, by which stand Isis and Nephthys. Facing its head are three of the forms of Osiris.

The resurrection of Osiris Khenti-Åmenti.
Mariette, *Dendérah*, IV, 90.

8. Osiris Ḥemaka, 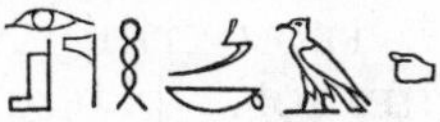, in the form of an unmummied man lying on a bier, by the foot of which stands Anubis. Nephthys kneels at the head, and Isis at the foot. Above the member of the god hovers Isis in the form of a hawk.

9. Åsår-Seker of Abydos kneeling in a kind of boat which is resting on a sledge.

10. Osiris rising revivified out of a kind of bowl which stands on a plinth between the outspread wings of Isis.

11. Osiris Khent-Åmenti, rising revivified from his bier, beneath which is placed a series of his crowns.

CHAPTER XVI.

THE BOOK OF MAKING THE SPIRIT OF OSIRIS,[1] OR THE SPIRIT BURIAL.

THE FORMULA FOR MAKING THE SPIRIT OF OSIRIS[2] IN ÅḲERTET, WHICH SHALL BE MADE (*i.e.*, RECITED) FOR THIS GOD, THE LORD OF ABYDOS, AT EVERY FESTIVAL OF OSIRIS, AND AT EVERY APPEARANCE [OF THE GOD] IN THE TEMPLES . . . . IT SHALL MAKE GLORIOUS HIS SOUL, IT SHALL STABLISH HIS BODY, IT SHALL MAKE HIS SOUL TO SHINE IN THE SKY, AND SHALL MAKE HIM TO RENEW HIS YOUTH EACH MONTH, IT SHALL STABLISH HIS SON HORUS UPON HIS COFFER. THIS FORMULA WAS RECITED BY THE SISTER [OF THE GOD]. IT WILL BENEFIT A MAN IF HE RECITETH IT, FOR HE SHALL BECOME A FAVOURED ONE OF OSIRIS UPON EARTH AMONG THE LIVING; HIS SON (?) SHALL BE ESTABLISHED IN HIS HOUSE EVERY DAY, AND HIS CHILDREN UPON THE [EARTH]. THIS FORMULA WAS RECITED BY ISIS AND HER SISTER NEPHTHYS, AND ALSO BY HER SON HORUS. AND IF IT BE RECITED FOR OSIRIS, IT WILL CAUSE THE SOUL OF THE DECEASED TO LIVE IN ÅḲERTET EVERY DAY, IT WILL GLADDEN HIS HEART, AND WILL OVERTHROW ALL HIS ENEMIES; AND IT SHALL BE RECITED DURING THE IVTH MONTH OF THE SEASON AKHET,[3] FROM THE XXIIND DAY TO THE XXVITH DAY THEREOF. [Here follow the commemorative sentences.]

Come to thy house, come to thy house, O Ån. Come to thy house, O Beautiful Bull, the Lord of men and women, the beloved one, the lord of women. O Beautiful Face, Chief of Åḳertet, Prince, First of those who are in the Other World, are not [all] hearts drunk through love of thee (O Un-nefer) triumphant? . . . .

[1] From a papyrus at Paris, a portion of which has been edited by Pierret (*Ét. Égyptologiques*, 1873), and see Brugsch, *Religion*, p. 626 ff.

[2] Or, commemorating Osiris.

[3] Choiak.

The hands of men and gods are lifted on high seeking for thee, even as those of a child [are stretched out] after his mother. Come thou to them, for their hearts are sad, and make them to appear as beings who rejoice. The lands of Horus[1] exult, the domains of Set are overthrown through fear of thee.

Hail, Osiris, First of those who are in the Other World! I am thy sister Isis. No god hath done [for thee] what I have done, and no goddess. I made a man child, though I was a woman, because of my desire

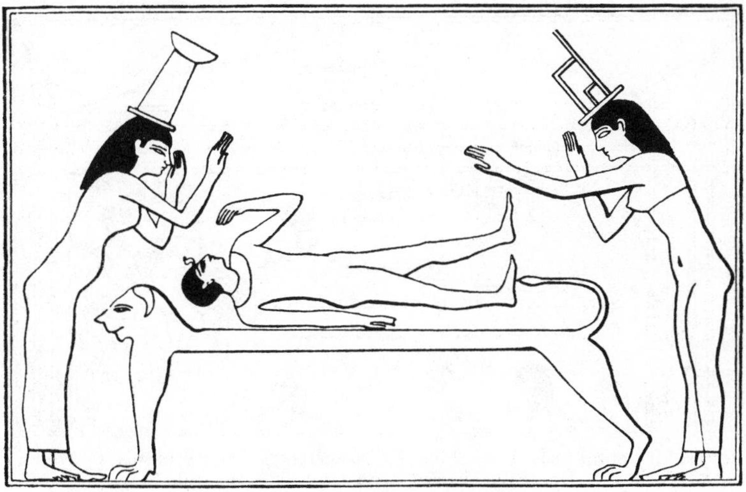

Isis and Nephthys bewailing the death of Osiris.
From a bas-relief at Philae.

to make thy name to live upon the earth. Thy divine essence was in my body; I placed him on the back of the earth (*i.e.*, brought him forth). He pleaded thy case, he healed thy suffering, he decreed the destruction of him that had caused it. Set hath fallen before his sword (or, knife), and the Smamiu fiends of Set have followed him. The throne of Ḳeb is to thee, O thou who art his beloved son!

Hail, Seker-Osiris! This calamity happened to thee in the primeval time. There have been made for thee mighty chambers in Ṭeṭṭu (Busiris). The god Uṭekh[2] embalmed thee and made sweet the smell of thee. The

[1] *I.e.*, the temple estates.

[2] .

god Ȧnpu (Anubis) toiled for thee in the place of purification, and performed all the things which he had to perform. I and my sister Nephthys kindled a lamp at the door of the *urit* chamber, so that [we] might snare in a net Set like a goose. Anubis came forth from the place of purification and overthrew all thine enemies. The mourners, male and female, made for thee their lamentations. Horus hath overthrown the Sebȧu fiends, and hath cast fetters about Set. The gods stand up and utter groans by reason of the great

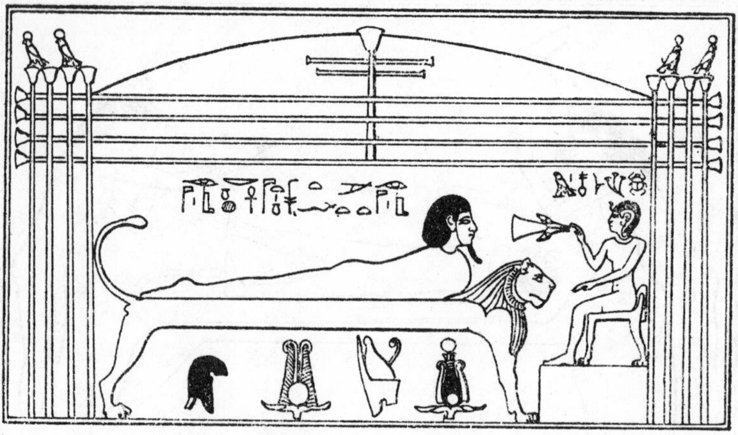

Osiris, king of the gods, Lord of life, Osiris smelling a flower presented by Horus. Under the bier are the four crowns of the god.
Mariette, *Dendĕrah*, IV, 65.

calamity which hath happened to thee, and they send forth their loud cries unto heaven. Those who dwell in the horizon hear the goddess making lamentation over the motionless one, they see what that accursed one hath done unto thee.

Thoth standeth at the door of the pure chamber in order to recite his formulae which shall give life to the soul each day. The Ploughing of the Earth[1] hath been performed for thee on the XXVIth day of the fourth month of the season Akhet. Thou comest forth in the Ṭuat. The Sons of Horus are with thee. Horus is before thee [with] the rope in his hands. The divine-

[1] *I.e.*, the sacrifice of human beings whose blood was used to moisten the earth.

father priests and the servants of the god prepare thy two ways (?) in the pure [chamber]. Thy mouth is opened by the "Book of Opening the Mouth." The Kher-ḥeb priest and the chief of the libationer priests, with their books of making [the soul] to live in their hands, recite the formulae over thee. The Setem priest hath opened thy mouth, Seker in the Ḥennu-Boat hath triumphed, thine enemies are overthrown.

Hail, Osiris Khenti-Åmentiu, come to thy sister, O (Un-nefer) triumphant, come to thy wife!

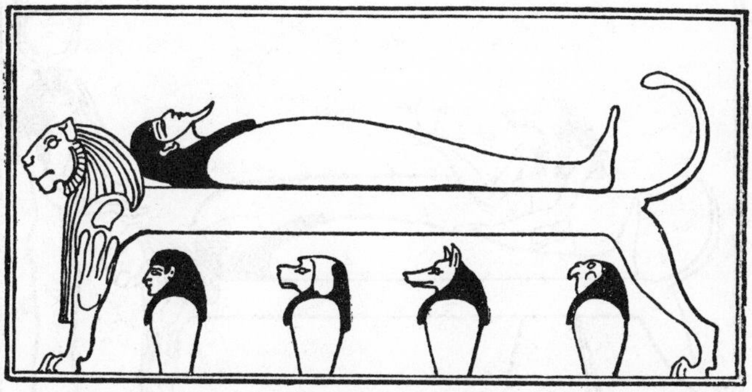

Osiris on his bier under which are the vases containing his intestines.
Mariette, *Dendèrah*, IV, 70.

Hail, Osiris Khenti-Åmentiu, the gods and the goddesses, with their heads on their knees, await thy coming to them; men with outcry and shouting call out: "O thou who art invisible, come to us." O Soul, perfect to all eternity, thy members are in a state of well-being, thy sufferings are relieved, every evil thing [in thee] is done away. Thy limbs are rejoined, thou art protected, thou hast no defect; thy limbs are rejoined, and not a member of thine is wanting.

1. Hail, Osiris Khenti-Åmentiu! O Form, thou hast thy head, O god of the lifted hand, [thy] crown and thy hair are [made of] genuine lapis-lazuli.

2. Hail, Osiris Khenti-Åmentiu! O Form, thou hast thy two eyes, thou seest with them; the Maāti goddesses love to protect thee.

3. Hail, Osiris Khenti-Åmentiu! O Form, thou

hast thine ears, wherewith thou shalt hear prayers for millions of years.

4. Hail, Osiris Khenti-Ȧmentiu! O Form, thou hast thy nose, thy nostrils snuff the breezes.

5. Hail, Osiris Khenti-Ȧmentiu! O Form, thou hast thy mouth; thou speakest therewith; Horus has pressed for thee thy mouth.

6. Hail, Osiris Khenti-Ȧmentiu! O Form, thy jaw-bones are on thee, firmly fixed.

Anubis anointing the mummy of Osiris with Isis giving directions.
Mariette, *Dendérah*, IV, 70.

7. Hail, Osiris Khenti-Ȧmentiu! O Form, thy beard [is made of] crystal which emitteth rays of light.

8. Hail, Osiris Khenti-Ȧmentiu! O Form, thy lips are of flint and thy teeth are turquoises.

9. Hail, Osiris Khenti-Ȧmentiu! O Form, thy tongue is the pilot of the Two Lands, it licketh up thine enemies.

10. Hail, Osiris Khenti-Ȧmentiu! O Form, thy body is of natron, it perisheth not.

11. Hail, Osiris Khenti-Ȧmentiu! O Form, thy neck beareth ornaments and amulets which reach to thy throat.

12. Hail, Osiris Khenti-Ȧmentiu! O Form, thy hands are firm on the staff, which is stable in thy abodes (?).

13. Hail, Osiris Khenti-Åmentiu! O Form, thy sinews (?) and thy vertebrae (or, joints) are stablished firmly.

14. Hail, Osiris Khenti-Åmentiu! O Form, thy belly, thy secret place, hideth that which is in it.

15. Hail, Osiris Khenti-Åmentiu! O Form, thy two shoulders are stablished firmly on thy back.

16. Hail, Osiris Khenti-Åmentiu! O Form, thou hast thy member and thy genitals that thou mayest copulate.

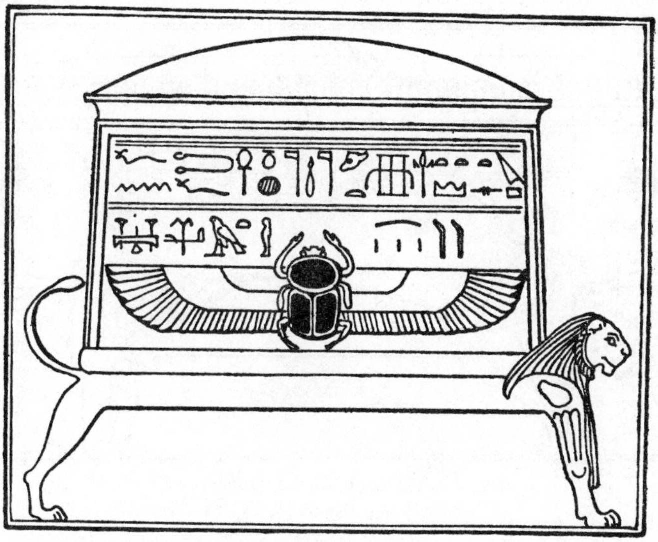

The bier and coffer of Fenth-f-ānkh Khenti Åbti.
Mariette, *Dendérah*, IV, 72.

17. Hail, Osiris Khenti-Åmentiu! O Form, thou hast thy backbone and thy buttocks, thou sittest upon the throne every day.

18. Hail, Osiris Khenti-Åmentiu! O Form, the soles of thy feet are on the earth, the water flood appeareth with them, O Osiris Khenti-Åmentiu!

Hail, Osiris Khenti-Åmentiu! Isis and Nephthys say :—

" Thou hast received thy head, thou hast united in " thy embrace thy flesh, thy limbs thou hast brought " unto thyself, thou hast gathered together thy members, " and they have come into thy mummified form. Thou "hast become like the god Sebeq, the Lord of the dead "body.

"Hail, Osiris Khenti-Åmentiu! There is health in "thy members, thy wounds are done away, thy suffering "is relieved, thy groaning shall never return. Come to "us the sisters, come to us; [our] hearts will live when "thou comest. Men shall cry out to thee, women weep "for thee with gladness at thy coming to them. [The "Two Lands] shall not lack thy name, and thou shalt be "stablished in the nomes of the gods for ever.

A local form of Osiris of Abydos, worshipped in Peḥu.
Mariette, *Dendérah*, IV, 72.

"Hail, Osiris Khenti-Åmentiu! Rise up, rise up! "Be thou not motionless. Thy son Horus over-"throweth thine enemies. Rise thou up into heaven, "unite thyself to Rā. The mariners of the divine boat "ascribe praises unto thee. The mouths of the gods of "the horizon utter glad words. Throats follow thee. "Thy love is in their hearts, thy terror is in their "breasts, when thou enterest into the Utchau, and "unitest thyself thereto. Those who are on the earth "and [those who are] in the Ṭuat flourish . . . Moon. "O Bull, who renewest youth in the sky each day, "creator of . . . and the Great Company of the Gods. "The Utchat goddess . . . filling of the mouth. . . . "At [thy] entrance into the Utchat the Sekhem (*i.e.*,

"Power) of Osiris, that is to say, Thoth, cometh into "being. When thou risest in the sky calamity "departeth, and when thou art seen in the sky on this "day bulls fecundate the cows and very many concep-"tions take place.

"Hail, Osiris Khenti-Åmentiu! Thou becomest a "child in the horizon of heaven each day, and thou "becomest old at every one of thy periods. Ḥāp (the "Nile) appeareth by the command of thy mouth, making "men and women to live on the effluxes which come "from thy members, making every field to flourish. At "thy coming that which is motionless groweth, and the "green plants of the marsh put forth blossoms.

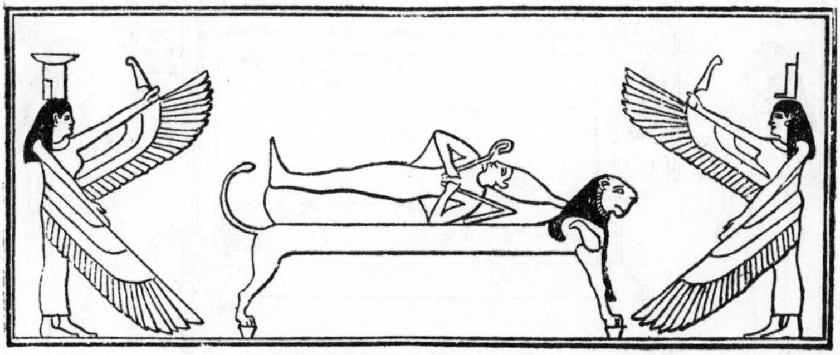

Isis and Nephthys providing Osiris with air.
Mariette, *Dendērah*, IV, 75.

"Hail, Osiris Khenti-Åmentiu! Thou art the Lord "of millions of years, the lifter up of the wild animals, "the Lord of cattle; every created thing hath its "existence from thee. To thee belongeth what is in "the earth, to thee belongeth what is in the heavens, "to thee belongeth what is in the waters, to thee "belongeth whatsoever is in them in thy name of 'Ḥāp.' "Hail to thee, in thy name of 'Inert one, chief of "Ḥet-urit.' Thou art the Lord of Truth, the hater of "sinners, who makest them to be overthrown in [their] "sins. The two Maāti goddesses are with thee, on no "day do they depart from thee. Sins (or, sinners) "cannot draw nigh unto thee in any place wherein thou "art. To thee belongeth whatsoever appertaineth to "life [and to] death. To thee belongeth whatsoever "appertaineth to men [and to] women.

"Hail, Osiris Khenti-Ȧmentiu! The mourners "weep, both men and women, and they lament. The "magical fluid of thy bier protecteth thee at [all] "seasons, thy members are guarded. All thine enemies "are overthrown. Thy throne is stablished firmly each "day like the throne of Rā, with mighty sovereignty, "by his ruling to his son's son. Shu and Tefnut were "with him in primeval time."

"Shu saith: 'O son of a son, I am thy son. Thou "renewest thy youth at the word (or, voice), it is I who

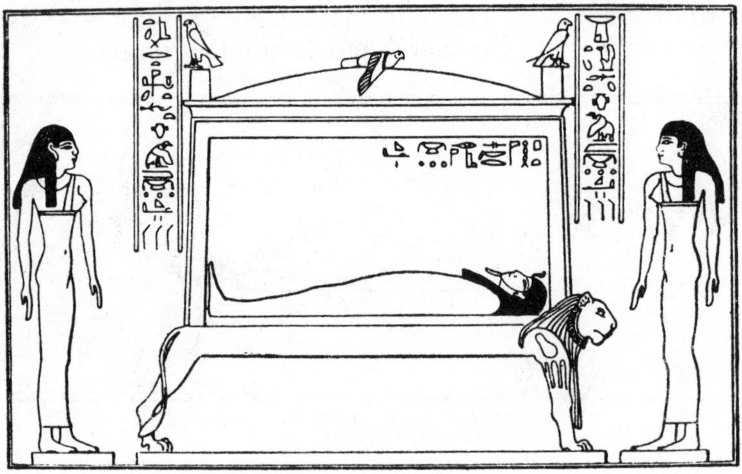

Seker-Osiris in his funerary coffer.
Mariette, *Dendérah*, IV, 89.

"give air to the throat which is closed, and from it "proceedeth life to the throat. Thou art Sovereign "among the gods, the Prince at the head of the Company of the Gods.'

"Tefnut saith: 'There is not to thee thy mother "who conceived by her father, on the day . . . giving "birth [to thee] with gladness. I made the form of the "*ȧmit* fire to overthrow all thine enemies. Likewise "all the . . . which I made for my father Rā in "primeval time I have made for Osiris Khenti-Ȧmentiu, "in order to create his form anew. I am the mother of "thy mother, I am (?) thy eldest daughter; thou art "[my] Sekhem.'" (?)

Men and women sing hymns of praise [when] thou risest on us at the season of thy departure. The beings of the South and the beings of the North must not be without a sight of thee. The beings of the West and the beings of the East are settled in the fear of thee, and they [bear tribute] on their heads each day. They shall never separate from thy Majesty by reason of their desire to see thee.

Hail, Osiris Khenti-Åmentiu! Come to me; I am thy sister Isis. Rise up, rise up, come at my call.

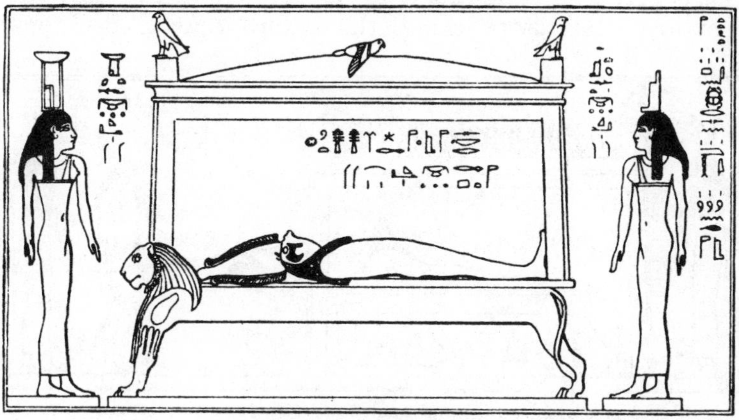

Seker-Osiris of Busiris.
Mariette, *Dendĕrah*, IV, 89.

Hearken thou to the recital of the things which I have done for thee, which I have done for thee [and] thy name in all the nomes, and in every domain, and how they hold thee in fear. They cry out unto thee at the time of thy departure. [Their] hearts are not wearied because of [their] love for thee. Be not afar off, come thou to us.

Hail, Osiris Khenti-Åmentiu! Thy mother Nut gave birth to thee in Thebes, and thou didst become a young man. As soon as thou didst rise on the earth as a child there was a shout of joy, and Rā heard it in his abode (?) in the Land of the North; hearts rejoice at thy birth. Thou arrivest at Ḥet-sutenit[1] on the night of the twentieth day of the month, and the fifteenth day of

[1] Xoïs.

the moon (*i.e.*, at full moon). Rā saw thee, thy love entered into his heart in this royal seat. He gave to thee the throne of thy father Ḳeb. Thou art his son whom he loveth. Thou enterest into the temple, into thy hidden abode, in Ḥet-Benben.[1] The gods in Ȧat-tcha-Mut[2] rejoice at the sight of thee. The city of Memphis[3] is with thee every day, and thou livest there in the form of Ȧtem-Kheperȧ, the Prince in Ȧnu (Heliopolis). Abydos is thy city in the Land of the South; thou art there in it every day in the form of Osiris Khenti-Ȧmentiu, the Great God, the Lord of Abydos. Isis stops the paths before that Evil One at

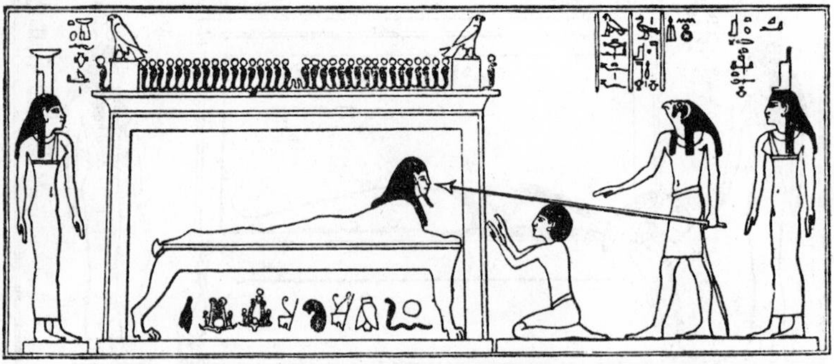

Horus opening the mouth and two eyes of Osiris with a spear.
Mariette, *Dendérah*, IV, 88.

Abydos, thy son Horus overthroweth thine enemies every day. Thou renewest thy youth in Ṭeṭṭu (Busiris). The goddess Nebt-ḥetep protecteth thee, the goddess Shenȧt keepeth off the fiend Set. The Temple Ȧnti [is full of] loud acclamations, and Re-stau [is full of] splendour.

The god Khnemu protecteth thee in Metchet (Elephantine). He poureth out for thee water in the Ḥetep Chamber in the Metchet temple, appearing in it anew, appearing from thee. The city of Beḥuṭet (Apollinopolis) is stablished under thy name, Horus overthroweth Set. The city of Horus of the West (Asphynis) rejoiceth at the sight of thee. The temple of

[1] The House of the Obelisk, *i.e.*, Heliopolis.
[2] Pasemis.
[3] Res-ȧneb-f.

Åptet (Ombos) hath joy of heart. The Spirits who dwell in Nekhent cry out with joy. The goddess Nekhebit protecteth thee in Nekhebet (Eileithyiaspolis). Splendid is thy rising up as the Lord of the South and North.[1] She is like a vulture in effecting thy protection, and she is like an uraeus serpent stablished on thy head; she maketh thee to rise like Rā every day. Offerings [to thee], with joy, with joy!

The god Ån purifieth thee in Ḥet-sekhemu (Diospolis Parva). Isis protecteth thee in Denderah (?), Nifu-urt[2]

Osiris Ṭeṭ of Busiris.
Mariette, *Dendérah*, IV, 88.

rejoiceth because of thee, thou art on the roads which are in it. The Two Companies of the Gods exalt thee high on thy standard. The gods look upon the two Merti (?) goddesses who are before thee, thy two Uatchti goddesses are in thy following, thou art never deprived of them. The city of Shenā-ḥennu rejoiceth at the sight of thee. Those who are in the East rejoice at thy KA (*i.e.*, double), and the cities of Åpu (?) and Khent-Menu utter many loud cries of joy. Hathor protecteth thee in Hierakonpolis, thou livest in Shaås-ḥetep (Hypselis).

Thou buildest up men and women, thou art the guide of the gods in thy name of Khnemu. Thy members are gathered together in Ḥet-Erṭuu, and the gods who dwell

1 .

2 A district of Abydos.

therein overthrow thine enemies. The god Thoth reciteth the Book of making the Spirit for thee in Khemenu (Hermopolis), and the Eight Gods of Hermopolis ascribe to thee praises as they did for thy father Rā. The gods of the city of Ḥesert rejoice in thee from the time thou enterest till thou departest. Ḥensu (Herakleopolis) adoreth thy Souls, and An-aårrut-f is under thee every day. Mer-ur (Moeris) rejoiceth, Smen-Ḥeru (Ptolemaïs) rejoiceth at thy coming. Thou hidest thy body in Pa-Ḥennu[1] until Hathor of Aphroditopolis cometh.

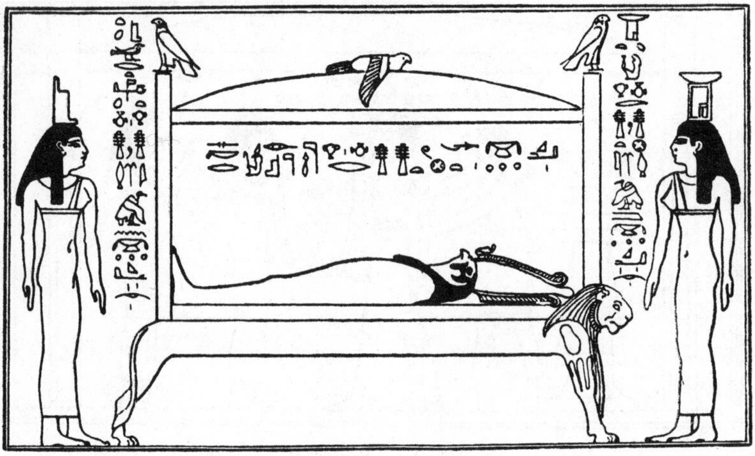

Seker-Osiris of Busiris, hawk-headed.
Mariette, *Dendĕrah*, IV, 90.

Memphis is established possessing thee. Kindled for thee is a fire in the hands of the goddess Rerȧt,[2] she performeth acts of protection for thee every day. Ptaḥ giveth air to thy nostrils. The Meriti-gods, chiefs of the Temple of Ptaḥ, protect thee. The sanctuary Shetat rejoiceth, the sanctuary Ḥennu is glad. The heart of Ptaḥ-resu-ȧneb-f is glad, he rejoiceth in thy love. The Temple of Sekhet resoundeth with music in thine honour. The Temple of Ȧqert rejoiceth possessing thee, and Horus overthroweth all thine enemies. The gods of Latopolis are full of the sight of thee. Thou art protected by Nut in the city of Apis, Momemphis

[1] The Temple of the Canal.
[2] The Hippopotamus goddess of the Nile.

rejoiceth in thine image. Thou suckest in pure life with the milk of the Cow-goddess Sekha-Ḥeru, and the Town of the Cow is full of happiness. The goddess Sekhmet protecteth thee in the lands of the Theḥennu, she defendeth thee; the queen of Mer-ur is glad.

The goddess of the Companies of the Gods tarrieth with thy name in the Temple of Neith, the city of Saïs is filled with glory at the sight of thee. Thou becomest hidden on the south side and on the north side, [thy] apparel is the work of the two Crocodile-gods. Thou

The goddesses Serqet and Ṭua (?) performing a magical ceremony for Osiris. From a bas-relief at Philae.

comest to Saïs, thou passest into the Temple of Ḥet-Khebit. The goddess Neith shooteth arrows from her bow to overthrow thine enemies utterly. Thou reachest Athribis, and thou appearest in the form of a bull upon his stand in thy name of Osiris-Uu, whilst Isis standeth before thee. She never leaveth thee. Thy name is in the mouth of her inhabitants, they praise thee where thou art all the day long, even as they praise Rā, the father of thy parents (*i.e.*, thy grandfather); the throne which thou lovest is in her (*i.e.*, Saïs). The Uraei-goddesses rejoice in thy image, and their sceptres bring thee healing season by season. The city of Pe rejoiceth at the sight of thee, and Ṭep bringeth hymns and praises before thy face. The goddess Uatchit, the Uraeus-goddess of the North, taketh up her place on thy head. Clusters of papyrus plants are presented unto thee in the city of Khebit;[1] all thine enemies are overthrown. The cities of Qebḥ-ḥer and Nai bow themselves down before thy face.

The children and young men come to thee from Heliopolis. The awe of thee filleth the temple of the god Sep, and thy name is spread abroad in . . . . The city of Kher-āḥa[2] is full of joy at the sight of thee, and

The Resurrection of Osiris.
From a bas-relief at Philae.

the Temple of Ȧmaḥet hath gladness of soul. Shenu-qebḥ is filled with joy of heart, and the holy city is glad; and under the form of Ḥetepit the goddess Hathor guardeth thee. Bast, the Lady of Bubastis, sendeth awe of thee among all men; thy strength against thine enemies is great. The town of Phacusa is glad. The god Sept, the Horus of the East, the Bull, the slayer of the Ȧnti, rejoiceth at the sight of thee. Ḥeru-Merti

[1] The Island of Khemmis of the classical writers.
[2] Babylon of Egypt.

protecteth thee, and overthroweth all thine enemies in the town of Sheṭen (Pharbaetus). The town of Tchān is glad, and the Land of Ḥāā is full of joy. The town of Remen keepeth a feast, the town of Horus in the North and Sma-Beḥuṭet rejoice in their hearts. The town of Theb-neter (Sebennytus) boweth low before thee, Ḥeru-Tema, with the lofty plumes, the lord of the crown, is the vanquisher of all thy foes. The town of Ḥet-Baiu (Thmuis) possesseth thy Ram, and thou appearest as

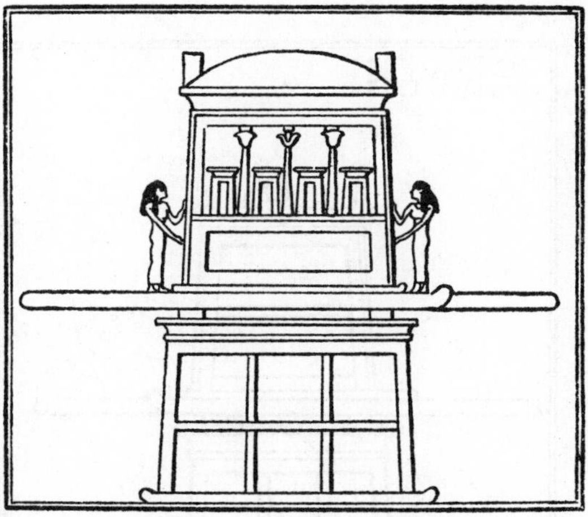

The Shrine Tenter on its sledge.
Mariette, *Dendérah*, IV, 65.

Ba-neb-Ṭeṭ (Mendes), the virile Ram, the master of virgins. The town of Hermopolis lieth under thy rule, and Thoth, the judge of the Two Combatants, stablisheth the writings which commemorate [the combat] . . . . Thou art in the place of Rā for ever.

THE LAMENTATIONS OF ISIS AND NEPHTHYS.[1]

THE BOOK OF THE COMMEMORATIVE SENTENCES WHICH ARE TO BE SAID BY THE TWO SISTERS [ISIS AND NEPHTHYS] IN THE HOUSE OF OSIRIS, KHENTI-ÅMENTIU, THE GREAT GOD, THE LORD OF ABYDOS, IN THE IVTH

[1] For the hieratic text and a French translation see J. de Horrack, *Les Lamentations*, Paris, 1866; for a hieroglyphic transcript see my *Egyptian Reading Book*, p. 78.

MONTH OF THE SEASON OF AKHET, ON THE XXVTH DAY OF THE SAME. THIS BOOK SHALL LIKEWISE BE RECITED IN EVERY SEAT OF OSIRIS DURING HIS FESTIVAL, FOR IT SHALL MAKE HIS SOUL TO BE A SPIRIT, SHALL STABLISH HIS BODY, SHALL MAKE HIS *KA* TO REJOICE, SHALL GIVE BREATH TO THE NOSTRILS AND AIR TO THE THROAT WHICH IS STOPPED, SHALL MAKE THE HEARTS OF ISIS AND NEPHTHYS HAPPY, SHALL PLACE HORUS ON THE THRONE OF HIS FATHER. IT IS BENEFICIAL TO RECITE THIS BOOK FROM THE HIEROGLYPHIC TEXT.

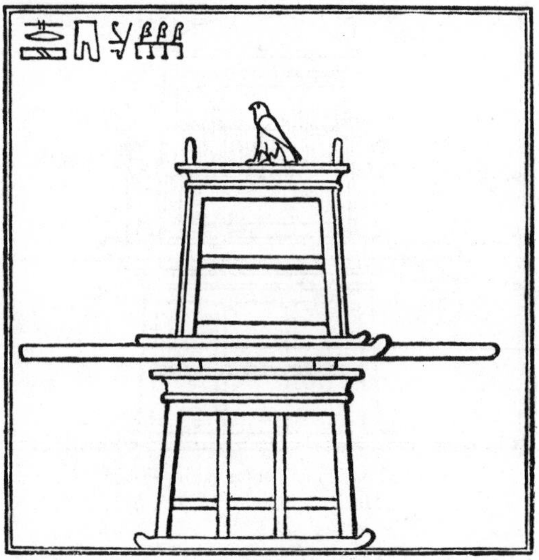

The Serekh Shrine containing remains of Osiris.
Mariette, *Dendĕrah*, IV, 67.

ISIS SAITH: "Come to thy house, come to thy "house. An, come to thy house. Thine enemy is "not. O beautiful Åḥi, come to thy house. Look "thou upon me, I am the sister who loveth thee, go not "far from me. O beautiful Boy, come to thy house, "immediately, immediately. I do not see thee, my "heart weepeth for thee, my two eyes follow thee about. "I am following thee about so that I may see thee. "Lo, I wait to see thee, I wait to see thee, Beautiful "Prince, lo, I wait to see thee. It is good to see thee. "it is good to see thee; O Ån, it is good to see thee, "Come to thy beloved one, come to thy beloved "one, Beautiful Being triumphant! Come to thy "sister. Come to thy wife. Come to thy wife, "O thou whose heart is still. Come to the lady of thy "house, I am thy sister by (?) thy mother. Go not "thou far from me. The faces of gods and men are "towards thee, they weep for thee all together. As "soon as I perceived [thee] I cried out unto thee, "weeping with a loud voice which penetrated heaven,

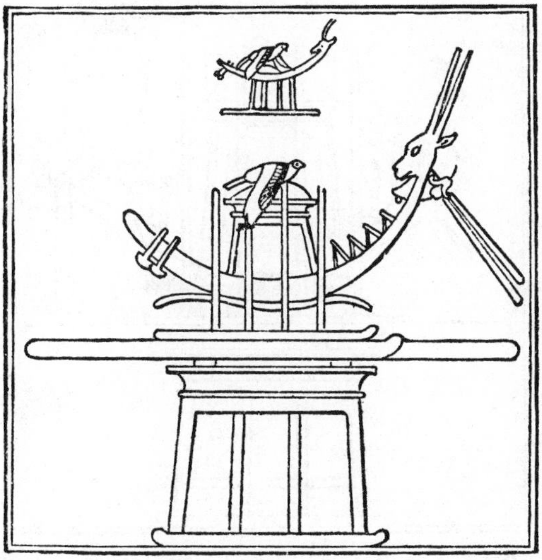

The Boat of Seker-Osiris on its sledge. It was drawn round the sanctuary at dawn. Mariette, *Dendérah*, IV, 64.

"and thou heardest not my voice. I am thy sister "who loved thee upon earth; none other loved more "than [thy] sister, thy sister."

NEPHTHYS SAITH: "O Beautiful Prince, come to thy "house. Let thy heart rejoice and be glad, for all "thine enemies have ceased to be. Thy two Sisters "are nigh unto thee, they protect thy bier, they address "thee with words [full of] tears as thou liest overthrown "on thy bier. Look thou at the young women, speak "to us, O Sovereign our Lord. Destroy thou all the "misery which is in our hearts. Thy *Shenit* nobles "among gods and men look upon thee [and say]:

"Turn thou to us thy face, O Sovereign our Lord!
"Life is [on] our face[s] in the seeing of thy face, turn
"not thou away thy face from us. The joy of our
"heart is in the sight of thee, O Beautiful Sovereign,
"our heart would see thee. I am thy sister Nephthys
"who loveth thee. Thy Sebȧu fiend hath fallen, he
"hath no being. I am with thee, and I act as a
"protectress of thy members for ever and ever."

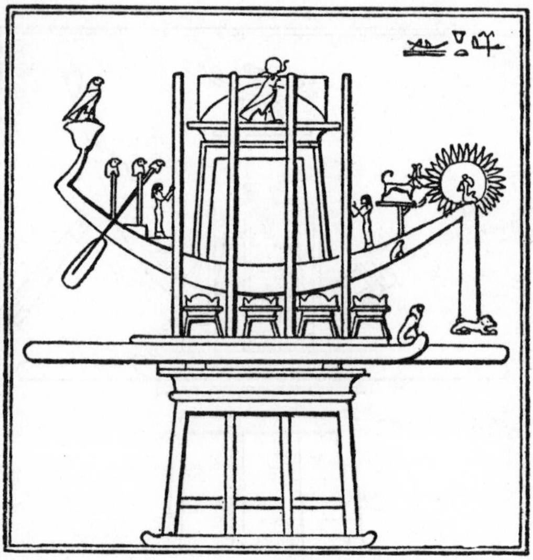

The Maāt Boat on its sledge. Harpokrates is seated on the prow.
Mariette, *Dendérah*, IV, 64.

ISIS SAITH: "Hail, thou god Ȧn, thou rollest up
"into the sky for us every day; we cease not to see thy
"beams. Thoth acteth as a protector for thee, he maketh
"to stand up thy soul in the Māāṭet Boat in thy name
"of Ȧāḥ. I have come to see thee and thy beauties
"within the Utcha in thy name of Ḥeb-enti-sȧs (?)
"(*i.e.*, the Sixth-day Festival). Thy *Shenit* nobles
"are round about thee, they depart not from thee.
"Thou hast conquered heaven by the greatness of thy
"majesty in thy name of 'Prince of the festival of the
"fifteenth day.' Thou risest upon us like Rā every
"day; thou shinest on us like Ȧtem. Gods and men
"live at the sight of thee. Thou risest on us, thou

“ illuminest the Two Lands. The horizon is covered
“ with the tracks of thy passings. The faces of gods
“ and men are turned to thee ; there is no evil thing
“ with them when thou risest. Thou sailest over the
“ sky, thine enemies exist not. I act as thy pro-
“ tector every day. Thou comest unto us as a babe
“ each month, we cease not to see thee. Thy divine
“ emanation glorifieth Saḥu (*i.e.*, the Orion god) in the

A Boat of Horus on its sledge.
Mariette, *Dendérah*, IV, 64.

“ heavens, rising and setting each day, and I am like
“ Sepṭet (*i.e.*, Sirius) behind thee, and I go not away
“ from thee. The holy and divine emanation which
“ cometh forth from thee vivifieth gods, men, quadrupeds,
“ and reptiles, and they live thereby. Thou sailest forth
“ to us from thy cavern at thy season to pour out the
“ seed of thy soul, to make abundant offerings for thy
“ KA, and to give life unto gods and men likewise.
“ Hail, thou Lord, there existeth no god who is like
“ unto thee. Heaven possesseth thy soul, earth pos-
“ sesseth thy similitudes, and the Ṭuat possesseth thy
“ secret things. Thy wife acteth as thy protectress,
“ thy son Horus is the Ḥeq (Governor) of the World.”

Nephthys saith: "Hail, Beautiful Sovereign! "Come to thy house, O (Beneficent Being) triumphant, come to Ṭeṭu (Busiris). Hail, Bull, thou "fertile one, come to Ānep (Mendes). O beloved one "of the sanctuary, come to the nome of Ḥāt-meḥit "(Mendes). Come to Ṭeṭṭet (Mendes town), the "place beloved of thy Soul. The Souls of thy fathers ". . . are to thee, thy son, the child Horus, brought

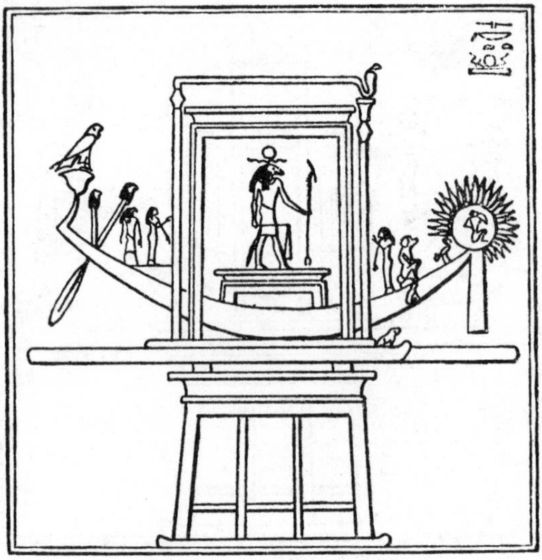

The Sektet Boat on its sledge with the shrine containing Osiris-Rā in the form of a ram-headed man. Harpokrates is seated on the prow.
Mariette, *Dendèrah*, IV, 64.

"forth by the Two Sisters, is before thee. I act as thy "protectress at dawn daily, and I never depart from "thee. Hail, god Ȧn! Come to Saïs; Sau is thy "name. Come to the nome of Sȧpi (?) (Saïtes), thou "shalt see thy mother Net (Neith); Beautiful Boy, "cease not to be with her, come thou to her breasts, "and drink deeply there, to thy fill. O Beautiful "Brother, depart not thou from her, O divine Son, "come to the city of Saïs. Come to Sȧpi, thy city. "Thy seat is the Temple of Ṭeb. Thou shalt repose "near thy mother for ever. She protecteth thy "members, she driveth away thy Sebȧu fiends, she

" acteth as the protectress of thy members for ever. " Hail, Beautiful Sovereign, come to thy house! O " Lord of Saïs, come thou to Saïs."

ISIS SAITH: " Come to thy house, come to thy " house! O Beautiful Sovereign, come to thy house! " Come, look thou upon thy son Horus, the king of " gods and men. He hath conquered cities and nomes " by reason of his august majesty. The heavens and " the earth are in fear of him, and the Land of Sti

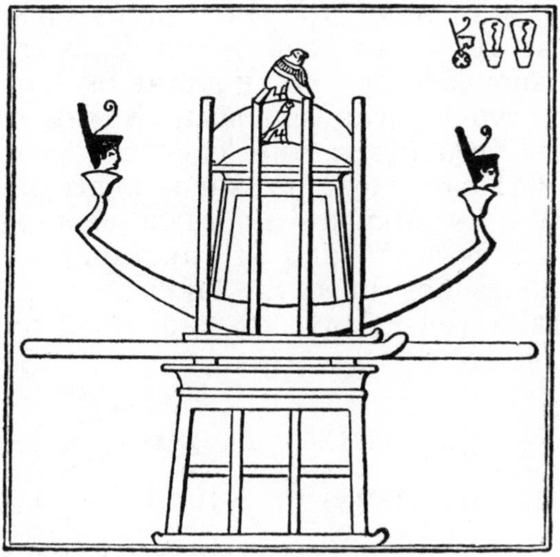

The Boat of the Âterti of the North.
Mariette, *Dendérah*, IV, 65.

" (Nubia) holdeth him to be conqueror. Thy nobles " among gods and men are to him in the Two Âterti,[1] " that they may perform what is to be performed for " thee. Thy Two Sisters are about thee to pour out " libations to thy KA. Thy son Horus maketh unto " thee the offerings which appear at the word—bread, " beer, oxen, geese. The god Thoth readeth the " service for thee, and he reciteth for thee his magical " spells. The [four] Sons of Horus act as guardians of " thy members, and make to be spirit thy soul every " day. Thy son Horus pronounceth thy name in thy " hidden chest, and placeth things (*i.e.*, offerings) to thy

[1] *I.e.*, the South and the North.

"KA. The gods hold in their hands the *nemmest* vases "to pour out libations to thy KA. Come thou to thy "nobles, O our Sovereign Lord, and depart thou not "from them."

RUBRIC: NOW AFTER THE ABOVE WORDS HAVE BEEN READ, THE PLACE BECOMETH MOST HOLY. LET NO HUMAN EYE (*I.E.*, NO MAN) LOOK ON OR LISTEN [AT THE READING] EXCEPT THE CHIEF KHER-ḤEB AND THE SETEM PRIEST. THEN TWO YOUNG AND FAIR WOMEN SHALL BE BROUGHT, AND MADE TO SEAT THEMSELVES ON THE GROUND BY THE CHIEF DOOR OF THE USEKHT CHAMBER. ON THE SHOULDER OF ONE THE NAME OF ISIS SHALL BE WRITTEN, AND ON THE SHOULDER OF THE OTHER THE NAME OF NEPHTHYS. AND CRYSTAL VASES FULL OF WATER SHALL BE PLACED IN THEIR RIGHT HANDS, AND CAKES MADE IN MEMPHIS IN THEIR LEFT HANDS, AND THEY SHALL PRESENT THEM AT THE THIRD AND AT THE EIGHTH HOURS OF THE DAY. THOU SHALT NOT CEASE AT ALL FROM THE READING OF THIS BOOK ON THE DAY OF THE FESTIVAL.

HYMNS TO OSIRIS.

I. THE HYMNS OF ANI THE SCRIBE.

1. Praise be unto Osiris Un-Nefer, the great god who dwelleth in Abṭu, king of eternity, lord of everlastingness, who passeth through millions of years in his existence. [He is] the firstborn son |

2. of the womb of Nut [and] was begotten by Ḳeb[1] the Erpāt. He is the lord of the Ureret Crown [and] the possessor of the lofty White Crown—the Sovereign of gods and men. |

3. He hath received the crook ⲋ [and] the whip, [and] the rank of his divine fathers. Let thy heart be glad, O thou who art in the funerary mountain, [for] thy son Horus is established on thy throne. |

4. Thou hast been crowned "Lord of Tattu" (Busiris), and "Ruler in Abṭu (Abydos). Thou makest the Two Lands (Egypt), to flourish triumphantly before.

[1] Strictly speaking, Ḳeb was the grandfather of Osiris.

5. Neb-er-tcher.[1] | He guideth that which hath not yet come into being in

6. his name "Ta-ḥer- | sta-nef." He draweth along the Two Lands (*i.e.*, Egypt)

7. with regularity in his name of "Seker." He is mighty in | . . . . and most terrible in his name of "Åsår" (Osiris).[2] The duration of his existence is an eternal *ḥenti* period[3] in his name of "Un-Nefer." |

8. Homage to thee, King of kings, Lord of lords, Governor of governors, Overlord of the Two Lands (Egypt), from the womb of Nut. He hath

9. governed | the countries [and] Åḳert. [With] limbs of silver-gold, and a head of lapis-lazuli, and turquoise all about him—thou god Ån of millions of years |

10. Extended of body, beautiful of face in Ta-Tchesert.[4] Grant thou glory in heaven, and power upon earth, and triumph in the Other World, and a sailing

11, 12. down the river | to Busiris in the form of a living | soul, and a sailing up the

13, 14. river | to Abydos like a Bennu bird, and a going in and a coming out |

15. without being repulsed at any of the gates | of the Ṭuat, and give thou

16, 17. | bread-cakes in the House of coolness, | and sepulchral offerings in Ånu

18. (Heliopolis), and a permanent | estate (or, possession) in Sekhet-Arui,

19. with wheat, barley, and | millet (*dhura*) therein —to the KA (*i.e.*, Double) of Osiris, the Scribe Ani.

II.

1. Praise be unto Osiris, the lord of everlastingness, Un-Nefer, Heru-Khuti, [whose] forms (or, transformations) are manifold, [whose] works are mighty.

[1] *I.e.*, the Creator and Sustainer of the universe, the Universal Lord.

[2] Here there is a play on the words *usr*, "strength," and *Åsår*, "Osiris."

[3] The ḥenti period consisted of two periods, each containing sixty years.

[4] Originally a part of Abydos, but subsequently the Other World in general.

2. He is Ptaḥ-Sekri-Tem in Heliopolis, and the Lord of the Sanctuary Shethit. He is the creator of Ḥet-ka-Ptaḥ (*i.e.*, Memphis) and the gods who are therein. [He is] the guide of the Ṭuat.

3. Thou art praised by them (*i.e.*, the Spirits of the Ṭuat) when thou joinest thyself to the night sky. Isis embraceth thee with content, she chaseth away the Tchai fiend

4. from the entrance of thy paths. Thou turnest thy face to Ȧmentet, thou illuminest the Two Lands (Egypt) with silver-gold light. The [souls who] are lying on their biers rise up to look upon thee, they snuff

5. the breezes [and] they behold thy face as the Disk rolleth on its horizon; their hearts are content at the sight of thee, O thou who art ETERNITY and EVERLASTINGNESS!

LITANY.

1. Homage to thee, O Lamp in Heliopolis, and Ḥenmemet-spirit in Kher-āḥa, Unti, who art more glorious than the gods of the Sheta Shrine in Heliopolis!

O grant thou unto me a path whereon I may journey in peace. I am righteous. I have not uttered lies wilfully. I have not acted a double part (or, dealt doubly).

2. Homage to thee, O Ȧn in Ȧntes (?). Great God, Ḥeru-Khuti, thou traversest the heights of heaven with spacious strides—thou who art Ḥeru-Khuti!

O grant thou unto me a path whereon I may journey in peace. I am righteous. I have not uttered lies wilfully. I have not dealt doubly.

3. Homage to thee, O Everlasting Soul, Ram-god, dweller in Ṭaṭṭu (Mendes), Un-Nefer, Son of Nut, who art the Lord of Ȧḳert.

O grant thou unto me a path whereon I may journey in peace. I am righteous. I have not uttered lies wilfully. I have not dealt doubly.

4. Homage to thee in thy dominion over Ṭeṭu (Busiris), the Ureret Crown is firmly fixed upon thy

head. Thou art One, thou effectest thine own protection. Thou restest in peace in Ṭeṭu (Busiris).

O grant thou unto me a path whereon I may journey in peace. I am righteous. I have not uttered lies wilfully. I have not dealt doubly.

5. Homage to thee, O Lord of the Nārt tree. The Seker Boat hath been placed upon its sledge. Turn back the Sebȧu Fiend, the Worker of evil, and make the Utchat to rest upon its throne.

O grant thou unto me a path whereon I may journey in peace. I am righteous. I have not uttered lies wilfully. I have not dealt doubly.

6. Homage to thee, O Mighty One in thine hour, Chief, Prince, President of Ȧn-ruṭ-f, Lord of Eternity, Creator of Everlastingness. Thou art the Lord of Suten-ḥenen (*i.e.*, Ḥensu, or Hânês).

O grant thou unto me a path whereon I may journey in peace. I am righteous. I have not uttered lies wilfully. I have not dealt doubly.

7. Homage to thee, O thou who art founded upon Truth. Thou art the Lord of Abydos, the members of thy body are joined to Ta-Tchesert. Thou art he to whom lies are abominations.

O grant thou unto me a path whereon I may journey in peace. I am righteous. I have not uttered lies wilfully. I have not dealt doubly.

8. Homage to thee, O thou who dwellest in thy Boat. Thou bringest the Nile forth from his cavern, and the Light-god rolleth above thy body. Thou art the dweller in Nekhen.

O grant thou unto me a path whereon I may journey in peace. I am righteous. I have not uttered lies wilfully. I have not dealt doubly.

9. Homage to thee, O Maker of the gods, king of the South and North, (Osiris), triumphant, Overlord of

the Two Lands (*i.e.*, Egypt), in thy seasons of beneficence. Thou art the Lord of the two Halves of Egypt.

O grant thou unto me a path whereon I may journey in peace. I am righteous. I have not uttered lies wilfully. I have not dealt doubly.

III. Hymn of Hunefer the Scribe.

1, 2. Praise be unto Osiris, and let adorations be made unto him! The Osiris Hunefer, the steward of the Palace of the Lord of the Two Lands, [(Men-Maāt-Rā), *i.e.*, Seti I] smelleth the ground before Un-Nefer, and toucheth the earth with his forehead before the Lord of Ta-Tchesert, and exalteth Him that is on his sand (*i.e.*, Osiris), saying:

3. I have come unto thee, O son of Nut, Osiris, Prince of Everlastingness.

4. I am among the followers (or body-guard) of Thoth, I applaud everything which he hath done [for thee]. He brought unto thee sweet breezes (*i.e.*, fresh air) for thy nostrils, and life and serenity to thy beautiful face, and he brought the north wind which proceedeth from the god Temu to thy nostrils, O Lord of Ta-Tchesert. He made the light of Shu to fall upon thy body. He illumined for thee [thy] path with splendour.

10. He destroyed for thee the defects which appertained to thy members by the magical power of the words of his mouth. He made the Two Horus Brethren[1] to be at peace with thee. He destroyed for thee the rain storm and the thunder and the lightning. He made the Two Reḥti Goddesses, the Two Sisters of the Two Lands, to be at peace before thee, he did away the hostility which was in their hearts, and each became reconciled to the other.

Thy son Horus is triumphant before the whole Company of the Gods; the sovereignty of the earth hath been given to him, and his dominion reacheth to the uttermost limit thereof. The throne of Ḳeb hath been awarded to him, and the full rank of the god

[1] Horus and Set.

Temu, and these are confirmed [to him] by the writings which are in the record chamber, and are engraved upon a block of alabaster (?), according to the decree of 15. thy Father Tanen on the Great Throne.

He (*i.e.*, Thoth) hath set his brother on that which Shu supporteth, to spread out the waters of the firmament, to [stablish] the mountains and hills, to make to germinate (or, flourish) the green things which grow on the untilled wastes, and the grain which shooteth up in the fields. He maketh offerings [to come] by water and by land. Gods celestial and gods terrestrial follow him [*i.e.*, Horus] into his hall, and every decree which he maketh in respect of them they accept and carry out forthwith.

Let thy heart be happy, O Lord of the gods, let thy heart rejoice exceedingly. Kamt (Egypt) and the Red Land give service to thy diadem. The temples and their properties are stablished in their places. Cities [and] nomes are founded (?) in their names. We pay unto thee the offerings which are obligatory, and oblations are made in thy name for ever.

20. Titles of praise are invoked upon thy name. Libations of cool water are poured out to thy Ka. Sepulchral meals are brought to the Spirits who are in thy train. Water is poured out on the bread (?) on both sides of the souls of the dead in this land. Every plan of thine which from the beginning was according to his (*i.e.*, Rā's) commands hath been carried out. 25. Therefore thou wast crowned, O son of Nut, like Neb-er-tcher at his coronation. Thou art a living being. Thou art established. Thou renewest thy youth. Thou art whole and perfect. · Thy father Rā maketh strong (or, protecteth) thy members. Thy Company of gods make adorations to thee. Isis is with thee, she never separateth herself from thee. Thou art not overthrown by thine enemies.

The Lords of all lands (*i.e.*, the world) thank thee for thy beauteous bounty as they thank Rā when he riseth up in the sky at sunrise. Thou art crowned like him that is exalted on his standard, and thy beauteous bounty exalteth the face and maketh long the stride. 30. It is thy father Ḳeb who hath given unto thee sovereignty, and it is he who hath created thy beauteous bounty. Nut, the genetrix of the gods, was she who caused thy members to come into being, and fashioned thee as the "greatest of five gods."[1] Thou art established king. The White Crown is upon thy head. Thou graspest the sceptre and the whip. Whilst thou wast in the womb, and before thou didst appear on the earth, thou wast crowned Lord of the Two Lands, and the Atef Crown of Rā was upon thy brow. The gods approach

The Boat of the Återti of the South.
Mariette, *Dendérah*, IV, 65.

thee bowing their backs because of the fear in which they hold thee, and their bodies swaying about withdraw themselves when they see thee arrayed in the awful majesty of Rā, and the victory of thy Majesty is in their hearts. Life is with thee, offerings follow in thy train, and the statutory offerings are offered up before thee.

Grant thou that I may have my being as a follower of thy Majesty, even as I lived with thee upon earth. Let my soul be called, and let it be 35. found near the Lords of Truth. I have come into the City of God, the territory of primeval time, Ba-soul, Double, and

[1] *I.e.*, Osiris, Isis, Set, Nephthys, and Horus or Anubis.

Spirit-soul in this land. The god thereof is the Lord of Maāt, the Lord of offerings, the Most Holy One. This land draweth unto itself every land. The South cometh sailing down the river, and the North steered by winds cometh each day to celebrate a feast, according to the decree of its God, who is the Lord of offerings (?) therein. And doth he not say :—Assuredly there shall be joy to him that performeth Maāt (or, maketh the offerings which are due) to the god who is in it? He giveth old age to him that doeth this for him, and after

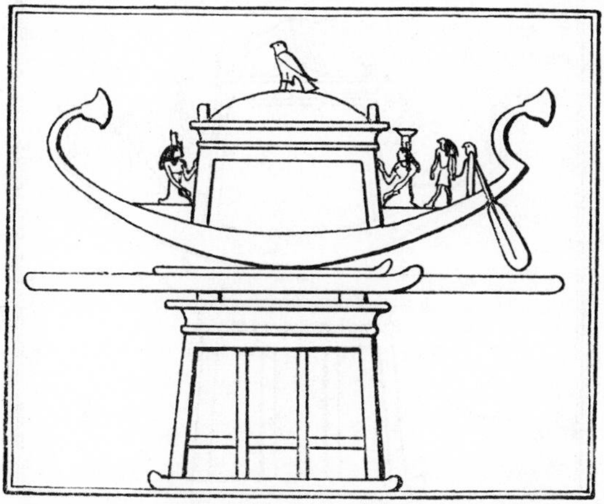

Boat with a shrine containing the body of Osiris; Nephthys kneels at the head and Isis at the foot.
Mariette, *Dendérah*, IV, 66.

him that followeth him loyally there shall follow offerings, and finally he shall attain to a beautiful funeral and shall be buried in the earth in Ta-Tchesert.

I have come unto thee, and my two hands hold Truth, and there is no falsehood in my breast. 40. I have set Truth before thee, for I know that it is that whereon thou livest. I have committed no sin in this land, and I have defrauded no man of that which is his.

I am Thoth, the perfect scribe, whose hands are pure, the lord of purity, the destroyer of evil, the righteous scribe whose abomination is sin. Behold, I am the writing reed of Neb-er-tcher, the lord of laws, who giveth forth the word of wisdom and understanding, whose speech founded the Two Lands (Egypt). I am

Thoth, the Lord of Truth, I make the feeble one to triumph, and I avenge the oppressed one by punishing him that wronged him. I have scattered the darkness, I have rolled away the thunder storm, I have brought air to Un-Nefer, the beautiful breeze of the north wind, which came forth from the womb 45. of his mother, and I have made Horus to enter into the Hidden Shrine to vivify the heart of the god of the Still-Heart Un-Nefer, the Son of Nut, triumphant.

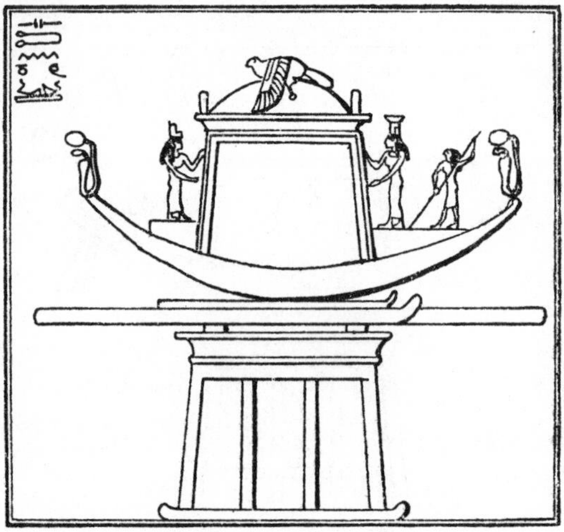

The Sethenu Boat of Osiris on its sledge.
Mariette, *Dendérah*, IV, 67.

IV. Hymn of Sutimes.

The Osiris Sutimes, the libationer and president of the altar chamber in the Åpts, the president of the scribes of the temple of Åmen, triumphant, saith :—

Homage to thee, O thou God, holy one, great in beneficent deeds, thou Prince of Eternity, who presideth over his place in the Sektet Boat, thou Mighty One of risings in the Āṭet Boat! Praises are ascribed unto thee both in heaven and upon earth. The Pāt beings and the Rekhit beings exalt thee, and the greatness of thy awe is in the hearts of men, the Spirits, and the Dead. Thou placest thy Souls in Ṭeṭṭeṭ (Busiris or Mendes) and thine awe is in Suten-ḥenen. Thou placest the visible emblems of thyself in Heliopolis, and the greatness of thy forms in the Place of Purification. I come to thee, my heart bearing truth, and my breast containing no falsehood. Grant thou that I may have my existence among the living, and that I may float down and sail up the river among thy followers.

V. Hymn to Osiris.[1]

Homage to thee, Osiris, Lord of eternity, King of the Gods, whose names are manifold, whose forms are holy, thou being of hidden form in the temples, whose KA is holy. Thou art the Governor of Ṭaṭṭu (Busiris), and also the mighty one in Sekhem (Letopolis). Thou art the lord to whom praises are ascribed in the nome of Ati, thou art the Prince of divine food in Ȧnu. Thou art the Lord who is commemorated in Maāti, the Hidden Soul, the Lord of Qerrt (Elephantine), the Ruler supreme in White Wall (Memphis). Thou art the Soul of Rā, his own body, and hast thy place of rest in Ḥenensu (Herakleopolis). Thou art the beneficent one, and art praised in Nārt. Thou makest thy soul to be raised up. Thou art the Lord of the Great House in Khemenu (Hermopolis). Thou art the mighty one of victories in Shas-ḥetep, the Lord of eternity, the Governor of Abydos. The path of his throne is in Ta-tcheser (*i.e.*, a part of Ȧbydos). Thy name is established in the mouths of men. Thou art the substance of the Two Lands (Egypt). Thou art Tem, the feeder of the KAU (Doubles), the Governor of the Companies of the gods. Thou art the beneficent Spirit among the spirits. The god of the Celestial Ocean (Nu) draweth from thee his waters. Thou sendest forth the north wind at eventide, and breath from thy nostrils to the satisfaction of thy heart. Thy heart reneweth its youth, thou producest the . . . . The stars in the celestial heights are obedient unto thee, and the great doors of the sky open themselves before thee. Thou art he to whom praises are ascribed in the southern heaven, and thanks are given for thee in the

[1] See Chabas, *Rev. Arch.*, 1857, p. 65; Ledrain, *Monuments*, Plate XXII ff.; Budge, *First Steps*, pp. 179–188.

northern heaven. The imperishable stars are under thy supervision, and the stars which never set are thy thrones. Offerings appear before thee at the decree of Ḳeb. The Companies of the Gods praise thee, and the gods of the Ṭuat (Other World) smell the earth in paying homage to thee. The uttermost parts of the earth bow before thee, and the limits of the skies entreat thee with supplication when they see thee. The holy ones are overcome before thee, and all Egypt offereth

The Boat containing the head box and standard of Osiris.
Mariette, *Dendĕrah*, IV, 68.

thanksgiving unto thee when it meeteth Thy Majesty. Thou art a shining Spirit-body, the Governor of Spirit-bodies ; permanent is thy rank, established is thy rule. Thou art the well-doing Sekhem (Power) of the Company of the Gods, gracious is thy face, and beloved by him that seeth it. Thy fear is set in all the lands by reason of thy perfect love, and they cry out to thy name making it the first of names, and all people make offerings to thee. Thou art the lord who art commemorated in heaven and upon earth. Many are the cries which are made to thee at the Uaḳ festival, and with one heart and voice Egypt raiseth cries of joy to thee.

Thou art the Great Chief, the first among thy brethren, the Prince of the Company of the Gods, the stablisher of Right and Truth throughout the World, the Son who was set on the great throne of his father Ḳeb. Thou art the beloved of thy mother Nut, the mighty one of valour, who overthrew the Sebȧu fiend. Thou didst stand up and smite thine enemy, and set thy fear in thine adversary. Thou dost bring the boundaries of the mountains (?). Thy heart is fixed (or, determined),

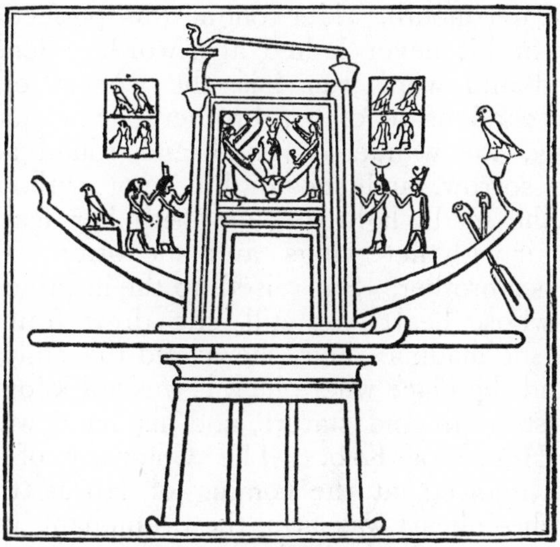

The Mākhet Boat on its sledge.
Mariette, *Dendérah*, IV, 68.

thy legs are set firm. Thou art the heir of Ḳeb and of the sovereignty of the Two Lords (Egypt). He (Ḳeb) hath seen his splendours, he hath decreed for him the guidance of the world by thy hand as long as times endure. Thou hast made this earth with thy hand, and the waters, and the winds, and the vegetation, and all the cattle, and all the feathered fowl, and all the fish, and all the creeping things, and all the wild animals thereof. The desert is the lawful possession of the son of Nut. The Two Lands (Egypt) are content to crown thee upon the throne of thy father, like Rā.

Thou rollest up into the horizon, thou hast set light over the darkness, thou sendest forth air (or, light) from thy plumes, and thou floodest the Two Lands like the Disk at daybreak. Thy crown penetrateth the height of heaven, thou art the companion of the stars, and the guide of every god. Thou art beneficent in decree and speech, the favoured one of the Great Company of the Gods, and the beloved of the Little Company of the Gods.

His sister [Isis] hath protected him, and hath repulsed the fiends, and turned aside calamities (or, times [of evil]). She uttered the spell with the magical power of her mouth. Her tongue was perfect (or, well-trained), and it never halted at a word. Beneficent in command and word was Isis, the woman of magical spells, the advocate of her brother. She sought him untiringly, she wandered round and round about this earth in sorrow, and she alighted not without finding him. She made light (or, air) with her feathers, she created air with her wings, and she uttered the death wail for her brother. She raised up the inactive members of him whose heart was still, she drew from him his essence, she made an heir, she reared the child in loneliness, and the place where he was was not known, and he grew in strength and stature, and his hand was mighty in the House of Ḳeb. The Company of the God rejoiced, rejoiced, at the coming of Horus, the son of Osiris, whose heart was firm, the triumphant, the son of Isis, the heir of Osiris. The sovereign chiefs of Maāt, and the Company of the Gods, and Neb-er-tcher himself, and the Lords of Maāt, gathered together to him, and they assembled in the [Great House of Ȧnu]. And verily, those who repulse sin rejoice in the House of Ḳeb to bestow its dignity upon the Lord thereof and the sovereignty of Truth.

CHAPTER XVII.

Osiris and the African Grave.

As the priests of Osiris and the regulations made by them for his cult forbade the decapitation and mutilation, or dismemberment, of the bodies of worshippers of this god, it was obviously necessary to provide tombs for such bodies, and to place them in graves, where they would be protected from the attacks of human, animal, and other eaters of the dead. The making of a good tomb, however simple, demanded the expenditure of money, or its equivalent, and thus it follows, as a matter of course, that only kings, chiefs, nobles, or men of high position, who could command the services of slaves, would be buried in a tomb, and that all the poor, or common people, would go without burial. As a result of the excavations which have been made in Egypt during the last thirty years, thousands of graves have been brought to light, but these, after all, must represent a very small proportion of the graves which would be necessary for the burial of even the upper classes of the Egyptians during the long period of the history of the country, which covers some thousands of years. The Egyptians had to solve the same difficulty as their kinsmen in other parts of Africa, namely, what to do with the dead, and it is probable that they solved it, in the earliest times at least, in the same way that the peoples in the Sûdân solve it at the present day. Rightly has Schweinfurth said: "Not a custom, not a superstition "is found in one part which is not more or less accurately repeated in another; not one contrivance of "design, not one weapon of war exists of which it can "be declared that it is the exclusive property of any one "race. From north to south, and from sea to sea, in "some form or other, every invention is sure to be "repeated; it is the thing that hath been."[1]

[1] *Heart of Africa*, Vol. I, p. 313.

Before the time of Osiris some of the Egyptians probably ate their dead, and used some of them up in making "medicines" of a magic character. Even after the cult of Osiris was established we read that the *erṭu* of his body, *i.e.*, the fluids which came forth from it after death, gave life,[1] and it is well known that in Africa at the present day the brains and fat of the dead are used in making charms. Thus the Borfimor "medicine" was a harmless substance enough until human fat was added to it, when it became an all-powerful fetish. This fat was procured from the intestines of men who were killed by the Human Leopard Society.[2] The infamous Tembandumba[3] pounded her child which she was feeding at her breast in a mortar, with roots, leaves, oils, etc., and made an ointment, with which she is said to have rendered herself invulnerable. Her subjects killed their male children also, and turned them into ointment, some of which was preserved till Winwood Reade's time, and was called "Magija Samba."[4] The Mpongwe sever the head from the body of a partially decomposed man, and suspend it above a mass of chalk which is placed to receive the moisture that drops from it. By rubbing the chalk on the foreheads of the living it is thought that they will acquire the brain power of the man whose brains have dropped on the chalk.[5] The eater of the brain becomes endowed with bravery.[6] Miss Kingsley found in a fetish bag a human hand (fresh), three big toes, four eyes, and two ears.[7]

The dead among the Egyptians who were not eaten by men were disposed of by the crocodiles in the rivers, by the hyaenas and jackals in the desert, and probably some of them by burning; at all events, judging by the graves which remain, the number that were buried were comparatively few. It seems from allusions in the Egyptian

[1] Budge, *Liturgy of Funerary Offerings*, p. 53.

[2] Alldridge, *The Sherbro and Its Hinterland*, p. 153.

[3] Or, Temba-Ndumba.—Burton, *A Mission to Gelele, King of Dahome*, 1864, Vol. I, p. 71.

[4] *Savage Africa*, p. 367.

[5] Nassau, *Fetichism in West Africa*, pp. 158, 162; Wilson, *Western Africa*, pp. 393, 394; Winwood Reade, *Savage Africa*, p. 248.

[6] Du Chaillu, *Adventures*, pp. 168, 169.

[7] *Travels in West Africa*, London, 1897, p. 273.

texts as if the custom of burning the dead was commoner in early times than has been generally supposed. In the Book of Overthrowing Āpep, this archfiend and his associates are burnt by the flames of the Sun-god and consumed.[1] In the Book Åm-Ṭuat, the bodies, souls, shadows and heads of the enemies of Rā are burnt and consumed daily in pits of fire.[2] In the Book of the Dead several allusions to burning occur. Thus the Rubrics of Chapters XVIII and XX say that the recital of these Chapters will enable a man to "come forth (*i.e.*, escape) from the fire." In Chapter XVII we read of the monster who feeds on the dead, and watches at the Bight of the Lake of Fire, and in Chapter LXXI are mentioned the Seven Beings who work slaughter in the Lake of Fire, who cut off hands and hack necks to pieces, and seize hearts and tear them out of the breasts. In Chapter LXIIIA the deceased prays in one version that "he may neither be burnt up nor destroyed by fire," and in the other he states that Osiris escaped from the fire and was not burnt. In Chapter CXXVI the deceased addresses the four apes who sit one at each corner of a rectangular lake of fire, "by the fire from whose mouths the gods are propitiated," and beseeches them to allow him to enter Åmentet. The Lake of Fire was no doubt a lake of boiling water, the drinking from which the deceased wished to avoid at all costs. A legend referred to in Chapter CXXV mentions that the abode of Osiris has a covering of fire, that its walls are living serpents, and that it rests on water ; whether the water is boiling or not the text does not say. These passages make it quite clear that the cult of Osiris forbade the burning of the body, and that at one time certain Egyptian peoples must have burnt their dead. The custom had not entirely died out in the Sûdân in the first or second century of our era, for in 1902 I found at the Pyramids of Meroë several pots containing ashes of the dead and calcined bones.[3] According to Frobenius, the Madgo tribes who live near the Mañbattu burn the bodies of the dead, and scatter their ashes.[4] As regards the other ways of disposing of the

[1] Budge, Papyrus of Nesi Amsu (in *Archaeologia*, Vol. LII).

[2] Division XI.

[3] Budge, *Egyptian Sudan*, Vol. I, p. 343.

[4] *Die Heiden-Neger des ägyptischen Sudan*, Berlin, 1893, p. 437.

dead followed by modern peoples in Africa, almost everywhere the common, or very poor, or very old, folk are thrown "into the bush" for the kites and hyaenas to devour. The Masai wholly decline to bury the dead, for they believe they would poison the soil;[1] this may be due to the fact that they believe in annihilation.

The oldest form of the African tomb is a pit dug in the ground, on the bottom of which the dead person was placed. Attempts were made at a very early period to protect the body from contact with the earth, for it was sometimes wrapped up in a reed mat, and sometimes in the skin of some animal. Another method of protecting the body was to place it in a hollow made in one side of the pit at the bottom, and this hollow subsequently developed into the sarcophagus chamber of the Egyptian tomb. In the Sûdân no stone buildings or tombs of any kind could be built because of the want of lime,[2] and therefore from the earliest period to the present time the essential characteristics of the African tomb have remained unchanged in that region. In Egypt several general modifications and developments took place in tombs at a very early period, but from first to last the essentials for all tombs were: 1. A funerary chamber, usually at the top of the pit, where offerings were placed. 2. A pit. 3. A chamber for the body or mummy, usually called the sarcophagus chamber, or mummy chamber.

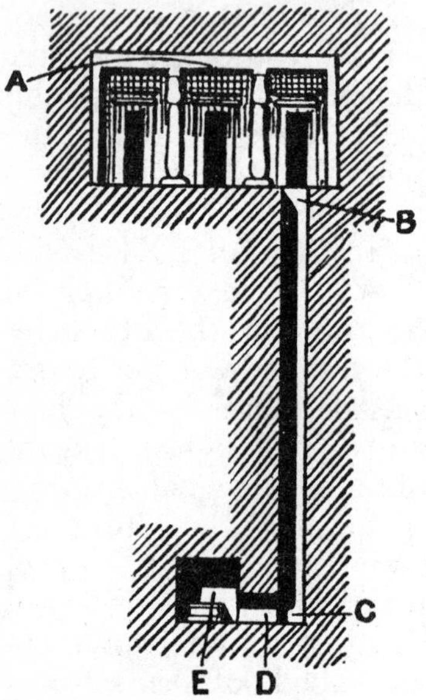

A, Tomb above ground.
B, C, Pit or shaft.
D, Corridor leading to mummy chamber.
E, Mummy chamber.

Sometime between the XIIth and XVIIIth dynasties, when a great development in the cult of Osiris took

[1] Joseph Thomson, *Through Masai Land*, London, 1885, p. 444.
[2] Schweinfurth, *Heart of Africa*, Vol. I, p. 208.

place throughout Egypt, the view became general that Osiris was buried at Abydos. How or why this happened is not known, but it may have been due to the revival of an ancient tradition to this effect. Be this as it may, quite early in the XVIIIth dynasty, the Egyptians felt sure that the body of Osiris rested at Abydos, and they identified a tomb of one of the kings of the Ist dynasty as the tomb of Osiris. This tomb was made for a king whose Horus name is written with a sign which I believe to have been read "Khent,"[1] and it is possible that those who made the identification connected in their minds this name with "Khenti-Ȧmenti," an old god of the dead of Abydos, whose position and attributes were absorbed by Osiris. From the XVIIIth dynasty onwards this tomb enjoyed great repute as the shrine of Osiris, and offerings poured into it in abundance. Between the XXIst and XXVIth dynasties a massive granite bier, on which was cut in high relief a figure of Osiris, was placed in the tomb, which for a considerable time afterwards continued to be regarded as the veritable tomb of Osiris. Whether this view was correct or not does not concern us here, for it is as a tomb merely that we are considering it. This tomb was discovered and excavated by M. E. Amélineau in the winter of 1897–8, and he has published a long detailed account of his labours in connection with it.[2] It was a rectangular building, the east and south walls of which were about 8 feet thick, and the west and north walls a little thicker. The walls were of brick. It resembled a house built on the north, south, and east sides of a court, and in the north-west corner was a flight of steps which enabled visitors to descend into the tomb, and to reach the tops of the fourteen chambers which were built on its three sides. The north and south walls were about 42 feet 6 inches long, and the

[1] Prof. Naville thinks the sign should be read SHEST or SHESTȦ, probably identifying it with 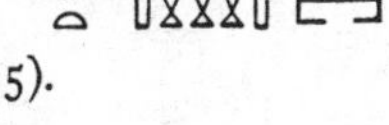 (Pepi I, ll. 196, 682) or  (Tetȧ, l. 225).

[2] *Le Tombeau d'Osiris*, Paris, 1899; see also Petrie, *Royal Tombs*, Part II, 1901, p. 8.

east and west walls about 38 feet 6 inches long; their original height is unknown, but when M. Amélineau discovered their remains they were all about 8 feet high. In this rectangle, supported on layers of sand, bricks, and wood, the tomb chamber was built; it was made of

wood, and was probably about 28 feet square. In the small chambers were found large jars, most of them broken, but on some of them there remained the earthenware caps which served to close their mouths, and which were stamped with the Horus name of King Khent.

On January 2, 1898, M. Amélineau found a head, which he believed to be that of Osiris, and on the same day his workmen excavated the granite bier of Osiris already mentioned. This bier, which is now in the Egyptian Museum in Cairo, is of grey granite, and is about 5 feet 4 inches in length, and about 3 feet in width. The bier resembles in form the *angarêb* bedstead which is found all over Egypt and the Sûdân, and had lion legs with a lion's head on the top of each, and they rest on a pedestal. On the bier lies a figure of Osiris, wearing the White Crown, and holding  and  in his hands. Above his head are figures of two hawks, and at his feet are two more. On the centre of his body is another hawk, which represents the goddess Isis, and is intended to commemorate the union of Isis and Osiris which, according to the legend,[1] took place after the death of Osiris. The fruit of this union was Horus, whom Isis brought forth in the Delta, where she reared him and taught him that it was his duty to avenge his father's murder. This interesting monument belongs obviously to a comparatively late period, but it is possible that it was a copy of an earlier bier which may have existed in this tomb.

The tomb of Khent certainly belongs to the period of the Ist dynasty, and it has importance in connection with

[1] It is as old as the VIth dynasty. In an address to Osiris it is said: 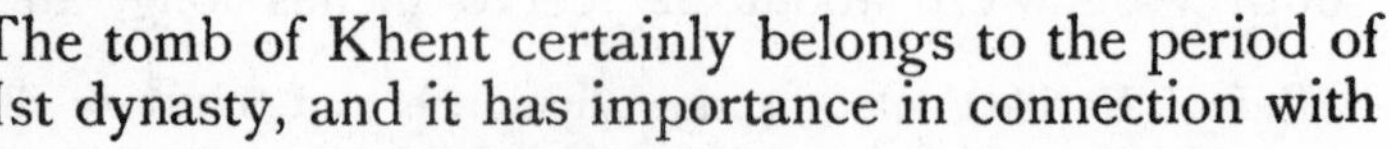
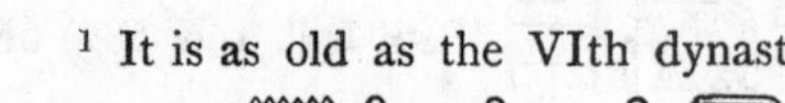. Pyramid of Tetȧ, l. 277.

the history of Osiris, for it satisfied the requirements of the tradition which identified it with the tomb of Osiris. Also we see in it the three essentials of the African tomb, the place for offerings, the pit, and the chamber for the dead. In this case the place for the offerings consisted of several chambers which were in the pit itself, but the inconvenience of this arrangement was readily recognized, and very soon after the Ist dynasty the place for the offerings was formed by a chamber made at the top of the pit.

The most perfect Egyptian form of the African tomb is the *maṣṭabah*, in which the chamber for offerings stands immediately over the pit and the mummy chamber, which was made on one side at the bottom of the pit, from which it was separated by a very short passage. When the mummy had been placed in its chamber this passage was blocked carefully, or built up, and thus the mixture of stones, sand, and mud, with which the pit was filled afterwards, did not force its way into the mummy chamber. In the great pyramid tombs the pit takes the form of a diagonal or horizontal corridor ; at the entrance is the hall for offerings, called the Ṭuat chamber, and at the end in the ground is the mummy chamber. When the tomb is hewn in the mountain the pit may also take the form of a horizontal or diagonal corridor, or series of corridors, and the mummy chamber is hewn at a considerable depth in the bowels of the mountain. In such cases the chamber for offerings is some distance from the outside of the mountain, and may be approached by going down a corridor or flight of steps. In all cases, however, the chamber for offerings, the pit, and the mummy chamber are the chief features of the tomb. We may now compare the facts about ancient Egyptian tombs given above with the details of tombs which are found scattered through the writings and reports of African travel made by competent travellers during the last hundred years.

The Dyoor graves are made close to the huts of the living. The ground is levelled by means of a piece of bark about 3 feet long, and a circular mound, some 3 or 4 feet high, indicates the last resting-place of a Dyoor, so long as the violence of the rain allows it to retain its shape. After a few years all traces of them disappear.[1] The Bongo grave is a pit 4 feet deep, with a niche hollowed in one side of it, so that the sack containing the corpse may not have to sustain any vertical pressure from the earth which is thrown in to fill up the grave. After the grave is filled in, a heap of stones is piled over the spot in a short cylindrical form, and this is supported by strong stakes, which are driven into the soil all round; on the middle of the pile is placed a pitcher, probably that from which the deceased drank. The graves are close to the huts, and their sites are marked by a number of long forked branches, carved with numerous notches and incisions, and having their points sharpened like horns. The Mittû and Madi and Musgû graves are somewhat similar. Among the Musgû arrows are shot into the stakes and are left sticking in the wood.[2] Schweinfurth could not learn from the natives what these notched stakes signified, but it is probable that originally each notch represented a year,[3] and that they collectively represented a great number of years, and signified the wish of relatives of the deceased that he might live for ever in the Other World. The A-Zande, or Niam-Niam, also bury the body in a niche in the pit, and when this is filled in with clay and stamped down a hut is built over it.[4] The Muslims have copied the old African custom, and carefully bury their dead in niches in the pit. The grave of the Moro chief, in Neambara, which Petherick saw, was a slightly oval hole, which varied from 2 feet 2 inches to 2 feet 6 inches in diameter, and was 5 feet deep. On the south side a cavity 4 feet 6 inches long, 4 feet wide and 1 foot 6 inches high was excavated, and in this the body was placed; a piece of basket work was placed along the side of it to keep the earth from the body when the pit was filled in. A tree trunk was dropped into the grave, and set upright, and round the top of it, which projected 3 feet above the level

[1] Schweinfurth, *Heart of Africa*, Vol. I, p. 212.
[2] *Heart of Africa*, Vol. I, p. 304.
[3] Like the Egyptian ; compare , "eternity."
[4] *Heart of Africa*, Vol. II, p. 35; Johnston, *George Grenfell*, Vol. II, p. 651.

of the ground, a conical mound was built; when this was covered with dry thorny branches, the grave was complete. Two large fires were kept burning at the grave day and night, and eight or ten persons kept guard over it for a week.[1]

Among the Bahima peasant folk are buried in holes dug at the doors of their huts.[2] Among the Banyoro a king's grave is dug 12 feet deep, and 5 feet in diameter;[3] the Basoga grave is 15 feet deep.[4] Thirty-six kings of Uganda were buried each on a wooden bier which was set on the ground in a large house, with a huge conical thatched roof resembling a pyramid in shape.[5] The Baziba grave is a deep narrow pit, just large enough for the body to stand or sit in;[6] the Manyema grave is a pit 10 feet deep and 10 feet square.[7] The Karamojo bury rich men in their own houses.[8] The Shula bury the dead in pits near the houses, and lay on them stones on which offerings are placed.[9] The Madi grave, according to Emin Pasha, is circular, and is 5 feet deep, and $3\frac{1}{2}$ feet in diameter.[10]

Of the cemetery of a village of Mbinda, Stanley says: The grave mounds were neat, and by their appearance I should judge them to be not only the repositories of the dead, but also the depositories of all the articles that had belonged to the dead. Each grave was dressed out with the various mugs, pitchers, wash-basins, teapots, kettles, glasses, bottles, etc., and above the mound thus curiously decorated were suspended by the branch of a tree the various nets of palm fibre in which the deceased had carried his ground-nuts, cassava bread, and eatables. All articles had been rendered useless, *i.e.*, broken.[11] The grave of a Lendu chief is dug in his hut, and one end of it is prolonged into a tunnel under the floor, in which the

[1] Petherick, *Travels in Central Africa*, pp. 271–273.
[2] Cunningham, *Uganda*, p. 11.
[3] *Ibid.*, p. 30.
[4] *Ibid.*, p. 117.
[5] For a picture of this see Cunningham's work, p. 251.
[6] *Ibid.*, p. 284.
[7] *Ibid.*, p. 314.
[8] *Ibid.*, p. 344.
[9] Frobenius, *Die Heiden-Neger*, p. 334.
[10] *Ibid.*, p. 378.
[11] *Through the Dark Continent*, Vol. II, p. 453.

deceased is placed.[1] In Western Africa the graves of chiefs and kings are "nice roomy apartments generally about 12 feet by 8 feet by 14 feet, but in Benin, I am told, the graves have a floor about 16 feet by 12 feet, with sides tapering to an aperture that can be closed by a single flag-stone."[2] When a Bari dies he is buried in the yard. A few ox-horns and skulls are suspended on a pole above the spot, while the top of the pole is ornamented with a bunch of cock's feathers.[3] In Dahomey the body is placed in a niche offsetting from a circular pit.[4] Battell, who wrote at the close of the sixteenth century, says that the African grave is made like a vault. A little way down the pit is undermined and made spacious within.[5] The Juiga graves are merely pits covered with mounds of stones, on which are placed cooking and drinking vessels; they are made by the sides of frequented paths, and the points where cross roads touch are favourite burial places.[6] Around the grave of Sekote, a Batoka chief, seventy large elephants' tusks were planted, with their points turned inwards, and there were thirty more set over the resting-places of his relatives.[7]

The Bangala rarely buried anyone. When they did commit a person to the earth the grave was only a foot deep, and its exterior was covered with provisions for the dead man's future existence. The Mañbattû buried warriors where they fell, and erected huts over their graves, to which friends and relatives[8] brought baskets of provisions and jars filled with water. The Abarambo chief, Mburo, thought it degrading for a chief like himself to be brought into close contact with the earth, and, therefore, ordered that his body should be placed in the upper part of a great tree near his house, with his face turned towards heaven. This is related

[1] Johnston, *Uganda Protectorate*, Vol. II, p. 554.
[2] Kingsley, *West African Studies*, p. 452.
[3] Baker, *Albert N'yanza*, p. 58.
[4] Burton, *A Mission to Gelele*, Vol. II, p. 164.
[5] *Strange Adventures*, p. 74.
[6] Livingstone, *Missionary Travels*, p. 424.
[7] *Ibid.*, p. 518.
[8] The following notes are from Johnston, *George Grenfell*, Vol. II, p. 649.

on the authority of Casati. An Ababua killed in war is cremated to prevent his body being eaten, and his ashes are carried to his village and buried there. The Bahuana grave is about four or five feet deep, and a small hut is erected over it. Grenfell notes that the Bakete mark a grave by means of an uprooted tree stuck into the earth with the trunk top downwards.

CHAPTER XVIII.

AFRICAN FUNERAL CEREMONIES AND BURIALS.

THE tombs of Egypt and their inscriptions supply an extraordinary amount of information about the funeral ceremonies and customs of the Egyptians from the beginning to the end of the Dynastic Period. And if we compare the details derived from these sources with the facts about funerals recorded by travellers in Africa, we shall find that whenever material means permit, and when allowance has been made for differences in the physical products of the country, there is a very close resemblance between the funeral of a really great modern chief in Central or Western Africa and that of an ancient king of Egypt. The Egyptians removed the intestines and brain, and embalmed the body with great skill, and then swathed it in linen, and laid it in a coffin or sarcophagus. The modern African removes the more perishable parts of the body by ways which will be described further on, and dries or smokes the corpse very effectively. He also anoints it with unguents, and wraps it up in much cloth, and then places it in a coffin or on a bier. The modern African grave contains all the essentials of that of the Egyptian, but as the modern African is not a skilled mason, and as mountains of stone are not always available, he is obliged to make almost all his graves in the earth. The sacrifice of human beings, or animals, the funeral feast, the pomp and ceremony, the wailings and the noise and the dancing which accompanied the burial of a king of Egypt are all paralleled in the great modern African funeral. The Egyptian king built his funerary chapel and endowed it, and made arrangements for the regular supply of sepulchral offerings, and for a perpetual service of priests to recite the appointed formulae daily, and to make all the necessary preparations for the commemorative festivals. A glance at the history of Dahomey, and of Congo-land, and of Uganda, is sufficient to show that the kings of these countries made exactly similar arrangements, and it is becoming clearer, the more the subject is investigated, that the beliefs which underlie the funeral ceremonies of Ancient Egypt and the Sûdân are identical. In some cases the customs of the ancient Egyptian are explained by those of the modern Sûdânî, and in their light certain passages in early Egyptian literature receive a new significance. Of this the following is an example :—

In the Liturgy of Funerary Offerings[1] which is found in the pyramid of Unȧs, a king of the VIth dynasty, we find the phrase : "O Unȧs, thy two jawbones which were separated have been established." In Chapter CXXXVIB (l. 10) of the Book of the Dead the deceased says : "I have come, I have brought to him "the jawbones in Re-stau, I have brought to him the "backbones in Ȧnu." In Chapter XCIX (l. 27) the deceased says that the god is equipped and that he is equipped ; that the god is provided with jawbones, and that he is provided with jawbones. In Chapter CLXXVIII (l. 28) it is said to the deceased : "Horus "hath avenged thee, he hath destroyed the jawbones[2] of "thine enemies." From the extract from the Liturgy we gather that some unpleasant thing had been done with the jawbones of Unȧs, and that owing to what the priest had said and done this unpleasantness had been done away. And from the passages from the Book of the Dead we learn that jawbones were taken to Re-stau, that the deceased rejoiced in his jawbones, and that Horus had smitten the jawbones of his enemies. So far as I know there is no Egyptian text which explains the allusion to the jawbones in any one of these passages, and it is not until we examine the funeral customs of the modern Sûdânî tribes that we gain any inkling as to their meaning. When a king of Uganda died the body was handed over to the official executioner and to the keeper of the royal tombs, and it was taken to the country of Emerera, where it was placed in a house. The under jaw of the dead king was then cut off and

[1] Ed. Budge, p. 65.

[2] *Ārti*, .

placed in a wooden dish, and the executioner having caused a *kibuga*, or enclosure containing a few houses, to be built, deposited the jaw in one of the houses, and appointed the chief who built the *kibuga* to be its guardian. Before the jaw was finally installed, it was decorated with *kauri* shells. No king of Uganda before Mtesa had been buried with his under jaw in its natural place,[1] and before he died he ordered all the jawbones of the kings to be collected and buried. The Wahŭma dried their kings for months, till they were like sun-dried meat, before they buried them, and they cut out the lower jaws, and covered them with beads and preserved them.[2] Among other objects brought at the celebration of the "So-sin Custom" of the king of Dahomey was the Agranhohwe, or "jaw umbrella," the white top and lappets of which were thickly studded with human jawbones.[3] Skertchley says that the jawbones are 84 in number, and that they are arranged chevronwise.[4] In Ashantee, before the return of the army, the general in command sends to the capital the jawbones of the enemies who have been slain.[5]

Thus we see that the Baganda and other modern African peoples cut out the jawbones of their dead kings and preserved them with honour, and the passage in the text of King Unȧs suggests that the Egyptians must have treated the jawbones of their dead kings in primitive times in a somewhat similar manner. Now the cult of Osiris prohibited the mutilation of the human body, and therefore the custom of cutting out the jawbones became obsolete. And the statement that Horus destroyed the jawbones of the enemies of the deceased is illustrated by the custom in Ashantee and Dahomey of wrenching the jawbones from the heads of dead foes and sending them to the kings. It may be noted in passing that Frobenius figures a trumpet ornamented with human jawbones, and that he refers to a curious use made of the lower jawbone by the New

[1] Cunningham, *Uganda*, p. 226.
[2] Speke, *Journal*, p. 394.
[3] Burton, *A Mission to Gelele*, Vol. II, p. 53.
[4] *Dahomey as It is*, p. 259.
[5] Ramseyer and Kühne, *Four Years in Ashanti*, p. 115.

Pomeranians.[1] Colonel Ellis notes that the Awunas, an Eastern Ewe tribe, say that the lower jaw is the only part of the body which a child derives from its mother,[2] and he mentions horns decorated with human jaws. It will have been noticed that the word used in Egyptian for jawbones is *ārti*, and that it is in the dual, and is determined by two jawbones , but I believe that the lower jawbone only is referred to. Some ancient peoples believed that the lower jawbone consisted of two bones which were joined at the chin, and 'Abd al-Laṭîf, the famous physician who flourished in the fourteenth century of our era, spent a good deal of time in examining skulls in Egypt, in order to be able to refute by personal observation the opinion of those who held this view. The determinatives of the Egyptian word suggest that the primitive Egyptians agreed on this point with the opponents of 'Abd al-Laṭîf.[3]

Some interesting light also is thrown on the umbilical cord and phallus of Osiris by customs concerning the preservation of these things which obtained until quite recently among the people of Uganda. In Chapter XVII of the Book of the Dead (l. 39 f.) we read :—" I have " done away my impurity, I have destroyed the evil things " in me." The commentary says : " What does this mean ? " The answer is : " It is the cutting off of the " umbilical cord[4] of the Osiris, the scribe Ani, triumphant " before all the gods, and the driving away of all the evil " things which belong to him." The commentary says : " What does this mean ? " The answer is : " It is the purification [which takes place] on the day of his birth." From this we learn that the umbilical cord of Osiris was

[1] *Childhood of Man*, pp. 61, 167 and 174.

[2] *The Yoruba-speaking Peoples*, p. 131 ; *The Tshi-speaking Peoples*, p. 257.

[3] See the translation of De Sacy, p. 419 ff. Tous les anatomistes s'accordent à dire que cette mâchoire est composée de deux os qui sont fermement réunis vers le menton . . . . . nous avons employé toute sorte de moyens pour nous assurer de la vérité, et nous n'y avons jamais reconnu qu'un seul os.

[4] 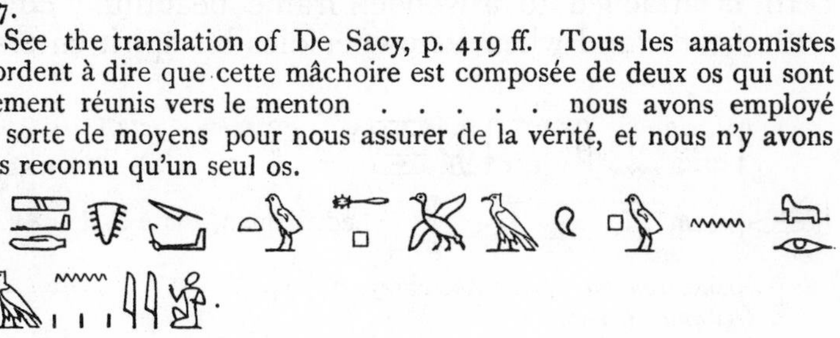

cut off, and that this cutting symbolized an act of purification whereby the god was freed at his birth from impurity. In the Westcar Papyrus we are told that when the three sons of Ruṭ-ṭeṭet were born, the four Meskhenit goddesses who were present at their birth washed in turn each child, cut off his umbilical cord, and placed it in a four-sided cloth which was laid in a stone box.[1] From the fact that the goddesses preserved the cord and wrapped it up in cloth and laid it in a box we are justified in assuming that they attached great importance to it, and that they intended to preserve it. Now Osiris was a king from his birth, and the three sons of Ruṭ ṭeṭet were destined to become kings, and it is therefore clear that under the Ancient Empire, and long before, the Egyptians were in the habit of preserving the umbilical cords of kings and great personages. What they did with them the texts do not say, but the customs of Uganda and Unyoro throw some light on the matter, for the Baganda and Banyoro have been in the habit of preserving the umbilical cords of kings for untold generations. Thus Speke tells us : " The umbilical cords are preserved from birth, and, at death, those of men are placed within the door-frame, while those of women are buried without, this last act corresponding with the custom of the Wahiyow."[2] Mr. Cunningham describes an interview between King Mtesa and the Namasole, or Queen Mother, who sat side by side on a sofa. An attendant brought to her the king's umbilical cord, and having taken it and held it for a moment in her hand, she placed it on the couch by her side.[3] The reason for preserving the cord is given by Mr. C. W. Hattersley, who says that the umbilical cords of kings are kept in receptacles called Balongo. Each umbilical cord is attached to a wooden frame beautifully covered with beads, and when its owner dies his spirit enters the

1 
, ed. Erman, Plate X, l. 12 ff.

2 Speke, *Journal of the Discovery*, p. 394.

3 *Uganda*, p. 190.

wooden frame, and lives there with the cord for ever.[1] If the frame be destroyed the spirit departs.

The investigations made in Uganda by the Rev. J. Roscoe supply a number of most important facts about the preservation of the lower jawbone, umbilical cord and phallus of kings in Uganda.[2] He says: "The cord seems to be to the afterbirth what the lower jawbone is to the person to whom it belonged; that is, the ghost of the person attaches itself to the jawbone after death, and the ghost of the afterbirth attaches itself to the bit of cord. Every person is born with a double, viz., the afterbirth, which has its ghost, and the umbilical cord in some way connects the ghost of the afterbirth with the living child . . . . At the ceremony of naming the child the bit of umbilical cord is brought out and dropped into a bowl containing a mixture of beer, milk, and water. If the cord floats the child is legitimate and the clan accepts it as a member; should the cord sink the child is disowned by the clan and the woman is punished for adultery. The cord is either preserved by the clan or buried at the roots of the plantain tree with the afterbirth. In the case of princes the cord is carefully preserved, and the fortunate prince who becomes king has the cord decorated and made into a "twin" (mulongo). This is kept by the Kimbugwe, who each month, after the new moon appears, brings in the "twin" wrapped up in bark-cloth to the king, who holds it for a moment or two and then returns it to him. It is carried in state to the Kimbugwe's enclosure, drums are beaten in the procession, and the "twin" is honoured as a king. When it is returned to its house it is not put inside, but is placed by the door and guarded all night; next morning the Kimbugwe comes and rubs butter on it, and restores it to its usual place inside the temple or hut. The jawbone and the umbilical cord must always be kept together to fulfil the requirements of the ghosts after the death of the king.

The stool on which the god Kibuka sits is also of

[1] Hattersley, *The Baganda at Home*, 1908, pp. 14, 15.

[2] See *Journal Inst. Anthropological Society*, Vol. XXXI, p. 117 ff.; Vol. XXXII, p. 25 ff.; and *Kibuka, the War God of the Baganda*, in *Man*, No. 95, 1907, p. 161 ff.

interest in connection with Osiris. Instead of the usual seat there is a basin 8 inches in diameter, and 4 inches deep, fitted into this. In this basin were kept the lower jawbone of the god, stitched into a leather case, and with this were two smaller leather cases containing the genital organs; each case is decorated with shells and beads. These were put in a bag tied with string made from the fibre of aloes, which was placed in the basin on the stool. The whole stool with its contents stands 22 inches high.[1] Now if we look at the vignettes in papyri of the Book of the Dead we shall find that in most cases the side of the seat, or stool, of the god is made to resemble the front of a tomb, and that the doors, with their bolts, resemble those which are painted on sepulchral coffers and chests which contain *ushabtiu* figures and the viscera of the dead. In other words, Osiris sits upon what is intended to represent a sepulchral coffer. And if the stool of Osiris were a sepulchral coffer it must have contained some portions of the body of the god, and such portions might well have been his genital organs and his lower jawbone, as was the case with Kibuka, the War-god of the Baganda. At all events, the custom followed by the Baganda in respect of the stool of Kibuka certainly throws some light on the stool or throne of Osiris and its sepulchral character. The texts are silent as to the fate of the phallus of Osiris, and Greek writers, being ignorant of the customs of the Sûdân, state that it was never found, and that Isis made a model of it which was worshipped in the temples. Allusions to the phallus of Osiris and the phallus of Rā occur in the Book of the Dead,[2] and we may be certain that the phallus of Osiris must have played a very prominent part in the beliefs of the Egyptians concerning the resurrection, otherwise the phallus of the deceased would not have been identified with Osiris in the Chapter of the Deification of Members of the body (Chapter XLII).

[1] See the illustration to Mr. Roscoe's paper in *Man*.

[2] XVII, 61, 143; XCIII, 2, 3, that of Beba, 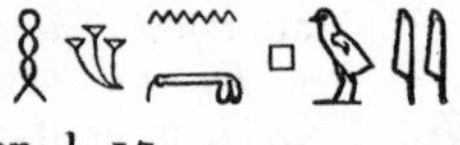
 is mentioned in XCIX, Introduction, l. 17.

The chief authorities for the methods of procedure followed in funerals by the Egyptians are the bas-reliefs and paintings which decorate the tombs of their nobles, especially those which belong to the period of the New Empire, say from B.C. 1600 to B.C. 600. Of special importance are the tombs of Western Thebes, for whole series of funerary scenes still remain in them in a wonderful state of preservation. Most valuable evidence is also supplied by such works as the Liturgy of Funerary Offerings and the Book of Opening the Mouth, which are well illustrated by the scenes depicted on the walls of the tombs of Rekh-mȧ-Rā (XVIIIth dynasty), Seti I (XIXth dynasty), and Ȧmen-em-Ȧp (XXVIth dynasty). Also the vignettes of the great illustrated copies of the Theban Recension of the Book of the Dead, *e.g.*, the Papyri of Nebseni, Nu, Iuȧu, Ani, Hunefer, Ȧnhai, Nesi-ta-neb-Asher, etc., and the Rubrics, describe and explain many interesting customs and ceremonies. When these authorities are examined, and the information given by them generally is compared with the descriptions of comparatively modern African funerals and methods of sepulture given below, the similarity in both customs and ceremonies will be found to be so marked that it is impossible not to conclude that they are the result of beliefs which are common to the ancient Egyptians and to modern Sûdânî tribes. This similarity is due not to any borrowing by the Sûdânî tribes from the Egyptians, but to indigenous, fundamental African beliefs which have remained unchanged in all essentials from the end of the Neolithic Period in Egypt until the present day.

THE BURIAL OF KAMRASI, KING OF UNYORO.—Immediately after the death of Kamrasi, his body was laid upon a framework of green wood, like a gigantic gridiron, over a slow fire, until it was quite dry and resembled "an over-roasted hare." It was then wrapped in new bark-cloths, and made to lie in state in a large house which had been specially built for the purpose. As long as the succession to the throne is undecided, the body remains unburied, but as soon as the victor in the civil war, which breaks out on the king's death, is hailed as king, he goes into the house where his father's body lies, and, standing near it, drives his spear into the ground, and leaves it near the right hand of the king. The victor next buries his father. A huge pit, capable of holding several hundred people, is dug, and neatly lined with new bark-cloths. Several wives of the late king are made to seat themselves together at the bottom, to bear upon their knees the body of their departed lord. On the night previous to the funeral, the king's own regiment, or bodyguard, surrounds many dwellings and villages, and seizes indiscriminately the people as they go out in the early morning. They are taken to the mouth of the pit, and, when their arms and legs have been broken with clubs, they are thrown into it, on the top of the king's body and his wives.

A mighty din of drums, horns, flageolets, whistles, mingled with the yells of a frantic crowd, drowns the shrieks of the sufferers, upon whom the earth is shovelled and stamped down by thousands of cruel fanatics, who dance and jump upon the loose mould so as to form it into a compact mass, through which the victims of this horrid sacrifice cannot grope their way, the precaution having been taken to break the bones of their arms and legs. At length the mass is buried and trodden down beneath a tumulus of earth, and all is still. The funeral is over.[1]

According to Mr. Cunningham, the grave of an Unyoro king was five feet in diameter and twelve feet deep. The king's bodyguard seized the first nine Unyoro men they met, and threw them alive into the pit. The body of the king was then wrapped in bark-cloth, and sewn up in the skin of a cow newly killed, and let down into the pit. Another cow-skin was stretched tightly across the opening, and pegged down all round; a covering of grass was laid over the skin, and a temple was built over the grave. A headman was appointed watcher, and some of the dead king's servants were ordered to live there, they and their descendants after them, and food was supplied as a matter of course by the people. The position of the dead body was the same for king and peasant. The body lay on its left side, with the hands, the palms facing, under the head, and the legs drawn up to the body. The poor people

[1] Baker, *Ismailïa*, p. 316.

were wrapped in grass, and spirit-houses were built over their graves.[1]

Dagara's Burial.—When Dagara, king of Karagŭé, was dead, the people sewed his body up, as was the custom in the case of kings, in a cow-skin, and placed it in a boat floating on the lake, where it remained for three days, until decomposition set in, and maggots were engendered. Then it was taken up and deposited on the hill Moga-Namirinzi, where, instead of putting him underground, the people erected a hut over him, and, thrusting in five maidens and fifty cows, enclosed the doorway in such a manner that the whole of them subsequently died of starvation. Rohinda the Sixth, father of Dagara, was buried in the same way. Out of his heart a young lion emerged, which guarded the hill and was the ancestor of all the lions in Karagŭé! These lions became subject to Dagara, and whenever he went to war he took an army formed of them instead of men, and was always victorious.[2] Rŭmanika, son of Dagara, sacrificed a cow yearly at his father's grave, and placed pombé and grain on it, because he thought they would secure for him good crops in the coming year.[3]

The Bongo Burial.—The dead body is placed in a crouching position, with the knees forced up to the chin, and is firmly bound round the head and legs. It is then sewn up in a skin sack and placed in a deep grave. The faces of men are turned towards the north and those of women towards the south.[4]

The Niam-Niam Burial.—The dead body is adorned, as if for a festival, with skins and feathers. It is usually dyed with red wood. Men of rank have their aprons fastened to them, and they are buried either sitting on their beds or enclosed in a kind of coffin which is made from a hollow tree. The earth is not allowed to touch the body, which is placed in a specially prepared niche in the grave. The men have their faces turned towards the east, and the women's are

[1] *Uganda*, pp. 30, 31.

[2] Speke, *Journal*, p. 181. Of the maggots of Dagara three were taken to the palace, where they turned into a lion, a leopard, and a stick.

[3] *Ibid.*, p. 197.

[4] Schweinfurth, *Heart of Africa*, Vol. I, p. 303.

towards the west.[1] The relatives shave their heads and destroy their headdresses.

THE MORO BURIAL.—The uncovered body was carried to the grave on a strong wicker frame; a number of mourning women went in front, and the wives went behind, and women chanted to the tom-toms. On the way many of the wives turned somersaults, and tried to throw themselves into the grave. The body was laid on its right side, in a bent position, as if asleep. A ligament of bark was tied to the little finger of the left hand, and the other extremity was drawn to the surface, and there attached to a peg driven in the ground. This was to enable the dead man to communicate with his children. The grave was filled up and a mound raised over it, with a pole in the centre, to the top of which was fastened the falcon's feather which was worn by the deceased when alive. The women threw their ornaments on the grave, and the relatives and friends of the deceased proceeded to hack in pieces with a spear the carcases of two bulls and to eat them.[2]

THE BAHIMA BURIAL.—The dead body is washed, and the arms and legs are doubled up against it by breaking the joints; the neck is broken, and the head is bent over the chest. The body is then tied up in a mat, forming a sort of bundle, and buried in the great village manure heap, within eight or ten hours after death. An ordinary man is buried in a hole dug at the door of his hut.[3]

THE BANABUDDU BURIAL.—The male relatives stand on the right-hand side of the body, and the females on the left, and then, beginning with the head, smear it with butter; it is then wrapped round with bark cloth, and carried to the grave in the neighbouring garden. The clay all round the grave must be pushed in with the elbows, and not with the hands and feet.[4]

[1] Schweinfurth, *op. cit.*, Vol. II, p. 34; Johnston, *George Grenfell*, Vol. II, p. 650.

[2] Petherick, *Travels*, p. 270 ff. Dr. Brownell was buried in a grave in an ant hill, fully four feet deep, with a niche for the body, which was protected from contact with the earth by means of several sticks which covered the opening of the niche. *Ibid.*, p. 140.

[3] Cunningham, *Uganda*, p. 10.

[4] *Ibid.*, p. 67.

The Basoga Burial.—The body is first rubbed with pulp made from the banana tree, and whilst this is being done no one must be present as witness of the operation. It is then rolled up in bark cloth and laid in a grave 15 feet deep, dug in the deceased's house. All the bark cloth which the relatives can get is stuffed into the grave, which is sometimes filled to the mouth with this material; earth is then thrown on top and stamped down flat. As soon as the grave is filled up the women leave the house, and having shut it up it remains unoccupied, and eventually tumbles down.[1]

The Basoga perform a curious ceremony in connection with a man who dies away from home. The relatives go into the bush and bring out a branch or long reed. This is thrown on the ground, and they say to it, having called out the dead man's name, "We have come to bring you home for burial." The branch or reed is then wrapped in bark cloth and carried home, and, when news is brought into the village that it is approaching, the women scream and wail until the branch is laid in the grave. The usual funeral ceremonies are then observed. In some places in Basoga the head of the dead person is washed, and his lips are smeared with oil,[2] which calls to mind one of the ceremonies in the Book of Opening the Mouth, in which the mouth of the deceased was anointed with oil by the Egyptians.

Formerly, before European influence modified any of the customs of the country, the successor of a dead king of Bukole, a district of Basoga, sent a large number of soldiers to range the country for miles round the chief's village, and slay any person they met. During the raid every attempt was made to capture a young man and a girl. On the second day after the chief's death they were killed, their pudenda were removed, and together with those of a bull, were put into the interior of a large fetish drum called "Kideye." The hole in the drum through which this tribute had been inserted was sown up, and the drum was beaten to

[1] Johnston, *Uganda Protectorate*, Vol. II, p. 715; Cunningham, *Uganda*, p. 117.

[2] Johnston, *op. cit.*, Vol. II, p. 718.

announce the chief's death.[1] Similar mutilations of a young man and a girl were made in order to make a sacrifice to the sacred stream on the death of a chief. Sometimes the man and maid after mutilation were thrown into the Nagua River as a sacrifice to the water spirit.

Burial of Kings in Uganda.—Formerly the dead king was carried to Emerera and dried, and when the lower jaw had been cut out,[2] it was wrapped up in many layers of bark cloth, and placed on a bedstead which stood on the floor of a large new house, with a conical thatched roof. The door was then shut and was never opened again. The king's cook, the headman of the beer-pots, and chief herdsman of the king's cows, and three women of rank equivalent to these, were seized, and dragged before the door of the closed tomb and slaughtered. The bodies were not buried, but left for the vultures to eat.[3]

The Basukuma Burial.—A king or chief is wrapped up in an ox-skin and buried in a sitting position. Ordinary folk are wrapped up in the leaves of the nghali tree, and buried in the centre of the kraal. At the funeral of a chief the people mourn for two days, and then eat the ox, in the skin of which the chief is buried.[4]

The Manyema Burial.—A chief is buried in a square pit 10 feet deep, wrapped in bark cloth. At the bottom of the grave ten living women with their arms and legs broken are laid, and on them the chief is placed; ten men, with their arms and legs broken, are next brought and laid on top of the chief.[5] The grave is then filled up with earth, and the burial is complete.

The Lendu Burial.—The body of a chief is, by means of many strips of bark cloth, made to take a sitting position, and is then placed on a bed of skins inside a tunnel-like excavation in the grave, which is dug

[1] Johnston, *Uganda Protectorate*, Vol. II, p. 716.

[2] The body was placed on a board which rested on the mouth of an earthen pot heated by fire from below. The drying process lasted three months.—Speke, *Journal*, p. 207.

[3] Cunningham, *Uganda*, p. 226.

[4] Cunningham, *Uganda*, p. 307.

[5] *Ibid.*, p. 314.

inside the hut of the deceased. This hut, with sometimes the whole village in which it is situated, is then abandoned.[1] Ordinary folk are buried immediately after death near the side wall of the hut. The body is put into the earth naked, and no coffin of any sort is used. The Alulu tribe wrap the body in the skin of a freshly killed bull or cow. Over the grave of a chief a tree is sometimes planted.[2]

THE SENGA BURIAL.—When a man dies everyone utters mournful cries. The body is washed, clothed, decorated with beads, and wrapped up in a piece of calico soaked in saffron. Then it is left two days, when it begins to decompose. It is then placed in a bag of rushes of three layers, and buried in a hole in the ground of the hut about five feet deep, and covered over with thorns and earth. On the grave they put a large earthenware urn containing a little flour, while a roast chicken is placed by the side of it. The natives clap their hands by way of adieu, and abandon the hut, and everyone who has touched the body goes and washes in the river. The members of the family cut their hair, and deposit the cuttings in a place where two roads meet; they put on black beads, and if possible black clothes. Three months after the death the friends assemble for a great feast. Having prepared a large quantity of beer, they take it to the hut in which is the grave, and digging a large hole outside, they set down in it a pot of beer, covering it with a plate, on which they sprinkle a little flour. Then they go into the hut, taking with them a sheep. They remove the urn which was placed over the head of the grave, dig a little hole and pour in beer; they also kill the sheep, and let the blood run down into the hole. They take the sheep outside, shut the door, and eat the carcase, and then they wash their hands in the pot of beer which they have left outside. One of the dead man's wives, who is called the "spirit" (musimo) is carried away on a man's shoulders, and they give her beer which she drinks under her veil. They next go to the hut of the chief widow, where a large hole has been dug and cemented; in this they pour the beer, and lie down on

[1] Johnston, *Uganda Protectorate*, Vol. II, p. 555.
[2] Cunningham, *Uganda*, p. 337.

their bellies and drink it. A great feast follows, with dancing and music.[1]

THE LOWER NIGER BURIAL.—In the case of a king or chief, the body is smeared with a decoction of certain plants, and then rubbed over with camwood oil and spirit, and wrapped in mats. The favourite method is to smoke-dry the body. Bodies are usually buried in the earth, but the Andoni use mud altars and platforms in trees; in graves the bodies are just laid flat upon the ground. The possessions of the deceased are buried with him, as well as the sacrificial victims, both human and animal.[2]

THE WANYAMWESI BURIAL.—When the last Sulṭân, Mkasiwah, died, they dug a large pit, in which they placed the chief in a large bark box, in a sitting posture, with one hand at his face and one of the fingers of the other pointing upward; beside him were placed two living men and two living women, and then the whole was covered over. They look upon the graves of their chiefs as sacred, and carry food and pray there.[3]

THE FJORT BURIAL.—The dead body is dried over a smoky fire, and is then wrapped up in endless lengths of cloth according to the wealth of the deceased; and after some months it is buried. When a king dies the body is smoked and watched, and the process may take years. First it is shaved and washed with water or palm wine. It is then placed upon rush mats for a day, then swathed in long pieces of cloth, and laid upon a framework bed, underneath which a hole is dug to receive the water, etc., which runs out of the body. A fire is lighted at the head and foot of the bed, so that the smoke may keep off the flies. The body is next covered with acaju leaves, then wrapped up in more cloth, then placed in a coffin, which is put in a shimbec or hut. There the body may lie for years. Formerly slaves and wives were buried with a chief or king.[4]

THE GAGA BURIAL.—The dead man was buried in a pit, sitting on a seat. Two wives, with broken arms and

[1] Decle, *Three Years in Savage Africa*, p. 234.
[2] Leonard, *Lower Niger and Its Tribes*, p. 175.
[3] Thomson, *To the Central African Lakes*, Vol. II, p. 258.
[4] Dennett, *Notes on the Folklore of the Fjort*, London, 1898, pp. 23, 111.

legs, were thrown in with him, and the grave was then covered over, and palm oil and goats' blood poured on the grave.[1]

THE PYGMY BURIAL.—The body is washed, painted, dressed in new clothes, and then seated on a seat of earth, with his beads and "the most part of his goods" with him. The blood of goats and wine are poured over the grave.[2] Memorial feasts for the dead are celebrated four or five times each year.

THE CONGO BURIAL.—The body is washed with a strong decoction of manioc, which whitens the skin. It is then placed in the fetish attitude : the face towards the setting sun, the knees bent, the left foot raised behind, the right arm hanging by the side, the fingers of the left hand separated, crooked, and pointing eastward. A small fire is kept burning under the body till the intestines are dried up like parchment. The body is then plastered over with red clay, and rolled up in cloths till it becomes a shapeless mass. The richer the person the more the cloth. Finally the body is buried in a large grave, over which is erected a hut without a roof. In Loango, the body is smoked on a scaffold over a green fire, like elephant meat. It is exposed in a sacred house for from six to twelve months, the relatives coming at stated intervals to mourn there. The body is then placed in a coffin shaped like a barrel, and is drawn to the grave in a kind of car.[3]

It is the earnest desire of a Congo man to be buried in a great quantity of cotton cloth, and to have a grand funeral. For this he trades, and works, and sins, and spares no pains. He shivers with cold in the dry season, but will not put on his back the coat or blanket which is reserved for his shroud. He suffers all this for the sake of display at the funeral. When a friend dies it is the proper thing to take a present of cloth for his shroud. A man's rich enemies may ruin his family at his death by their lavish donations for his shroud, which his family will never be able to repay. A great man is often buried in hundreds of yards of cloth, and it all goes underground

[1] Battell, *Strange Adventures*, p. 34.

[2] *Ibid.*, pp. 74, 78 : Johnston, *Uganda*, Vol. II, p. 539.

[3] Winwood Reade, *Savage Africa*, p. 542.

to rot, and be eaten by the white ants. The expense of a funeral is so great in the case of an important man that his own accumulations are never sufficient. The corpse has therefore to be kept for a considerable time. To this end a grave-like hole, two or three feet deep, is dug in the house in which a man dies. The body is placed in the hole, and over the hole a mat is spread; the mat is then covered with an inch and a half of earth. Fires are lighted by the sides of the hole, and are tended night and day by the wives of the deceased, who ought not to leave the house until the funeral. For the first few days the house is crammed with wailing women. The heat of the fires, the closeness of the crowded hut, combine with the smell of the decomposing body to create an atmosphere almost indescribable; but fifty or or sixty women will crowd in, and sit with tearful eyes, wailing and chanting their mournful dirges night and day.

After a day or two the wailing moderates, but at ten o'clock at night, and at five o'clock in the morning, a special wailing is set up, to the beat of the native gong and a small drum. In the early night the young people take the great town drum to the house, and dance for some hours; so that with laughter at the antics of a dancer outside, and tears as the wail surges and falls, the hours pass. The wives put on an old cloth, and sit and sleep on the ground. They never wash, nor comb or cut their hair for months; pot black and oil are rubbed into their skin and hair. A few yards of cloth are wrapped round the corpse before it is put into the drying pit. The heat of the fires goes down into the ground, and so a slow dry heat is set up; in time most of the moisture of the body evaporates or runs into the soil. It is then removed from the pit, wrapped in more cloth, and placed on a shelf in the house. In the dry season the body may be buried by the side of the house six or eight inches below the surface, and the place covered with the thorny bases of palm fronds to keep the jackals away.

Meanwhile the relatives of the deceased have been doing their utmost to raise money for the funeral, and the younger members of the family are often pawned. As the day for the funeral approaches the wailing is resumed. The drum is beaten nearly all night, and in the early morning the gong and the chant can be heard. At dawn for several days there is heavy firing. The body is then wrapped in its shroud, and around this a "glorious cloth" is wound, and then with the thunders of the big drums and a dirge, it is brought to the great square of the town so that all may see it. Six strong men raise the body as high as they can to "show" it, in different parts of the square. It is then taken to the grave amid screams and wailings, and when the women have laid their hands on it, two men jump into the grave to receive the body and put it carefully in its final resting-place. As soon as this is done, all weeping and wailing and tears cease as if by magic. The daughter turns aside, dries her streaming tears, and walks away chatting lightly.[1]

The Bateke, who live to the north of Stanley Pool, often bury a man in the floor of his own house. The shroud is cut over the mouth, and in filling up the grave, after the interment, a pole is placed with one end on the mouth of the body, and the other end sticking out from the grave. When the earth is properly filled in and trodden down, the pole is withdrawn, and so a clear hole is left to the mouth of the body. Into this hole, from time to time, palm wine is poured, that the deceased may not lack the liquor which used to gladden his heart when living.

On the Upper Congo a man of importance has a number of slaves, who follow him about, paddle his canoe, and generally serve him. When he dies, it is not fitting that he should enter the Spirit-world unattended, as though he were only a slave. Wives will be needed to cook and care for him; so, when the time for burial comes, these conveniences are provided for him. The dead man is washed, rubbed with oil and powdered camwood, which makes him red all over. His face is decorated, one eye and cheek being made yellow with ochre, and the other white with pipeclay; coloured lines are drawn on the forehead. A broad line in white, bordered with black, is brought down each of his red arms. Dressed in fine cloth, his hair well braided, his body sits in state on his stool, his pipe in his mouth. Men and women come to look at him, while the wives and their friends sing a dirge, rattle their rattles, and beat

[1] Bentley, *Pioneering on the Congo*, Vol. I, p. 176 ff.

the gongs. In a house near by are ten men, their necks secured in forked sticks  and firmly tied; they are to accompany him. Among the weeping wives are three or four who are chosen to attend him in the Spirit-world. Great crowds assemble on the day of the funeral, and each person is in full paint and finery, and several people dance. The body is brought out, and the crowd gathers in an open space where there is a strange wooden seat. The ten slaves are brought, and one of them is placed in the seat and fastened to it. A tall flexible pole is stuck into the ground, at some distance behind the seat, and from its top is suspended by a cord a sort of cage. The pole is bent down, and the cage is fitted to the man's head. He is blindfolded, and the executioner commences to dance, and make feints, and at last, with a fearful yell, he decapitates his victim, with one sweep of the huge knife. The pole, thus released, springs into the air. The crowd yells with delight and excitement. The body is unbound, and a new victim is placed on the seat, and this horror is repeated, until the ten slaves have joined their dead master. The heads are thrown into a pool of water beside the river, until the flesh comes off, and then the skulls are placed in the house over the master's grave. The bodies of the slaves are carried to the grave, and laid in order on the bottom. Four women are then seized, and their arms and legs are broken with blows from a heavy stick, and then, still alive, they are placed in the grave. The body of their lord is laid upon them, and the grave is then filled in. Higher up the river these customs would be considered poor and mean without a cannibal feast, and the body would be kept until a hunt for victims could be organized. Among the Bakuba on the Upper Kasai, three hundred slaves have been killed at the death of the king or his sister.[1]

THE BALUBA BURIAL.[2]—The dead man is buried in a wicker basket with a lid, the body being in the position of a man squatting and embracing his knees. The grave

[1] Bentley, *Pioneering on the Congo*, Vol. I, p. 253.

[2] The facts given in the following nine paragraphs are taken from Johnston's *George Grenfell*, Vol. II, p. 646 ff.

is dug in the forest in the evening, and the body is hurriedly buried. The house of the deceased is burnt down, but a small hut is built near the place where it stood, and there the spirit of the dead man will come to hold converse with the living. Before the hut a ditch is dug, which is filled with flour and water. By its side is dug another, in which is placed a pot pierced at the bottom; in this palm wine is poured.

THE MUYANZI BURIAL.—The body is washed and painted. The legs are bent in such a manner as to raise the knees as high as possible, and are kept in that position by bands of tree bark or native cloth. The body is then dressed in the richest clothes of the deceased, and placed before his hut, where for ten days all come to admire it. The people dance funeral dances, sing songs, fire off guns, and beat drums; this goes on all day, and palm wine circulates freely. When decomposition is far advanced the body is buried in the entrance to the house, clothes and all.

THE MONGO BURIAL.—The body is washed and placed in a hut for one, or even two months. It is then enclosed in a box, which is carved, painted, and mounted with points resembling horns, and carried through the neighbouring villages with songs and dances, and then buried.

THE BANGATA of the Equator put the dead body in communication with the living by means of a tube, as do the people of the Cataract region of the Lower Congo.

THE BAPOTO BURIAL.—The body is decorated with collars, bracelets, glass trinkets, etc., and is buried by mourning women who wear bands of green leaves round their bodies.

THE ARUWIMI BURIAL.—The body is buried in a shallow grave made in the house, and one or two slaves are killed, so that their spirits may go to Spirit-land with their master.

THE MAÑBATTÛ BURIAL.—The warrior is buried where he falls. A hut is built over him, and there the relatives and friends bring baskets of food and jars of water at intervals, and they keep the grave clean. The bodies of the poor are left for the ants and hyenas.

The Bantu Burial.—The Ababua and the Baieu (Babati) of the Wele-Bomo-Kandi bury the dead on a bed, at a depth of three feet; after a month they are exhumed and buried in another place. This ceremony is repeated as long as the parents live, and when the bed is worn out another is provided; at each exhumation lamentation is made. The gifts to the dead consist of food only, and all the property of the deceased is buried with him. The Baieu eviscerate the body and dry it.

The Nilotic-Negro Burial.—On the north-east Congo the body is buried in a square pit dug in the house, and is placed in a sitting position with the arms folded and wrists fixed to the shoulders. When the pit is filled in, the grave is sprinkled with ox blood or beer.

The Banziri Burial.—The body is arranged in a doubled-up position on a kind of gridiron of poles, and a fire is lit under it; earthen pots are placed to receive the fat which runs out of it. Those present rub their faces and hands with this fat, rinse it off with warm water, and the relatives drink the rinsings, thinking thereby to absorb the virtues of the deceased. What remains of the fat is either sent to absent relatives, or kept in the dead man's house. The body is not buried until decomposition is far advanced.[1]

The Ndolo Burial.—The body is covered with a coating of red bark paste, and is provided with a new loin-cloth; the eyebrows are blackened with charcoal. It is then hoisted up on to a platform twelve feet high, and set in a sitting position; a stick supports the head, and the hands are spread on the knees. The women and girls chant a dirge.[2]

The Bahuana Burial.—The body is placed in a sitting position in a grave about five feet deep, with the face towards the west; food, palm wine, and all the clothes and weapons of the deceased are buried with him. In a small hut above the grave are laid the fragments of his pots, which are broken at the

[1] Mr. Torday's information.

[2] Father Heymans, of New Antwerp (*George Grenfell*, Vol. II, p. 652).

funeral; here the brother of the deceased often places an offering of food. Women have their pots buried with them. A man killed by lightning is buried lying on his back. The foreheads of the men mourners are painted black, but the women paint the whole face black.[1] The mourning colour of the Bayaka women is red.[2]

THE BALUBA BURIAL.[3]—When an important Luba chief expires, every one, great or small, must mourn in a subdued tone; the members of all the brotherhoods come before the house where the body lies to perform dances; the women violently strike their hatchet and hoe against each other. This deafening hubbub lasts a day. The relatives then make a distribution of beads among all the dancers, and the tumult ceases. During this time a young slave is obtained; his neck is broken by a blow, and he is laid by the body for two days. He is the chief's boy attendant. The chief's wives, squatting near him, do not cease their lamentations. Some days pass in this way without other incidents; after which the stiffened limbs are forcibly bent and the body placed in its wicker coffin. In the house two stages are raised, one above the other; on the upper one is placed the coffin, on the lower a large earthen pot. The body decomposes; a noxious liquid infested with maggots escapes from it and falls into the receptacle; it is left there for several weeks. When the body is ready, that is to say, when the nails can be taken off easily, the Musungi (*i.e.*, the "peacemaker"), the provisional "executor" of the deceased, raises the lid of the coffin, removes all the nails from the feet and hands, and the belt of hippopotamus hide, the badge of greatness, cuts off the middle finger of the right hand and a great toe and places them together in a hollowed fruit, which is placed in a small basket with a cone-shaped cover. The bundle is entrusted to the nephews of the deceased; they proceed to hang it up in

[1] Torday and Joyce, *Notes on the Ethnography of the Ba-Huana*, p. 290.

[2] *George Grenfell*, Vol. II, p. 655.

[3] The following account by a Belgian missionary is printed in *George Grenfell*, Vol. II, p. 655.

the ancestral hut. One of the nephews has it under his special care, and is responsible for the whole under pain of death or banishment. At this time they sacrifice a slave ; his death announces the event.

Finally the burial is proceeded with. The important men of the village, followed by some relatives, proceed by day and night towards a shallow marsh, carrying the remains of the deceased. A great chief can never go thus into the Other World without taking away a portion of his slaves ; and so whenever the funeral procession is set in motion, two men are beaten to death with clubs and thrown across the public road without burial ; it is their mission to tell passers-by that their master has gone along that way to his last dwelling. As soon as the site of the grave has been selected, the men build a large square barrier of grass and weed, drain off the water which is within, and set to work with feverish activity to dig a deep ditch of about six feet, taking care to keep the side walls well hollowed out ; and forthwith two female slaves of the dead man, who have as a preliminary been decked in their finest attire, descend of their own accord (or by force, and in spite of their laments and sobs) to the bottom of this tomb, lie on their sides face to face, and stretching out the arm which is next the ground, embrace the decomposed remains of their master. The jar containing the liquid and worms I have described is emptied and broken in the grave. These poor women, mad with misery, do not always show themselves eager to fulfil the task required of them at the funeral ; for that reason they are usually bound, or sometimes their skulls are mercifully broken. During that time, six slaves brought for the purpose are butchered, and their bodies placed in the hollowed walls ; then the ditch is quickly filled up, and the marsh water, escaping over the barrier, makes its way in and covers this sad spot with a silence which will be broken for a moment, some months later, by the piercing cries of new victims. In short, the same grave-diggers will return to the grave, bringing a man in bonds, whom they will force to build a wooden enclosure on the edge of the marsh ; when he shall have completed his task, one of them will drive into his breast the head of his lance, crush his head, and lay him in a ditch beside the chief. Then a few days before the arrival of a successor at the dead man's village, they will go again with a slave, and some jars of beer, force the wretched man to pull out all the stakes and drop all the jars in a small ditch; then they will kill him likewise, and bury him on the other side of the grave. The departed is satisfied; his successor may come.

THE NSAKARA BURIAL.—On a bed, in an immense circular ditch, his head resting on the arm of his favourite wife, is laid the body of the deceased, dressed in his richest attire; around him, attached to stakes, the strangled bodies of the wives who have been unwilling to survive their husband; thrown pell-mell in the ditch the bodies of slaves and servants who have worked for the dead man; such is the hideous spectacle presented to a crowd craving for pain and slaughter. The ditch is filled up, and on the newly-piled earth begins the sacrifice of the victims destined for the feasts celebrated in memory of him whom they are lamenting . . . . These repasts of human flesh last many days.[1]

THE UPPER CROSS RIVER BURIAL.—The old and helpless members of the community are hit on the head by their fellows, who carefully smoke-dry their bodies. These are afterwards pulverized, and formed into small balls by the addition of water in which Indian corn has been boiled for some hours. This mixture is dried in the sun, or over fires, and is then put away for future use as an addition to the family stew.[2]

THE ARAB BURIAL.—Sir Samuel Baker attributed to the Arabs the grave which, as has been seen above, is of purely African origin. He says: "The graves of the Arabs are an improvement upon those of Europeans. What poor person who cannot afford a vault has not felt a pang as the clod fell upon the coffin of his relative? The Arabs avoid this. Although there is no coffin the earth does not rest upon the body. The hole being dug similar in shape to a European grave, an extra trench is formed at the bottom of the grave about a foot wide.

[1] From the Report of a Belgian missionary, printed in *George Grenfell*, Vol. II, p. 657.

[2] Kingsley, *West African Studies*, pp. 555, 556.

The body is laid upon its side within this trench, and covered by bricks made of clay which are laid across; thus the body is contained within a narrow vault. Mud is then smeared over the hastily-made bricks, and nothing is visible, the tomb being made level with the bottom of the large grave. This is filled up with earth, which, resting on the brick covering of the trench, cannot press upon the body. In such a grave my best man was laid—the Slave women raising their horrible howling, and my men crying loudly . . . . I was glad to see so much external feeling for their comrade, but the grave being filled, their grief, like all loud sorrow, passed quickly away, and relapsed into thoughts of buffalo meat; they were soon busily engaged in cutting up the flesh."[1]

The Abyssinian Burial.—When a person is seized with the fever, the relatives set in front of him all the ornaments of gold and silver and fine clothes which their respective friends can collect, making at the same time as much noise as possible with drums, trumpets, and loud outcries, which is done with the view of "driving out the devil" of the man, for most Abyssinians believe that most diseases are caused by demoniacal possession. When it is seen that the sick man is about to die, the drums and trumpets cease, and all present set up mournful howls. And when death is announced, they tear out their hair, scratch the skin from their temples, and throw themselves with sobs and screams on the ground; they show such agony that one would imagine that the very existence of the universe was threatened by his death. Relatives, friends, acquaintances and servants together produce indescribable confusion. Soon after death, the body is carefully washed, fumigated with incense, and sewn up in one of the cloths which the deceased wore when he was alive, and is then carried to the grave, in which it is laid whilst the priests recite appropriate prayers. On the following day the relatives and friends celebrate the feast in honour of the dead. An image of the deceased is made up and dressed in rich garments, and is placed on his favourite mule, and carried in procession through the town to the tomb. A

[1] Baker, *Albert N'yanza*, p. 36.

number of professional wailing women join the procession, and keep up a terrible noise the whole time, saying: "Why did you leave us? Had you not houses and lands? Had you not a wife who loved you?" Arrived at the tomb the cries and wailings are redoubled, the priests shout "Hallelujahs," and the relatives scream in concert. The whole party then goes back to the house of the deceased, and partakes of a huge meal of meat, and drink is provided in such quantities that every member of the party eventually becomes drunk.[1]

From the statements contained in the above descriptions of modern African funerals the reader will see that the similarity between them and the funerals of the ancient Egyptians is too close and too widespread to be the result of accident. The indigenous Egyptians being Africans buried their dead like Africans. A settled government enabled the craft of the undertaker to develop and flourish to a degree undreamt of in Central Africa, but it may be safely asserted that the well-preserved condition of Egyptian mummies and funerary furniture is due far more to the protection of the limestone hills and the sandy deserts than to the art of the embalmer and his colleagues. Everything put into the ground of the Central African forest perishes through damp and insects, and the same is the case in the fertile Delta of Egypt; only in those parts of Egypt where tombs can be hewn in the mountains or in the stony bed of the desert have mummies and funerary furniture been satisfactorily preserved.

[1] Salt, *Voyage to Abyssinia*, p. 422.

CHAPTER XIX.

THE AFRICAN DOCTRINE OF LAST THINGS.

IMMORTALITY.

THE offerings found in the pre-dynastic tombs of Egypt prove that the indigenous inhabitants of the country believed in existence after death, and the persistent allusions to "everlasting life" and immortality which are found in the texts of all periods show that the belief in a resurrection was general. Two or three passages are sufficient to prove how definite this belief was, and it is unnecessary to quote more than the following: To Unȧs, a king of the VIth dynasty, it is said, "Hail, "Unȧs! Assuredly thou hast not gone as one dead, "but as one living to sit upon the throne of Osiris."[1] Again, the same king is declared to be the son of the god Temu, the Father-god and Creator, and it is said: "He "(*i.e.*, Temu) liveth, this Unȧs liveth; he dieth not, this "Unȧs dieth not."[2] That this life beyond the grave was everlasting is proved by the words of Thoth, who said to the deceased: "Thou shalt exist for millions of years, [thy] period of life shall be millions of years."[3] The deceased says that his soul is both God and eternity,[4] therefore God is eternal and His servant

1 
. Unȧs, l. 206.

2 
. Unȧs, l. 240.

3 . Book of the Dead, Chapter CLXXV, l. 16.

4 . Book of the Dead, Chapter LXXXIV.

partakes of the attributes of the Deity and lives for ever with Him.

The Ka or Double.

Having proved by their own words that the Egyptians believed in a future life, we have to try to find out from their religious literature (1) what portion of a man's entity it was which lived after the death of his body; (2) what form it lived in; and (3) where it lived. These questions are full of difficulties, for however closely we may examine the texts, we still find there are many points about which they give no information at all, and the confusion and contradictions which meet us in many documents prove that the writers of them were as much puzzled when they tried to harmonize their statements as we are. The Egyptians more than most peoples tried to explain the unknowable, and, of course, failed. The physical body of a man was called KHAT, , a word which sometimes has as its determinative a mummy, , or a mummy lying on a bier, ; the word seems to mean something which decayed. The god Osiris had such a body, and it lay in Ȧnu (Heliopolis).[1] When the body was born there came into existence with it an abstract individuality or spiritual being, which was wholly independent and distinct from the physical body, but its abode was the body, whose actions it was supposed to direct, and guide, and keep watch over, and it lived in the body until the body died. No healthy child was ever born without this spiritual being, and when the Egyptians drew pictures of it they always made it resemble the body to which it belonged; in other words, they regarded it as its "DOUBLE." Its name in Egyptian was KA, and the hieroglyph which represents it is , *i.e.*, two human arms extended at right angles to the breast as if ready to embrace someone;[2] in late times KA simply meant

[1] 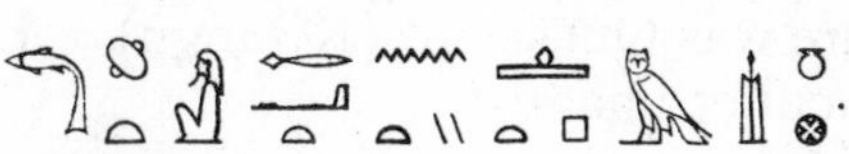. Book of the Dead, Chapter CXLII.

[2] The word exists in Coptic under the form ⲕⲱ, *statuae*, *idola*.

"person," or "self," and the Romans, had they understood the true meaning of the word, would probably have translated it by "genius natalis." When the body died the Ka did not die with it, but continued its existence; whether it was supposed to live for ever cannot be said. The body was preserved in a tomb, so that the Ka might come and visit it whenever it pleased, but it could not be considered the dwelling-place of the Ka after its death. Therefore the Egyptians prepared a figure or statue of the dead person to whom the Ka belonged, taking great pains to give it all the characteristics of the deceased, so that the Ka might recognize it as an image of its body and be pleased to enter into the figure and take up its abode there. The Egyptians placed the figure or statue so prepared in the tomb with the body, sometimes in a niche, and sometimes in a very small chamber behind a stone partition with an opening in it, so that the Ka might see and hear all that was going on in the tomb when visitors came there to pay visits in its honour. The figures set up in memory of the dead by many modern African peoples are in reality Ka figures, only the original purpose of them has been forgotten. Dr. Schweinfurth rightly says that such figures are not idols, and in describing those which were on the grave of Yanga, the Bongo chief, he mentions rough-hewn figures, as large as life, which were carved to represent the chief followed by his wives and children. Some figures of this kind have bead necklaces and rings, and hair is fixed in appropriate places on the body.[1] No pains are spared in making such figures as life-like as possible. In the case of a very great man such a figure is placed in the middle of the town or village, in order that the living may benefit by consultation with the Ka when it visits it. Thus in the town of Cashil, in the Jaga country, there was such an image 12 feet high in the centre of a circle of elephants' tusks, and the natives were in the habit of making offerings of palm oil and goats' blood to it. The name of the figure was Quesango (Kizangu). Elsewhere were several smaller images.[2]

[1] *Heart of Africa*, Vol. I, p. 286.

[2] Andrew Battell, *Strange Adventures* (1901 edition), p. 46.

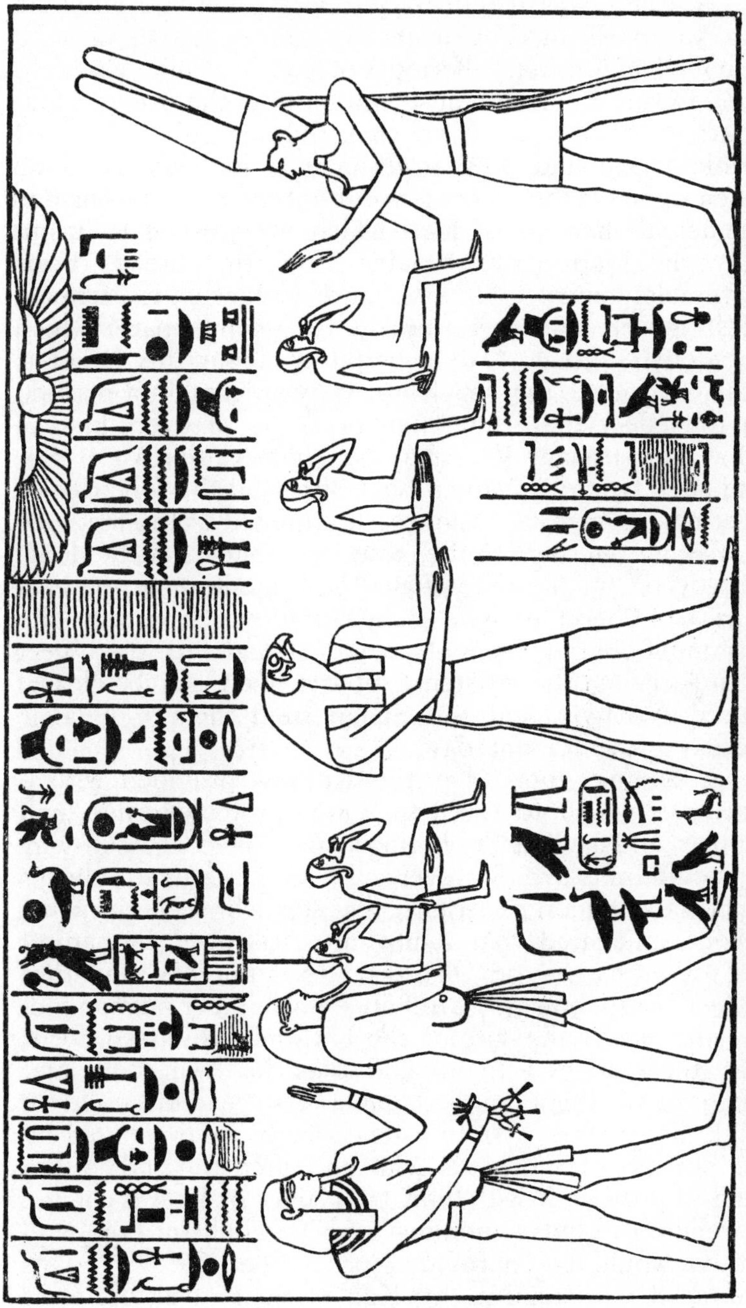

The gods Ḥāp, Hekau and Horus presenting the royal child Åmen-ḥetep III and his Ka, or double, to Åmen-Rā.
From a bas-relief in the Temple of Luxor.

Not only was it necessary to provide a figure for the Ka to dwell in, but if it was not to perish of cold, hunger, and thirst, offerings of meat, drink, clothing, etc., must be placed in the tomb by the friends and relatives of the dead, so that the Ka might eat and drink, anoint and dress itself, even as its body had done when upon earth. The Ka did not, of course, consume the actual offerings of food which were given to it, but only the spirits, or "doubles," of the bread, beer, vegetables, meat, oil, etc., and similarly it arrayed itself in the spirits of the suits of linen apparel which were offered to it. No uncertainty about this belief is possible, for all the sepulchral prayers contain a petition to the effect that thousands of meals of every kind of good and pleasant food may be given to the Ka of So-and-so. In the Chapter on Osiris and the Doctrine of offerings, numerous instances are quoted of the methods of making offerings to the Kau, or Doubles of the dead, employed by the Egyptians and modern peoples in Africa. Therefore it is sufficient to say here that the custom of offering food, etc., to the dead with the object of preserving the existence of the Kau can be clearly traced in Egypt and the Sûdân from the Pre-dynastic Period to the present day.

Assuming, then, that the Ka was provided with a statue in which to dwell in a well protected tomb, and regular and sufficient offerings, there is no reason why it should not live for ever. It has, however, always been the common experience that sepulchral endowments become alienated, that tombs are destroyed by natural and other causes, or "usurped" by strangers, and that bodies perish, however carefully embalmed or mummified. In such cases the fate of the Ka was sad indeed, for it was then obliged to go and seek its own food, and hunger and thirst might compel it to eat offal and to drink filthy water. Its existence might be prolonged by the prayers of the pious who entreated the gods of the dead to provide it with food, but sooner or later a change of religion would come, men's ideas would change, and the Ka would be unprovided for. When the Egyptians embraced Christianity, the Kau of their ancestors must have starved, for the Egyptian Christians made no offerings to the dead, and they did not pray the magical prayers which in earlier times were believed to secure food for the dead. The Kau of dead Egyptians would meet with little charity at the hands of their descendants who embraced Islâm, for they had been "unbelievers," and the offspring of the "time of ignorance" (*jahilîyah*), who knew neither the God of Islam nor its great Prophet. On this point the words of the Ḳur'ân are quite definite:—Upon those who believe not, and who die in their unbelief, shall be the curse of God, and of the angels and of all men; they shall remain under it for ever, their punishment shall not be alleviated, neither shall they be regarded.[1] If, as seems likely, the fate of the Ka was bound up with that of the body, then many score millions of Kau must have perished when the ancient religion of Egypt came to an end, at least so far as ordinary people were concerned. We read of KAU in the kingdom of Osiris, but these, probably, belonged to kings and chiefs and nobles who were buried with elaborate rites and ceremonies, which conferred on them the privileges of the gods who lived for ever, or they may have belonged to the gods themselves.

A belief in the existence of the Ka exists among some modern African peoples. The Tshi-speaking tribes[2] use the word Kra to designate the spirit of a man, which enters him at birth, lives with him throughout his life, and leaves him at death. This spirit is entirely distinct from the man himself. The word Kra is generally interpreted "soul," but the Kra does not in any way correspond to the European idea of soul, and it has nothing to do with the soul which, on the death of the body, departs straightway to the Land of the Dead. The Kra is not the man himself, in a shadowy or ghostly form, that continues his existence after death in another world, but is a kind of guardian spirit, who lives in a man. The Ewe-speaking peoples have a similar belief, the indwelling spirit being by them termed a "Luwo." The Gã-speaking peoples assign to each individual two indwelling spirits called "Kla," one male and one female, the former being of a bad and the latter of a good

[1] Surah II (The Cow).
[2] See Ellis, *The Tshi-speaking Peoples*, p. 149.

disposition. And they give good or bad advice, and prompt good or bad actions, according to their respective dispositions.[1] The Bantu equivalent of the "Kra" or "Kla" is called "Manu."[2] The Ba-Huana believe that man is composed of body, *bun* (soul), and double (*doshi*). The Doshi is a shadowy second self, corresponding to the Kra of the Tshi-speaking tribes of the Gold Coast, and the Ka of the Ancient Egyptians. It leaves the body in sleep, and visits other people in dreams, and the Doshi of the dead appear to the living in the same manner. All people have Doshi, and animals also. At death the Doshi lingers about in the air, visits its friends and haunts its enemies; it will persecute the relations if the body has not received proper burial; there are no means of exorcising it.[3] The Bayaka of the Kwango-Kwilu also believe in the existence of an imperishable principle or soul, according to Mr. Torday, which they call "Doshi."[4]

Colonel Ellis says that when a man dies his Kra becomes a "Sisa," and a Sisa can be born again and become a Kra in a new human body. It can remain in the house with its dead body, and can annoy the living and cause sickness. If it fails to find a new body, it must go to the land of Insisa, where the Insisa (plural of Sisa) live and build houses. This country lies beyond the River Volta. Usually Insisa do no harm to the relatives of its dead body unless they have not buried it with proper care and ceremony; therefore are the dead buried with great care, for the relatives like to think that the Sisa of the dead relative is sitting with them comfortably in the hut, and not wandering about outside unprovided for. The Sisa lives near the house until the end of the period of mourning, when it goes to the country of Insisa. The Ahantas build special small huts for the Insisa, in which

[1] The Yorubas think that a man has three indwelling spirits: 1. The Olori, which dwells in the head, and is the protector, guardian, and guide of a man; to it offerings are made. 2. The Ipin ijeun, which dwells in the stomach. 3. The Ipori, which dwells in the big toe.—Ellis, *Yoruba-speaking Peoples*, p. 126.

[2] Kingsley, *West African Studies*, p. 200.

[3] Torday and Joyce, *Notes on the Ethnography of the Ba-Huana*, *Journal Anth. Inst.*, Vol. XXXVI.

[4] Quoted by Johnston, *George Grenfell*, Vol. II, p. 640.

they place a bundle of hair of the deceased, and meat and drink offerings.[1] These facts are of importance, for they show that the modern African holds about the Kra, and its later development the Sisa, views similar to those which the Egyptian held about the Ka, and the urgent necessity there was to bury the body with full ceremonies and to provide for the Ka.

The Spirit-Body (Sāḥu).

The fact that the Egyptians and many peoples of the Sûdân were in the habit of drying the body in the sun or embalming it, and swathing it in cloth of some kind, proves that its preservation was in some way necessary for the eternal welfare of its spiritual constituents. The Egyptians were a practical people, and they would never have gone to the expense and trouble of embalming the dead unless they had believed that it was absolutely necessary. There is no proof that they ever expected the physical body to rise again; on the contrary, the texts state clearly that the "soul is in heaven, the body in the earth,"[2] and "thy essence is in heaven, thy body in the earth";[3] and this, notwithstanding the texts say: "I germinate like the plants";[4] "my flesh, , germinateth";[5] "I am, I am, I live, I live, I germinate, I germinate";[6] and in the "Book of Breathings" it is said to the deceased: "Thy soul liveth, thy body "germinateth by the command of Rā, without diminution, "without defect, like [that of] Rā, for ever and ever." These statements taken together prove that the Egyptians believed that some kind of body rose from the dead, and continued its existence in the Other World. The pictures of the beatified as seen in papyri

[1] Ellis, *op. cit.*, p. 151.

[2] 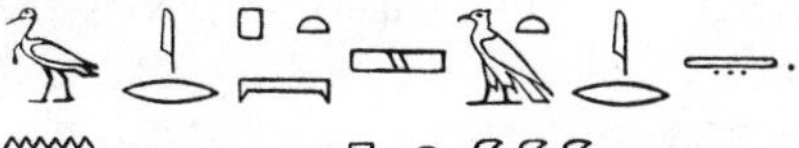. Pepi I, l. 85.

[3] 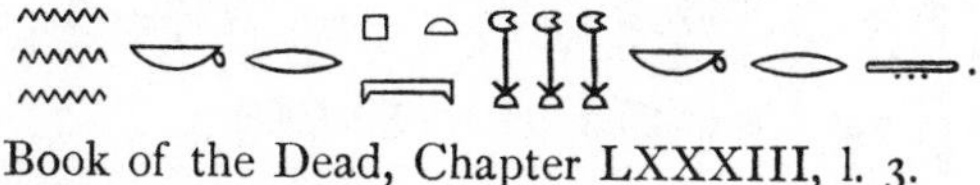. Pepi I, l. 304.

[4] Book of the Dead, Chapter LXXXIII, l. 3.

[5] *Ibid.*, LXIV, l. 49.

[6] *Ibid.*, CLIV.

show us that this risen body had the form and appearance of the physical body which had been mummified and laid in the grave. We know that the KA was maintained by the offerings of relatives and friends of the dead, but we have no information as to the means by which the Sāḥu,[1] or revivified body, was kept in existence. The word "sāḥu" seems to mean something like "free," "noble," "chief," and in this case it appears to be used as the name for a body which has, by means of the religious ceremonies that have been performed over it, obtained freedom from the material body and power whereby it has become incorruptible and everlasting. Hence arose the great importance of funeral ceremonies and offerings, which caused a spiritual body to spring from the physical body, and the KA to continue its existence after the death of the body to which it belonged. As the physical body formed the abiding-place of the KA and the soul, so the spiritual body was believed to afford a dwelling-place for the soul, for it is distinctly said[2] that "souls enter into their sāḥu." And the spiritual body had power to journey everywhere in heaven and on earth, for to King Tetȧ it is said: "Thou "hast received thy sāḥ, thy foot shall have no limit "set to it in heaven, thou shalt not be driven back on "earth."[3]

Modern African peoples also believe that the living man and the Kra become on the death of the man a ghost or shadowy man and a Sisa. On this point all the Tshi-speaking peoples agree.[4] The Tshi name for the shadowy man is "Srahman," plur., Asrahmanfo. The Srahman does in the Other World what he did when he lived here; the chief is a chief, the peasant a peasant, and the slave a slave. He has the same passions, appetites, needs, and necessities as living men, and he lives on and enjoys the intangible individualities of the offerings which are made at his grave.[5] The Yoruba

[1] 

[2] Book of the Dead, Chapter LXXXIX, l. 5.

[3] Tetȧ, l. 271.

[4] Ellis, *op. cit.*, p. 155.

[5] *Ibid.*, pp. 157, 158.

tribes call the "ghost-man" "Iwin," or "Okan," but the latter word also means "heart." The Iwin holds the position he held here in the Other World, if he reaches it, but this he only does if the prescribed funeral rites have been properly performed. If these be omitted the "ghost-man" wanders about the world, cold, hungry, and homeless, and he may be seized by evil spirits and cast into "the unseen world of potsherds."[1] Dr. Nassau tells us that the Uvengwa is the self-revivified spirit and body of a dead human being. It is an object of dread, and is never worshipped in any manner whatever. It is white in colour, but the body is variously changed from the likeness of the original human body.[2] The Baluba believe that the soul continues to reside unimpaired in the corpse, with the possibility of detaching itself, not freely and untrammelled, but in association with a vague, impalpable something, a kind of phantom or spectre which has the exact appearance of the dead body, but has not its real substance. It is under this shadowy form, which is, in short, the dematerialized body, that the soul will henceforth live in the realm of the dead. The Baluba believe the soul to be a principle distinct from the body, and endowed with a more ethereal nature, but unfit to exist alone without some veil or phantom. This phantom has not always the exact shape of a human being. Thus the phantom of a man whose flesh has been eaten by cannibals takes the form of a dried skeleton, and that of a man whose body has been burnt will for ever appear as a wreath of smoke dropping an ashy dust.[3] Thus the ancient and modern evidences taken together show that the Egyptians and Sûdânî peoples believed in a resurrection, and thought that the spirit body was enabled to rise from the physical body through the rites and ceremonies which were performed over it.

[1] Ellis, *Yoruba-speaking Peoples*, p. 127.
[2] *Fetichism in West Africa*, p. 71.
[3] Johnston, *George Grenfell*, Vol. II, p. 642.

The Shadow (Khaibit).

Closely associated with the body was its shadow, 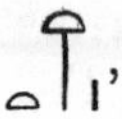, and the Egyptians appear to have thought it one of its most important attributes. We do not know what ideas they held about its functions when the man to whom it belonged was alive, but it is quite certain that they did not believe the resurrection of the spiritual body to be complete unless that phantom form was in possession of its shadow. The texts lead us to suppose that the Sāḥu was an immaterial form of the physical body, and it seems that the Egyptians thought it to be material enough to cast a shadow! In the text of Unȧs the shadow is mentioned in connection with the "form."[1] In the Theban Book of the Dead the deceased prays that his Ba and Khu and Shadow may not be shut in in the Other World,[2] and elsewhere[3] we read, "O keep not "captive my Soul (Ba), O keep not ward over my "Shadow, but let a way be opened for my Soul and for "my Shadow, and let [me] see the great God in the "shrine, on the day of the Judgment of Souls, and let "[me] recite the words of Osiris, whose habitations are "hidden, to those who guard the members of Osiris, "and who keep ward over the Khu (Spirits), and who "hold captive the shadows of the dead, who would "work evil against me, lest they work evil against me." In the vignette in the Papyrus of Ani we see Ani standing by the door of his tomb, and his soul in the form of a human-headed bird hovering over his spirit body. In a variant vignette[4] the soul is hovering over the shadow of the deceased, which is painted solid and black. Further on in the text of the same Chapter it is said: "Thou shalt have dominion over thy legs, and thou shalt advance to thy body straightway in the earth." These passages are important, for they show: (1) That there were believed to exist certain evil Shadows who would do harm to their fellow Shadows if they could;

[1] Line 523.
[2] Chapter XCI.
[3] Chapter XCII.
[4] Papyrus of Nefer-uben-f.

(2) That the Shadow was associated with the Soul; (3) That the Shadow had the power to move about and to go where it liked. The difference between the spirit-body and the Shadow is so slight that we can readily understand how easily one was confounded with the other in men's minds.

The Shadow is a recognized portion of man among modern African peoples. In West Africa the natives told Dr. Nassau that it was possible for a human being to have his *nsisim, i.e.*, shadow, stolen or otherwise lost, and for him to exist in a diseased or dying state. In this case his body would cast no shadow.[1] The same authority says there is a widespread belief among the natives in a "dual soul," which consists of a "spirit," which, as far as is known, lives for ever in the world of spirits, and a shadow, which for an uncertain length of time hovers around the mortal remains.[2] Here we seem to have a confusion between the spirit-body and the shadow of a man. The shadow, according to Miss Kingsley, is one of the four souls of man. She noticed that men would march happily enough through forest or grass land on a blazing morning, but when they came to a piece of open ground they would go round it, not across it, because they were afraid of losing their shadows. They only do this at noontime. On asking some Bakwiri why they were not anxious about losing their souls at night time, she was told that at night all shadows lay down in the shadow of the Great God, and so became stronger. Had she not noticed how long and strong the shadows of men, trees, and mountains were in the morning? Murders are sometimes committed secretly by driving a nail or a knife into a man's shadow.[3] The Nandi think that the human soul is embodied in a person's shadow, and it is firmly believed that after death the shadows of both good and bad people go underground and live there.[4] All the Nandi are afraid of a shadow.[5] At one time among the Bavili it was

[1] *Fetichism in West Africa*, p. 65.
[2] *Ibid.*, p. 230.
[3] *West African Studies*, p. 207.
[4] Hollis, *The Nandi*, p. 41.
[5] *Ibid.*, p. 148.

considered a crime for one person to trample upon or even to cross the shadow of another, especially if the shadow were that of a married woman. The shadow was supposed to sleep in the body of its owner at night, and if a sorcerer were to rob a man of his shadow it was equivalent to taking away his life. The shadow enters and leaves the body by the mouth, and is then likened to the breath of a man. When a man dies he has no shadow, and when he falls into a fit or trance the Bavili say it is because some sorcerer has taken his shadow.[1] According to the Fjort the Shadow ceases to exist on the death of the body.[2]

We have now described the physical body, the spirit-body, the double and the shadow, and it remains to consider the African beliefs about that portion of a man which we call the soul.

The Soul of the Ka, or Body-Soul.

To one of the constituents of man's spiritual economy the Egyptians gave the name of "Ba," , a word which, by general consent among Egyptologists, is translated "soul." Various attempts have been made to provide a derivation for the word, and it has been thought to mean something like "noble" or "sublime," but all such derivations are mere guesses, and it must be frankly admitted that the exact idea which the Egyptians associated with the word is unknown. The texts afford no explanation of it, but they give a certain amount of evidence which shows us generally what they thought the Ba to be, and this, especially when compared with modern African ideas of the soul, is invaluable. The Ba, it seems, was connected closely with the Ka with which it dwelt, and it appears to have been regarded as the soul of the Ka. It was not incorporeal, though its nature and substance were somewhat ethereal. It was gratified by the offerings made to the Ka of the dead body in the tomb, and perhaps it partook of their spirit entities. It revisited its Ka and the body in the tomb,

[1] Dennett, *At the Back of the Black Man's Mind*, p. 80.
[2] Dennett, *Folklore of the Fjort*, London, 1898, p. 116.

and it could take up its abode there at pleasure ; it was free to travel all over heaven, and to mix with and to hold converse with souls there, and it could take any form it pleased. The Ba of a man was represented by a bird with a bearded human head . As in the Pyramid Texts we read of a "living Ba,"[1] we must assume that there was such a thing as a dead Ba, in other words, that the Ba could die. The Ba could live in a body not its own, for at their pleasure the gods sent their Ba into the dead king Unȧs.[2] The Egyptians believed that more than one Ba belonged to a man, for the "Baiu" or "souls" of King Pepi were placed at the head of the Two Companies of the Gods.[3] The "souls" here referred to are, of course, the other portions of the spirit entity of man which resemble the Ba in nature and substance. The Egyptians believed that the Ba might, by the agency of evil spirits, be prevented from rejoining its Ka and physical body, and that it might wander away from them, and even be shut up with them and unable to get out. Therefore was written the LXXXIst Chapter of the Theban Book of the Dead, in which the deceased prayed: "If my Ba would tarry, let it be "brought to me from whatsoever place it may be in " . . . let me have my Ba and my Khu . . . let it look "upon its physical body, let it rest upon its spirit-body." From the same chapter we learn that the rejoining of the Ba to its Ka and body was supposed to take place in Heliopolis, where the Soul of Osiris rejoined itself to the body of that god. According to one view, when the Ba visited its Ka and body in the tomb it took with it air and food, which we may assume were intended for the Ka; this is proved by the vignette in the Papyrus of Neb-qeṭ,[4] in which the Ba, in the form of a human-headed bird, is actually seen descending the shaft of the

[1] Unȧs, l. 455. [2] *Ibid.*, l. 522.

[3] , l. 167.

[4] Ed. Devéria and Pierret, Plate 3.

pit of the tomb leading to the mummy chamber bearing with it air and water.

We have already seen that offerings were made to the Ka, and a passage in the Book of the Dead (Chapter XXIXc) suggests that the Ka, if needing food, had the power of making the Ba to bring it. The deceased says: "I am the Bennu, the Ba of Rā, the "guide of the gods of the Ṭuat. Their Baiu (souls) "come forth upon earth to do the will of their Kau, "therefore let my Ba come forth to do the will of my

The "Doubles" of Ani and his wife drinking water in the Other World.

"Ka." Now the vignette of this Chapter in the Papyrus of Ani is a heart 𓄣, which proves that in the XVIIIth dynasty the heart was somehow associated with the Ba and the Ka, and we must, it seems to me, conclude that the Ba was the soul of the Ka, and that its seat of being was in the Ka.

The Heart.

In Egyptian *ȧb*[1] 𓄣, which literally means "heart," is used to express wish, longing, desire, lust, will, courage, mind, wisdom, sense, intelligence, manner, disposition,

[1] The Semitic word for "heart" (Heb. לֵב, Syr. ܠܒܐ, Arab. لُبّ, Eth. ልብ:) may be connected with this word.

attention, intention, etc., and it is clear that the heart was regarded as the seat of life, and as the home of the passions, both good and bad, and as the seat of the pleasures derived from eating, drinking, and the carnal appetite. There appears to have been a soul which was connected with the heart. It was not, I believe, the soul as we usually understand it, but the heart-soul.[1] The importance of the heart to the deceased will be readily understood from the fact that no less than five Chapters of the Book of the Dead (XXVI–XXX) are devoted to its preservation. In one of these (XXVI) the deceased prays for a heart, for, if he has no heart, he says: "I cannot eat of the cakes of Osiris on the "east bank of the Lake of Flowers. . . . With the "mastery of my heart I am master of my arms and legs, "and I can do whatsoever my Ka pleaseth, and my "soul will not be fettered at the gates of the Ṭuat." Here, clearly, we see that the welfare of the soul depends upon that of the heart. In the XXVIIth Chapter the deceased appeals to the "stealers of hearts"[2] not to take his heart-soul away; and in the XXVIIIth he prays that his heart-soul may not be carried off by the War-gods of Heliopolis,[3] and that it may not be given to Suti (Set). The vignette represents the deceased seated and clasping his heart to his breast with his left hand, in the presence of a monster, the form of which appears to be derived from that of the ourang-outang, or the soko, of the forests of the Sûdân. In the XXIXth Chapter the deceased prays that his heart may be neither taken away from him, nor killed, and he identifies himself with Horus, the "dweller in hearts," and with the "lord of hearts, the slayer of the heart." In Chapter XXX he addresses with reverence the heart of Osiris, and the intestines [of the god] and the Four Sons of Horus, who protect the viscera. The contents of the famous "Heart-Chapter" (XXXB) have already been described; in this the heart and its soul are addressed by the deceased.

1 On the Heart-soul, *Ḥāti*, see *infra*, p. 137.

2 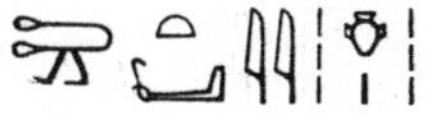

3 

Among modern African peoples the heart of both man and beast is regarded as the source of all life, emotion, passion, movement, and strength, and in the case of man the heart is often identified with the soul.[1] Thus the Ba-Huana call the soul and the heart by the same name—" Bun."[2] The priests of Ogun used to take out the hearts of human victims, and reduce them to powder, which they mixed with rum and sold to persons who wished to be endowed with great courage. Such people swallowed the mixture, and believed that by doing so they absorbed all the courage of the dead.[3] Among the Nandi the warrior always ate a small portion of the heart of the dead man in order to make himself brave.[4] The heart of the lion, the elephant, and other mighty beasts has always been prized, and eaten joyfully by the natives, and as a proof that the custom is still observed we may quote the experience of the unfortunate Lieut. Boyd Alexander. After he killed a lion, and the beast had been skinned, John, his cook, secured all but a little corner of the heart, and having dried it took it home to make strong the heart of his little son.[5]

The Spirit-Soul (Khu).

The exact meaning of the word Khu, or, as it is written in the Pyramid Texts *Åakhu*, is very hard to discover, and authorities have differed greatly in their translations of the word, and in their descriptions of what the Khu is. That it was a very important portion of a man is clear from texts of all periods, and there is no doubt that it was supposed to be eternal. The Pyramid Texts prove that the Khu of the gods lived in heaven, and thither wended the Khu of a man as soon as ever the prayers said over the dead body enabled it to do so. King Unȧs " stood at the head of the Khu,"[6] *i.e.*, he was the chief of all the Khu ; and when the souls of the gods transferred themselves from their own spirit-bodies to

[1] Ellis, *Yoruba-speaking Peoples*, pp. 126, 127.
[2] Torday and Joyce, *op. cit.*, p. 291.
[3] *Ibid.*, p. 69.
[4] Hollis, *The Nandi*, p. 27.
[5] *From the Niger to the Nile*, p. 61.
[6] Line 71.

Unȧs, their Khu were before Unȧs.[1] The god received the king as a brother, and placed him among the "imperishable Khu."[2] The last passage is important, for the hieroglyphic determinatives suggest that the Khu were beings of light, comparable to the stars, and the evidence of other passages supports this view, and indicates that the Khu of a man was the intangible, ethereal, transparent portion of his immaterial economy, to which modern nations have given the name of "spirit." The Khu is mentioned in connection with the Ba and the Khaibit (Soul and Shadow),[3] and with the Ba and the Ka (Soul and Double),[4] but it is clear that it is something quite distinct from the Ka, Ba, and Khaibit, though in some respects it must have possessed characteristics similar to these immaterial entities of man. We have seen that the texts speak of man having more than one "soul," and that the Egyptian, like the modern African, thought that he possessed three at least, the Ka, or Double, the Ba, or Heart-soul, and the Khu. The Khaibit or Shadow was confused at times with the Ka. It appears, then, that the Khu is the Spirit, or Spirit-soul of a man, which it was impossible to injure or kill, and that it was the vital principle of a man and was immortal. The Ka perished if offerings were not provided for it, and the Ba (Heart-soul) might, it was thought, also die, but the Khu was "imperishable."

Appertaining to the Khu was the Sekhem , the functions of which are not known exactly; the word means "power," and it may be an immaterial personification of the energy of a man. To King Pepi it is said: "Thy Sekhem cometh among the Khu";[5] "thy Sekhem is pure among the Khu";[6] "thou art pure, thy Ka is pure, thy Ba is pure, thy Sekhem is pure."[7] Osiris and every god had his Sekhem, and Rā is called the "Great Sekhem, the Sekhem among the Sekhemu."[8]

[1] Line 522.

[2] . Tetȧ, l. 289.

[3] Book of the Dead, Chapter XCI.

[4] *Ibid.*, Chapter CLXXXIII, l. 35.

[5] Line 13. [6] Line 113. [7] Line 112. [8] Unȧs, ll. 514, 515.

From the above facts we are able to state the following:—

When an Egyptian was born he was believed to possess a physical body (Khat) and an immaterial Double (Ka), which lived inside the body and was associated closely with the Ba, which dwelt in the heart, and which appears to have been connected with the Shadow of the physical body. Somewhere in the body lived the Khu or Spirit-soul, the nature of which was unchangeable, incorruptible, and immortal. When the body died there could be raised from it by means of words, holy or magical, and ceremonies performed by the priests, a

Isis giving bread and water to the Heart-soul.

Spirit-body called Sāḥu, which the Khu (Spirit-soul) could inhabit at pleasure. The Ka, Ba, or Heart-soul, and Shadow dwelt in the tomb with the body, or wandered about outside it and away from it, when they desired to do so. Their existence was finite, and appears to have terminated whenever funerary offerings failed to be made to them. As all tomb-endowments came to an end sooner or later, the destruction of the Ka and its soul and shadow was certain. On the other hand, the Sāḥu, or Spirit-body, which was revivified from the physical body, was wholly independent of offerings, for it derived its sustenance from the Khu, or Spirit-soul, and this was self-existent and immortal. Therefore it was the Sāḥu which entered heaven and lived with Osiris and the blessed for all eternity. This being so it is easy to understand why the Egyptians took such pains to preserve the bodies of their dead by mummification, and why the custom of embalming the dead continued in Egypt for some centuries after the introduction of Christianity into that country, in fact until the doctrine preached by Saint Anthony became known. This great ascetic taught men to believe that Christ would, at the Resurrection, give them back their bodies in a glorified state, and that therefore mummification was unnecessary for the genesis of the spiritual body.

If we consider the facts stated in the preceding paragraphs as a whole, and compare the Egyptian's belief about the constituent parts of his spiritual entity with the beliefs of other ancient peoples, we find nothing resembling it. It stands quite alone, and it is not until we come to examine the modern African beliefs concerning the soul that we find anything similar to it. It will be seen from the facts given below that among the tribes of the Sûdân and Western Africa exactly parallel beliefs exist, and we are driven to conclude that the eschatological ideas of the Egyptians were not peculiar to themselves, but belonged to the indigenous peoples of those parts of Africa.

The Dual-Soul of the Modern African.

Speaking generally, the belief in a future life among modern Africans is as universal as the belief in God. The Masai say that when a man dies and is eaten by a hyena, all is over with him, and that the soul does not come to life again. They say also, somewhat inconsistently, that when a medicine man dies, or a rich man, and is buried, his soul turns into a snake as soon as his body rots; and the snake goes to his children's kraal to look after them.[1] The Bari think that when a man dies, the person is gone absolutely, never to return, in fact that a man is "worn out."[2] The Bahima believe in the spiritual existence of chiefs,[3] according to Sir Harry Johnston, but Mr. Cunningham says that they have no

[1] Hollis, *The Masai*, p. 307. See also Johnston, *Uganda*, p. 832.
[2] Frobenius, *Die Heiden-Neger*, p. 137.
[3] Johnston, *Uganda*, Vol. I, p. 631.

belief in kings or warriors coming back.[1] Neither the Masai nor the Bahima appear to bury the bodies of ordinary folk, for the former throw them out into the bush, and the latter hang them on the branches of trees for the hyenas to eat,[2] but kings and chiefs are buried, because it is thought that their existence does not end with the death of their bodies. Although the African may say that he does not believe in the resurrection of the body, his acts prove that he takes the existence of the soul in another life for granted. Mr. Nassau found that the very people who were declaring unhesitatingly that men came to an end like goats, dogs, and chickens, took the greatest care of their family fetish, and sacrificed diligently to the spirits of their ancestors, and appealed to them for help in their family undertakings.[3]

In West Africa the belief in the DUAL-SOUL, *i.e.*, the soul of the body, and the soul, or, as we may call it, the "Spirit-soul," is well-nigh universal. The soul of the body, the Egyptian Ba, is mortal, but the Spirit-soul, the Egyptian Khu, is immortal. Nothing is soulless to the African, and even matter is thought to be a form of soul, of a low order it is true, which souls of a higher nature can make use of.[4] It is generally thought that, in addition to the Body-soul and the Spirit-soul, man possesses also a Life-soul and a Dream-soul. The Life-soul is viewed in different ways by different peoples. According to some it is of equal importance with the Body-soul and the Spirit-soul, but others regard it as a member of a class of spirits which is associated with man from his birth to his death. All agree that it has its abode in the physical heart, and that it can be drawn away from the heart by witchcraft; when the Life-soul is stolen from a man his body dies. Some regard the Life-soul as a sort of guardian spirit, and at times it is spoken of as if it were a man's conscience, and it is important to note that a kind of worship is accorded to it as to spirits. The general

[1] *Uganda and Its Peoples*, p. 12.
[2] *Uganda*, p. 632. There is no future life for women or common folk.—*Ibid.*, p. 832.
[3] *Fetichism in West Africa*, p. 53.
[4] Kingsley, *West African Studies*, p. 199.

drift of the evidence which we have about it suggests that this Life-soul is nothing more nor less than the soul of the heart, and that it was known to the Egyptians. In the Chapters of the Book of the Dead which deal with the heart are two words commonly rendered heart by translators. The first of these is *ȧb*, , and the second is *ḥāti*,[1] . Thus in Chapter XXXA the deceased says: "My *ȧb*, my mother! My *ḥāti*, my being!" It is quite easy to say that *ȧb* and *ḥāti* are synonyms, and to translate accordingly, but the Egyptian must have made some distinction in his mind when he used them, and it seems to me that in the earliest times *ȧb* meant the physical heart, and *ḥāti* the soul of the heart, or the state, or quality, or mental condition, of the heart. Both the *ȧb* and the *ḥāti* could be stolen, as the titles of the Chapters in the Book of the Dead prove, and the result would be in either case the same to the body, namely, death. The *ȧb* could be given to a man (Chapter XXVI), or carried away from a man (Chapter XXIX), or struck dead (Chapter XXIXA), or a model of it could be made in *sehert* stone (Chapter XXIXB), or it could be spoken against, or cursed, or bewitched (Chapters XXXA, XXXB). The *ḥāti* could only be carried off, or stolen, and the vignette of Chapter XXVII in the Papyrus of Ani proves that the deceased adored it, for we see him standing reverently before the *ḥāti*, which, in the form of a heart, is set upon a pedestal before him . In the scene of the weighing of the heart which is found in fine papyri, the heart seen in one pan of the Balance probably represents the Ḥāti, or Heart-soul.

The name "Dream-soul" is given to that part of a man which is thought sometimes to leave him during sleep, and to wander away into strange places, where it sometimes meets with remarkable adventures. Sometimes it enjoys its freedom so greatly, and so delights in its intercourse with other Dream-souls, that it forgets to come back to its body before the man wakes up. If it

[1] In Coptic ϨⲎⲦ.

does come back in time its reunion with its body dulls its faculties, and the person, in his efforts to remember or to tell what he has seen, relates only the vagaries of a dream. If it does not come back in time, the man to whom it belongs falls seriously ill,[1] and recourse must be had to a witch-doctor, if his life is to be preserved. The witch-doctor professes to be able to bring back the Dream-soul to its home, but there is a great deal of fraud connected with the process. It is most important for a man that every soul of his shall be in him, for any breach in the intercommunication of his souls is followed by the decay and death of his body. If the Dream-soul of a man has lost itself, a new one must be found to take its place, for the abode where it lives in a man must in no case be left empty, otherwise a "Sisa," *i.e.*, the soul of some person who has not been properly buried, will step into it and dwell there. Unfortunately a Sisa is usually accompanied by a crowd of devils, or evil spirits, and these enter a man with it, and produce illnesses of all kinds, fever, delirium, convulsions, etc., which must cause death unless they and the Sisa can be ejected from the body.[2] It is a prevalent belief that Dream-souls which lose themselves are caught by witch-doctors, who set traps for them in a systematic manner, and then sell them to their original owners at high prices. Though a man has a Dream-soul substitute in him, which in a general way is satisfactory, he is never really comfortable until he gets his own Dream-soul back, and he usually spares no pains to effect its capture. Sometimes the witch-doctor is paid by an enemy of the man to whom the Dream-soul belongs, to keep it in captivity and thereby to cause his death; in such cases it is not only caught and kept, but tortured, and hung up over the canoe fire, and so on.[3]

Yet another soul of man is believed to exist by the Africans, viz., the Bush-soul. It lives in some animal in the forest, a pig, or a leopard, and offerings are made to it; these are placed in small huts built far away in the forest. If the animal in which is a Bush-soul dies or

[1] Nassau, *Fetichism in West Africa*, p. 55.
[2] Kingsley, *West African Studies*, p. 203.
[3] Kingsley, *West African Studies*, p. 206.

is killed, the man who is connected with the soul dies also; and if the man dies or is killed, the animal containing his Bush-soul contrives to die or be killed also.[1] These three souls, the Life-soul, the Dream-soul, and the Bush-soul, appear to be phases of the Body-soul, and it seems to me that actually the Egyptian and the African only know of the Dual-soul, *i.e.*, the Body-soul and the Spirit-soul.

TRANSMIGRATION OF SOULS AND TRANSFORMATION.

The Egyptians believed in the transmigration of souls, and their priests composed a series of Chapters,[2] the recital of which enabled the souls of the dead to take any form they pleased. A soul could become a golden hawk, a divine hawk, a *tchatcha* chief, a god of light, a lily,[3] the god Ptaḥ, a Bennu bird, a heron, a "living soul," a swallow, a serpent, and a crocodile. It could remain in each of these so long as it pleased, presumably without losing its identity, and it could pass from one form to another at pleasure. By passing into the body of a Light-god it became an equal of the luminaries of heaven, as a bird it could explore the sky, as a serpent the earth, and as a crocodile it could travel whither it pleased in the waters. Among modern Africans the belief is current that the souls of men make periodic migrations into hyenas,[4] in order to attack and injure or kill those who have done their bodies harm. Dr. Junker's servant Ahmad told him a story of a woman in Sennaar who had been turned into a hyena[5] by witchcraft, an occurrence of which, he assured him, he had been an eye-witness.[6] The human soul which

[1] *Ibid.*, p. 208.

[2] See Book of the Dead, Chapters LXXVI–LXXXVIII.

[3] It is curious to find a flower mentioned in this category, for though the African gives a soul to vegetable matter, he denies to it mind and intelligence.—Leonard, *The Lower Niger*, p. 188.

[4] Schweinfurth, *Heart of Africa*, Vol. II, p. 322.

[5] The Nandi believe that hyenas talk like human beings and that they hold converse with the spirits of the dead. They say the hyenas are hermaphrodites, and they are supposed to put on spectacles, and an apparatus to assist their hearing; they are supposed to intercede with the spirits of the dead, so that the lives of children placed on their paths may be spared.—Hollis, *The Nandi*, p. 7.

[6] Junker's *Travels in Africa*, Vol. I, p. 333.

enters into an animal does not necessarily lose its human personality, or change into that of a beast, and the belief in this possibility does not include the idea of a permanent residence in the animal.[1] A human soul in an animal may do harm to members of its own family, as in the case of the soul-possessed elephant at Benita in 1867, which was laying waste a certain plantation. When the owner was asked why he did not shoot it, he said he dared not, as the spirit of his father who had died recently had passed into it.[2] The Wanyamwesi of East Africa believe in transmigration, both during life and after it. In Mashonaland they believe that both the living and the dead can change themselves into animals, either to execute some vengeance, or to procure something they wish for. Thus a man will change himself into a hyena or lion to steal a sheep and make a good meal of it, or into a serpent to avenge himself on some enemy.[3] According to the Barotse, the spirit of a chief takes up its abode in a hippopotamus, but yet they carry water to his tomb.[4] The tribes of the Lower Niger think that certain individuals can transform the human body into that of an animal, and *vice versâ*, and that human beings can be possessed by souls of animals. The human soul does not alter the character of the animal, but the animal soul in a man debases him.[5] This power of transformation is called "Ehehe." Major A. G. Leonard mentions the case of a woman of Utshi who was accused of causing the death of one Oru, who was devoured by a crocodile. This she was supposed to have done by projecting her Spirit-soul into the crocodile which devoured him, and not by transforming herself into the animal.[6] In Southern Guinea it is believed that a man can turn himself into a tiger and destroy the lives and property of his fellow men. He can also turn his enemy into an elephant and kill him.[7] Among the Yorubas a belief is current to the effect

[1] Nassau, *Fetichism*, p. 56.
[2] *Ibid.*, p. 58.
[3] Decle, in Nassau, *op. cit.*, pp. 71, 230, 231.
[4] Decle, *Three Years in Savage Africa*, p. 74.
[5] Leonard, *The Lower Niger and Its Tribes*, p. 189.
[6] *Ibid.*, p. 194.
[7] Wilson, *Western Africa*, p. 398.

that men can transform themselves into trees, shrubs, rocks, etc., as well as into animals.[1] Up and down the main Congo the Bantu populations consider it possible for the spirits of dead and living men to enter the bodies of buffaloes, leopards, and crocodiles, in order that they may inflict injuries on their enemies. The Busoko cannibals of the lower Aruwimi believe in a kind of transmigration of souls.[2] Thus from one side of Africa to the other we find that the belief in the transmigration of souls is general, but it may be noted that among modern peoples it is usually associated with evil intent. The object of all the transformations provided for the Egyptian was to do good to him, and to benefit him, and not to enable him to do harm to other people. Still, the facts prove that the Egyptians and the modern Africans held precisely similar views about the transmigrations of souls.

NEW BIRTH AND REINCARNATION.

There are at least two passages in the Theban Recension of the Book of the Dead which show that the Egyptians believed in the possibility of a "second birth." The first occurs in the LXIVth Chapter, in which the deceased identifies himself with the "God of the hidden soul, the Creator of the gods," and refers to his second birth,[3] and the second in the CLXXXIInd Chapter, wherein Osiris is addressed as "he who giveth birth to men and women a second time."[4] The context in the latter case suggests that the new birth or re-birth here referred to did not take place in this world, but in the kingdom of Osiris, and in the former case the new birth of the deceased seems to resemble the re-birth of Rā, the Sun-god, who, it was thought, was re-born daily. In neither case can the re-birth be considered as re-incarnation as the word is understood at the present time.

[1] Ellis, *Yoruba speaking Peoples*, p. 123.

[2] Johnston, *George Grenfell*, Vol. II, p. 632.

[3] 

[4] 

Among modern African peoples it is believed that a considerable number of the souls of the dead pass into the bodies of their descendants, and live there permanently.[1] The idea of reincarnation is very strong in the Niger Delta tribes. Among them, Miss Kingsley says: "Most—I think I may say all—human souls of the 'surviving soul' class are regarded as returning to the earth again, and undergoing a reincarnation shortly after the due burial of the soul.[2] When a baby arrives in the house after the death of a chief, articles which once belonged to deceased members of the house are presented to it, and then, according to the one it picks out, it is decided who that baby really is—See, Uncle So-and-so knows his own pipe, etc.,—and I have often heard a mother reproaching a child for some fault say: 'Oh, we made a big mistake when we thought you were So-and-so.'"[3] According to popular belief, a certain proportion of spirits, who have recuperated their evidently diminishing energy during their stay in spirit-land, are obliged to be re-born into their own family. Thus we have a belief in a reversion to the ancestral type. These spirits, who are chosen by the "dormant or self-existent Creator," are those of men of strong character and moral stamina, especially those who have been good domestic managers, traders, farmers, or hunters, but not necessarily men of commanding ability or marked individuality. The re-birth of the soul into the human body is not merely a belief, in the ordinary sense of the word, but a conviction, that neither argument, satire, nor ridicule will uproot or even shake. Proof of re-birth depends on physical and external similarities of appearance between the living or human and the departed or spirit elements, and in making comparisons particular attention is paid to birth-marks, scars, cicatrices, defects, deformities, etc. In addition, the expression of the intelligence and individuality is taken into consideration, and the testimony of the dream-soul communications, and the feeling of the absolute immutability of the creative principle. This conviction is so inflexible,

[1] Nassau, *Fetichism*, p. 56.
[2] *Travels in West Africa*, p. 461.
[3] Kingsley, *West African Studies*, p. 145.

handed down as it has been in uninterrupted succession for thousands and thousands of years, from father to son, and from mother to daughter, that when an infant having a mark of some kind on its body dies, and another happens to be born with a mark in any way similar, or bearing the slightest resemblance to it, it is at once said to be the same child born over again. It is the custom of the tribes all over the Niger Delta to give the child a name which implies "re-born."[1]

Many pygmy tribes think that their dead relations live again in the form of the red bush-pig,[2] and the Banza of the Western Mubangi basin believe that their chiefs are reincarnated in chimpanzis.[3]

Death.

The Egyptian theologians believed that there was a time when there was no death,[4] but that time was when the god Temu alone existed, and before he created the heavens and the earth, and men and "gods." How and why death came the texts do not tell, but, judging from the views which are held in the Sûdân at the present time, we may assume that the Egyptians regarded death as the means necessary to enable man to continue his existence after the breath left his material body. The present world was to them merely the ante-chamber of the Other World; a man's house in this world was a temporary abode, but his tomb was his "eternal house," .[5] The philosopher counselled men to enjoy themselves,[6] to anoint and scent their bodies, to wear garlands and lilies, to cherish the woman beloved, to sing and dance, to put away trouble and sorrow, and

[1] Leonard, *The Lower Niger and Its Tribes*, p. 210 f.

[2] Johnston, *Uganda*, p. 539.

[3] Johnston, *George Grenfell*, Vol. II, p. 632.

[4] . Text of Pepi I, l. 664.

[5] The Dahoman considers this present life as only a means of attaining an eternal status: Earth is only a temporary dwelling-place; Hades is their "home."—Skertchley, *Dahomey as It is*, p. 462.

[6] , "make a happy day."

to think only on things which yield pleasure, until the day when they must come into port in the land that loveth silence.[1] "Follow after enjoyment and forget care," was the advice given by his soul to the man weary of life,[2] and the dead lady That-I-em-ḥetep advised her husband to eat, drink, marry wives, enjoy himself, and to have no thought or care or sorrow so long as he lived. For, she adds, Åmenti is a place of stupor and darkness, and Death calleth every one to him, gods and men, and great and little are all one to him, and he seizeth the babe as well as the old man.[3] The ordinary Egyptian felt as did old Chinsunse, who said to Livingstone: "We live "only a few days here, but we live again after death. "We do not know where, or in what condition, or with "what companions, for the dead never return to tell us. "Sometimes the dead do come back, and appear to us in "dreams; but they never speak nor tell us where they "have gone, nor how they fare."[4] In spite of this, however, the Egyptian did not devote all his life to the pursuit of pleasure, and he who had the necessary means prepared an "eternal house" for himself, so that when death claimed him, he might have a "secret place" wherein to free himself from his material body, and rise in the Spirit-body, and depart to the Other World which, in spite of all the assertions of his priests, must ever have been a place of the deepest mystery.

The modern African believes that more than half the deaths which occur are caused by witchcraft,[5] and that usually a body only dies because someone has stolen one of its souls.[6] Among many tribes death is always supposed to be caused by witchcraft, but a few peoples are ready to admit that some deaths are due to the call of Njambi (*i.e.*, God, or Providence).[7] Here and

[1] *A.Z.*, 1873, p. 60.

[2] 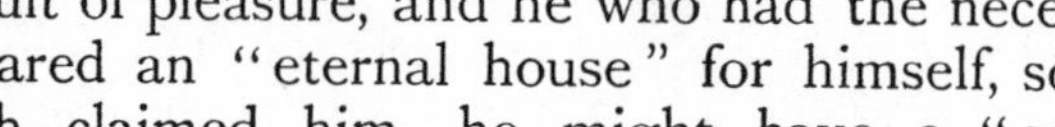 § 16.

[3] See the stele in the British Museum, No. 1027.

[4] Livingstone, *The Zambesi and Its Tributaries*, p. 121.

[5] Miss Kingsley says "sixty per cent."—*West African Studies*, p. 209.

[6] Frobenius, *Childhood of Man*, p. 155.

[7] Nassau, *Fetichism*, pp. 117, 170.

there a people, *e.g.*, the Wakamba, believe that death from natural causes is quite possible. If an old man dies they say, "he was due to die:" it is fate (inguè).[1] Livingstone in his definition of the primitive African faith says that "death is often a punishment of guilt, such as witchcraft."[2] The Bantu believe in a "spirit of death," and according to a legend of Kintu, the founder of the Unyoro-Uganda dynasty, it was attached to this king in the form of a young man, owing to an act of disobedience to God on his part.[3] Among them death is in no way regarded as a cessation of being. They have no idea of the resurrection of the body, for that is buried, but the spirit, the man himself, lives on. Where and how he lives they know not.[4] The Baluba of South Central Congoland think that death in no way causes a separation of soul and body; it is a stoppage of the heart produced by: (1) A fatal accident, or (2) the power of a sorcerer, or (3) the spirit of a deceased relative. Some have an idea that a spirit in the Other World complains to Kabezya-Mpungu that it is lonely, and asks that So-and-so who is living on earth may be sent to him. Kabezya-Mpungu then despatches a messenger who fastens on the person whom he has come to summon. This is sickness, and when God gives the signal this messenger begins to compress the heart, and continues to do so until it has ceased to beat. That is why they say of a sick man: "Such an one has seized him"; and of a dead man, "God "has visited him, the All-Powerful has got possession "of him"; or again, "his father has called him," or, "his mother has slain him."[5]

Among the tribes of the Lower Niger death is not only accepted and looked on as a spiritual causation, but death itself is personified, as with the Egyptians,[6] and dealt with as a powerful spirit, who gains the mastery over the life of the human *ego* by depriving the soul of the body, *i.e.*, ejecting the former, so that dissolution of the latter

[1] Decle, *Three Years in Savage Africa*, p. 491.
[2] *The Zambesi*, p. 521.
[3] Johnston, *Uganda*, p. 606.
[4] Bentley, *Pioneering on the Congo*, Vol. I, p. 252.
[5] Johnston, *George Grenfell*, Vol. II, p. 642.
[6] See the quotation from the Stele of That-I-em-ḥetep, p. 144.

supervenes. The native regards death as a relentless and inexorable demon who, although omnivorous and a glutton who is always gorging himself, is not so much a devourer of souls as a carrier away of them. With this description may be compared the passages in the XVIIth Chapter of the Book of the Dead, which describe: (1) The god with the face of a dog and the eyebrows of a man, who feedeth on the dead, who watcheth at the Bight of the Lake of Fire, who devoureth the bodies of the dead, and swalloweth hearts, who voideth filth, and remaineth unseen. The name of this being is "Devourer for millions of years." (2) The great god who carrieth away the soul, who eateth hearts, who devoureth offal, the guardian of the darkness, the dweller in the Seker boat. His name is either Suti, or Smam-ur, the Earth-soul. The latter passage suggests that the ancient and awful god Seker, who sat enthroned in darkness in the bowels of the desert west of Memphis, is Death himself. Though the native believes that in some cases death is due to some former act of omission or commission on the part of the deceased, and in others to natural decay, *e.g.*, senile decay, he thinks that nearly every death is, in the first instance, due to or associated with witchcraft.[1] When a person falls ill among the Nandi it is attributed to the anger of an ancestor, and when he is nearing death his male relatives say: "The soul has become very small." Mr. Hollis[2] records a Nandi myth to the effect that the early dwellers on the earth were threatened by a dog with death, unless they gave him milk from their gourd and beer through their straw. "If you do this," said he, "I will arrange for you to go to the river when you die, "and to come to life again on the third day." The people laughed at the dog, and gave him some milk and beer to drink off a stool. The dog was angry at not being treated like a human being, but he drank the milk and beer, and as he went away he said: "All people will die, and the moon alone will return to life." This is why the dead do not return, and why the moon reappears after three days' absence.[3] Two other causes of death

[1] Leonard, *The Tribes of the Lower Niger*, p. 171 ff.
[2] Hollis, *The Nandi*, pp. 69, 70.
[3] Hollis, *The Nandi*, p. 98.

are mentioned by Miss Kingsley, viz., some action on the part of the Bush-soul, and reincarnated disease. When a man falls ill, he sometimes thinks that his illness is the result of anger on the part of his Bush-soul, and therefore causes offerings to be made to it in a little hut in the forest built on the last place in which it was seen. As no one but an Ebumtup, or person endowed with the gift of second sight, can see his own Bush-soul, the services of a witch-doctor are obtained, and attempts are made by him to placate the Bush-soul. If these are not successful, the sick man dies. Or, the Bush-soul may through some rash act on its part become wounded or killed, and then its owner will die. A reincarnated soul may have suffered from some disease in a former state of existence in the body, and this having been reincarnated with the soul causes the death of the new body.[1]

[1] *Travels in West Africa*, pp. 459–461.

CHAPTER XX.

Spirits and the Spirit-world.

The Egyptians believed that the spirits of the dead, whose bodies had been buried with the proper rites and ceremonies, went ultimately to a region which was set apart for them and was called "Ṭuat," 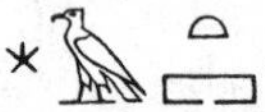. It follows of necessity that very few Egyptians could afford the expense incurred in embalming, in hewing a tomb in the rock, and in purchasing funerary furniture and offerings, etc., therefore the bodies of a very large number of people must have been disposed of by some means or other each year without "burial," as the high-class Egyptian understood the word. Kings and members of the royal family, nobles, and officials and priests were, no doubt, "buried," but the working classes, and peasants and slaves, must have been thrust into shallow graves in the sand on the edge of the desert, from which they were ultimately dragged by wild beasts and devoured. There is no *proof* that the dead were wilfully cast forth into the desert to be eaten by beasts, as the Masai cast their dead into the bush and invite the hyenas to come and eat them, but it is quite clear that the dead must have been got rid of by some such means. The cultivable land of Egypt was too valuable to be devoted to them, and the number of tombs which remain is remarkably small when we consider the scores of millions of human beings who lived in Egypt under thirty dynasties of Pharaohs. We have already seen that the Kau and Body-souls of the dead perished when the supply of offerings failed, or when the dead had no friends to recite the magical formulae which produced offerings, but there remained the immortal Spirit-souls of the dead, and these must have proceeded to the Land of Spirits when they departed from their bodies. Therefore this region must have been inhabited by the spirits of all the human beings who had ever been born in Egypt, and their number must have been millions. An obscure passage in the Book of the Dead[1] mentions 4,601,200, or 4,301,200, Spirit-souls (Khu),[2] but whether these represented all the inhabitants of the spirit-world of Egypt cannot be said. In the Short Version of the Chapter "12 cubits" are mentioned, and this may be the height of the spirits. If so, spirits must have been of varying heights, for the spirits who reaped the wheat and barley in the Second Division of the Domain of Osiris[3] were nine cubits in height, the wheat and barley being five cubits high. In the Fifth Division the spirits who lived on the helpless shadows of the dead had thighs (?) seven cubits long.

As the Egyptians believed that there was once a time when death did not exist, there must have been a time when there were no human souls in the Ṭuat, if it then existed. The great and unknown God alone had being, for the gods were not born until a later period. Now, we read in many funerary texts of the "Gods of the Ṭuat," so we must assume that after death entered the world, and souls began to go to the Ṭuat, they found there these gods, who had been created by the unknown God. Each of these appears to have had a separate entity ; their relationship with the unknown God is not clear, but they were like human beings and souls, inferior and subordinate to Him. As time went on these gods became more and more independent, and the unknown God appears to have allowed them to do as they pleased, and in the end they became the arbiters of the destinies of the souls of men. The cult of Osiris in no way interfered with this view generally, but the man who wanted his soul to go to the kingdom of Osiris after death was called upon to obey during his lifetime the commands of this god, and not to worship "gods" who were of no account. The gods of the Ṭuat possessed many of the qualities and attributes of men ; when pleased they were good-tempered and benevolent, and when angry they gratified their feelings of revenge.

[1] Chapter LXIV, Long Version, l. 21 ; Short Version, l. 7.

[2] 

[3] See Chapter CXLIX, Åat II.

They could be placated by service and offerings, and they showed their pleasure and gratitude by doing acts of kindness to their worshippers, and by assisting them when in trouble and difficulties. Those who were wise spared no pains in obtaining their help, and in disarming their opposition. The spirits of the dead were regarded with much the same feelings as the gods. Their power for evil was believed to be greater in the Ṭuat than upon earth, for their freedom from the body gave them greater facilities for doing harm to men. They could, moreover, move about unseen, and escape from invisible spirit-foes was well-nigh impossible. There were good spirits as well as bad, but the Book of the Dead practically ignores the former, and its magical formulae were directed entirely against the operations of evil spirits. Though naturally of a gay and light-hearted disposition, the Egyptian must have lived in a perpetual state of fear of spirits of all kinds, spirits of calamity, disease, and sickness, spirits of angry gods and ancestors, and above all the spirit of Death. His imagination filled the world with spirits whose acts seemed to him to be generally malevolent, and his magical and religious literature and his amulets testify to the very real terror with which he regarded his future existence in the world of spirits. Escape from such spirits was impossible, for they could not die.

The views of modern African peoples about spirits and their world throw much light upon the denizens of the Egyptian Ṭuat, and a few of them are here noted. Among the Nandi the Oiik, *i.e.*, devils, or spirits of departed kinsfolk, cause sickness and death, and when they move about underground earthquakes take place. They appear to men in dreams. They may be propitiated by offerings, and prayers must be made to them.[1] The people of the Congo believe that souls can act as demons, and must be propitiated. The lesser spirits, at any rate, are human in their intelligence, can be flattered, propitiated, deceived ; are sometimes kind to the individuals or clans they patronize, or who adopt them as protectors or allies.[2] Departed souls must be kept in a good

[1] Hollis, *The Nandi*, pp. 41, 69, 82, 100.
[2] Johnston, *George Grenfell*, Vol. II, p. 636.

humour, and must, if possible, be kept at a distance; food and drink must be given to them, and huts built for them.[1] In West Africa the natives mourn the loss of the bodies of their dead, whilst at the same time they drive away their spirits with yells and noises of every kind. These spirits are worshipped, with worship of a deprecatory character, but their continued presence is not desired.[2] The Dinka and Bongo tribes know no spirits except those which are evil.[3] The evil spirits in Ankole are very numerous, and they cause sicknesses.[4] Some spirits which have inhabited human bodies are supposed to have existed before birth as well as after death. It is considered possible for a minor evil spirit to be born with a man's soul, and to enter a man's body during sleep.[5]

The Ibo define the soul as the fruit of the body, and the spirit as the living or vital energy of a person, in other words, the soul whose material body has died or perished. They make no difference between soul and spirit.[6] In Northern Guinea the spirits of the dead are supposed to mingle freely with the living, and they convey warnings and admonitions to human beings in dreams.[7] Messages can be sent to spirits by dying people,[8] and Mr. H. Ward actually heard a message being given to a slave, who was to be beheaded, for a spirit by a man who said: "And tell him when you meet, that his biggest war-canoe, which I inherit, is rotten."[9] In Dahomey every act of importance was reported to the king's ancestor by the spirit of a man who was killed on purpose.[10]

The Egyptians speak in their religious texts of Heart-souls, Spirit-souls, Kau, or Doubles, Sāḥu, or Spirit-bodies, and Sekhemu as if they formed separate

[1] Frobenius, *Childhood of Man*, p. 158.
[2] Nassau, *Fetichism*, p. 59.
[3] Frobenius, *Die Heiden-Neger*, pp. 343, 361.
[4] Johnston, *Uganda*, p. 631.
[5] Kingsley, *West African Studies*, p. 200; *Travels in West Africa*, p. 230.
[6] Leonard, *The Lower Niger*, p. 140.
[7] Wilson, *Western Africa*, p. 211.
[8] *Ibid.*, pp. 220, 394.
[9] H. Ward, *A Voice from the Congo*, p. 144.
[10] Burton, *A Mission to Gelele*, Vol. II, p. 24; Skertchley, *Dahomey as It is*, p. 339.

orders of spirits, and we find that modern African peoples also arrange the spirits in different groups. In each case the grouping does not mean, it seems to me, that the nature and character of the spirits of the various groups are different, but only that their occupations are different. Dr. Nassau classifies the spirits of West Africa thus :—

The first class is known by the name of "Anina" or "Malina," and consists of souls or spirits, embodied and disembodied; they take a great interest in human affairs, and especially in those of the families of which they are or were members.

The second class is called "Abambo," which may be rendered "ghosts." Where they live and why they appear is unknown. They are never asked to appear, and are rarely worshipped, and their coming is dreaded. They are the spirits of dead tribal ancestors, as distinguished from the spirits of strangers. The natives cannot decide whether they are benevolent or malignant, or whether to love or hate them. The Abambo are the spirits which are supposed to possess men; they are cast out only with the greatest difficulty, When Abambo appear to human beings they rarely speak to them, they only terrify them.

The third class is the "Ombwiri," plural "Awiri." The Awiri resemble the fauns, dryads, and forest spirits, which live in rocks, trees, etc., and resent the trespass of human beings on their land. The Ombwiri is regarded as a guardian spirit, and each man has his own ombwiri, for which he provides a small house near his own. The Awiri are the only spirits which have no priesthood; they hold intercourse with men direct. They are kindly disposed towards men, but religious services, which really constitute an ancestral worship, must be performed in their honour.

The fourth class is the "Sinkinda," and consists chiefly of the spirits of people who were in a humble position in this world, and were distinguished neither for greatness nor goodness. Besides these, the class includes spirits, or perhaps demons, whom Njambi (*i.e.*, God) created, but to whom He never gave bodily existence. Almost all Sinkinda are evilly disposed.

One or more of them can enter into a human body, but sickness follows their coming; they are never visible to man. Sometimes they are called "Ivavi," *i.e.*, "messengers," and they bring tidings, good or bad, as the case may be; a "messenger" gives his information by the mouth of some living member of the family, whose body he is occupying temporarily. With such "messengers" may be compared the messengers  mentioned in the Book of the Dead. In the XXIXth Chapter the deceased calls upon the "messenger of every god" to retreat, and he says: "Even though thou hast come to carry off my living "heart-spirit, this living heart-spirit of mine shall not be "given to thee." And in the CXXVth Chapter[1] we read of the "messengers" which utter evil accusations, and make calamities to happen.

A fifth class of spirits, the "Myondi," are akin to those of the fourth class, but appear to be less under the control of the witch-doctor than other spirits. They cause sickness, and can help or harm men. They are worshipped always in a deprecatory way. They sometimes take possession of human bodies, and the Sinkinda, Awiri, and Ilâgâ (spirits of foreigners) are invoked to effect their expulsion.[2]

Authorities differ in their definitions of the powers and functions of the various classes of spirits, which are very difficult to determine, but all agree that some spirits, even those of the same class, are stronger and have greater power for good or evil than others. The powers of a spirit are limited: it cannot do everything. Usually a spirit attends to a particular kind of work, but it is thought that, on occasions, it may attempt to usurp the functions of a spirit of another class. Every class of spirits can be made helpers of man provided that they are entreated with humility, and made friendly by means

[1] Part III, ll. 16, 17.

[2] Miss Kingsley refers to another class of spirits which resemble the Lares and Penates of the Romans, and belong to the household, and descend by inheritance with the family. In their honour are secretly kept a bundle of fingers, or other bones, nail-clippings, eyes, brains, etc., accumulated from deceased members of successive generations.—*Travels in West Africa*, p. 444.

of offerings.[1] The existence of a sixth class of spirits is considered possible both by Dr. Nassau[2] and Miss Kingsley,[3] viz., those which enter the body of some animal, generally the leopard, with a definite purpose and for a limited time. This purpose is generally the killing of some enemy, and as the strength of the animal is directed by human intelligence and will, the spirit is enabled to carry out its evil design. Many murders are committed in this way, as in the cases of the German wehr-wolf and the French loup-garou. Mr. Bonham Carter, the eminent Legal Secretary at Khartûm, shows that this belief was in operation in the Sûdân in 1903. One Kwat Wâd Awaibung murdered his neighbour Ajak Wâd Deng, and, having pleaded guilty, he said :—"Ajak owed me a sheep and would not "pay me. He said he would show me some of his work, "and next day my son was eaten by a crocodile, which "was, of course, the work of Kwat, and for that reason "I killed him. We had a feud for years, as I was "a more successful hippopotamus-hunter than he was, "and for that reason he was practising witchery over "me and my family." The explanation of the murder is that Ajak believed that Kwat had sent his soul into the crocodile, which made the animal lie in wait near the river bank where Ajak's son usually bathed. When the youth came down to the river and entered the water, the crocodile obeyed its natural instinct, and dragged him down and drowned him and ate him. Several witnesses supported Ajak's statement, and their evidence proved that this belief was shared by the people generally.[4]

The Baluba believe in the existence of a great number of evil spirits called "Bashangi" or "Bakishi," who are probably the disembodied souls of wicked sorcerers. They wander about at night, appearing sometimes as shooting stars. They terrify men and scatter death among the villages; their sole aim is to injure, and their chief happiness is to make people

[1] Nassau, *Fetichism*, p. 64 ff.
[2] *Ibid.*, p. 70.
[3] *Travels in West Africa*, p. 445.
[4] *Egypt and the Sûdân* (Report), Egypt No. I, 1904, p. 89.

miserable.[1] A very large number of tribes in Africa believe firmly in the existence of a host of evil spirits, which they generally identify with the souls of the dead. Some African peoples, *e.g.*, those of Dahomey, have the curious belief that the same spirit can be in more than one place at the same time. Thus Gêzu's spirit was thought to be on his war-stool in his shed, and also in his own tomb, at one and the same time. A spirit will sometimes remain in Dead-land, and also come back to the earth in the body of a new-born infant; all the king's children were but the transmigrated spirits of the old kings.[2]

THE PLACE OF DEPARTED SPIRITS.

The Egyptians held several opinions about the places to which spirits departed after the death of their bodies. According to some they went and lived in the bodies of animals and birds, others thought they entered the stars and so lived in the sky, from which they could visit the earth from time to time, and others believed that they lived in the Boat of the Sun. The greater number, however, assumed that they went to a region called Ṭuat, which was thought to be situated on the other side of the range of mountains that surrounded the world. On the far side of the Ṭuat there was a similar range of mountains, and so we may say that the Ṭuat had the form of a long valley, very much like the Nile Valley; it ran parallel to both ranges of mountains and between them, and was on the same plane as the land of Egypt, or of the sky which was above it. In the range of mountains which enclosed Egypt were two holes; from the one on the east the sun rose, in that on the west the sun set. The Ṭuat began near the western hole and ended near the eastern hole; thus it was nearly circular in form. It was shut off from Egypt by mountains, and had neither sun, nor moon, nor stars, therefore it was a region of gloom and darkness and a place of fear and horror. A river flowed through the Ṭuat Valley, just as the Nile flows through

[1] Johnston, *George Grenfell*, Vol. II, p. 636.
[2] Skertchley, *Dahomey as It is*, p. 465.

Egypt, and its banks were inhabited by the spirits who had lived in the body in the various nomes of Egypt. The Ṭuat Valley was divided into sections. Thus there were the Ṭuat of Thebes, the Ṭuat of Abydos, the Ṭuat of Herakleopolis, the Ṭuat of Memphis, and the Ṭuat of Saïs ; then, bending eastwards, there were the Ṭuat of Bubastis, the Ṭuat of Heliopolis, the Ṭuat of Kher-āḥa, and so on. Each Ṭuat contained its own good and evil spirits, who might be well disposed towards native souls, but who were almost certain to be hostile to stranger-souls that came from other parts of Egypt. Thus the Ṭuat was a duplicate of Egypt, and the dwellers in it were as various as the living inhabitants of Egypt, but the spirits for the most part confined their movements to their own section. The man who wished his soul after death to have the power of moving about from one end of the Ṭuat to the other took care to make offerings to all the gods of all the Divisions of the Ṭuat during his lifetime, for such acts of worship were believed to secure for him their help both in this world and in the next. Each Division of the Ṭuat contained a town which was the seat of the god who ruled it ; this town was the equivalent of the metropolis of the nome on earth.

The Egyptian theologians realized at a very early period that the soul of a man would have great difficulty in making its way through the Ṭuat, therefore they compiled various books which they intended to form Guides to that region of darkness and difficulty. The oldest of these may be called the Book of the Two Ways, and copies[1] of it are found on the coffins of the Middle Empire. According to this a man might go to the abode of the blessed by two ways, by land or by water, but once having set out on one route, the soul could not change to the other ; for the two ways were separated by a river of fire. Another Book, called "Åm-Ṭuat,"[2] describes the journey of Rā through the Ṭuat. It was intended to illustrate the power of Rā over the kingdom of the dead, but incidentally it gives a considerable amount of information about the Ṭuat.

[1] See Schack, *Zweiwegebuch*, Leipzig, 1903.
[2] See my *Egyptian Heaven and Hell*, Vol. I, London, 1905.

Rā, or rather the dead body of Rā, makes the journey along the river of the Ṭuat in a boat, wherein is a crew of gods; each Division is supposed to represent one of the hours of the night, and the goddess of each hour in turn acts as the pilot. In the first hour Rā, or his flesh Ȧf, travels through the first Division, a distance of 120 *ȧtru*, when he reaches the gods of the Ṭuat. The Second and Third Divisions are each 309 (or 480) *ȧtru* in length and 120 *ȧtru* in breadth. In the Third Division the kingdom of Osiris is situated, and when there Ȧf is near Abydos. The Fourth and Fifth Divisions reach from Abydos to Ṣaḳḳârah, and include the kingdom of Seker, the god of Death. At this stage of the journey Ȧf is obliged to leave his boat, for the region is a waterless desert. The boat takes the form of a serpent, and so is enabled to pass through the sand. In the Sixth Division Ȧf again uses his boat, and sails to the city of Osiris, where this god was said to be buried. In the Seventh Division, which is the secret abode of Osiris, the boat of Ȧf is stranded because the river has run dry, and it is only moved along by means of the magical words of Isis and Semsu (firstborn gods?). The failure of the water is caused by the serpent Āpep, who has drunk it up. This monster is called "Stinking Face," Neḥa-ḥer, and is 450 cubits long. Ȧf does not destroy him, but casts a spell on him and then passes him by. The Eighth Division is a continuation of the Seventh, and contains the Secret Circles of Ȧment; it was situated near Busiris in the Delta. In the Ninth and Tenth Divisions the gods from the boat of Ȧf assist in preparing the boat for the last stage of the journey. In the Tenth Division Ȧf finds the Beetle into which he is to transform himself, and in the Eleventh he sees the pits of fire in which the bodies, souls, shadows, and heads of the foes of Osiris are being burnt. In the Twelfth Division the beetle is on the front of the boat, and when the boat has been dragged through the body of a huge serpent 1,300 cubits long, entering at its tail and coming out from its mouth, Ȧf is found to have transformed himself into the beetle, *i.e.*, into Kheperȧ, the morning sun. In the vignette to this Division we see that the dead body of Rā is thrown aside in the

Ṭuat, and that, in the form of the solar disk, Kheperȧ enters his boat in the sky, and begins his journey across heaven. As Rā, or rather Ȧf, passed through the Ṭuat he addressed words to all the beings who were on the banks of the river in each division, and provided them with food and drink. As he journeyed along he seems to have brought light with him, and the gods rejoiced in the temporary lightening of their darkness ; as he passed on gloom once more settled down upon them, and the blackness of night again covered them. Fortunate indeed were the souls who were able to secure a passage in the Boat of Ȧf, for then they would have no reason to fear the fiends on the river bank and the pits of fire. The Book Ȧm-Ṭuat was as useful to the living as to the dead, and every picture in it was regarded as the symbol of a magic power which was able to protect the body in this world and the soul in the next.

A third work also was compiled by the priests as a "Guide" to the Ṭuat, viz., the Book of Gates. In it the Ṭuat is divided into twelve Divisions, each of which is guarded by a huge fortified Gate, and each Gate is kept by warlike gods and fiery serpents. The kingdom of Osiris occupies a prominent place in this work, and we have in it representations of the Hall of Judgment of this god, and the occupation of the blessed, and the punishment of the wicked. From first to last the Book of Gates[1] represents the Ṭuat as conceived by the indigenous Egyptians, and the ideas and beliefs expressed therein agree with those of the Book of the Dead. These ideas and beliefs are purely African, and they suggest that the Egyptian Ṭuat was very much what the "God's Town" or "Njambi's Town" is to the African of to-day. They did not, I believe, grow up in Egypt, but in Central or West Africa. The frequent allusions to "making a way," or having a way made or opened for the deceased, which are found in the Book of the Dead, show that to reach

The deceased setting out for the Other World.

[1] See my *Book of Gates* (*Egyptian Heaven and Hell*, Vol. II), London, 1905.

the Ṭuat the soul was obliged to travel through a forest, in which it was easy to lose the path. The Yoruba "babalawo" (priest) to-day addresses the dead, saying: "May the road be open "to you . . . May you "find the road good when "you go in peace."[1] The road to the Ṭuat was so difficult to find, that unless the soul was conducted thither by the Wolf-god Åp-uat, the probability of its losing its way was very great. At times the mantis acted as guide, and in the LXXVIth Chapter of the Book of the Dead the deceased says: "I have come into "the House of the king; the mantis[2] led me hither . . . "I have made my way, and I have travelled thereon."

The deceased building himself a house in the Other World.

The Domain of the Ṭuat was, according to one opinion, divided into seven parts, each of which was guarded by a Gate; each Gate had its keeper, its watchman, and its herald. According to another view the Gates were ten in number, and some papyri enumerate fourteen or fifteen and some twenty-one. To pass through them it was necessary for the souls of the dead to know the names of the Gates and the names of the beings who guarded them, in fact, to possess the knowledge of a series of important words of power. Yet another opinion was that the Kingdom of the Ṭuat

[1] Ellis, *Yoruba-speaking Peoples*, p. 156.

[2] Commonly known as the "praying mantis," to which supernatural powers have been attributed by Africans, Arabs, and some European peoples. The Arabs say that it prays with its head turned towards Mekkah! "There were parrots . . . . . . and those most "entertaining stick-like little insects known as 'praying mantis,' that "hold up two long front legs in a supplicating and prayerful attitude if "one attempts to touch them."—L. Gerard, *Hyena of Kallu*, p. 134. "In the south of the Peninsula (Yucatan) you find that curious insect "the praying mantis, so-called in allusion to the attitude of its forelegs, "which are held as are hands in prayer. These creatures wage "remorseless war on one another and fight until the stronger literally "pulls its foe's head off."—C. Arnold and F. J. T. Frost, *The American Egypt*, p. 377. For an excellent drawing of the mantis see Johnston, *Uganda*, Vol. I, 412; and for a description of the species see Johnston, *George Grenfell*, Vol. II, p. 938.

was divided into fourteen Ȧats (Domains), of which only one was devoted to Osiris. One Ȧat was specially set apart for the gods and another for the Spirits; a third was a region of fire, a fourth contained roaring torrents of water, a fifth was the home of the Nile, a sixth was the home of the Hippopotamus-goddess, and so on. The Domain of Osiris was only one among many, but to the Egyptian it was the most important of them all. In it the god lived surrounded by his ministers and followers like an African king on earth; the former directed the work of the servants of the god, and the latter performed the duties which were assigned to them in the fields wherein grew the Maāt wheat, or the "staff of life." On this wheat Osiris and his followers lived. It was a form of Osiris himself, and those who ate it and lived upon it nourished themselves upon their god. The ministers of Osiris formed the aristocracy of Sekhet-Ȧaru, and their occupations were the same as those of an aristocracy on earth. The personal attendants of Osiris, and his servants, and his field labourers, lived in much the same way as they lived upon earth. Groups of souls belonging to the same family lived together, and the friendships of earth were continued in the Ṭuat. The souls of husbands and wives were reunited. There parents found their children again and rejoiced in their love, and faithful household servants and slaves ministered to the souls of their masters and mistresses in the Ṭuat as they had ministered to them upon earth. Many passages in the texts refer to the sexual union of souls, but there is no mention of the begetting of offspring. The population of the Ṭuat was recruited from the souls who left this earth day by day. The duties which souls performed for Osiris in nowise interfered with the interest which they took in their kinsfolk who lived on the earth, and they were able to watch their affairs and, when necessary, to afford them protection. This idea is well expressed in the following extract from a text of the XVIIIth dynasty:—

"Thou makest a way through the mountains of Kher-neter.[1]

"Thou lookest upon thy house of the living,

[1] The Other World.

"Hearing the sound of singing and music in thy hall on this earth.

"Thou workest protection for thy children for ever and ever."[1]

The connection between the souls of the living and the dead was very close, and the belief in it permeated every class in Egypt. If the Egyptians thought, like the modern African, that some men contained souls which had been twice born, they would feel that they had in their midst beings from the Other World, and the influence of such in the affairs of daily life must have been very great. Be this as it may, it is certain that the worship of ancestral and other spirits was always one of the most important factors in their religion, and that the belief in the Ṭuat and its spirit-dwellers was a fundamental feature of their spiritual constitution. The "gods," *e.g.*, Rā, Åmen, Ptaḥ, Khnemu, etc., were beings to revere and propitiate when necessary, but none of them ever really occupied in their minds the position of Osiris, King and Judge of the dead. The priests of Åmen attempted to force their dogma of the sovereignty of their god over the dead into the minds of the people, but they failed, and the cult of Osiris flourished centuries after they had passed away. The Ṭuat was an indigenous African conception, and all its features and characteristics were African, and Osiris its overlord ruled after the manner of an African king.

Under the IVth dynasty every man in Egypt belonged to the king, every yard of ground was the king's; the king was Egypt, and Per-āa (Pharaoh), the "Great House," was the house in which all men lived. The king disposed of men's lives as he pleased, and their bodies were only buried by his favour. The absolutism of the king of Egypt at that time is well

1  Sethe, *Urkunden*, IV, 1064.

illustrated by the views about kings and chiefs which were current in Africa not many years ago. Among the Manyema a subject shows his submission to a chief by rubbing dust on his shoulders.[1] Baker says that there was never a more supreme despot than Kamrasi. Not only the property, but the families of his subjects were at his disposal. He boasted that "all belonged to him."[2] Speke saw the subjects of Mtesa throw themselves flat upon their bellies before him and cover their faces with earth;[3] the same writer says that in Uganda every man adores the king as a deity.[4] "Uganda is "personified by Mtesa, and no one can say he has seen "Uganda until he has been presented to the king."[5] To the king all territorial chiefs owe allegiance as overlord.[6] Among the Barotse the people kneel before the king, raise their hands high in the air, and cry out "Great king." Chiefs kneel down and pour water or sand into their hands, and spread it over the king's arms. Then they strike their heads on the ground, and clapping their palms together sing his praises. Personal freedom and personal property are alike non-existent. All the people are the slaves of the king.[7] In Shoa the king is absolute lord and master of the land, and of the bodies and lives and possessions of all his people.[8] The Basango regard their chief as a god, and fear to say anything wrong lest he should hear them. They fear both before him and when out of sight.[9] In Dahomey the men touch the ground with their heads and lips before the king. When a man appears before the king he must cover his head and the upper part of his body with dust, as much as to say, "I am nothing but dirt before thee."[10] And every man belongs to the king.[11]

1 Cunningham, *Uganda*, p. 324.
2 *Albert N'yanza*, p. 408.
3 *Journal* (Dent's Reprint), p. 238; and see p. 267.
4 *Ibid.*, p. 245.
5 *Ibid.*, p. 255.
6 A. R. Tucker, *Eighteen Years in Uganda*, Vol. I, p. 86.
7 Decle, *Three Years*, p. 72.
8 Krapf, *Travels*, p. 35.
9 Livingstone, *Last Journals*, Vol. II, p. 77.
10 Burton, *A Mission to Gelele*, Vol. II, p. 341.
11 Skertchley, *Dahomey as It is*, p. 487.

And thus it was with Osiris, Overlord of the Ṭuat. Every soul in his kingdom belonged to him absolutely, and drew its means of support from him. In the Book Ȧm-Ṭuat we see the god seated on his throne watching the slaughter of those who have rebelled against him; their limbs are fettered, and then they are dragged into the presence of the god and their heads cut off. Treason to the mind of the African king is the gravest of all offences, and is always punished by death, which is usually accompanied by tortures, and thus was treason punished in the Ṭuat. The headsman of Osiris and his assistants in the Ṭuat were as busily occupied as are the executioners in the service of African kings at the present day.

With the brief description of the Ṭuat and of the life led by souls in it given in the preceding paragraphs we may compare the accounts given by travellers of modern African ideas about the Spirit-world. The Bahima believe that the spirits of the dead go to Mitoma, and to arrive there they have to enter the great Ankole forest, and pass under German East Africa. The whiz and hum of passing spirits[1] are frequently heard as they enter the forest on their way to Mitoma. Good and bad go there, but no slaves are admitted, for there is no work to do there. There are no cows there, and no clothing is needed; in fact, the beings there have no wants. The spirits of white men cannot enter Mitoma.[2] The Egyptians were not so exclusive, for their Ṭuat contained the souls of the Āamu, *i.e.*, the dwellers in the Eastern Desert, the Libyans (Themeḥu) and the Negroes (Neḥesu).[3] According to Dr. Nassau the Spirit-world is all around us, and does not differ much in its wants and characteristics from this earthly life, except that it is free from some of the limitations of material bodies. Spirits require food, but only its essence. They have passions good and bad. They have wives, but there is no procreation by spirits in the Other World. The

[1] Among the Akikuyu they say: "You can hear the spirits; they come together from different places, and dance in the wilds and make a noise. Spirits make a whirring sound, they do not say words."—Routledge, *With a Prehistoric People*, p. 240.

[2] Cunningham, *Uganda*, p. 23.

[3] Budge, *Book of Gates*, pp. 151–153.

natives having no system of rewards or punishments believe not in heaven or hell. All the dead go to Njambi's Town, and live there together, the good with the bad, as they lived together on earth. The hell which some speak of is not a native conception, but is probably the result of the teaching of Portuguese Roman Catholic missionaries three hundred years ago. Departed spirits (Musimo) never die, and they are to be feared and driven away by noise.[1] The Akikuyu believe that some spirits pass into animals, that others wander about, and that some go to the Land of the Dead, Miirîniya Mikongôi. This land is regarded as the residence of the dead of bygone generations, and is a place from which spirits cannot emerge, and is dark. They have no god of evil, but there is a dwelling-place where live a vast number of bad spirits, men, women, and children. These possess many cattle, sheep, and goats. It is terribly cold there, and its inhabitants have no clothes except a scrap of skin, the size of the palm of the hand, which they place over their faces when they sleep. To approach a fire is for them an absolute impossibility.[2]

The Spirit-world of the Tshi-speaking peoples is called "Srahmanadzi." It resembles this world, and like the Egyptian Ṭuat has towns, villages, forests, mountains, rivers, etc. It is beneath the earth, and is less bright than the world of the living. A proverb says: "A corner in the world is better than the whole of Srahmanadzi." When the sun sets in this world it rises in Srahmanadzi. There the old become young, a young man becomes a boy, and a boy a baby. They grow and become old, but age brings no weakness or wasting of the body. When they reach the prime of life they remain in that condition, and never change. A chief in this world is a chief there, and a slave a slave. Srahmanadzi is a duplicate of this world, and life there is only a continuation of the life here. It is this belief which is at the bottom of the custom of killing wives and slaves on the death of a king or chief, so that their souls may depart to the Spirit-world and minister to his wants there. This custom is not the result of a blood-

[1] Nassau, *Fetichism in West Africa*, pp. 56, 59, 62.
[2] Routledge, *With a Prehistoric People*, p. 243.

thirsty disposition, but arises from feelings of affection, respect, and awe for the dead, and the desire that the departed may suffer no inconvenience or lack comfort in his new abode.[1] The entrance to the Tshi Other World is "just east of the middle Volta, and the way down is difficult to follow."[2] The souls who arrive there do not cease to take an interest in mundane affairs, for they not only have local palavers, but try palavers left over from their earthly existence. And when there is an outbreak of sickness in a Fanti town or village, and several inhabitants die off, the opinion is often held that there is a big palaver going on down in Srahmanadzi, and that the spirits are sending upon earth for witnesses, subpœnaing them as it were.[3]

The Other World of the Ibo is much the same as this, but it is full of gloom, for there is no day there. The earth is similar, and there are in it forests, hills, valleys, rivers, and roads leading from one town to another, and houses and farms. Roads lead from this world to it, and on these souls travel to their final home. The land of the dead has no connection with the land which swallows up the sun, for it is dark, whilst the place where the sun is is always light. The king, the rich man, the poor man, the working man, and the farmer will all be as they are here. Certain places are set apart for the spirits of murderers, suicides, and men of violence. Whether good or bad here, the man who is properly buried will go to the land of spirits. Some souls are good and are well-doing, but those who belong to criminals and outcasts are regarded as demons. The head of a house here will there have authority over the fate of his own household, and it is necessary to be on good terms with him; this may be secured by gifts, offerings, and sacrifices made to his soul. Negligence in respect of such a soul will beget neglect on its part, and may even render it hostile to the interests of its kinsfolk on earth.[4] The souls in the Other World not only converse with each other, but they have assemblies and

[1] Ellis, *The Tshi-speaking Peoples*, p. 157 f.
[2] Kingsley, *Travels in West Africa*, p. 488.
[3] *Ibid.*, p. 519.
[4] Leonard, *The Lower Niger*, pp. 185–189.

palavers in order to discuss the more public affairs of the community, arguing, wrangling, and even quarrelling, as they did in this world. Unlike humanity, however, they keep their own counsel, and their quarrels to themselves. As they neither speak of their affairs to human beings nor give them counsel, they are inquisitors pure and simple. Thus, the ancestor becomes the great spirit inquisitor of his family, who can and does inflict injury and evil upon it ; this belief is the root of the whole idea of moral punishment.[1]

According to the Yorubas the spirits of all the dead go to Ọrun, the heavens. It is divided into two parts ; in one, the heaven of peace and happiness, live the souls of the blessed, and in the other, which is called the "world of potsherds," live the spirits of the wicked.[2] The Bantu believe that the spirits of the dead live in a dark forest, which is commonly spoken of as the "forest" or "the land of the dead."[3] In Dahomey the "nidon" or spirit goes to "Kutomen" or "Dead-land," where there is neither reward nor punishment. The king here is a king there, and every soul has the social status which its body had on earth. Kutomen is, in fact, a "Swedenborgian reproduction of this world, and "it is placed under the earth. The departed often "returns to earth in the body of a child, and yet remains "in Dead-land—an idea which some travellers have "confounded with metempsychosis."[4] The priests say that life in the Other World is much the same as in this, and that there are there wars, palavers, feasts, dances, etc., as here. The clothes in which a man is buried accompany him to Kutomen.[5] The oldest idea in Central Congo-land is that the spirits of the dead live in a dark forest. Until recently the Congo tribes on the coast believed that their dead went to a world at the bottom of the sea, and there spent their time as slaves to the white man, making cloth and trade goods.

The Bayanzi think that the souls of the dead go to

1 *Ibid.*, p. 190.
2 Dennett, *At the Back of the Black Man's Mind*, p. 268.
3 Bentley, *Pioneering on the Congo*, Vol. I, p. 252.
4 Burton, *Mission to Gelele*, Vol. II, p. 158.
5 Skertchley, *Dahomey as It is*, p. 465.

the sky.[1] Some ancient Egyptians also held this view. They thought that the sky was the floor of heaven, and that it rested on two mountains, Bakha and Manu, which are the mountains of Sunrise and Sunset respectively. Another view was that it rested on four pillars, which formed the four cardinal points and were held in position by the four Sons of Horus. In the former case souls made their way to one or other of the mountains, and climbed to the top, and so stepped on to the crystal sky, and then joined the souls who were already there. In the latter case the Egyptians thought that souls could only reach the sky by means of a ladder. There is a legend[2] to the effect that Osiris only succeeded in getting into the sky by means of a ladder which was provided by Rā. Osiris was assisted to mount it by Rā and Horus, or Set and Horus, each of whom pushed him up with one finger. In the tombs of the Ancient and Middle Empires models of ladders have been found, and it was believed that when deceased persons had pronounced over them the appropriate words of power, these models increased in length and strength, and became actual ladders, and reared themselves up so that they might mount them, and so ascend at will from their graves to heaven. The ladder also appears in the Book of the Dead, and the deceased says: "I set up a ladder among the gods,"[3] and the "Light-god hath made me to be vigorous by the two sides of the ladder."[4] Elsewhere it is said: "He shall come forth upon your ladder "which Rā hath made for him, and Horus and Set "shall grasp him firmly by the hand."[5] Finally, when men no longer placed models of ladders in tombs, the priests provided for the necessity of the dead by painting a ladder on papyri containing copies of the Book of the Dead.[6] In connection with this belief in the ladder as a means of communication between heaven and earth, it is interesting to note that the Fernando Po people think that at one time a ladder, "like the one you get

[1] Johnston, *George Grenfell*, Vol. II, p. 643.
[2] Unȧs text, ll. 192, 579, and Pepi text, ll. 200, 422, and 471.
[3] Chapter CXLIX.
[4] Chapter XCVIII.
[5] Chapter CLIII.
[6] *Papyrus of Ani*, 2nd edit., Plate 22.

palm-nuts with, only long, long,' reached from earth to heaven, so that the gods could come down and attend personally to mundane affairs. One day a crippled boy began to ascend it, and when he was a long way up his mother saw him, and started in pursuit. The gods, being horrified at the idea of the invasion of heaven by boys and women, threw down the ladder, and have since left humanity severely alone.[1] It is possible that the idea of a ladder reaching from earth to heaven may have drifted across Africa from the Christians in Abyssinia, but it is hardly likely, and it is probable that it forms a part of the tradition current all over West Africa that there was once a time when a direct means of communication between gods and men existed upon earth.

[1] Kingsley, *Travels in West Africa*, p. 507.

CHAPTER XXI.

Magic (Witchcraft), White and Black.

The Egyptians, like the modern Africans, believed that the government of this world was, practically speaking, in the hands of a considerable number of "gods" and spirits, and that, in order to have success and happiness here and hereafter, it was necessary to obtain their good-will and help. The performance of the duties and ceremonies connected with the proper worship of ancestral spirits was performed by a member of each family, who in dynastic times was called the "servant of the ka," 𓍛𓂓, and the direction of the worship due to the local god was committed to the care of the "servant of the god," 𓍛𓊹. The chief of every large village, or town, or district, usually attached to his service a man who was believed to be able to hold communication with the spirits of the "gods," and to have influence with them, and also to possess powers of an occult character with which, when necessary, he could control, limit, or abrogate the action of evil spirits. In many cases the chief, and even the king of the whole country, must have owed his position to the influence of this man and his assistants, who posed as interpreters of the divine will, and the acts and policy of the chief were often directed by them. The chief was supreme in all temporal matters, and the man who possessed occult powers was equally supreme in all spiritual matters. The chief was in primitive times the strongest and bravest man in the community, the most fearless hunter, and the fiercest fighter, and was, in fact, the embodiment of physical strength. The man of occult powers was, on the other hand, the incarnation of intelligence, agility of mind, thought, cunning, shrewdness, and foresight, and, when the Egyptians had acquired the art of writing, he added to his other powers the ability to read and write, and he possessed a thorough knowledge of the sacred books. This condition of things exists among the communities of West Africa at the present day, for Sir Harry Johnston says that among those where there has been no recent interference of the white man, and no conversion to Islâm or Christianity, there are two pillars of society—the Chief (king, judge, magistrate, leader in battle), and the Magician (sorcerer, medicine-man, priest, lawyer). Sometimes, but rarely, the functions of the two are combined. Usually, the chief leaves the laws, police, medicine, meteorology, prophecy, and practical science of the tribe to a distinct functionary, the magician, the wise man, or woman, the "Nganga" of Bantu Africa.

The title of the man who possessed occult powers and was recognized by the King of Egypt as the official director of religious and magical ceremonies, was "Kher ḥeb," , and his influence was very great and far-reaching. He was well versed in the knowledge of all the sacred books, he knew how to perform both magic and religious ceremonies, and how and when to recite spells with the proper tone of voice, he was able to draft prayers, incantations, spells and magical formulae, he could foretell the future, explain auguries and portents, interpret dreams, assign causes to illnesses, and declare the name of the spirits of the dead which caused them, he knew the great secret names of the gods whereby they existed and maintained order in the world, he knew how to cause death and to make the dead to live, to concoct potent medicines, to take the form of anything animate or inanimate in earth, air, water and sky, to render himself invisible at pleasure, and to cast out devils. Such are the powers which the literature of ancient Egypt ascribes to the Kher ḥeb. The use of these powers for a good purpose and with the object of doing good to the living or the dead may be described as White Magic, and the employment of them with the view of doing harm or injury to anyone as Black Magic.

The legitimate use of White Magic took place chiefly in connection with the dead, and the Kher ḥeb was held to be justified in using his powers to effect the preservation of their bodies and souls, and to make the Spirit-soul to join the Spirit-body. The formulae which he composed and recited protected the grave, and kept away hostile beings, living and dead, from it, and caused supplies of offerings, on which the KA and the Heart-soul lived, to appear regularly and constantly in the offerings-chamber. When written upon the walls of tombs, coffins, sarcophagi, wooden boards, amulets, etc., they became "words of power" of irresistible might, for they transferred to them some part of the invisible and almighty power which was believed to maintain life in the gods, and to support all creation. The Kher ḥeb was the channel by which this mysterious and wonderful power was made useful to man, and his most sacred function was to act as mediator between the spirits of gods and of the beatified and the living. He was himself a great amulet or charm, for at times the spirits of the gods made his body a temporary abode, and all that he did and said on such occasions was thought to be inspired by divine beings and to have divine authority. At such times he spoke as if he were indeed the god who possessed him, and in addressing the evil spirit, or crocodile, or serpent, or fiend, he bade him depart, or fall helpless, or die because he was that god.

Thus in the Book of the Dead we have: "Get thee, "back, crocodile Sui, for I live by the magical power (*ḥeka* "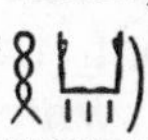). My mouth hath power over the *ḥeka*" (Chapter XXXI). "I am Osiris. I am Horus. I am Ȧnpu. "I am the priest in heaven" (Chapter XXXI). "Get "thee back, Crocodile, I am Set. Get thee back, "Crocodile, I am Osiris. Get thee back, Crocodile, "I am Sepṭ. Get thee back, Crocodile, I am Tem. "Get thee back, Crocodile, I am Uatch-Merti, I "am Rā" (Chapter XXXII). "O serpent, I am the "Lynx" (Chapter XXXIV). "I command the spirits" (Chapter XXXVIIIA). "I am the two lion-gods. I "stand in the Boat of Rā, and I recite his commands, "and announce his words" (Chapter XXXVIII). "Depart from me, O Āpshait, for I am Khnemu, and "I carry the words of the gods to Rā" (Chapter

XXXVI). "I am the Great One, son of the Great "One. I am fire, the son of Fire" (Chapter XLIII). "I am Yesterday, To-day, and To-morrow. I shall "be born a second time. I am the Soul who created "the gods, and I feed the beings in the Ṭuat" (Chapter LXIV). "I am the Fire-god, brother of the Fire-god; "I am Osiris, brother of Isis. I am Orion. I am "Anubis. I am Horus. I am Tem. I was in the "birth-chamber of Osiris. I was born with him. I "renew my youth" (Chapter LXIX). "I am the "girdle of the robe of Nu. I rescued the Eye of Rā "when it grew dim. I judged Sut. I turned the night "into day" (Chapter LXXX). "My tongue is the "tongue of Ptaḥ" (Chapter LXXXII). "I created "myself like Kheperȧ. I am Khensu (Moon-god), who "beateth down all opposition" (Chapter LXXXIII). "I am the Soul, which is God. I am the Souls of "everlastingness, and my body is eternity. My form "is everlastingness" (Chapter LXXXV). "I know the "hidden ways and the doors of Sekhet-Ȧarru" (Chapter LXXXVI). "I am the serpent Sata. I die and I am "born each day" (Chapter LXXXVII). "I am the "divine crocodile dwelling amid terror" (Chapter LXXXVIII). "I smite with terror the powers of the "rain and thunder" (Chapter XCV).

In several of the magical texts which contain spells reference is made to various calamities which befell the gods or goddesses, and the rubrics say that the spells there written were the identical spells which were recited to effect the deliverance or relief of the injured deities. Thus Horus was stung by a scorpion, but Isis, by the advice of Nephthys and Serqet, prayed to Rā, who stopped his boat, and sent Thoth to heal the child. Thoth came bearing with him magical power (*ḥeka*) obtained from Rā, and the poison having been expelled from the body of Horus, the suffering child recovered. If a person who was stung by a scorpion would bear this story in mind, the poison would leave his body, as it left the body of Horus. Or, if anyone recited this story over a man stung by a scorpion he would be healed.[1]

[1] This story is told on the Metternich Stele (ed. Golénischeff).

Another great source of the magician's power was the secret names of the gods, which he professed to know. The existence of every god, and indeed of every being, was bound up in his secret name, and he who knew these names and how to utter them was their master. The importance of the name is well illustrated by the following legend of Rā and Isis.[1] When Rā reigned on earth as well as in heaven, Isis was seized with the desire to know his secret name, which was the source of his life and sovereignty. She knew everything except this name. Rā was old, and dribbled at the mouth, and catching some of his spittle she kneaded it with earth and made a serpent, which she placed on the path of the god so that it might bite him when he passed by. When Rā came along with the gods, this serpent bit him, and as the poison flowed through his body he suffered great pain, and was about to die. Then Isis came and asked the god to tell her his secret name, but though he enumerated many of his names, his great and secret name was not among them. Meanwhile his agony increased, and when his body became filled with the fire of the poison, and he was unable any longer to bear it, he promised that his secret name should be transferred to Isis; this apparently took place, for Rā recovered, but what the name was we do not know. The knowledge of names plays a very prominent part in the Book of the Dead. Thus, to be acquitted in the Judgment Hall of Osiris, it was necessary for the deceased to know the names of the Two-and-Forty gods who were there. To obtain a passage in the magic boat (Chapter XCIX) it was necessary for him to know the secret name of every part of it, and to be able to utter them correctly. To pass through the Seven Halls and the Pylons of the Kingdom of Osiris he had to know not only their names, but also the names of their Porters, Watchers, and Heralds (Chapters CXLIV–CXLVIII). Before he could escape from the net of the catcher of souls he was obliged to know and declare the names of every part of it (Chapter CLIIIA). As specimens of magical names may be quoted the following: Sharesharekhet, Shapuneterarika, Shaka Amen

[1] See Lefébure, *A.Z.*, 1883, p. 27 ff.

Shakanasa, Atareamtcherqemturennuparsheta, Kasaika Arethikasathika, Amennaankaentekshare, Retasashaka, Ireqai, Mārqatha, Rerei, Nasaqbubu, Thanasathanasa, Shareshathakatha, Haqahakaḳaḥer, Ānrauaaqersaanqrebathi, Kherserau, Ḥarepukakashareshabaiu (Chapter CLXII ff.). In the Magical Papyrus (B.M., No. 10,042) we have the following words of power :—

Atir-Atisau, Atirkaha-Atisau, Smauimatemu-Atisau.
Smautanenmui-Atisau, Smauttekaiu-Atisau.
Smauttekabaiu-Atisau, Smauttchakaratcha-Atisau.
Tāuarhasaqinahama, Sennfetta, Bathetet, Satitaui.
Anrahakathasatitaui, Haubairhuru (?), Haari (Col. XII).

Pāpāluka, Pāpāruka, Pāpālur (Col. VII).

In a spell in the same papyrus we read : "I am the "chosen one of millions of years, who cometh out of the "Ṭuat, whose name is unknown." If this name be "cut" (*i.e.*, uttered) on the river bank, it will slice it away ; and if it be cut on the ground a fire will break out. The power of this spell was very great. If a man repeated it four times,[1] and held in his hand at the same time a drawing of the Eye of the Sun with a figure of Ȧn-Ḥer in it, the earth would collapse into the celestial ocean, and the South would become the North. A man who knew the next spell in the papyrus became like one who had seventy-seven eyes and seventy-seven ears (Column VII). The most remarkable use of the name of a god as a word of power is related in the Book of Overthrowing Āpep (British Museum, No. 10,188). In this the god Tem describes how he created the world and all the generations thereof. There was a time, he says, when no one and nothing existed except himself. A desire came over him to create the world, and he carried it into effect by making his mouth utter his own name as a word of power, and straightway the world and all therein came into being.[2] The things which came

[1] The Gallas to this day recite their semi-magical prayers four times. See Paulitschke, *Ethnographie Nordost-Afrikas*, 1896, Vol. 2, p. 45.

[2] 

into being as the result of the utterance of the secret name of Temu contained some of the power of that name, which existed henceforward in the secret names which they possessed. What the secret name of Tem really was the papyrus does not say, but it is quite clear that the Egyptians thought that heaven, earth, and the Other World, and every being and thing which were in them, existed by virtue of it. To possess the knowledge of the secret names of God, and those of the gods, and of things animate and inanimate, was the magician's chief object in life, and his desire to acquire it is easy to understand; for, according to the belief of the period, it made him master of all the powers in this world.

The power of the spell, or incantation, or of any word of power, was greatly increased by the use of magical pictures and amulets which contained either a portion of *ḥeka* power, or an indwelling spirit. Thus, if a certain kind of wreath was laid on the face of a dead person, and the Kher ḥeb recited the words of power which formed the XIXth Chapter of the Book of the Dead, whilst incense was being burnt, that dead person would never lack food, and would always overcome his enemies. The fumes of the incense rising heavenwards was supposed to bear the words of power with them to Osiris, who heard them and did as the petitioner desired. Again, to cause the spirit of the dead man to have power like Osiris in the Other World, it was necessary to perform elaborate ceremonies and to use amulets, as well as to recite four potent spells. Four lamps, with wicks made of *āṭmā* cloth which had been steeped in Libyan unguent (*ḥātet*), were kindled, and these were held in the hands of four men, each of whom had written on his shoulder the name of one of the Four Sons of Horus. Four troughs were made of earth on which incense had been sprinkled, and these were filled with the milk of a white cow. After the lamps had been burning for a time in the sun-light, they were

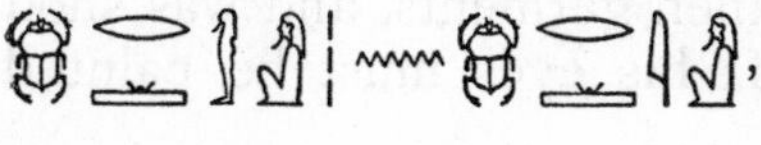
, Col. XXVIII, l. 22.

quenched, each in one of the troughs of milk. The performance of this ceremony was to be witnessed by none save a man, or his father, or his son. A ṭeṭ of crystal, a figure of Anubis, a figure of a mummy, and the model of a palm tree, seven cubits in height, each mounted on a small mud brick inscribed with its own spell, were then placed in the east, west, north, and south walls of the tomb respectively, and the text of the CXXXVIIth Chapter of the Book of the Dead was recited. How the power of these amulets worked, and what exactly the ceremonies were supposed to do we know not, but the general evidence of the Chapter itself suggests that they made the soul of the dead man to ascend into heaven in the form of Osiris or Rā. The Rubric says that the figure of the mummy is to be smeared with bitumen and set fire to, and we may assume that, as the body of the deceased is thus burned symbolically, his spirit rises in the flame, and mingles with the flames of the four sacred lamps of the Four Sons of Horus, and is thus united to the soul of Osiris, which, it seems, sometimes took the form of a flame of fire. These ceremonies are said to be "an exceedingly "great mystery of Åmentet, and a type of the hidden "things of the Other World." More than once the Rubrics order that such ceremonies as these are not to be witnessed by the "dwellers in the papyrus swamps," *i.e.*, the fen-men of the Delta, who were also not to be allowed to know the texts which related to them, or even to see copies of them (Chapters CLXI and CXC).

The Rubrics to the magical texts make clear another very important fact in connection with the working of magical ceremonies and the reciting of spells by the Kher ḥeb, viz., that before undertaking anything of the kind he must make himself ceremonially pure. The things described in the Rubrics to Chapter CXXXVII were ordered to "be performed by a man who is washed "clean and is ceremonially pure, one who has neither "eaten meat nor fish recently, and has not had inter-"course with women." The famous Judgment Chapter was to be recited "by a man who was washed clean and "purified, who was clad in linen garments, and was shod "with white leather sandals; his eyes must be painted "with antimony, and his body anointed with *ānti* "unguent" (Chapter CXXV). The spiritual faculties of the magician were rendered more keen by abstention from carnal pleasures, and the words of the man who was clean "within and without, before and behind," were believed to possess greater power, and to be followed more quickly by the desired effect, than those of him to whom personal cleanliness was of small account. The higher the degree of cleanliness of his mind and body, the greater was the influence of the magician over the spirits whom he summoned to help him. The White Magic of the Egyptians, notwithstanding the ceremonies and spells, and figures and amulets, which were associated with it, was sanctified by the chief object for which it was employed, namely, the resurrection of the Spirit-body and the rejoining of the Spirit-soul to it in the kingdom of Osiris. Besides this, it was used to heal sicknesses and to drive out devils and evil spirits from suffering humanity, and the general trend of its influence was for good. In every important event in the life of the Egyptian, from his cradle to his grave, White Magic played a prominent part. It brought to him at his birth good spirits, who watched over him and protected him, it gave him amulets which brought the living power of his gods to his body as he grew up, it provided beneficent spells which guarded his wife and children, and house, and farm, and animals, and other possessions, its precepts led him to worship his ancestral spirits and gods, and when he died its rites and ceremonies were employed to secure the admission of his soul into the kingdom of spirits.

There were, however, in Egypt many men who professed the art of Black Magic, the object of which was to do harm. In their hands the powers of magic were generally misused, and disastrous results, if we may believe the papyri, were the consequence. One of the commonest ways of working evil was by means of the wax figure. A man employed a magician to make in wax a figure of his enemy, whose name was cut or written upon it, and then to work magic upon it by reciting spells over it. If the spells contained curses, they were supposed to take effect upon the living man;

and if the figure were stabbed, or gashes made in it with a knife, the living man suffered terrible pain, or wounds appeared in his body. If the figure were destroyed by fire or by any other means, the death of the living man ensued. The Westcar Papyrus tells us that the wife of one Āba-àner committed adultery in his garden with one of his servants. When the news of this was brought to him, he made a model of a crocodile in wax, and told his servant to go and place it in the river at the spot where his guilty wife's paramour was in the habit of bathing. As soon as this man entered the water on the following day, the wax crocodile turned into a huge living crocodile, which quickly devoured him. The Rollin Papyrus states that certain evil men succeeded in stealing a book of magic from the Royal Library, and that by following the directions contained in it they succeeded in making wax figures, on which they worked magic with the view of injuring or killing the king of Egypt. This was held to be treason in the first degree, and the malefactors seem to have suffered the death penalty. The use of the wax figure was not disdained by the priests of Àmen-Rā at Thebes, for they regularly burnt a wax figure of the fiend Āpep, who daily endeavoured to prevent the sun from rising. This figure was in the form of a serpent of many folds, on which the name Āpep was written or cut. A case made of papyrus inscribed with spells containing curses was prepared, and, the wax serpent having been placed inside it, both case and figure were cast into a fire made of a special kind of plant. Whilst they were burning the priest recited curses, and stamped upon them with his left foot until they were rendered shapeless and were finally destroyed. This magical ceremony was believed to be very helpful to Rā, the Sun-god, who uttered over the real Āpep spells which paralysed him, and then killed him by the fiery darts of his rays, and consumed him.

Further information about the powers said to be possessed by Egyptian magicians is given by the Westcar Papyrus. Thus in the reign of Seneferu one Tchatcha-em-ānkh divided the water of a lake into two parts, and placed one part upon the other, in order to allow a singing woman, who was rowing the royal boat with the king in it, to recover a jewel which had dropped from her into the water as she rowed and sang. Another magician, called Teti, who lived in the reign of Khufu, could make a lion follow him without leading him by a rope, and knew certain mysteries connected with the sanctuary of Thoth, and could rejoin the head of a man to his body after it had been cut off, and make him live again. He was brought into Khufu's presence by Prince Ḥeruṭāṭāf, and the king commanded that a prisoner should be given to him, so that he might exhibit a proof of his magical powers before His Majesty. Teti, however, suggested that some animal should be substituted for the prisoner, and a goose was brought in. Having cut off its head, he placed the head and the body in different parts of the room, the former on the west side and the latter on the east. He then uttered words of power, and the head and the body began to move towards each other; when they came close together, the head leapt back to its place on its body, and the bird quacked. Another kind of bird was treated in the same way, and its head rejoined its body as in the case of the goose. An ox was then brought and its head was cut off, and the words of power of Teti caused it to rejoin its body.

As the worker of White Magic used the hidden names of gods and good spirits as words of power, so the sorcerer used the hidden names of devils and fiends as spells which produced evil. The knowledge of these names made him master of the devils who entered the bodies of the living and produced diseases of every kind, and who unhesitatingly performed his commands. The names of Set and his fiends could be made to produce thunder, lightning, storm, cold, famine, pestilence, and death. The use of the names of the spirits of poisonous plants enabled him to concoct deadly poisons, and decoctions made from parts of savage animals and venomous reptiles, and liquid from dead human bodies, formed ingredients in his baleful "medicine." Like the modern fortune-teller, he professed to read the future, and a complete calendar of the lucky and unlucky days of the year, of which we have one complete copy[1] and one

[1] See Budge, *Egyptian Hieratic Papyri in the British Museum*, Plates XXXI and XXXII.

incomplete,[1] enabled him to declare what day, and what part of it, would be propitious for undertaking any proposed work. He professed to be able to hold intercourse with the spirits of the dead, and to have an intimate acquaintance with all that took place in the Other World. Thus in the Second Tale of Khā-em-uas[2] we read how one Setme went into the Ṭuat, and having passed through its various halls he saw Osiris seated in judgment, with Anubis on his left hand and Thoth on his right, whilst the Assessors were on both sides of him. He saw the Balance standing there, and learned that the men whose good deeds exceeded their evil deeds entered among the lords of Ȧmentet, whilst their souls went to heaven. Those whose evil deeds exceeded their good deeds were delivered to the Devourer, and their souls and bodies were destroyed for ever. This same tale describes the magical powers which were possessed by Setme's son, Sa-Ȧsȧr. Thus he could read books without opening them, and he told the king the contents of a letter which an Ethiopian had brought to him. The magician Hor made a model in wax of a litter for four bearers, and, having pronounced a spell over it, ordered it to go to the Sûdân and bring back the Viceroy, so that he might be beaten with 500 stripes, and to return in six hours; and it is related that the litter did so.[3] During a contest between this same Hor and an Ethiopian magician, the Ethiopian caused fire to appear in the palace; in reply Hor recited a spell, and a shower of rain came and put out the fire. The Ethiopian then caused the heavens to become black, so that no man could see his neighbour, whereupon Hor recited a spell and made the darkness to pass away. Then the Ethiopian made a huge vault of stone, 200 cubits long and 50 cubits broad, to be above the heads of Pharaoh and his princes, and it threatened to crash down and kill them all; when the king and his people saw this they uttered piercing shrieks. Hor, however, uttered a spell, which caused a great phantom boat, apparently made of papyrus, to come into being, and he made it carry the stone vault away to the Great Water of Egypt (Lake Moeris).

[1] Sallier Papyrus No. IV (No. 10,184).
[2] Ed. Griffith, p. 46.
[3] *Ibid.*, p. 59.

From the works of Greek writers of the Graeco-Roman Period we know that Egyptian sorcerers at that time were supposed to be able to send terrifying dreams to men and women, to steal the mind and senses from a man, to rob the lover of his beloved's love, to alienate a wife's affections from her husband, to fill men and women with longings for illicit love, to cause sickness and death, to raise the dead, to take the forms of animals, birds, reptiles, etc., to make themselves invisible, to involve men in loss or ruin, to control the powers of heaven and earth, etc. There is nothing strange in this, for powers to perform all these things were claimed by ancient Egyptian magicians. In the Ptolemaïc Period, magicians began to cast nativities and to make horoscopes, and to claim the power of explaining the alleged influences of the Seven Planets, and the Twelve Signs of the Zodiac, and the Thirty-six Dekans, on the lives of men. Nectanebus, the last native king of Egypt, was reputed to be the greatest of magicians, for he knew what was in the depths of the Nile and the sea, he could work the astrolabe, read the stars, cast nativities, foretell the destinies of men, and he slew his enemies by sea and by land by the use of words of power and mighty names and wax figures. He made wax models of ships and their crews, and of regiments of soldiers, some representing those of his own country and others those of the enemy, and setting them face to face he recited over them his words of power. The figures of the soldiers or sailors, as the case might be, then began to fight, and as the wax figures of his troops slew and routed those of their opponents, his living enemies were destroyed. One day his words of power failed to produce their customary effect, and, realizing that the gods of Egypt had forsaken him, he collected all the money he could carry and fled by ship to Macedon, where by magical means he seduced Olympias, and became, according to Pseudo-Callisthenes, the father of Alexander the Great. He went to the fields and collected a number of plants which possessed magical properties, and, having pounded them and squeezed out their juice, he made a figure of Olympias, and wrote her name upon it; he then poured the juice of the plants over it and laid it down in the attitude of sleep by the fire. Nectanebus recited spells and names over the figure, and the result of these was to cause Olympias to dream that a spirit called Åmen came to her and was united with her, and that she conceived a man-child by him. Shortly after this Nectanebus disguised himself as Åmen and went to the queen's chamber, and, believing him to be the god who had appeared to her in her dream, she admitted him to her embrace.[1]

The Egyptian Christians were nearly as much addicted to the use of magic as their "pagan" ancestors. With them the Cross took the place of the ānkh ☥, and its name became a word of power. The sign of the Cross terrified the devil, drove away fiends, and healed the sick, and the Name of Christ possessed untold power. The Devil fled before it "like a sparrow before a hawk," and a hippopotamus which ravaged the crops, being adjured by it to depart, ceased to do harm, and departed and was no more seen. The Christian Fathers asserted that even laymen might drive away devils by the Name of Christ and the Sign of the Cross. Macarius, by the sprinkling of holy water, restored to her human form a woman who had been transformed into a mare. Paul the Simple cast out from a man a devil, who took the form of "a mighty dragon seventy cubits long." The monk Apollo cast spells upon certain priests and people who were worshipping an image, and they remained powerless to move under a blazing sun, until he prayed over them and removed the spell. A friend of this Apollo called Ammon appealed to Christ to destroy a serpent, and as soon as the reptile heard this name it burst asunder. Bessarion walked on the water, and made the sun to stand still. Petarpemotis made a dead man to speak, and walked upon the water, and entered into a chamber where the brethren were "in the air by the power of the angels," and visited Paradise and saw the saints, and brought back figs therefrom. When the people mixed the sand which he had blessed with the sterile soil in their land, crops grew straightway

1 *Ethiopic Version*, ed. Budge, p. 10 ff.

which were larger and more abundant than those of any other part of Egypt.[1]

With the description of the alleged powers of ancient Egyptian magicians set forth in the previous pages, we may now compare the statements made by various travellers about the medicine-men and witch-doctors and their doings in Central and Western Africa in recent years. According to Schweinfurth, the creed of the Dinkas centres in an institution called "Cogyoor," which embraces a society of necromancers and jugglers by profession. They are expert conjurers and ventriloquists, and are familiar with the ghosts of the dead.[2] The Matabele recognize two kinds of witchcraft. One kind includes the "making of medicine" to cause rain and the performance of ceremonies to appease the spirits of ancestors. The other kind consists of evil practices which were supposed to cause sickness and death.[3] If a man wants to cause his enemy to be speared, he makes a clay figure, which is supposed to represent him, and pierces it with a pin. Anyone can be bewitched by spreading medicine on his path or in his hut. He who possesses the liver and entrails of a crocodile can cause the death of anyone he pleases. There are two kinds of witch-doctors. One kind works his magic by throwing three bones, and watching the positions in which they fall; the other kind chants his spells and oracles in a shrill voice. Both kinds hold intercourse with the spirits of the dead. The blood and gall of a black ox were used by the witch-doctors in the charm for making rain.[4] Among the Bongo many of the chiefs are magicians, or medicine-men, and they owe much of their influence over their peoples to the fact that they are believed to possess power over the spirits of the dead, all of whom are supposed to be capable of doing mischief. As the Bongo have no belief in the existence of good spirits it follows that the only magic they know is Black Magic. The Bongo medicine-man holds communication

[1] For the statements in this paragraph see my *Paradise of the Holy Fathers*, Vol. I, p. XLIX ff.

[2] *Heart of Africa.* Vol. I, p. 169.

[3] Nassau, *Fetichism*, p. 117; Decle, *Three Years*, p. 152.

[4] Decle, *Three Years*, p. 153.

with spirits by means of certain roots, decoctions and preparations of which are used to do harm to living persons.[1] Among the Baganda each tribe or clan has its own Muchwezi, or sorcerer (*i.e.*, medicine-man, or witch-doctor), who conducts the worship of ancestral spirits. There are, however, besides many doctors in white or black magic.[2] The men who attend to the worship of the various gods and ancestral spirits were termed "Bamandwa." They were also diviners, and were able by superstitious means to answer questions as if they were oracles. The Mandwa would listen to the question, and having made the sign of the cross with a strip of leather on which were sewn nine kauri shells (called "Engato"), and flung this object before him, would answer it as one inspired. The priests of Mukasa, the god of Lake Victoria, carried a paddle as an emblem of their office,[3] just as do twelve of the gods in the pictures in the Egyptian Books of the Other World.[4] In Kavirondo witchcraft is of two kinds, "obufira," *i.e.*, white magic, or the use of hypnotism and divination for innocent purposes; and "obulugo," which is little else than killing people by poison, or fright.[5] Their witch-doctors are great experts in the lore of omens derived from the appearance of the entrails of sheep. Besides ancestral spirits two gods are worshipped by the Ba-Kavirondo: Awafwa, the god of good spirits, and Ishishemi, a sort of devil.[6] The right side is lucky and the left unlucky,[7] as in ancient Egypt. The witch-doctors among the Basoga of the island of Bavuma recognize two classes of spirits, one good[8] and the other bad,[9] and each spirit has its own priest. They are

[1] Schweinfurth, *Heart of Africa*, Vol. I, p. 306; Frobenius, *Die Heiden-Neger*, p. 361.

[2] Johnston, *Uganda*, Vol. II, p. 589.

[3] *Ibid.*, p. 676.

[4] Budge, *Åm-Ṯuat*, p. 189; *Book of Gates*, p. 276.

[5] Johnston, *Uganda*, Vol. II, p. 751.

[6] *Ibid.*, p. 750.

[7] *Ibid.*, p. 751.

[8] These are: Nasamba, Walumbe, Waitambugwe, Kintu, Maganda, Maero, Bugingo, Takwe, Kisalumkaba, Kirongo, Lukamaembe, Nalango, Kitako, Kalesa, Duungu, Nabisana, Kigulu, Kaliro, Naigombwa, Lumbui, Kamiantumbe, Kakua, Kambuzi.

[9] These are: Irukoma, Isōdzi, Buvuma, Kasota, Wesege, Nambaga, Kitiko, Meru, Buyegu, Nabirie.—See Johnston, *op. cit.*, II, p. 718.

worshipped by offerings which are placed for them in "fetish huts." Among the Jalas there exists a kind of magic called "Jamkingo," which is practised by a sort of secret society, and which means to all intents and purposes secret poisoning. Among the Gemi tribe the magicians are blacksmiths, which fact calls to mind the blacksmiths[1] (*mesentiu*), or metal workers, who assisted Horus in performing the ceremonies connected with the resurrection of Osiris.

The Juju[2] priests of New Calabar were said to be able, by their devilish arts, to change a man's face and appearance to such a degree that his mother would not recognize him; to cause a tree on the river banks to bend its trunk and lower the topmost branches so that they could absorb water from the river; to take upon themselves the form of birds and fly away, and to be able to disappear at pleasure.[3] When the Juju priest performed a ceremony of great importance he wore nothing but "a superb dark-coloured and greasy-looking "rag about his loins, barely sufficient to satisfy the "easiest-going of European Lord Chamberlains."[4] This also was the case with the Kher ḥeb magician in ancient Egypt, for when performing certain of the ceremonies connected with the "Opening of the Mouth" he wore nothing but a loin cloth.[5]

Among the Masai all medicine-men belong to the Kidongi family of the Aiser clan, and they are descended from Ol-Oimooja, or E-Sigiriaishi, the sons of Ol-le-Mweiya. They have four methods of divining: (1) By a buffalo or ox horn and a handful of stones. (2) By examining the entrails of a goat. (3) By getting drunk and prophesying. (4) By dreams.[6] Among the Nandi the Orkoiyot or principal medicine-man is chief of the

[1] *Ibid.*, Vol. II, p. 792.

[2] Derived not from "joujou," as is commonly supposed, but from a local West African word "egugu," which means "idol," "sacred emblem."—Leonard, *Lower Niger*, p. 115.

[3] Kingsley, *West African Studies*, p. 499.

[4] *Ibid.*, p. 505.

[5] The chief Kapufi was not allowed to wear anything but a single loin-cloth of the plainest cotton.—Thomson, *Central African Lakes*, Vol. II, p. 221.

[6] Hollis, *The Masai*, p. 325.

whole race. His methods of divining are similar to those of the Ol-oiboni, or medicine-man of the Masai. He can interpret omens and avert ill luck. He tells the people when to plant their crops, he obtains rain for them, he makes women and cattle fruitful, and the success of a war or raid depends on his approval. His approval is shown when he gives one of the leaders a club which has been smeared with a concoction called *setanik*, and this club is carried in front of the party. The person of the Orkoiyot is absolutely sacred. No one may approach him with weapons in his hand, or speak in his presence unless first addressed ; his head must never be touched, lest his powers of divination depart from him. He is thought to be able to detach his head from his body, and to send it to watch his troops wherever they may be engaged in fighting. He never prays to Asista, but only to the spirits of his deceased ancestors. Besides the Orkoiyot there are two classes of lesser medicine-men, one of whom is called Kipsakeiyot, and the other Kipungut. The magicians bewitch people by "catching" their footprints, or by means of portions of their clothing which they have worn, or a bead, or by their hair, nail parings, teeth, spittle, or anything which has fallen from their bodies. The rain-makers cause rain by soaking the root *kiptakchat* in water.[1]

Among the Gallas the magician or medicine-man has great power, and is called "ogêssa," *i.e.*, "learned man," or "doctor of the book."[2]

The position and authority of the magician in Western Africa is well summarized by Wilson, who says that the person who has a knowledge of witchcraft is supposed to possess little less than omnipotence. He is master of the lives and destinies of his fellow men, and of sea and land, and of the elemental forces of nature, and of the wild beasts of the earth. He can change himself into a tiger, elephant, shark, etc., and withhold rain, and fill the land with want and distress and pestilence. He can cause sickness, poverty, insanity, and death. The art of witchcraft may be exerted with

[1] Hollis, *The Nandi*, p. 52.

[2] Paulitschke, *Ethnographie*, Vol. II, p. 62.

or without any material agency; the wish and the word of the magician can perform anything. No one knows the source of his power; some suppose that it is derived from the spirits, and others believe that he obtains it by eating the leaves or roots of a forest tree.[1]

The art of the magician, or medicine-man, or witch-doctor, is employed by the natives in every event of life, and is used publicly and privately. Before Mtesa went to war the priests of the Musimu, or evil spirits, about one hundred in number, used to bring the war charms for him to touch with his forefinger. These charms consisted of dead lizards, bits of wood, hide, nails of dead people, claws of animals, beaks of birds, with compounds of herbs and leaves carefully placed in vessels ornamented with beads. During the fight these magicians chant spells, and exhibit their "medicines" to the foe, and their associates shake large numbers of gourds filled with pebbles, and create an awful din.[2] Among the Garenganze in South-east Africa the side that is beaten at once acknowledges that the medicines of the enemy are stronger than their own.[3] The war-fetish of the Batanga is a spear with prongs, which is thrust into the head of a dead man, which is afterwards cut off from its body, and carried to the house of the medicine-man. Whilst the man does this he must be naked. The spear is then boiled in a pot with some of the blood of a cock, and several magic ingredients, including the human head, and the warriors are sprinkled with some of the water from the pot. A mess composed of cock's blood, red-wood, a cock, oil, gourd seeds, plantains, etc., is then cooked in the pot, and the medicine-man and the warriors eat it. The warriors are sponged on their breasts, and are then ready to fight, feeling assured of victory. The spear is, presumably, carried before them as they march.[4]

Before going hunting the members of the party would fetch a medicine-man, who put the fat of zebra, eland, and other game, mixed with dirt, in a pot. Hot coals

[1] *Western Africa*, p. 222.
[2] Stanley, *Through the Dark Continent*, Vol. I, p. 327.
[3] Arnot, in Nassau, *Fetichism*, p. 175.
[4] Nassau, *op. cit.*, p. 177 f.

were then placed on the fat, and clouds of dense smoke arose. Into this the men thrust the muzzles of their rifles through the smoke, and sniffing the smoke each called on the hunting spirit Saru, saying, "Saru, I must kill game." The medicine-man next placed a bowl of the "medicine" water on the hunter's head, and whilst the latter repeated the names of the animals he wished to kill, the former stirred the water. If the water splashed over and ran down on the hunter's face success was assured to him; if none left the bowl he might as well go home. Among the Matabele the medicine-man made a mark with medicine water on the forehead of each hunter, and this gave him authority over the beasts. When going on a journey a travelling fetish is prepared. This is a spear with roots of a sweet herb tied round the blade. Wood splinters are then tied to it in such a way that they form a little cage, and in this are placed a bit of human skin, bits of the claws of a lion or leopard, food, beer, and magical roots. A cloth is sewn over the cage, and when the king has spit on it and blessed it, the spear is ready to be carried before the caravan. The human skin gives power, the claws of the animals protect from claws, the food and beer secure a supply of meat and drink, and the roots and the king's spittle give health to the party.[1] Success in trade is obtained by mixing with water the brains of a dead man who was wise, and rubbing the mixture on the face; brains mixed with oil are also rubbed on the hands. Another trade medicine is made by putting into an antelope's horn the ashes of the skin of a flying fox, the leaves of the kota tree, the nail from a human finger, the tip of the tongue, menstrual fluid, red-wood powder, and the tail feathers of the kilinga bird. The mouth of the horn is closed with gum, but the feathers are allowed to project through the gum. When about to trade the owner of the horn secretly pulls out a feather, and rubs a little of the liquid from the horn on the tip of his nose.[2] The native merchant who is in a hurry to get rich sometimes employs the Okundu medicine, which is of a very terrible character. The merchant or his witch-doctor

[1] *Ibid.*, p. 174.
[2] *Ibid.*, p. 180.

kills someone in order that his spirit may be set free to go and use its influence on the merchant's behalf with the white men with whom he is about to trade.[1]

Modern Africans of all kinds, like the ancient Egyptians, firmly believed that every sickness and disease were caused by some evil spirit, either as a punishment for some neglect or insult to it on the part of the stricken man, or as the result of the machinations of some witch-doctor. Dr. Nassau distinguishes three kinds of disease-causing spirits, viz., the Nikinda, Ombwiri, and Olâgâ. The first are supposed to be the spirits of the dead who were undistinguished when living, the second the spirits of kings, chiefs, nobles, etc., and the third the spirits who had been raised to the rank of angels in the Spirit-world. In treating the diseases supposed to be caused by these spirits the medicine-man tries to find out from the patient which kind of spirit it is who is vexing him, and when he has satisfied himself on this point he proceeds to concoct medicine from the herbs and roots which are suitable. The three classes of spirits mentioned above are probably the equivalents of the three classes of beings mentioned in the Egyptian texts, viz., the *ḥenmemet*, *pāt*, and *rekhit*.[2] These, apparently, all lived in heaven, but whether the Egyptian associated them with causation of disease cannot be said.

The making of love-philtres is a very common occupation of the witch-doctor, to whom both men and women apply for means whereby they may enjoy the love of some particular person. Many men and women make their own love-philtres, and the essential in most of them is some portion of the body of the woman or man, from which when mixed with herbs a decoction is made, to be administered in some form or other to the person whose love is wished for.[3] Sir Harry Johnston has given us a number of most interesting facts about the witch-doctor's methods in various parts of Africa. The Baluba magicians say they can make themselves invisible by means of certain charms, and once invisible they indulge

[1] *Ibid.*, p. 181.

[2] 

[3] For full descriptions see Nassau, *Fetichism*, p. 184 ff.

in horrible "ghoulish practices or in disgusting immoralities." The magician fills the body of the large Goliath beetle, or a small horn, with small human knuckle-bones, and scrapings of red camwood. He puts this in his mouth and becomes invisible. He then fills a Tragelaphus horn with magic ingredients, and encloses this in the very long pod of the Kigelia tree. He covers the beetle or small horn with charcoal paste, as he utters his spell, and then ties the pod up in cloth. He then buries the magic horn in a hole dug in front of the door of the man whom he wants to bewitch, fills the hole up, and covers it with twigs. Immediately the inmate of the house on going out touches one of the twigs, his leg contracts, his sinews shrivel, and he falls back dying on his mat. Or the magician takes straws from the house and path of the victim, and throws them into his supply of water; as the water evaporates the victim pines away. Or he takes grass from under the tree which has often sheltered his victim, and binding it in small bundles hangs them up in his house; when these are dry his enemy is dead. Or he makes a wooden figure of his victim, cuts it in pieces, which he throws one by one into boiling water; when the last is thrown in the man is dead. The Baluba magician also asserts that he can steal a man's personality from him, and the natives are fully convinced that their souls can be stolen from them.[1] This belief was common among the ancient Egyptians, as we have already shown. Magicians in all parts of Africa profess to be able to drive out spirits from those possessed, and their operations are everywhere characterized by noise, dancing, singing, drumming, and feasting. The story of the casting out of an evil spirit from the daughter of the chief of Bekhten by the priests of Khensu proves that the ancient Egyptian priest pretended to possess the same powers as the modern African witch-doctor.

The wide-spread belief that almost every death is caused by witchcraft gives to the medicine-man or witch-doctor a power over his fellow creatures which is well-nigh absolute, for he can accuse any man he likes of causing the death of another, and the accused person is forthwith put to death, unless he is willing to undergo the "ordeal

[1] Johnston, *George Grenfell*, Vol. II, p. 660.

of the red-water." The "red-water" is a decoction of the inner bark of a large forest tree of the mimosa family; it is reddish in colour, and has an astringent taste, and analysis shows that it is both an astringent and a narcotic, and, when taken in large quantities, an emetic. The accused, with a cord of palm leaves only about his waist, sits near the pots containing the red-water, and all the people gather round about and form a circle. After his accusation has been pronounced, he makes a formal acknowledgment of all the evil deeds of his past life and, invoking the name of God three times, calls down His wrath upon himself if he is guilty of the crime laid to his charge. He then steps forward and drinks freely of the red-water; if it produces nausea in him, and causes him to vomit freely, he is at once declared innocent. If it produces vertigo, and he loses self-control, he is regarded as guilty, and the people fall upon him, kick him, buffet him, stone him, and finally drag him through bushes and over rocks until he is practically torn to pieces. The man who is declared innocent enjoys a higher position in society than he did before the ordeal, and a few days after, dressed in his finest clothes, he progresses with his friends in triumph through the village or town, and receives gifts from admirers and friends. He then arraigns his accusers before the chief men of the place, and they must either undergo the ordeal, or pay a fine. The natives believe that red-water itself possesses intelligence, and that it is capable of clear discrimination in all doubtful cases.[1] They think that when it enters the stomach it at once lays hold of the element of witchcraft, and destroys the life of the accused. The quantity of red-water which the accused is made to drink depends upon the popular feeling at the time; if he is "very bad man," the quantity of water alone is sufficient to kill him, to say nothing of the extract of bark in it. Sometimes the accused is allowed to go away after drinking the usual quantity, and then he, no doubt, takes an emetic, and soon becomes well. Or, owing to family influence,

[1] This is the Nkasa of Western Congo-land, Mwavi of Nyasa-land, Chifafa of Luba-land, Ibunu of the Bateke, Mbondi or Nkā of the Upper Congo, Mondenge of the lower Aruwimi, and Samba of the Lokele.—Johnston, *George Grenfell*, Vol. II, p. 689.

or friendship, the witch-doctor may make the decoction very weak, which is certain to produce nothing but nausea and vomiting.[1] Du Chaillu saw a decoction of Mbundu leaves administered, and "the poor drinker fell down dead, with blood gushing from his mouth, eyes, and nose, in five minutes after taking the dose."[2] Messrs. Joyce and Torday have proved that the poison of the ordeal is far more often made from the bark or roots of a *Strychnos* than from *Erythrophlaeum quineense* of Zambezia and Nyasa-land.[3] Many other ordeals are known and practised,[4] but the issue of each is practically in the hands of the witch-doctor.

In several parts of Africa sand plays a prominent part in magical ceremonies. In connection with this it may be noted that in the performance of the ancient Egyptian ceremony of Opening the Mouth, the statue of the deceased was placed upon a small mound of sand, with its face towards the South,[5] and that in the CXXXVIIth Chapter of the Book of the Dead, a wholly magical Chapter, the Kher ḥeb is ordered to say a formula over one of the mud bricks, beginning: "I am the collar (or, field) of sand, round the things which are hidden."[6] Junker relates that, when in Kordofân, he came across a native who divined the future by means of sand. The seer strewed sand smoothly on the ground, and then made various marks and finger impressions in the sand, from which he read his augury.[7] Mr. R. G. Anderson says that the Falatah of Kordofân still have recourse to sand-gazing, but that they use it for predicting the course, treatment, and issue of an illness,

[1] See the excellent account of the red-water ordeal in Wilson, *Western Africa*, p. 224, and the remarks on its terrible effects on the population of the country by Nassau, *Fetichism*, p. 224. See also Bentley, *Pioneering on the Congo*, Vol. I, p. 276; Winwood Reade, *Savage Africa*, p. 215 (1864 edit.); Leonard, *Lower Niger*, p. 480.

[2] *Adventures in Equatorial Africa*, p. 257.

[3] Quoted by Johnston, *George Grenfell*, Vol. II, p. 689.

[4] They are summarized by Johnston, *George Grenfell*, Vol. II, p. 692 f.

[5] 

[6] 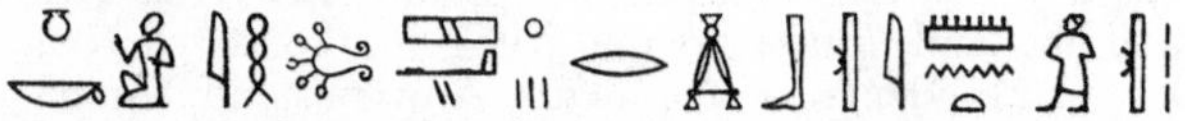

[7] *Travels in Africa*, Vol. III, p. 417.

the medium being a small boy who has never been bitten by a dog nor burnt in the fire. The boy gazes on the word "Allah" in the centre of a Khatim, or seal, traced in the sand, and under the controlling eye of a Fiḳi calls to the "King of the Devils," who, on his arrival, will answer any questions put regarding the sick, through the medium of the child, by this time sunk into a trance.[1] Among the Vai and Mandingo in Liberia, divination by means of sand is also practised. The sand is sifted through the fingers or sprinkled on the ground, and the magician draws his conclusions as to the future from the forms into which the sand falls. Sir Harry Johnston says that sand divination is practised throughout Muḥammadan Africa, from the Senegal to the Red Sea, and from Egypt to Nyasa.[2] In the oldest form of sand divination, the signs used were triangles and circles and lines with dots made inside and outside them in sand on the desert floor; from the combination of dots the magician made his augury. In the next form the sand was scattered by hand, and the augury was derived from the forms which it assumed. In the Graeco-Roman Period the triangles, circles, and lines were drawn on a board, and counters were made to take the place of the dots; in this form it passed into use among the Arabs among whom the Ḍarb-al-raml, or "striking of the sand," is a common means used in divining.[3] Burton saw an Arab "sand board" (*takht-*

[1] *Third Report of the Wellcome Research Laboratories*, 1908, p. 295.

[2] *Liberia*, Vol. II, p. 1064.

[3] In the *Golden Silence*, by C. N. and A. M. Williamson, London, 1910, we read that the lady Lella M'Barka always carried about with her the sand which she used in divining. It came from Tuggûrt, and was mixed with a little sand from Mekkah (p. 260). It would only yield up its secret in star-light (p. 266). It was tied up in green silk, lined with a very old Arab brocade, purple and gold, and was in quantity as much as could have been heaped on a soup plate. The heroine took a handful and held it over her heart, and framed a wish whilst it was there, and then sprinkled it over the rest. M'Barka trailed her fingers lightly over the sand until she had made three long wavy lines, the lower ones rather like telegraphic dots and dashes. The heroine then laid her forefinger on three of the figures in the lines, and after consulting a little old note-book M'Barka also measured spaces between the figures the girl had touched and counted monotonously. And having uttered her prophecy she then smoothed away the tracings in the sand (p. 273).

al-raml) in use in Dahomey, and says that it was 2 feet long, 8 inches broad, and that it had a dove-tail handle. On one side of it were sixteen primary figures, called "mothers," and on the other sixteen secondary figures, called "children"; each figure was in an oblong of cut and blackened lines, and at the top were circles, squares, etc. The counters were thrown on the board, and according to the positions in which they fell, so was the augury.[1] Whether the ancient Egyptians used sand in divining cannot be said, but there seems to be little doubt that they regarded it in the light of a substance which possessed magical qualities. They were probably well acquainted with the mighty masses of sand which move from north to south and from south to north in the Western Desert, ruthlessly burying whole villages in a few hours, and they, no doubt, believed that sand contained a spirit which had to be propitiated. At all events, it is impossible to think that they could have placed the statues of the dead, which were intended to become abodes of their Doubles (KAU), upon mounds of sand without some good traditional reason.

The power of the witch-doctor is exhibited to its fullest extent when he is called on to "smell out" the witch in a community in which a man of importance has died suddenly and without apparent reason. He is often fetched from a great distance, and when he has come and performed his magic, and has declared that such and such a man has witched out the life of the dead man, no earthly power can save the accused from a cruel death. Du Chaillu has vividly described the appearance of a witch-doctor who came to find out who had caused Ishungui's death, and he says that he never saw a more ghastly object. He had on a high head-dress of black feathers. His eyelids were painted red, and a red stripe from the nose upward divided his forehead into two parts. Another red stripe passed round his head. The face was painted white, and on each side of his mouth were two round red spots. About his neck hung a necklace of grass and also a cord, which held a box against his breast. This little

[1] See Burton, *Alf Laylah wa Laylah*, Vol. III, p. 269; Burton, *Mission to Gelele*, Vol. I, p. 332.

box is sacred and contains spirits. A number of strips of leopard and other skins crossed his breast, and were exposed about his person ; and all these were charmed and had charms attached to them. From each shoulder down to his hands was a white stripe, and one hand was painted quite white. To complete this horrible array, he wore a string of little bells around his body. He sat on a box or stool, before which stood another box containing charms. On this stood a looking-glass, beside which lay a buffalo-horn containing some black powder, and said, in addition, to be the refuge of many spirits. He had a little basket of snake-bones, which he shook frequently during his incantations ; as also several skins to which little bells were attached.[1] An official medicine-man seen by Mr. Torday had a tuft of blood-red feathers on his head, numerous skins about his loins, his body painted with white ochre, his hands holding three spears, a whisk made of an antelope's tail, an axe, and an executioner's knife.[2] Baertand Werner describes the dress of a "fetish man" of a Mongwandi village on the Dua-Ebola River thus : Two or three red loin-cloths woven of raphia palm-fibre encircle his thighs ; bells, feathers, and iron bracelets ornament his ankles and wrists ; a collar of white feathers surrounds his neck ; a score more large feathers of various colours are bound in the shape of a tail in his hair ; all his body is daubed red, his face painted white ; his hands shake little bells.[3] There is no proof that the Kher ḥeb magician of the ancient Egyptians ever arrayed himself in such apparel as that described above, but it is quite possible that the magic-doctors who worked magic for the lower classes of the people dressed themselves in a fantastic fashion in order to impress them with a sense of their supernatural powers, and to awe them. The bulk of the population of Egypt must always have been devout believers in magic, both black and white, and their belief, no doubt, found expression in the same way as the belief in magic of the modern peoples of the Sûdân.

[1] *Adventures in Equatorial Africa*, p. 241.
[2] Torday, in Johnston, *George Grenfell*, Vol. II, p. 661.
[3] *Ibid.*, p. 663.

CHAPTER XXII.

Fetishism.

Various writers on comparative religion have described the religion of the ancient Egyptians as "fetishism," and have regarded their gods as "fetishes." It seems, however, to me wholly wrong to call the propitiatory ceremonies which they performed before certain of their spirits, and the worship which they paid to certain sacred animals, and even the worship of figures of the gods, by the name of fetishism, for by so doing they use the word to describe forms of worship to which it cannot rightly be applied. Neither a spirit, nor an animal, nor a figure of a god, is a fetish, for, properly speaking, "a fetish is something tangible and inanimate, which is believed to possess power of itself."[1] The misuse of the word "fetish" practically begins with Bosman, who often uses it in his "Description of Guinea." In one place he says: "Fetiche, or Bossum in the Negro language, derives itself from their false God, which they call Bossum," and elsewhere he states that "all things made in honour of their false gods, never so mean, are called Fetiche." De Brosses, a later writer, called everything worshipped by the negroes of West Africa "fetishes," and their system of worship "fetishism," but, as Colonel Ellis has shown, he mixed up Animal Worship and Nature Worship with the worship of tangible and inanimate objects, and termed these three distinct forms of worship "fetishism." Both Bosman and De Brosses perpetuated a mistake made by the early Portuguese travellers to West Africa who visited that country between 1440 and 1500. At that time their native country was filled with relics of saints, charmed rosaries, images, crosses, etc., which were, in the majority of cases, regarded by their wearers as amulets or charms. Such articles were termed by the

[1] Ellis, *Tshi-speaking Peoples*, p. 178.

Portuguese *feitiços*, and a manufacturer or seller of them was termed a *feiticeiro*. When, therefore, the Portuguese found the natives reverencing or worshipping certain objects such as those tenanted by tutelary deities they naturally spoke of them as the *feitiços* of the natives. They had no other word commonly in use with which to describe charms, or that which they supposed the natives to regard as charms or amulets. The Portuguese only applied the term *feitiço* to tangible and inanimate objects, and to the wooden figures, stones, and cones of earth believed by the natives to be the abiding-places of indwelling gods, etc. They would never have called an iguana a *feitiço*, nor the local spirit of a hill or river, etc. Since, therefore, a *feitiço* is only, properly speaking, a tangible and inanimate object, fetishism can properly only mean the worship of such objects. The confusion which has resulted from the improper use of the term fetish is extreme, and is now probably irreparable. The natives never worshipped, and do not now worship, rocks or rivers, but the gods who dwell in them ; and rocks, rivers, trees, etc., are only reverenced as the abiding-places of gods. True fetishism, *i.e.*, the worship of tangible and inanimate objects, as Colonel Ellis rightly says, is not characteristic of primitive peoples, or of races low in the scale of civilization. It is only arrived at after considerable progress has been made in religious ideas, and when the older form of religion becomes secondary. It owes its existence to the confusion of the tangible with the intangible, of the material with the immaterial ; and to the belief in the indwelling god being gradually lost sight of, until the power, originally believed to belong to the god, is finally attributed to the tangible and inanimate object itself.[1]

According to Major A. G. Leonard fetishism and idolatry are the two chief branches of the main channel of ancestral worship which forms the foundation of naturism.[2] The spirit or deity symbolized in any object, be it tree, stone, animal, etc., is in every case the

[1] Ellis, *op. cit.*, p. 190. And compare Nassau, *Fetichism*, p. 75 ; Wilson, *Western Africa*, p. 211 ff., and Frobenius, *The Childhood of Man*, p. 182.

[2] *The Lower Niger*, p. 114.

personification of the ancestor.[1] In the Delta of the Niger fetishes and idols are merely religious adjuncts that have grown out of the one main ancestral idea.[2] Material forms are considered by the native to be essential for all ancestral spirits whose services are utilized or whose memories revered. These, to them, constitute the great and radical difference between those spirits from whom human treatment may be expected, and the malignant demons who wander about formless, always ready to perpetrate evil and evil only. It is in the act and purpose of this materialisation, in other words, of this emblemism of spirits, which we speak of as fetishism and idolatry, that much misconstruction has been placed, principally by missionaries and travellers, who, although their own Christian religion has been evolved from the same identical germ, and on somewhat similar lines, have been the greatest offenders in this respect. Emblemism is merely an external formula of an inner cult of worship.[3]

Turning now to the ancient Egyptian religion, it may be asked, Was there fetishism in it? and if so, To what extent? If we compare the worship or reverence paid by the Egyptians to the spirits of certain trees, or to the spirit of the Nile, or to the spirits of the gods, with the worship of spirits of like character by modern African peoples, we find its theory and practice to be identical. The Egyptians worshipped their ancestors, whose spirits they located in statues and figures, and Nature-spirits of all kinds, and spirits of gods, who when it pleased them took up their abode in symbolic figures, in living animals, and in totems, living or dead, but from first to last there is no evidence whatsoever that they worshipped a figure or symbol, whether made of metal, wood, stone, porcelain, or any other substance, unless they believed it to be the abode of a spirit of some kind. So far from fetishism being peculiarly characteristic of the Egyptian religion, it seems to me that this religion, at all events in its oldest form, was remarkably free from it. There is plenty of evidence that the Egyptian of the Middle and

[1] *Ibid.*, p. 115.
[2] *Ibid.*, p. 116.
[3] *Ibid.*, p. 278.

New Kingdoms did not know what many of the sacred emblems or symbols represented, a fact which is clearly proved by the way in which they drew them on papyri, or fashioned them in various substances.

Thus in the case of the symbol ☥ *ānkh,* which certainly means "life," the Egyptians do not appear to have known what object the picture represented, and no modern Egyptologist has satisfactorily identified it. Again, the Egyptians associated the so-called "Buckle" of Isis, 𓎬, with the blood and magical words of power of that goddess, and they believed that the object would protect the wearer against evil,[1] but there is no evidence that they knew in late times what object it symbolized. The suggestion that the picture represents a buckle or belt has nothing to recommend it, and it is far more likely that 𓎬 is a conventional representation of some member of the body of the goddess than anything else.[2] Of the ṭeṭ, 𓊽, which is the symbol of Osiris, or his emblem, more is known. The text of the CLVth Chapter of the Book of the Dead associates it with the backbone, , and vertebrae, , of the god, and it is clear that 𓊽 is a conventional representation of a part of his spinal column. The oldest form of this part was probably represented by the symbol 𓄦, which seems to represent a part of the back with portions of the ribs attached to it. As time went on the funerary artist drew a stand with a broadened base under it, and made the ribs straight, and at length the form 𓊽 came into being. It is possible that when the Egyptians had forgotten what objects these three pictures, ☥, 𓎬, and 𓊽, symbolized, and only remembered that the first gave

[1] Book of the Dead, Chapter CLVI.
[2] See above, p. 276 (Vol. I).

life, and the second the virtue of the blood of Isis, and the third the stability of the backbone of Osiris, the god who rose from the dead, the lower classes and the ignorant came to regard them as fetishes in the true sense of the word; but this is not by any means certain. There is no evidence that the Egyptians ever forgot that figures of gods and sacred animals and pictures, and amulets of all kinds, were the permanent or temporary abiding-places of spirits, who, if cherished, would be kind and helpful to them, and who, if slighted or neglected, would do them harm. The 𓊽 and the 𓎬 certainly represent the ancestral idea which seems to me to have been the root of the cult of Osiris, for, as we have seen, the former symbolizes a part of the body of Osiris, himself the great ancestor-god, and the latter is connected with the womb, that is to say, the very life of Isis, the great ancestress-goddess.

Many of the amulets are connected with the bodies of the father-gods, or with incidents in their lives, to reproduce which was always beneficial to the dead, and sometimes to the living also. There was, no doubt, among the Egyptians a class of men who were conscious or unconscious impostors, and who supplied them with charms, or amulets, or objects which were supposed to contain powers derived from familiar spirits over which such men claimed to have absolute or special control. Even in such cases the alleged powers must have been assumed to be of a spiritual character, for neither buyer nor seller would be foolish enough to imagine that a piece of carnelian, or a bit of porcelain, or a wooden figure, would, of and by itself, bring protection to the wearer. It was to the interest of both that the amulet or charm should contain a Spirit-power, for without the spirit they were "dead" things. The natives all over the Sûdân and in West Africa will sell the traveller dead fetishes and amulets, but they will not willingly part with those in which they think the spirits still live. Amulets and charms which were inherited from parents or relatives might, of course, easily become fetishes, just as they do in Africa at the present day, in which case the possessors worshipped them for themselves alone. On the other hand, the present possessor might think that the Spirit-power which was in them when they were in the hands of former possessors was increased by the addition to it of the Spirit-powers of such possessors, and if this were so he would regard them as very potent objects. Wherever we find fetishism it seems to be a corruption or modification of some former system of worship rather than the result of a primitive faith. The worship of the Sun-god Rā which was introduced into Egypt by the priests of Heliopolis was, no doubt, adopted by the upper classes of the Egyptians, but the masses never forsook their cult of the spirits who dwelt in ancestral figures, sacred animals, amulets, and totems living or dead. Similarly the cult of Åten, which was rejected even by the priesthood, made no impression on the Egyptians of the lower classes, and the only effect it could have upon them would be to make them cling closer to their belief in the great ancestor-god Osiris. In cases where their priests adopted the cult of the sun under any form, and therefore ceased to teach the doctrine of the in-dwelling spirit in ancestral figures, etc., the people might forget the doctrine, and their ancestral figures, amulets, etc., would then degenerate into fetishes.

All this is only theory so far as the Egyptians are concerned, but authorities on modern African religions tell us that this is exactly what has taken place among the peoples of West Africa. Thus Colonel Ellis says that there is more fetishism among the negroes of the West Indies, who have been Christianized for more than half a century, than amongst those of West Africa; for side by side with the new religion have lingered the old superstitions, whose true import has become forgotten or corrupted. Hence the belief in Obeah, still prevalent in the West Indies, which formerly was a belief in in-dwelling spirits which inhabited certain objects, has now become a reverence or worship paid to tangible and inanimate objects, which of themselves are believed to possess the power to injure.[1] Dr. Nassau says that the West African accepted baptism as a powerful charm. For each and all of his heathen fetishes the Christian

[1] Ellis, *Tshi-speaking Peoples*, p. 193.

priest simply substituted a relic. The ignorant African, while he learned to bow to the Virgin, kept on worshipping also a fetish. The Virgin was only just another fetish, and Christian priests only another set of powerful fetish-doctors. The heathen in becoming a baptized "Christian" left behind him only the names of his fetish ceremonies. Some new and professedly more powerful ones were given him, which were called by Christian names, but which very much resembled what he had been using all his life. His "conversion" caused no jar to his old beliefs, nor change in its practice, except that the new fetish was worshipped in a cathedral, and before a bedizened altar.[1]

[1] *Fetichism in West Africa*, p. 212.

CHAPTER XXIII.

Spitting as a Religious Act.

The ancient Egyptian texts contain many allusions to spitting, and whether employed in blessing or banning it was certainly regarded as a religious act of no small significance. Under certain circumstances it was considered to be a creative act. Thus when, according to a legend which is as old at least as the Pyramids, the god Tem had had union with himself he spat, and his spittle was the gods Shu and Tefnut; he then placed his arms round them, and his Ka, or Double, entered into them.[1] This legend is repeated in the Papyrus of Nesi-Åmsu,[2] and, no doubt, was accepted in the Ptolemaïc and Roman periods. In the XVIIth Chapter of the Book of the Dead we read that the Eye of Rā, *i.e.*, the Sun, was seriously injured by a violent assault made upon it by Set, but Thoth came forward, and, having spit upon the Eye, the trouble disappeared, and the Eye soon recovered.[3] In this case spitting was used as a curative act. From a book of magic we learn that spitting was sometimes made an act of cursing. Thus in the Book of Overthrowing Āpep we have a Chapter entitled "Of spitting upon Āpep," and its opening words are: "Be spit upon, Āpep," which are to be said four times. When the wax figure of Āpep was cast into the fire the priest spat upon it as it burned, and then trampled upon it with his left foot. On another occasion the priest said: "Look thou, Rā, hear

1  Pepi II, l. 663.

2 See Budge, *Egyptian Hieratic Papyri*, p. XIV.

3 , l. 74.

"thou, Rā, verily I have destroyed thine enemy, I have "trampled upon him, I have spit upon him." The case in which the wax figure was sometimes burnt was, according to the Rubric, "to be stamped on with the "left foot, and spit upon four times in the course of every "day." In this case spitting is an act of banning. The following illustrates the use of spitting as a curative act. In Kordofân the operator kneels over the outstretched patient, and after making a silent prayer he reads aloud the opening Surah of the Ḳur'ân, and then spits over the body three times; having said Amîn (Amen) he rises to his feet. Descendants of the Prophet possess the powers of curing by spitting, but holy men in general have them. And any human spittle is supposed to contain curative properties. Sometimes the saliva is mixed with sand and is applied to the nostrils, eyes, and forehead of the sufferer, and at other times it is mixed with water and carried to the bed-ridden as a remedy. Roots are often chewed to a pulp in the mouth and then applied to the nostrils.[1] Spitting has many significations in the Sûdân generally, and the universality of the custom is proved by the following remarks of travellers.

Schweinfurth says that spitting betokens the most affectionate goodwill. Among the Dyûr it was a pledge of attachment, an oath of fidelity; it was to their mind the proper way of giving solemnity to a league of friendship.[2] The chief of the Jangaes gave Petherick a goat, requesting that he would spit in the hand of his son, expressing a belief that if he did so his son would be enabled to throw a spear with power. Petherick cordially did so amid the acclamations of the tribe, and the youth received the congratulations of all.[3] Among the Barotze relatives take leave of each other with elaborate ceremony. They spit upon each other's faces and hands, or, rather, pretend to do so, for they do not actually emit saliva. They also pick up blades of grass, spit upon them, and stick them about the beloved head. They also spit on the hands; all this is done to warn off evil spirits. Spittle also acts as a kind of *tabû*. When

[1] R. G. Anderson, *op. cit.*, p. 294.
[2] *Heart of Africa*, Vol. I, p. 205.
[3] *Travels in Central Africa*, Vol. I, p. 105.

they do not want a thing touched, they spit on straws, and stick them all about the object.[1] Among the Bantû when the priest introduces the newly born child to the ancestral spirits, he spits on it as he makes each petition on its behalf.[2] The Masai formerly attached much importance to the act of spitting, and among them and the tribes of the Nandi and Sûk to spit at a person is a very great compliment. When the Masai came to Sir Harry Johnston, each of them before extending his hand to him would spit on the palm. Before they entered his house they would spit to the north, east, south, and west. Every unknown object which they regarded with reverence, such as a train, they would spit at. Newly born children are spit on by every one who sees them.[3] The people of the Kytch tribe return thanks by holding your hand and *affecting* to spit upon it ; which operation they do not actually perform, as I have seen stated in works on the White Nile.[4] Before parting a ceremony had to be performed by Katchiba. His brother was to be our guide, and he was to receive power to control the elements as deputy-magician during the journey, lest we should be wetted by the storms, and the torrents should be so swollen as to be impassable. With great solemnity Katchiba broke a branch from a tree, upon the leaves of which he spat in several places. This branch, thus blessed with holy water, was laid upon the ground, and a fowl was dragged about it by the chief. Katchiba handed the branch to his brother, who received it with much dignity, in addition to a magic whistle of antelope's horn which he suspended from his neck. Every native had a whistle, with which he could attract or drive away rain at pleasure. No whistle was supposed to be effective unless it had been blessed by Katchiba.[5] One day Speke went out shooting, but though he fired at several animals he failed to kill any of them. All his men were surprised, and the

[1] Nassau, *Fetichism in West Africa*, p. 213; Decle, *Three Years*, p. 77.

[2] Johnston, *Uganda*, Vol. I, p. 587.

[3] *Ibid.*, p. 833.

[4] Baker, *Albert N'yanza*, p. 48.

[5] Baker, *Albert N'yanza*, p. 211.

villagers who were escorting him in the hope of getting flesh, were so much annoyed that they offered to cut his forefinger with a spear and spit on it for good luck.[1] When Rebmann was leaving a chief, he and the Wanika and Suahili were favoured with "dirty expectoration" by the natives as a sign of farewell, and then they were told to "go in peace."[2] When Miss Kingsley said farewell to a woman whom she visited, the old lady took her hand, turned it palm upwards, and spat upon it. She consulted Dr. Nassau on the subject, and he told her that the spitting was a by-product of the performance which consisted in blowing a blessing.[3]

Thomson says: Spitting has a very different signification with the Masai from that which prevails with us or with most other tribes. With them it expresses the greatest goodwill and the best of wishes. It takes the place of compliments of the season, and you had better spit upon a damsel than kiss her. You spit when you meet, and you do the same on leaving. You seal your bargain in a similar manner. The Masai flocked to me, and the more copiously I spat upon them, the greater was their delight . . . How could I, for instance, resist the upturned face of a young unmarried woman, as with her bright eyes she would look the wish she longed to utter. And what better reward could I have than the delighted glance of the nut-brown maid when I expectorated upon the little snub nose so eagerly and piquantly presented?[4] Among the works of the European travellers to Africa in the seventeenth century which mention spitting may be noticed Claude Jannequin's *Voyage to Lybia in* 1697, p. 33.

The Wearing of Tails by Men and Women.

Everyone who has examined the bas-reliefs in Egyptian temples, and the coloured vignettes in papyri containing copies of the Book of the Dead, cannot have failed to notice that gods and kings are often repre-

[1] *Journal of the Discovery*, p. 462.
[2] Krapf, *Travels*, p. 262.
[3] *Travels in West Africa*, p. 288.
[4] *Through Masai Land*, p. 290.

sented wearing very long tails, with an elongated tuft at the end. And if we look at the statues of kings we shall find that in many of them also the tail is represented, especially in seated statues. In the case of the seated statues of Ȧmen-ḥetep III in the British Museum,[1] the tails are supposed to have been brought under the body, and parts of them, with the tufts, will be seen sculptured on the flat surfaces between the legs. In reliefs the tail is attached to the girdle and tunic, or loin-cloth, of which it probably, at one time, formed part. In primitive times gods, kings, and magic-doctors, all over the Sûdân and in other parts of Africa, wore the skins of animals when they were performing solemn ceremonies, and the tails of such skins hung down behind them; the tail in the Egyptian bas-relief and in the vignette is a survival of this ancient skin dress. The god Thoth was incarnate in the ibis, and Horus in the hawk, yet the Egyptians saw nothing unusual in representing the former as an ibis-headed man wearing a long tail, and the latter as a hawk-headed man wearing a long tail.[2] Animal gods, *e.g.*, the Jackal-god Anubis, when represented with a human body, are also given tails. The custom of wearing a tail has passed down the ages from the primitive to the modern African peoples, who, as will be seen from the following extracts, attach considerable importance to it.

The Bongo men and women wear girdles, the former adding a strip of stuff which they fasten to the girdle, allowing the ends to fall down before and behind. The latter attach to the girdle a supple bough with plenty of leaves, and perhaps a bunch of grass. Now and then a tail, like a black horse-tail, composed of the bast of the Sanseviera, is appended to the back of the girdle.[3] The usual costume of the Niam-Niam is formed of skins which are fastened to the girdle and form a picturesque drapery about the loins. The finest and most variegated skins are chosen for this purpose, those of the genet and colobus being held in the highest estimation; the long black tail of the quereza monkey is also

[1] Nos. 412, 413.
[2] See the Judgment Scene in the Papyrus of Ani.
[3] Schweinfurth, *Heart of Africa*, Vol. I, p. 294.

fastened to the dress.[1] Escaryac de Lanture was told of the existence of Lake Koeidabo, to the west of which lived the Mala-gilageh, or men with tails ; they were of small stature and reddish complexions, and covered with long hair.[2] The dress of the Moro women is of the scantiest description, and consists of a plaited wisp of straw of the strictest economical dimensions, and is drawn up between the legs and attached to a slender waist-belt. This also sustains at the back a bunch of green leaves, about the size and shape of the tail of an ostrich, which gives the wearer a jaunty appearance.[3] The men of Uregga wear skins of civet and monkeys, with the tails hanging downwards.[4] Among the Bantu negroes both sexes usually wear a waist-belt of beads, and the married women who have borne children wear a lower string of beads, to which is attached a tiny little apron of leather embroidered with beads, and also a long tail made of strings of fibre derived from a marsh plant. The tiny apron in front is sometimes made of short strings of the same fibre, instead of being a piece of leather sewn with beads. Very great importance is attached to this tiny square of fibre or beadwork, and to the tail behind. If a man of the same tribe should touch this, the only covering worn by a married woman, a great offence has been committed, even if the man be the woman's husband. Unless the sacrifice of a goat is made it is thought that the woman will die of the insult. If, however, these coverings are touched or torn off by an enemy or a stranger no harm is done.[5] Among the Nilotic negroes, when a woman is married she puts on a tail of strings. After marriage it is considered very bad manners for a woman to serve food to her husband without putting on this tail. On the other hand, if the husband or any other man should touch the married woman's tail, it is considered that he wishes to bewitch her, and such an offence must be atoned for by

[1] *Ibid.*, Vol. II, p. 6.

[2] *Ibid.*, Vol. II, p. 137 ; see also Frobenius, *Die Heiden-Neger* p. 385.

[3] Petherick, *Travels in Central Africa*, p. 277.

[4] Frobenius, *Die Heiden-Neger*, p. 146.

[5] Johnston, *Uganda*, Vol. II, p. 728.

the usual sacrifice of a goat.[1] As a sign of mourning a black tail, fringed with white strings, is worn for about a month.[2] The women of the Shîr and Kytch tribes wear small lappets of tanned leather as broad as the hand. At the back of the belt, which supports this apron, is a tail which reaches to the lower portions of the thighs. This tail is formed of finely cut strips of leather, and the costume has doubtless been the foundation for the report I had received from the Arabs that "a tribe in Central Africa had tails like horses."[3] The Bari women wear a neat little lappet, about six inches long, of beads, or of small iron rings worked like a coat of mail, in lieu of a fig-leaf, and the usual tail of fine shreds of leather or twine, spun from indigenous cotton, pendent behind. Both the lappet and tail are fastened on a belt which is worn round the loins, like those of the Shîr tribe; thus the toilette is completed at once.[4] The Latuka women wear exceedingly long tails, precisely like those of horses, but made of fine twine and rubbed with red ochre and grease.[5] The Yergum on the Niger told Mr. Boyd Alexander that the Gazum people have tails about six inches long, for which they have to dig a hole in the ground when they sit down, a statement which he doubted.[6] The Wahele women who can afford it dress almost entirely in beads, wearing innumerable strings round their loins. Nothing else is worn in front, while behind it would be considered indecent to appear without a piece of hide ornamented with beads, and cut away so as to resemble a tail.[7] The Wakavirondo also make tails for themselves of grass or fibre.[8]

[1] *Ibid.*, p. 783.
[2] *Ibid.*, p. 793.
[3] Baker, *Albert N'yanza*, p. 54.
[4] *Ibid.*, p. 59.
[5] *Ibid.*, p. 135.
[6] *From the Niger to the Nile*, p. 78.
[7] J. Thomson, *To the Central African Lakes*, p. 218.
[8] Hattersley, *The Baganda at Home*, p. 144.

CHAPTER XXIV.

MISCELLANEOUS.

1. Illness Caused by an Offended Deity.

It has already been shown that the Egyptians believed that sicknesses were caused by spirits, good or bad, and that the modern Africans hold a similar belief. The sickness may be a punishment inflicted on a human being by an offended or outraged deity, or may be caused by a minor evil spirit who has been induced to cause it by the operations of a magician, or witch-doctor. As an example of the belief that a sickness was caused by the anger of a deity may be quoted the following :—A stele at Turin[1] which was made for one Nefer-Åābu bears a text in which the deceased confesses the sins which he committed against the goddess Mer-seḳert,[2] who was called Ṭeheni-Åmenti,[3] the "Forehead of Åmenti," and whose shrine was situated near the Ramesseum at Thebes "Whilst "I was on earth," he says, "I was an ignorant and a "senseless man, knowing neither good nor bad, and I "transgressed against Ṭeheni. And she corrected me, "and I was in her hand both by night and by day, and "I sat upon the tiles like a woman who is with child. I "cried out for air (or, breath) but none came to me, for "I was fast bound by Ṭeheni-Åmentet, the strongest of "all the gods, the goddess of the city. Behold, I say to "everyone, great and small, among the officials, Take "good heed to Ṭeheni, for there is a lion inside her, "and it smiteth like a savage lion, and she pursueth "whosoever sinneth against her. Then I cried out to "my Lady, and she came to me in the form of sweet air, "she made peace with me, and she made me to perceive "her hand, she came back to me with feelings of peace,

[1] No. 102. Published by Lanzone, *Dizionario*, Plate CXXV; and see Maspero, *Bibl. Égyptol.*, tom. II, p. 405.

[2] 

[3] 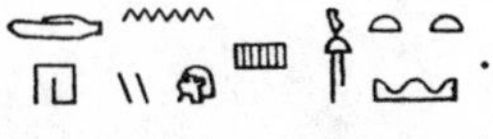

" she made me to forget my suffering, and I had air to " breathe. Now Ṭeheni-Åmentet maketh peace with " him that crieth out to her, and Nefer-åābu saith : " Behold, listen, O all ye ears which are upon the earth " —take good heed to Ṭeheni-Åmentet." The stele on which this text is found was, no doubt, set up by a man who, when suffering from bronchitis or asthma, or both together, went to the shrine of the goddess, and, confessing his sins, implored her forgiveness and help. The goddess answered him graciously, and came to him in the form of air, *i.e.*, she gave him power to breathe easily, and in grateful remembrance of her help, he had an account of his cure written and set up near her shrine for all to see.

2. Illness Caused by the Spirit of a Dead Wife.

A papyrus at Leyden, published by Maspero,[1] supplies some very interesting information on the causation of sickness by spirits. This document contains a copy of a letter which was written by a widower to the spirit of his deceased wife, and placed by him on a sepulchral figure. In it he says : " What harm did I ever do to " thee that I should come to the terrible plight I am in ? " What harm have I done to thee that thou shouldst lay " thine hand upon me, seeing that no evil hath been done " to thee ? From the time when we were married have " I ever hidden anything from thee ? Thou didst " become my wife when I was a young man, and I have " lived with thee ever since. Though I was promoted " to dignities of all kinds I still lived with thee, and I " never left thee, nor did I cause thy heart any pain. " When I was set over the soldiers of Pharaoh and the " men who followed his chariot, did I not cause thee to " come so that they might do homage to thee, and did " not they give thee beautiful gifts of all kinds ? When " thou wast ill I went to the chief physician, and he did " for thee everything which thou saidst he ought to do. " When I went with Pharaoh to the Sûdân I was " thinking the whole time of thee, and I passed the eight " months which the expedition lasted without desire to

[1] *Études Égypt.*, tom. I, p. 145 ff.

"eat or to drink because of thee. When I came back "to Memphis I asked leave of Pharaoh, and I returned "at once to thee, and I and my people mourned for thee "before my house. I made funerary apparel for thee, and "linen swathings, and provided an abundant supply of "offerings." The concluding words of this extraordinary document are obscure, and it is impossible to say what their meaning is. The sheet of papyrus on which this letter was written was rolled up and attached to a sepulchral figure, not of the wife to whom it is addressed—she was called Ānkh-ȧri[1]—but of another woman. This fact is difficult to explain, and it has been supposed that the letter was attached to the wrong figure by mistake. Another explanation is possible. The figure to which it was fastened may have been that of a woman who died some time after Ānkh-ȧri, and the widower may have attached it to her figure with the view of getting the spirit of this woman to convey its contents to the spirit of his dead wife in the Other World. The text says nothing about the reason why the letter was written, but it seems quite clear that the widower, finding himself sick and depressed, consulted a magician, who told him that his illness was caused by the spirit of his dead wife. Towards the close of his letter the widower seems to say that he did not enter his house for three years, and we may assume that, having waited all this time for peace, he at last consulted a magician, and made his appeal to his dead wife's spirit. Further, the magician may have promised him to cause the contents of the letter to reach the Other World without fail.

3. Marriage.

Of the betrothal and wedding ceremonies of the ancient Egyptians nothing is known, but it is most probable that they resembled those which are common among Africans at the present day.[2] Social formalities

[1] 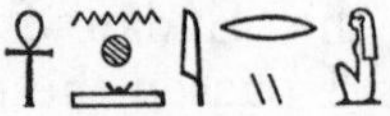.

[2] See Johnston, *George Grenfell*, Vol. II, p. 674 ff.; Bentley, *Pioneering on the Congo*, Vol. II, p. 44; Johnston, *Uganda*, Vol. II, pp. 609, 687, 747, 790, 822, 878; Hollis, *Masai*, pp. 121, 129, 170,

made the marriage legal, and it is unlikely that there was any religious ceremony. Under the New Empire women of high degree took care to have suitable provision made for them before they married, and carefully worded legal contracts safeguarding their interests were drawn up and executed. Apparently any man might marry any woman, for there seems to have been neither family nor tribal totem *tabû*, at least in the Dynastic Period. Polygamy was very common. Among the upper classes a man frequently married more than one wife for purely official and social reasons, which were often connected with property of various kinds, and the inscriptions mention a few cases in which two wives rule in a man's house at the same time. Kings, of course, married several wives for political and State reasons, and they and their nobles usually kept large *harîms*. Among the lower classes in the great towns sexual morality was not of a high order, and men frequently lived with women who were not their wives. Then, as now, they entered into "temporary marriages, and as often as not they called the women who lived with them their "sisters." In all classes men sometimes married their actual sisters, and they appear to have done so in order to keep property in the family. This kind of incest was authorized by the cult of Osiris, for according to the legend the two brothers Osiris and Set married their sisters Isis and Nephthys. Another legend quoted by Plutarch makes Osiris to have union also with Nephthys, the result of this intercourse being Anubis. The Ptolemies adopted the custom of sister-marriage, though the Greeks in general abhorred it. Among modern African peoples marriage between brother and sister is practically unknown. In West Africa marriage within any degree of consanguinity is forbidden, and marriage of cousins is impossible ;[1] in modern Egypt the marriage of cousins is regarded as a fitting arrangement, and all parties are satisfied. The religious texts show that the spirits of the Other World

201, 238, 299, 302, 309, 331 ; Hollis, *Nandi*, p. 60 ff. ; Kingsley, *Travels in West Africa*, p. 225 ; Decle, *Three Years*, pp. 78, 158, 233, 294, 346, 430, 445, 490 ; and especially Nassau, *Fetichism*, p. 4.

[1] Nassau, *Fetichism*, p. 8.

rejoiced in marriage, though there is no mention made of spirit offspring. Thus in the text of Unȧs (Vth dynasty) we read of the king marrying a young and beautiful woman in the kingdom of Osiris,[1] and also the goddess Isis,[2] and he carries off women from their husbands whenever he pleases, and makes them his wives[3] in any place he pleases.

Adultery was as common in Egypt as it is at the present time in many parts of Africa, and was sometimes punished by death. Thus in the Westcar Papyrus we find that the adulterous wife of Āba-ȧner was, by royal command, burnt by the north wall of the palace, and her ashes thrown into the canal, or river, and the Tale of the Two Brothers says that after Ȧnpu had heard the true account of his wife's wickedness from his brother he went home and killed her, and threw her body to the dogs, or jackals.[4] Among modern African peoples adultery is punished by death, or mutilation, or a heavy fine. Prostitution was common, and among the ranks of courtesans were large numbers of married women whose husbands had left them, and who travelled up and down the country practising their profession. This is proved by a passage in the Maxims of Ani, wherein the young man is warned to guard himself against the woman from outside whose town is not known. The

1 , l. 182.

2 . Tetȧ, l. 277 = Pepi I, l. 30.

3 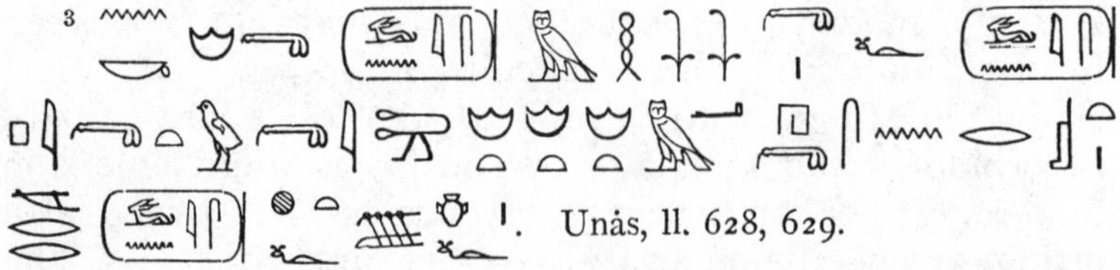. Unȧs, ll. 628, 629.

4  (VIII, 7).

5 .

writer also mentions the woman whose husband is far away from her,[1] and who writes every day to the man she has set her heart upon. If there is no one looking she stands up and spreads out her net. "Do not look "at her, do not follow her, have no commerce with her. "She is like a whirlpool in a current leading man "knoweth not where. To listen to her is an abominable "and deadly thing." The modern parallel to this is supplied by the Babangi women, who used to group themselves in little bands of courtesans, who plied their trade up and down the Congo between the Equatorial region and Stanley Pool.[2] The courtesan and concubine were such important members of ancient Egyptian society that even the pious Egyptian expected to meet his friends among these classes in the Other World. On a coffin at Cairo the deceased Sepȧ says: "Behold, "O great Creator, make Sepȧ to rejoin his sons and "daughters, and his concubines whom it is his heart's "desire [to meet]," and he hoped to find in heaven his grandparents, parents, sons, daughters, brethren, sisters, uncles, aunts, cousins, friends, servants, "and the concubine whom he loved and knew."[3] Among some African peoples, *e.g.*, the Busoga, seduction is heavily punished; curiously enough, among the Bantu Kavirondo marriage is consummated in the presence of a large number of girls and women.[4] The "chief wife," whether in palace or farm, was a great power, and she ruled the household as she pleased. The reverence paid to the mother was always very great, and under the Ancient and Middle Empires men invariably traced their descent from their mothers. On a funerary stele the name of the father of the deceased is rarely mentioned, but great care is taken to record that of the mother. It has been customary in Africa from time immemorial to trace descent through the mother rather than through the father, probably because there never can be any doubt as to a man's parentage on his

1 

2 Johnston, *George Grenfell*, Vol. II, p. 678.

3 *Recueil de Travaux*, 1904, pp. 67–72.

4 Johnston, *Uganda*, pp. 719, 747.

mother's side. Kinship was reckoned very far on the female side. Thus in the "Stele of the Enthronement"[1] the pedigree of the mother of Aspelta is reckoned for seven generations, while of his male ancestors only his father is mentioned. This is the case also among some modern African peoples, *e.g.*, the Bambala, who reckon kinship on the female side; on that of the male not beyond the uncle and grandfather.[2] In the Camma (Nkama) country also descent is traced from the mother.[3] The Maxims of Ani tell a man to make offerings to his father and mother when they rest in the tomb,[4] but he is most solemnly warned by them to be most careful how he treats his mother, who suckled him for three years,[5] and carried bread and beer to him every day when he was at school. The writer says: "Give thy mother no cause to be offended at thee, lest "she lift up her hands to the God, Who will hear her "complaint"[6] and will punish thee.

4. Respect for the Aged.

Respect for the aged was a characteristic of the Egyptian, and it is found among a large number of

1 Mariette, *Monuments Divers*, Plate 9.

2 Johnston, *George Grenfell*, Vol. II, p. 699.

3 Du Chaillu, *Adventures*, p. 251.

4 

5 See Winwood Reade, *Savage Africa*, p. 205. "The mother is "treated with great respect, and is exempt from all labour while she "continues to suckle her child, which she does as long as her milk lasts "—generally two or three years. During this time and also from the "moment that impregnation becomes apparent, the mother no longer "cohabits with her husband." Compare also Livingstone, *Last Journals*, p. 51, where he says that women have no intercourse with their husbands when *enceinte*, and for three years afterwards.

6 

modern African tribes at the present day. The Maxims of Ani say: "Sit not down when another is standing up if he be older than thou, even if thy rank in life be higher than his."[1] With this compare: Young men never enter the presence of an aged person without curtseying, and passing in a stooping attitude, as if they were going under a low door. When seated in his presence, it is always at a humble distance. If they hand him a lighted pipe or a mug of water, they fall on one knee. If an old man, they address him as *rera*, "father"; if an old woman, as *ngwe*, "mother."[2] The aged must only be addressed in terms of flattery and adulation. Any disrespectful deportment or reproachful language towards such persons is regarded as a misdemeanor of no ordinary kind. And there is nothing which a young person so much deprecates as the curse of an aged person, and especially that of a revered father. This profound respect for aged persons, by a very natural operation of the mind, is turned into idolatrous regard for them when dead. They are not divested of their power and influence by death, but, on the contrary, they are raised to a higher and more powerful sphere of influence, and hence the natural disposition of the living, and especially those related to them in any way in this world, to look to them and call upon them for aid in all the emergencies and trials of life.[3]

5. Purification After Birth.

Soon after a child was born among the ancient Egyptians, he or she was washed with water and, in the case of well-to-do people, was probably anointed with oil. The washing with water was, no doubt,

1 

2 Reade, *Savage Africa*, p. 208.

3 Wilson, *Western Africa*, p. 393.

originally a symbolic act, and was equivalent to the sprinkling with water which took place during the performance of religious and magical rites and ceremonies. The anointing oil was probably of a special kind, and must have been thought to possess peculiar properties, like the Seven Holy Oils used in the Opening of the Mouth. Whether the washing of the child with water was regarded in the same way as we regard baptism we do not know. Among many modern African tribes there remain traces of a ceremony resembling baptism, which may have been derived from the Jews or Christians of East Africa. Dr. Nassau found traces of the ceremony on Corisco Island about 46 years ago, and he says that it had been very prevalent in other parts of the Gabûn country before that time.[1] Mr. Wilson states that in Western Africa a public crier announces the birth of a child, and claims for it a name and place among the living. Someone else, in a distant part of the village, acknowledges the fact, and promises, on the part of the people, that the child shall be received into the community, and have all the rights and immunities pertaining to the rest of the people. The population then assemble in the street, and the babe is brought out and exposed to public view. Dr. Nassau gives a picture of the babe lying on a plantain leaf.[2] A basin of water is provided, and the headman of the village or family sprinkles water upon the child, giving it a name, and invoking a blessing upon it, such as, that it may have health, grow up in manhood or womanhood, a numerous progeny, possess much riches, etc.[3] Among the Banyoro the Muchwezi, or sorcerer, visits the newly born child, and as he prays that it may have long life, riches, and health, and may be a firm believer in the tribal and ancestral spirits, he spits on its body as he utters each petition, and pinches it all over.[4] The priest's saliva is, of course, sacred. Bishop Tucker found in Uganda a ceremony very like baptism; oil was poured on the

[1] *Fetichism*, p. 212.
[2] *Crowned in Palm-Land*, p. 102.
[3] Wilson, *Western Africa*, p. 399.
[4] Johnston, *Uganda*, Vol. II, p. 587.

child's head, and a name was given to it.[1] Among the Yorubas a remarkable ceremony of purification is performed over both mother and child seven days after its birth. The water which is always in the earthen vessels placed before the images of the gods is brought to the house and thrown upon the thatched roof, and as it drips down from the eaves the mother and child pass three times through the falling drops. The *babalawo* (priest) next makes a water of purification with which he bathes the child's head, and he repeats three times the name by which the infant is to be known, and then holds him in his arms so that his feet touch the ground.[2]

When in the Oasis of Khârgah in 1909, I was informed by the Omdah that the inhabitants, though Muslims, baptize their babies on the second or third day after birth. The child is placed in a flat basin (*tisht*) and water is poured over it, whilst a name is given to it. This custom dates from pre-Muslim times, when the dwellers in the Great Oasis were Christians, and they have preserved it along with several other customs, apparently of Christian origin. Thus they decorate the tops of the walls of their houses with palm branches once a year on a day which is equivalent to Palm Sunday, and for weeks before Easter they collect eggs, and save them and dye them pink with a decoction of permanganate of potash, and as "Easter eggs" they eat them on Easter Sunday.

6. Circumcision.

The mummified bodies of the ancient Egyptians which are available for examination prove that circumcision was general at all periods in Egypt. As, however, the texts say little or nothing about the ceremony itself, or its significance, we must assume that it had no religious importance, at least in Dynastic times, and that, if the earlier inhabitants of the Nile Valley ever regarded it as an act of worship, this view of it was ignored by their descendants or forgotten. Originally, circumcision must have had a religious significance, and there is little doubt

[1] *Eighteen Years in Uganda*, Vol. I, p. 85.
[2] Ellis, *Yoruba-speaking Peoples*, p. 153.

that the portion cut from the body of the boy was regarded as an offering which was made to one or other of the gods of virility or generation, just as it is to-day among many of the tribes of Africa. A representation of the performance of circumcision, probably the oldest known, is found on a relief in a tomb at Ṣaḳḳârah,[1] and it dates from the period of the VIth dynasty. The act is performed by a "priest of the KA,"[2] but whether this official was a member of the boy's family, or a professional priest, cannot be said. A god of circumcision appears to be mentioned in the text of Tetȧ (VIth dynasty), but in exactly what connection is not clear.[3]

According to the accounts of travellers circumcision is not universal in Africa at the present time. All the males of the Congo Pygmies seen by Sir Harry Johnston were circumcised,[4] and so were the Mbuta and Bantu-speaking negroes of the Congo Forest, from the Semliki Valley to the Upper Congo.[5] Among the Nandi youths are circumcised between the ages of ten and twenty, and only boys are so treated if they are fairly rich orphans, or if their fathers are old men. The commonest age is between fifteen and nineteen.[6] Among the Masai the age is between thirteen and seventeen, but orphans and the children of the poor wait till they are twenty.[7] Among the Lendu the age is seven or eight, and the part cut from the boy is carefully buried in the ground.[8] In some parts of West Africa the

[1] See Capart, *Une Rue de Tombeaux à Saqqarah*, and a notice of the work by Scott-Moncrieff in *P.S.B.A.*, Vol. XXX, pp. 34-36.

[2] 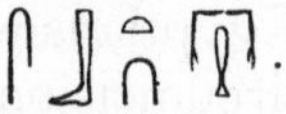.

[3] 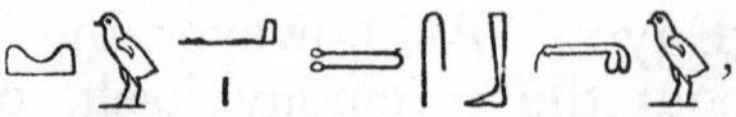, or 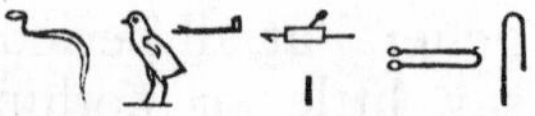 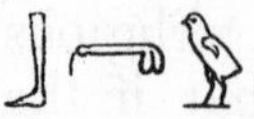 (l. 292). The root 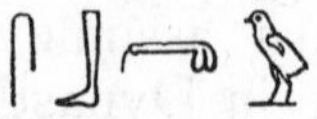 appears in Coptic under the forms ⲥⲃ̅ⲃ̅ⲉ, ⲥⲃ̅ⲏⲧ, ⲥⲉⲃⲏⲧ, ⲥⲉⲃⲓ, ⲥⲟⲩⲃ̅ⲉ.

[4] *Uganda*, Vol. II, p. 538.

[5] *Ibid.*, p. 556.

[6] Hollis, *Nandi*, p. 52 ff. The elaborate ceremonies performed by the Nandi, as described by Mr. Hollis, are full of interest, and merit careful study.

[7] Hollis, *Masai*, pp. 262, 296.

[8] Johnston, *Uganda*, Vol. II, p. 554.

operation is performed from two to twelve days after the child's birth, in others after a period of three or four months, and in others the rite is evaded. No Lunda man can become chief until he has been circumcised. Some of the tribes of forest negroes of the north-east borderland of the Congo basin,[1] and a few of the Mongo tribes, and the Bambala and Bahuana of the Kwilu-Kasai, and many of the wild negroes of the south and south-east, do not circumcise. The Kruboys of West Africa entirely repudiate the idea.[2] Among the Bongos circumcision is not practised, and a circumcised man cannot hope to make a good marriage.[3] The Basukuma do not circumcise,[4] but the Lendu do.[5] According to Stanley, some of the tribes of the great African forest circumcise, and others do not;[6] the forest embraces twelves degrees of longitude. The Wakamba, like most East African tribes, circumcise.[7] In Andrew Battell's day the people of Angola were circumcised.[8] The Waiyau used to circumcise their males, and after the performance of the ceremony boys took a new name.[9] The people of the Sherbro also gave their boys a name after circumcision.[10]

As to whether there is any religious or "fetishistic" idea connected with circumcision in the minds of the modern African opinions differ. Bentley thought there was not, but according to Mr. Torday some tribes in south-west Congoland attach a "distinct fetishistic importance" to the operation. Sir Harry Johnston also thinks that in some parts of Congoland "vestiges of

[1] As to the peoples of the Batwa information is not forthcoming. The names given to them are: Dongo, Matimba, Obongo, Bakka-Bakka, Kenkab, Betsan, Mala-Gilagah, Tikki-Tikki (by the A-Sandê), Akka (by the Mañbattû), Affifi (by the Mounfu), Wotsehua, Wambuttu, etc. —Frobenius, *Heiden-Neger*, p. 456.

[2] Johnston, *George Grenfell*, Vol. II, p. 576; *Liberia*, Vol. II, p. 978.

[3] Schweinfurth, *Heart of Africa*, Vol. I, p. 294.

[4] Cunningham, *Uganda*, p. 309.

[5] *Ibid.*, p. 326.

[6] *Darkest Africa*, Vol. II, p. 90.

[7] Krapf, *Researches and Missionary Travels*, p. 144.

[8] *Strange Adventures* (Hakluyt Society), p. 57. Livingstone says that the Bechuanah and Caffre tribes circumcise, but not the Negro tribes beyond 20 degrees south.—*Missionary Travels*, p. 146.

[9] Livingstone, *Last Journals*, Vol. I, p. 81.

[10] Alldridge, *Sherbro and Its Hinterland*, p. 125.

superstition or religion" are attached to it in the minds of the people.[1] He also thinks that the practice "arose in connection with religious belief somewhere in Egypt, Arabia, Syria, or the Mediterranean coast-lands, and gradually made its way south into Africa, assisted very considerably during the last thousand years by the spread of Muhammadanism."[2] It is, however, quite certain that circumcision was practised by the Blacks, or Negroes, in Predynastic times; this is proved by the green slate object in the British Museum,[3] on which is a representation of a fight between Egyptians and Blacks. The men who are vanquished have curly wool for hair, and are bearded and naked, and it is evident that they are circumcised. These enemies of the Egyptians, who are certainly Sûdânî folk, may have borrowed circumcision from Egypt, but if it is so, it is quite clear that the borrowing was very ancient, for it took place at least 6,000 years ago. Strabo says: "All the Troglodytes are circumcised, and the cripples among them are mutilated" (iii. 31). The general trend of the evidence suggests that circumcision was practised in the Sûdân, as well as in Egypt, from time immemorial, that it had nothing to do with considerations of health, that it had a religious significance, and that it was originally connected with some kind of phallic worship.[4]

In many parts of the Sûdân girls also are circumcised. According to Mr. R. G. Anderson the circumcision of girls is of two kinds. The first is called *Ṭahûrat Sunna*, *i.e.*, the "purification of the law," and the second *Ṭahûrat Farohîn*, *i.e.*, the "purification of the Pharaohs." In the first the clitoris and labia minora are removed; this kind is in vogue among Egyptian women, but in the Sûdân is mostly restricted to the Baḳḳârah tribes. In the second the upper two-thirds of the labia majora are

[1] *George Grenfell*, Vol. II, p. 576.

[2] *Ibid.*

[3] No. 20,790, Third Egyptian Room, Table-case L.

[4] An excellent description of the operation of circumcision as practised in Kordofân is given by Mr. R. G. Anderson in *Third Report of the Wellcome Research Laboratory*, p. 318, with good illustrations. The peculiar character of Masai circumcision is shortly stated by Johnston, *Uganda*, Vol. II, p. 804.

also removed; this kind of circumcision is believed to have been practised by the ancient Egyptians under the Pharaohs, and is thought to have survived despite the innovation of Muslim Law.[1] Strabo mentions the circumcision of girls (καὶ τὰ θήλεα ἐκτέμνειν), but he does not go into details. W. G. Browne, who was in the Sûdân between 1792 and 1800, supplies some interesting information in his narrative of his travels, and describes the operation and its effects.[2] The whole subject has been investigated with great care and learning by Dr. Ploss, who shows that the practice is common in Egypt, Nubia, Abyssinia, Sennaar, and the Sûdân, and among the Gallas, Agows, Gaffats, Gongos and many other peoples of East Africa. It is also found in the Little Oasis, where to be called the "son of an uncut woman" is a serious insult, and in West Africa, *e.g.*, in Sierra Leone, Benin, Congo-land, Accra, the Gold Coast, Old Calabar, Loando and in the lands of the Masai, Wakuasi, and Betchuanas. It is interesting to note that Dr. Ploss considers infibulation, which follows the operation in Africa, quite peculiar to Africa, for he says that outside North and Central Africa he has found it practised in no other country in the world.[3]

[1] *Third Report*, p. 320.

[2] "Mihi contigit nigram quandam puellam, qui hanc operationem "subierat, inspicere; labia pudendi acu et filo consuta mihi plana "detecta fuere, foramine angusto in meatum urinae relicto. Apud "Esne, Siout et Cairo, tonsores sunt, qui obstructionem novaculâ "amovent, sed vulnus haud raro lethale evenit" (p. 347). Of the operation necessary before marriage, he says: "Cicatrix, post excisionem "clitoridis, parietes ipsos vaginae, foramine parvo relicto, inter se "glutinat. Cum tempus nuptiarum adveniat, membranum, a quâ "vagina clauditur, coram pluribus pronubis inciditur, sponso ipso "adjuvante. Interdum evenit ut operationem efficere nequeant, sine "ope mulieris aliquae expertae, quae, scalpello partes in vaginâ "profundius rescindit. Maritus crastinâ die cum uxore plerumque "habitat; unde illa Araborum sententia, 'Lêlat ad-dukhla mithl lêlat "al-futûḥ, *i.e.*, post diem aperturae, dies initus. Ex hoc consuetudine "fit ut sponsus nunquam decipiatur, et ex hoc fit ut in Aegypto "Superiori innuptae repulsare lascivias hominum parum student, "dicentes, 'Tabûsni walâ takhurḳani,' sed quantum eis sit invita haec "continentia, post matrimoniam demonstrant libidine quam maxime "indulgentes" (p. 332).

[3] *Das Weib in der Natur- und Völkerkunde*, ed. Bartels, Seventh edition, Vol. I, p. 227 ff.

7. Twins.

It is well known that in several parts of the Sûdân the advent of twins is regarded as a calamity, and that they are promptly killed, and that in others twins are welcomed and are allowed to grow up like other children. The Egyptians had no hostile feelings to twins, for their gods and goddesses Osiris, Isis, Set, Nephthys and Horus were all children of one birth, and Osiris and Set were always regarded as twin brethren, and Isis and Nephthys as twin sisters. And the Egyptians were as tolerant of twins in daily life as they were in their mythology, as the following facts will show. In the reign of Ȧmen-ḥetep III the whole of the monuments and temple buildings on the west bank of the river at Thebes were under the direction of an eminent "Clerk of the Works," called Suti, and those on the east bank, including the royal residence, were under the direction of another eminent "Clerk of the Works," called Ḥeru. These facts we learn from the stele in the British Museum (No. 475) which was found at Thebes in a tomb that probably contained both their bodies. The principal text on the stele is a hymn to the Sun-god, and on the sides of this are given a few biographical details of the two men. After describing his love of truth and his hatred of falsehood, Ḥeru says that "his brother" was like himself in this respect, and that he "came forth from the belly with me."[1] Thus Ḥeru and Suti were brothers, and if the words quoted mean anything at all it is that they were twins. Here we have a proof that under the XVIIIth dynasty at least twins were not regarded as a calamity, and their names, Ḥeru and Suti, suggest that the gods Horus and Set were held to be the patron gods of male twins. We may now note the usages as to twins in other parts of Africa.

In one town of the kingdom of Benin, the name of which Miss Kingsley was unable to obtain, twins and their mother were sacrificed to a demon who lived in a

[1] . Birch, *Trans. Soc. Bibl. Arch.*, Vol. VIII, p. 157.

wood near the town. In Old Benin the law was mercilessly carried out in the case of the poorer class of natives, but wealthy people often bribed the Juju priests, and the twins were spared.[1] Women who bore twins or who died in child-birth were supposed to have committed adultery with spirits.[2] In Nguru, one of the sister provinces of Unyanyembe, twins are ordered to be killed and thrown into water the moment they are born, lest droughts and famines or floods should waste the land. Should any one attempt to conceal twins, the whole family would be murdered by the chief. In the province of Unyanyembe, if a twin or twins die, they are thrown into the water for the same reason as in Nguru. When a twin dies, the mother ties a little gourd to her neck as a proxy, and puts into it a trifle of everything which she gives the living child, lest the spirit of the dead twin should torment her. On the death of the child she smears herself with butter and ashes, and runs frantically about, tearing her hair and bewailing piteously. The men use the foulest language to her, as if in abuse of her person, but they do so merely to frighten away the demons who have taken the child. Speke was told of a Myoro woman who bore twins that died, and who kept two small pots in her house as effigies of the children, into which she milked herself every evening, lest the spirits of the dead should persecute her. The twins were placed in pots, which were taken to the jungle and placed by a tree, with the mouths downwards.[3] Among the Matabele twins are put to death,[4] but the Senga, Chinyai, Tuwala, and the Goa, *i.e.*, the principal native races of the Portuguese Zambesi, have large families, and do not kill twins.[5] Whilst Du Chaillu was in an Apingi village a woman gave birth to twins, and one of the children was immediately killed, the Negroes holding that if both twins are permitted to live the mother will die.[6] Twins are killed among all the Niger Delta tribes, and, in districts out of English control, the mother

[1] *West African Studies*, p. 455.
[2] *Ibid.*, p. 148.
[3] *Journal of the Discovery*, Dent's edition, pp. 425, 426.
[4] Decle, *Three Years*, p. 160.
[5] *Ibid.*, p. 231.
[6] *Strange Adventures*, p. 456.

too, except in Omon, where the sanctuary is. There mothers and their twins are exiled to an island in the Cross River. In some places the mother of twins is kept in a hut for a whole year after their birth. Then there is a great dance, and certain ceremonies take place, during which the mother and the doctor, not the husband, have their legs painted white. After this the woman returns to her ordinary avocations. When a twin dies a wooden image is made and placed near it so that the spirit of the dead twin may have some place to live in if it needs it. Elsewhere Miss Kingsley found that the mother of twins, if allowed to live, was regarded as a thing accursed, and an outcast. She had to live by herself in a hut, into which no one would enter, no one would eat or drink with her, or partake of the food or water which she had cooked or fetched. Remarriage and giving birth to a child acceptable to the natives were the only things which could rehabilitate her. The bodies of mothers of twins, and of women who have died in their confinement without the child being born, are cast far into the bush, and not near the path, where the bodies of the children are thrown in order that their souls may choose new mothers from the women who pass by.[1] In Old Calabar twins are buried alive.[2] Among the tribes of the Lower Niger a woman on giving birth to twins is not allowed to touch the cooking utensils.[3]

According to Major A. G. Leonard the destruction of twins is a purely religious custom, the origin of which is lost in antiquity. The birth of twins is regarded as an unnatural event, which is to be ascribed solely to the influence of malign spirits, acting in conjunction with the power of evil. It is an offence against the ancestral gods, and must be removed, together with the offending cause, the woman. It implies a spirit duality, or enforced possession by some intruding and malignant demon, in the yielding and offending person of a member of the household, consequently an outrage committed upon the domestic sanctity. The natural product of two human energies, as a single unit, is only

[1] Kingsley, *West African Studies*, pp. 472, 473.
[2] Hutchinson, *Ten Years' Wanderings among the Ethiopians*, p. 49.
[3] Leonard, *Lower Niger*, p. 311.

endowed, or provided, with one Soul-spirit. The Ibo and Brassmen always allow the first-born twin to live, and this custom is a practical admission of this view. In every home in the Delta the advent of twins causes terror, for it will provoke the anger of the gods and bring punishment. Twins are therefore thrown into the bush, or set adrift in rivers and creeks in roughly-made baskets of reeds and bulrushes, where they are drowned or devoured by sharks and crocodiles. The mothers are considered unclean for the rest of their lives, and are compelled to live in "Twin Towns."[1]

In Alladah and Whydah twins were regarded as a sure proof of the infidelity of the mother, as the people considered that no woman could have two children at once by one husband. The twins were thrown into the water, and the mother impaled and her breasts cut off.[2] Among the Nandi the birth of twins is looked upon as an inauspicious event, and the mother is considered unclean for the rest of her life. One of the twins is always called Simatua (a kind of fig tree) and the other receives the name of an animal.[3]

On the other hand, the Bantu and the Nilotic negroes consider the birth of twins to be a very lucky event; among the former people it is celebrated by an obscene dance, which, however, is only lewd in its traditional gestures.[4] Among the Masai, Turkana, Sūk, etc., the birth of twins is considered lucky, but, at the same time, to be rather a tempting of Providence. And the mother of twins must live away from her husband's village for some months, and on no account go near the kraal where the cattle are kept. One cow is reserved for her use, and she drinks its milk.[5] The Igarra in the Niger Delta hail the birth of twins with joy and acclamation, and it is thought to be brought about by good and not evil spirits. The twins are treated exactly alike, eat alike, dress alike, and are married on the same day. It is thought that twins

[1] *Ibid.*, p. 458.
[2] Skertchley, *Dahomey as It is*, p. 500.
[3] Hollis, *Nandi*, p. 68.
[4] Johnston, *Uganda*, Vol. II, pp. 748, 778.
[5] *Ibid.*, p. 878.

cannot be poisoned, and that whilst children they can declare the sex of an unborn child.[1] Up till 1874 twins were brought from Cape Coast to the wells of the god Kottor-krabah to be named by the two famous silk-cotton trees, called "N'ihna-attah."[2] In Garenganze the people delight in twins, and the fathers and mothers of twins used to bring their offspring and present them to the king. Men and women came wearing scant clothing, and the king made them presents of cloth. Among the Benga tribe if a twin died, a wooden image was substituted in the bed or cradle box for the dead twin; if both children die the mother must have two wooden images. In the Gabûn country special ceremonies must be performed for the safety of their lives, or, if they die, to prevent further evil. Among the Egba tribes of the Yoruba country they become objects of worship.[3]

An interesting fact in connection with twins is reported by Speke, who says:—To-day a tremendous commotion took place in Mûsa's tembê amongst all the women, as one had been delivered of still-born twins. They went about in procession, painted and adorned in the most grotesque fashion, bewailing and screeching, singing and dancing, throwing their arms and legs about as if they were drunk, until the evening set in, when they gathered a large bundle of bulrushes, and, covering it over with a cloth, carried it up to the door of the bereaved on their shoulders, as though it had been a coffin. Then, setting it down on the ground, they planted some of the rushes on either side of the entrance, and all kneeling together, set to bewailing, shrieking, and howling incessantly for hours together.[4]

8. Steatopygous Women.

The pictures of Egyptian women which are found on the walls of tombs, etc., prove that the majority of women in Egypt, at least of the upper classes, were slender in figure, with long arms, hands, legs, and feet. Among

[1] Leonard, *Lower Niger*, p. 462.
[2] Ellis, *Tshi-speaking Peoples*, p. 43.
[3] Nassau, *Fetichism*, pp. 205–208.
[4] Speke, *Journal*, p. 98, Dent's edition.

the dolls and portrait figures of women which have come down to us this type is well represented, but among them we also find figures of women, both tall[1] and short,[2] with abnormally developed hips and thighs. In one of the reliefs which formerly adorned the temple of Ḥātshepset at Dêr al-Baḥarî, and is now in the Egyptian Museum in Cairo,[5] the artist depicted the King of Punt, his queen, two sons, and a daughter. The figure of the queen, with its curved back, massive arms and legs, and huge hips, is very remarkable, and

The steatopygous Queen of Punt.
From a bas-relief in the temple of Ḥātshepsut at Dêr al-Baḥarî (now in the Egyptian Museum, Cairo).

that of the daughter suggests that when she grew older she would be like her mother. At one time this figure was thought by some to be a caricature of the queen drawn by an ill-natured Egyptian artist, but recent investigations have proved that, so far from this being the case, his representation of the queen is strikingly faithful, especially when we compare it with modern pictures of modern steatopygous women. All that can be said against it is that the curve of the back is, perhaps, unduly emphasized, but, even so, the

[1] See the dolls and portrait figures exhibited in the Fourth Egyptian Room in the British Museum.

[2] See the bone figure of a pygmy woman, No. 42, Table-Case L, in the Third Egyptian Room in the British Museum.

[3] See Maspero, *Guide to the Cairo Museum*, edit. 1910 (Room I, No. 309), p. 130.

conventional limitations imposed on the artist must be taken into account.

The reliefs in the pyramid-chapels at Shendî, or Shindî, represent funeral processions of women with extraordinary girth of body and development of hip, and the great "Candace" queens of Meroë are seen to be even larger. They resemble in many respects the queen of Punt, but they are taller, and their backs are straight. In and around Shendî at the present day many young women succeed in attaining great girth of body by drinking milk, in which a certain herb has been steeped, in large quantities daily, and the works of travellers contain many allusions to the great corpulency of African beauties in all parts of the Continent. Thus Ibn Baṭûṭah extols the beauty of the women of the Bardâmah, a Berber tribe, and says they were the whitest and stoutest women he had ever seen. They drink night and morning a mixture of milk and water and crushed millet, uncooked.[1] Mungo Park says that a woman of even moderate pretensions must be one who cannot walk without a slave under each arm to support her, and "a perfect beauty is a load for a camel." The girls eat large quantities of *kuskus*, and drink a large bowl of camel's milk each morning, and mothers used to beat their daughters for not eating enough.[2] Schweinfurth saw fattened women among the Bongos, whose thighs were as large as a man's chest, and whose measurements across the hips recalled to his mind the "Hottentot Venus" in Cuvier's *Atlas*.[3] Baker, describing Kamrasi's retreat, says that he appeared with a great number of women (his wives), several of whom were carried on litters, being too fat to walk.[4] Speke visited the chief Wazézéru and found him sitting with his wife on a grass-strewn bench of earth, with numerous wooden pots of milk in front of them. The lady was so immoderately stout that she could not rise, and so large were her arms that, between the joints, the flesh hung

[1] *Voyages d'Ibn Batoutah*, ed. Defrémery et Sanguinetti, tom. IV, p. 438.

[2] *Travels in the Interior of Africa*, Dent's edition, p. 116.

[3] *Heart of Africa*, Vol. I, p. 295.

[4] *Albert N'yanza*, p. 385.

down like large, loose-stuffed puddings. Wazézeru, when asked what they did with so many milk pots, pointing to his wife, replied: "This is all the product of these pots; "from early youth upwards we keep those pots to their "mouths, at it is the fashion at court to have very fat "wives."[1] On another occasion Speke visited a sister-in-law of Rŭmanika and found her to be "another of these wonders of obesity, unable to stand excepting on all fours." Her measurements were: height, 5 feet 8 inches; round arm, 1 foot 11 inches; chest, 4 feet 4 inches; thigh, 2 feet 7 inches; calf, 1 foot 8 inches. "Mean-"while, the daughter, a lass of sixteen, sat stark-naked "before us, sucking at a milk-pot, on which the father "kept her at work by holding a rod in his hand, for, as "fattening is the first duty of fashionable female life, it "must be duly enforced by the rod if necessary."[2] The only occupation of Kamrasi's sisters consisted in drinking milk, each one consuming daily the produce of from ten to twenty cows. They cannot walk, and should any one of them wish to go and see a relative, eight men are required to help her on to a litter.[3] Mr. J. Thomson also speaks of the "monstrously" fat wives of Kapufi, king of Karague, who were fed entirely on milk.[4] This peculiarity of the women of Central and Southern Africa is discussed by Dr. Ploss, who quotes many authorities, and prints a number of illustrations from drawings, photographs, etc., and adds remarks on its physiological aspect.[5]

9. The Poisoning of Rā.

In the Legend of Rā and Isis we read that the goddess Isis wished to become like Rā and to have dominion over the whole universe, and that, having meditated long on the matter, she at length decided she could only gain the power of Rā by obtaining the knowledge of his secret name from him. She therefore caused the god to be bitten by a serpent, and when he

[1] *Journal*, p. 172.
[2] *Ibid.*, p. 189.
[3] *Ibid.*, p. 420.
[4] *To the Central African Lakes*, Vol. II, p. 219.
[5] *Das Weib*, Vol. I, p. 202 f.

was in great agony he was persuaded to let his name pass into her. The "magnificent serpent" which bit the god was fashioned by Isis out of the dust of the ground, mixed with the saliva that fell from the mouth of Rā, and she made it to have poison fangs, and set it on the path by which Rā went forth each day to inspect the heavens and the earth. When the god came forth, accompanied by his train of gods, he passed along the road of heaven as usual, and when he arrived at the spot where the serpent lay coiled up waiting for him, it reared itself up, and bit him, and drove the poison of its body into him.[1] In placing the serpent on the path of the Sun-god, Isis employed a stratagem which is in use by buffalo hunters among the Banyoro at the present day. The Chiope hunters in the north of Unyoro told Mr. G. Wilson, the Collector of the District, that expert hunters were in the habit of catching puff-adders in a noose. They nailed the living snake by the tip of its tail in the middle of a buffalo track, and when a buffalo went by the snake struck at it and killed it. As many as ten buffaloes were killed in one day in this manner. The body of the first buffalo was discarded as being poisoned, but the bodies of the other victims were eaten.[2] The puff-adder attains a considerable size, for Sir Samuel Baker saw one which, though only 5 feet 4 inches in length, was rather more than 15 inches in girth. Its head was flat, its tail blunt, it had eight teeth, and Sir Samuel secured five poison fangs, the two most prominent being an inch in length.[3] When Rā had transferred his secret name to Isis, the goddess, presumably, administered to him an antidote, just as a modern witch-woman would do, for many "doctors" in Africa are well acquainted with antidotes to snake-bite.[4]

10. Osiris Restored to Life by Isis.

According to one of the legends of Isis and Osiris, the goddess by enchantments and other means succeeded

[1] Lefébure, *A.Z.*, 1883, p. 27.

[2] Johnston, *Uganda*, Vol. II, p. 584.

[3] *Albert N'yanza*, p. 233. A good coloured picture of the Gabûn puff-adder is given by Johnston, *Uganda*, Vol. I, Plate facing p. 94.

[4] Johnston, *Uganda*, p. 795.

in making Osiris to return to life sufficiently long to beget Horus. An interesting modern parallel to this story is given by Mr. Dennett, who prints a story to the effect that Fullafulla, one of the three wives of Nenpetro, after the death of her husband collected herbs and plants, and by their means restored him to life. The juices of the plants and herbs were applied to his body by her, and she, presumably, recited incantations as she used them. It is impossible to think that the legend of Isis and Osiris is known in West Africa, and we can only conclude that modern "wise-women" or "witch-women" claim to do what was done by Isis, the great enchantress.

11. The Spitting Serpent.

In the Eighth Section of the Book of Gates a picture is given of a monster speckled serpent called "Kheti," , with seven undulations, in each of which stands a god. The mouth of the serpent is open, and through it he belches a stream of fire into the faces of the enemies of Rā, whose arms are tied behind their backs in agonizing positions. Horus says to the serpent: "Open thy mouth, distend thy jaws, belch forth thy fire "against the enemies of my father, burn up their bodies, "and consume their souls by the fire which issueth from "thy mouth, and by the flames which are in thy body." In the Book Åm-Ṭuat (IXth Division) we also have a group of twelve little serpents, the duty of which was to pour out fire from their bodies, which was to light the dead Sun-god on his way. It is easy to explain away these creatures and their fire-spitting qualities by saying that the word fire is only figuratively used here, and that the pictures are merely representations of serpents shooting out poison from their fangs. It was formerly thought spitting serpents did not exist, and that the Egyptian drawings were the result of the artist's imagination. Livingstone, however, killed a serpent of the species *picakholu*, which was 8 feet 3 inches long, and was so copiously supplied with venom that it continued to distil clear poison from the fangs for hours after its head was cut off. He says, "This was probably that which passes "by the name of 'spitting serpent,' which is believed to "be able to eject the poison into the eyes when the "wind favours its forcible expiration."[1] Bentley tells us that one of the ladies of the Mission at Vivi went to look for eggs in the fowl-house, and that she nearly put her hand on a "spit-adder," which spat at her. The poison entered her eyes, and for a while it was feared that she would lose her sight; the pain was very great.[2] The Egyptian artist clearly had this serpent in his mind when he drew Kheti spitting venom in the faces of the wicked. The question of the "spitting serpent" is discussed by Dr. F. Werner, who says that he saw a full-grown specimen of the Naja Nigricollis which had been brought to him in Gondokoro, spitting directly at his friend Dr. Sassi. The saliva has, he says, no fatal effect on the unbroken skin, nor on the mucous membrane of the eyes, which are, however, liable to severe inflammation, provided that it be washed away at once.[3] Another serpent, Naja hajae, is supposed by some to spit, but Dr. Werner has no evidence on the subject. This serpent is probably the "asp" of Cleopatra, and, no doubt, the snake which Moses made to become rigid in the presence of Pharaoh. Modern snake-charmers give similar exhibitions of their power over it in Egypt at the present day.

12. The Insect Sepa.

In various places[4] in the text of Unȧs there are series of spells which were recited with the view of keeping off from the king's body in its tomb the attacks of serpents, scorpions, and other venomous reptiles. Among such reptiles is mentioned the "Sepa [5] of Horus" or, as in line 537, "Sepa" , without any reference to Horus. In Tetȧ, line 302,

[1] *Missionary Travels*, p. 143.
[2] *Pioneering on the Congo*, Vol. I, p. 393.
[3] *Third Report of Wellcome Research Laboratories*, p. 174.
[4] Line 301 ff., and l. 532 ff.
[5] Or, . Unȧs, l. 329; Tetȧ, l. 300.

we have  , and in line 304, "the great Sepa" . In the Middle Empire we have the form ,[1] and in Theban papyri of the Book of the Dead  ,[2] .[3] The variant forms of the determinative which are placed after the word show that the scribes had no very clear idea of the form of the *Sepa*, but the determinative in Unȧs, l. 329, proves conclusively that *Sepa* was a many-legged reptile or insect, which had poison fangs, or bags, one on each side of its vicious mouth. On submitting a copy of this determinative to the Hon. Walter Rothschild he at once pronounced it to represent a caterpillar of an allied family to the South American "Megalopygidae." He showed me a specimen of this family, and the accuracy of the Egyptian representation of a member of the allied family was seen to be remarkable. The creature is about three inches long, and is covered with a mass of orange-coloured hair, about half an inch thick. Each hair is capable of ejecting poison into the hand of anyone who touches it incautiously; the contents of even a single hair produce very severe inflammation, whilst the discharge into the human body from many hairs would be followed by death. These characteristics of the Sepa caterpillar-family enable us to understand why the Egyptians classed it with venomous serpents, scorpions, etc. Witch-doctors are said to make use of the poison distilled from caterpillars in their "medicines," but details of the effect of it are hard to acquire. We may note in passing that the spells against serpents, etc., in the text of Unȧs prove that when they were written Egypt must have been overrun with venomous snakes, reptiles, and insects, just as is the Congo Forest at the present day. Sir Harry Johnston enumerates some of these, viz., mosquitoes, tsetse fly

[1] *Recueil*, tom. XXX, p. 187.
[2] Chapter XVII, l. 87.
[3] Chapter LXIX, ll. 7 and 9.

(causer of sleeping sickness), sand flies, hippo flies, jiggers or burrowing fleas, driver ants, brown ants, ants that stink, cockroaches two inches long, locusts four inches long, mason wasps, wasps with an almost deadly sting, beetles, caterpillars that produce a skin disease by the slightest contact with their poisonous hairs, aromatic bugs, shrieking locustids, pouncing crickets, mantises, spiders, ticks, the huge Pandinus scorpion six inches long, centipedes eight inches long, with a very poisonous sting, and huge, but harmless millipedes.[1] The adult millipede ejects a dark liquid which stains the hands, and is said to be poisonous, if taken internally.[2]

13. Snake-worship.

The Egyptians regarded certain kinds of snakes with reverence, and their religious books contain many allusions to them ; on the other hand, the mythological writings show that some snakes or serpents were regarded as incarnations of evil. Among these are the serpents the names of which are given in the text of Unȧs, and several others are mentioned in the Book Ȧm Ṭuat and the Book of Gates ; but all of them appear to have been regarded as forms of the monster serpent Āpep 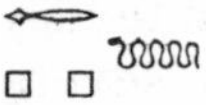, which was the type of all physical and moral evil. In short, the serpent was either a power for good or the incarnation of diabolical cunning and wickedness. Similar views are held concerning the serpent by modern African peoples, as the narratives of travellers testify, and if we had sufficient information we should probably find that the snakes which were revered in old days are revered now, and that those which were regarded as evil beings are still so regarded. The Book of the Dead mentions (Chapter CVIII) the serpent Ȧmi-hemf, which lived on the top of a mountain and was thirty cubits[3] long, and the Papyrus Golénischeff[4] also mentions a serpent thirty cubits long, which had a

[1] *George Grenfell*, Vol. I, p. 232, Vol. II, p. 937.
[2] Nassau, *Fetichism*, p. 199.
[3] About forty-five feet.
[4] *Recueil de Travaux*, tom. XXVIII.

beard two cubits long, and which conversed with the ship-wrecked mariner on the enchanted island. The longest serpent now living in Africa seems to be the python, which is, however, less than 45 feet long, as the following instances prove. Du Chaillu's men ate a python 13 feet long;[1] Schweinfurth saw a python 15 feet long;[2] Sir Harry Johnston's longest python was 17 feet long;[3] a python of Du Chaillu was 18 feet long;[4] Mr. Hunter Reid killed a python near Boma, the skin of which when dry was 25 feet 2 inches long and 2 feet 7 inches wide;[5] Bentley says the python sometimes attains a greater length than 30 feet; Mr. Alldridge saw a dead python 33 feet long and 6 inches in diameter, which was being carried away by a crocodile;[6] and the longest skin measured by Miss Kingsley, a damaged one, was 26 feet. She mentions a python which was brought into Creek Town in the Rev. Mr. Goldie's time which must have been over 40 feet in length.[7] The Egyptians represented certain snakes with a head at each end of the body,[8] and Miss Kingsley mentions one serpent which the natives declared to have "a head at each end."[9] The Egyptians drew figures of serpents with human heads and legs, and the wings of a bird, but this is not very remarkable when we remember that even Herodotus and Aristotle believed in "flying serpents." Reverence is still paid to the serpent in many parts of Africa. Thus the Dinkas revere pythons,[10] and call snakes in general their "brethren";[11] they wash them with milk and anoint them with butter.[12] The python is

[1] *Adventures*, p. 57.

[2] *Heart of Africa*, Vol. I, p. 83.

[3] *Uganda*, Vol. I, p. 118.

[4] *Adventures*, p. 145.

[5] *George Grenfell*, Vol. I, p. 270. Its stomach contained one peck of brass, copper, and iron rings. The natives walked along its back as on a big log.

[6] *Sherbro and Its Hinterland*, p. 109.

[7] *West African Travels*, p. 547.

[8] Ȧm-Ṭuat, Division X.

[9] *West African Travels*, p. 161.

[10] Stanley, *Darkest Africa*, Vol. I, p. 424.

[11] Schweinfurth, *Heart of Africa*, Vol. I, p. 158.

[12] Stanley, *Darkest Africa*, Vol. I, p. 424; and see Frobenius, *Heiden-Neger*, p. 344.

the great Juju snake of the Brassmen, and their titular guardian angel, and no Brass king would sign a treaty with the British Government that did not include a clause by which any European who killed or molested a python was made liable to a fine.[1] The Gallas pay great reverence to the serpent, which they regard as the mother of the human race, and they in this respect follow the example of the Pagan Ethiopians, whose deity was a huge serpent.[2] The Bârî think that a python called Yukanye was the mother of their tribe, and they keep tame serpents in their houses, and all over the Blue Nile district a certain kind of python is venerated. The Dinkas work witchcraft by means of snakes, and the snake-magician is believed to be able to cause his snake to injure a man, or his family, or cattle. If a man is injured by a snake in any way, he promptly tries to find out who is its "master," so that he may propitiate him.[3]

14. The Crocodile.

The Egyptians reverenced the crocodile from the earliest times, but their reverence was the result of fear, and the creature was always regarded as the incarnation of a terribly evil power which manifested itself in the destruction of human and animal life. The Egyptians endeavoured to placate the Crocodile-god by means of offerings and sacrifices, and many modern African peoples follow their example. Shrines dedicated to the crocodile existed in some of the cities of the Delta under the Ancient Empire, and under the Middle Empire the cult of the creature was common in Egypt. The Book of the Dead contains a spell (Chapter LXXXVIII) which gave the deceased the power to assume the form of the "divine crocodile, which dwelleth in terror, and seizeth its prey," and the belief is common in Africa at the present day that a human spirit can take possession of a crocodile, and direct the creature to carry out some purpose, good or bad.[4] Two

[1] Kingsley, *Travels in West Africa*, p. 483.
[2] Krapf, *Travels*, p. 81.
[3] Anderson, *Third Report*, pp. 355, 356.
[4] Kingsley, *Travels in West Africa*, p. 538.

other spells (Chapters XXXI and XXXII) enabled the deceased to drive away the four crocodiles which dwelt in the four quarters of the world, and attacked the dead in order to seize upon the *ḥeka*, or magical powers and words, on which they depended for existence in the Other World. In the Book of Gates (Division IX) we find that Āpep, the monster serpent which endeavoured to prevent the sun from rising, and the cause of storms, whirlwinds, thunder and lightning, is accompanied by a fiend in the form of a crocodile, which has a tail terminating in the head of a serpent, and is called Shesshes, or Sessi.[1] This is, undoubtedly, the crocodile of which figures were burnt at stated intervals on certain days, in the great temples of Egypt, down to the Ptolemaïc Period, with the view of preventing the brewing of storms in the skies, and of assisting the Sun-god Rā to rise in the sky. In beliefs connected with the cult of Osiris the crocodile appears as a friend of this god and of his son Horus, but the fact remains that the creature was held sacred in some parts of Egypt, and was slain as a noxious reptile in others.[2] The centre of its worship in Roman times was the city of Arsinoë (Crocodilopolis), where the sacred crocodile was kept by itself in a lake, and was fed with bread, flesh, and wine by its priests; bracelets were placed on its fore-legs, and gold ear-rings in its ears.[3] Another place famous for the cult of the crocodile was Thebes, and reverence for it seems to have persisted in the Thebaïd till the eighteenth century of our era, for at that time the "king of the crocodiles" lived at Armant, eight miles south of Thebes.[4] According to Wiedemann,[5] a gigantic crocodile was venerated at Kharṭûm in the reign of Muḥammad Alî. It would be interesting to know if this crocodile was an ordinary *Crocodilus niloticus*, or a Slender-snouted crocodile (*Crocodilus cataphractus*), or a Short-headed crocodile (*Crocodilus*

1 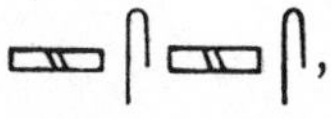, or 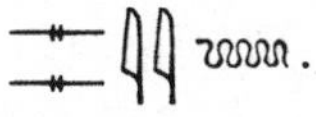.

2 Herodotus, II, 69.

3 Strabo, I, § 38.

4 Sieber, *Beschreibendes Verzeichniss*, Vienna, 1820, p. 59; Pückler, *Aus Mehemed Ali's Reich*, III, p. 250.

5 *Muséon*, Vol. VI, 2, pp. 113–128.

osteoloemus).[1] In size the crocodile is often over-estimated, and Sir Harry Johnston says that the biggest his party ever shot in Uganda was 15 feet long.[2] The largest measured by Miss Kingsley was 22 feet 3 inches long,[3] and Bentley killed one which was 17 feet 6 inches long.[4] At Dixcove and in the Lower Congo the crocodile is worshipped,[5] and in some parts of West Africa its intelligence is believed by the natives to be of a very high order. Thus Stanley tells us that the chief of Ukara had a crocodile which was as docile and obedient to his master as a dog, and as intelligent as a man. The chief coveted a pretty woman who was in the house of Lukongeh, but could find no way of getting possession of her. At length he told his crocodile of his wishes, and told it to lie in wait in the rushes near Msossi until the woman came to the lake to bathe, and then to seize her and bring her over to him. The next day at noon the woman was in the house of the chief of Ukara! It was also said that Machunda, the father of Lukongeh, owned a crocodile that stole an Arab's wife and carried her across the country to the king's house.[6] The Christian monks of Egypt made use of crocodiles, and Palladius tells us that Apellen ordered a crocodile to carry him across the river and that the creature did so twice.[7] Among many Sûdânî tribes a belief in the efficacy of the genitals of the crocodile as an aphrodisiac is current, and portions of them are powdered and swallowed by men who wish to be blessed with large families. Mr. Bousfield says that the penis of the crocodile eaten with spices is considered to be the most potent means of increasing sexual power in the male.[8]

[1] These are the three chief classes mentioned by Johnston, *George Grenfell*, Vol. II, p. 929.

[2] *Uganda*, Vol. I, p. 406.

[3] *Travels*, p. 546.

[4] *Pioneering on the Congo*, Vol. II, p. 249.

[5] Kingsley, *West African Studies*, p. 140.

[6] *Through the Dark Continent*, Vol. I, p. 253.

[7] Budge, *Paradise of the Holy Fathers*, Vol. I, p. 354.

[8] Bousfield, *Native Methods of Treatment of Diseases in Kassala* (*Third Report of the Wellcome Research Laboratories*, p. 274).

15. The Use of the Net in Fowling, Fishing, and Hunting.

At a very early period in their history the Egyptians believed that the spirits of the dead, in journeying from this world to the next, would encounter beings equipped with nets which they used for catching unwary souls who were travelling. To guard souls against this danger, the priests drew up a series of spells, copies of which form Chapters CLIIIa and CLIIIb of the Book of the Dead. They also provided the former Chapter with the picture of a magical net, every part of which had a magical name, and in the accompanying text all the names are given. Apparently souls flew through the air to their abode in the Other World, and they were sometimes caught in the net of the "fierce fowler whose fingers are hidden,"[1] but he who was provided with the proper spells was able to avoid him altogether, or to escape from him. The name of this great fowler was Ḥer-f-ḥa-f, or Maa-ḥa-f,[2] who ferried the dead over the Egyptian Styx, and he was assisted by the "fowlers," who on some great occasion had caught the fiends and the Khetiu-ta in his net. The net depicted on the papyrus was a picture of the net used by him, but if the deceased knew the names of all its parts it would be powerless to enmesh him. In the Book of Gates (Division IX) we see the net being used by those who are going out to work spells on Āpep and Shesshes, the enemies of Rā. The company consists of six men, four apes, and four women, and in front of them stand three men armed with harpoons.

The net is employed in hunting by many African peoples just as it was by the Egyptians. Thus, among the Bongos, nets are used in all the *battues* for game, and the people devote as much attention to the construction of these nets as they do to the weaving of their fish-

1  Chapter CLIIIa, l. 7.

2  or 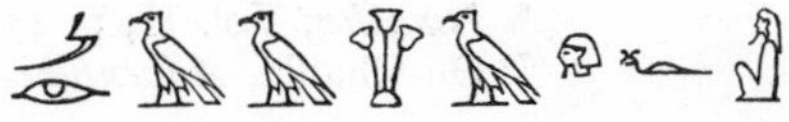.

snares and basket pots.[1] The king of Toro's men were provided with extensive nets, and they caught a large chimpanzee in one of them,[2] and the Bantu negroes sometimes catch antelopes in nets.[3] The Sango and Mongwandi are fond of eating monkeys and chimpanzees, and when they go hunting, they frighten these creatures into isolated trees, and then drive them into nets which they spread about the feet of them.[4] The Ababua drive game, with the help of dogs, into enormous nets, where the killing takes place.[5] At Fatiko, Sir Samuel Baker says, the favourite method of hunting was by means of the net. Every man in the country was provided with a net of strong cord. This was twelve yards long and about eleven feet wide, if stretched to its maximum. The meshes were about six inches square.[6] All the Bakalai tribes enjoy *ashiga* or net hunting, The nets are made of the fibre of the pineapple plant, or of the fibres of a kind of tree, with which stout threads are mixed. They are from sixty to eighty feet long and five feet wide, and every village possesses several.[7]

16. Strong Names.

A king of Egypt under the Middle and New Empires usually possessed five names, and each of these proclaimed his strength, valour, and power. He bore the first name as the successor of Horus, the second as the chosen one of the goddesses Nekhebit and Uatchit, the third as the Golden Horus, the fourth as the King of the South and North, and the fifth as the son of Rā. The various names which are given to Rameses II may be counted by the dozen, and the custom of giving such "mighty names" to the king of Egypt finds its parallel in the custom which is widespread among many modern African peoples of calling the chief or king by "strong names." Thus the king of the Bavili has seven titles, one

[1] Schweinfurth, *Heart of Africa*, Vol. I, p. 272.
[2] Johnston, *Uganda*, Vol. I, p. 357.
[3] *Ibid.*, Vol. II, p. 586.
[4] Johnston, *George Grenfell*, Vol. II, p. 780.
[5] *Ibid.*, p. 776.
[6] *Ismailïa*, Vol. II, p. 439.
[7] Du Chaillu, *Adventures*, p. 106.

of which he does not receive until after his death.[1] Among the "strong names" of Daho, the "Omniscient," king of Dahomey, 1625—1650, were "Donun," "the all-wise," "Akwazhu," "the leveller of his enemies," etc. Gêzu, 1818—1858, had many strong names, among them being :—

Bodun-ganu-minh, *i.e.*, "fetish conquering everything."

Eganu-menseh-Minhwe Gêzu, "he conquered all his enemies, so everybody comes to Gêzu."

Gan kaka de jeh, "a conqueror for whom everybody will wait."

Vokhe Mau, "the scarlet bird of the gods."[2]

Among the titles of Gelelê, the successor of Gêzu, were :—

Glere, "heavy," *i.e.*, the "king who cannot be moved."

Kini-kini-kini, "dragon with claws," *i.e.*, "he tears all in pieces."

Tenge makan fenkpon, "rock, finger-nail cannot scratch it."

Ahorsu Yemabu, "Shadow-king," *i.e.*, "he who will never be lost in his kingdom."[3]

The king of Dahomey is double, not merely binonymous, nor dual, like the spiritual Mikado and the temporal Tycoon of Japan, but two in one ; he is king of the city, and he is king of the Bush, *i.e.*, of the farmer folk and of the country as opposed to the city. This Bush-king, Addokpon, though a wholly imaginary person, enjoys all the pomp and state of a real king. The Bush-king double of Gelelê had his palace at Akpwe-ho, a few miles from Abomey, on the Toffo road, an official mother, a chief executioner, a master of ceremonies, male and female officers, eunuchs, and wives. And a number of criminals and victims were set apart to be slain at this Bush-king's So-Sin Customs. The idea of the Bush-king is said to have been evolved by Gêzu, the father of

[1] Dennett, *At the Back of the Black Man's Mind*, p. 100.
[2] Skertchley, *Dahomey as It is*, p. 451 ff.
[3] Burton, *Mission to Gelele*, Vol. II, p. 333.

Gelelê, for the purpose of enabling the king to trade and to carry on commercial enterprises ; but evidence in support of this view is wanting. The idea of the "double" is a very ancient one in Africa, as we have seen, and it has always been there. The existence of the Horus name among the ancient Egyptians proves that the king had a special "double," which must have been supposed to exercise sovereignty in some way, and to have been honoured by the people as a king. An interesting passage occurs in the LXXXVth Chapter of the Book of the Dead which seems to indicate that the deceased expected to have two existences, one as a dweller in the city, and the other as a dweller in the country. He says: "I am a young man in the city, and a youth in the country ; as for my name, my name is the 'Imperishable one.'"[1]

17. The Election of a King.

On the Stele of the Coronation[2] is an account of the election of the Nubian king Åspelta. Four groups of officials assembled with the Royal Brethren who were eligible for the throne, and introduced them into the presence of the god Åmen-Rā of Napata, who, however, selected none of them. They then introduced Åspelta by himself to the god, who at once "selected," *i.e.*, touched him, and declared him to be the man whom he had chosen to be king, and the officials and all the people at once accepted him as their lord. A modern parallel to this election is found in Uganda. On the death of the king, the Katikiro, or chief officer of state, at once summons the Kasuja, or Keeper of the Princes, and in the presence of the chiefs asks him who among the Princes is most qualified to reign. Having given his opinion, the chiefs order him to collect the Princes. When this is done he forms them up into line, and

1 

2 Mariette, *Monuments Divers*, Plate 9.

touches one of them with his hand, and the prince so touched becomes at once king of Uganda, and makes all arrangements for the burial of the dead king.[1]

18. Pottery Made by Hand.

During the Predynastic Period and the early dynasties the Egyptians made their pottery, even the largest vessels, by hand, and the use of the potter's wheel appears to have been unknown. Their skill in this craft was remarkable, and the proportions of the vessels which they turned out are so true, and the circular shapes so exact, that it is sometimes almost impossible to believe that they did not employ some mechanical means in their pottery work. Many modern peoples in Central Africa possess similar skill in the craft of the potter, *e.g.*, the Dyoor, of whose work Schweinfurth says: "It is remarkable how they manage with the mere hand to turn out immense vessels which, even to a critical eye, have all the appearance of being made on a wheel.[2] Among the Bongos the women, without the help of any turning-wheel, succeed in producing most artistic specimens of pottery. The larger water bottles are sometimes a yard in diameter. Handles are uniformly wanting, and to compensate for this want, their whole outer surface is made rather rough by being ornamented by a number of triangles and zig-zag lines, which form all manner of concentric and spiral patterns. The gourd-platters and bottles are generally decorated with different dark rows of triangles.[3] In all Congoland the potter's wheel is unknown; all pottery is made by hand, and women are the potters. In the west beautiful and elaborate designs and careful choice of colours and materials make their appearance: this is probably due to the influence of the Sûdânî peoples in the north and of the early Portuguese.[4] The only implements used by the Nandi in pottery making are: The handle of a hoe, which is employed for pounding and stirring the clay,

[1] Cunningham, *Uganda*, p. 224.
[2] *Heart of Africa*, Vol. I, p. 212.
[3] *Ibid.*, p. 292.
[4] Johnston, *George Grenfell*, Vol. II, p. 812.

the shoulder-blade of an ox, a stone, a seed pod, some plaited grass, and three pieces of straw, with which the pots are smoothed and ornamented.[1] At Stanley Pool the natives had no idea of the potter's wheel, but putting a piece of calabash under a lump of clay, to make it turn freely, they very deftly turn it round slowly by hand, and make some very thin regular ware. It is hard sometimes to realize that the articles have not been "thrown" on the wheel, so round are they, and even.[2] The Obbo people have no knowledge of the potter's wheel, and the circular form is obtained entirely by hand.[3] The Bubis of Fernando Po also make their pottery without a wheel.[4] Of native pottery in general Dr. Livingstone says: "The pots for cooking, holding water and beer, "are made by the women, and the form is preserved by "the eye alone, for no sort of machine is ever used."[5]

19. Finger-Nails.

In one of the Chapters of the Daily Cult[6] which deals with the placing of the hands on the coffer to "make purification," the priest declares to the god that he has "done away," *i.e.*, cut, his nails, in imitation of Thoth, who, on a certain occasion, cut his nails. These words show that the cutting or cleansing of the nails was an important act in making the body of the priest ceremonially pure. What exactly was the idea which underlay this act of purification cannot be said, but its importance is evident. In connection with this it is interesting to note that the cannibal Makarakas, among other cleanly habits, include that of keeping the finger-nails tidy.[7]

20. Figures and Counting.

The Egyptians counted from one to nine by means of short strokes, and they had signs for ten ∩, hundred 𓍢,

[1] Hollis, *Nandi*, p. 35.
[2] Bentley, *Pioneering on the Congo*, Vol. II, p. 37.
[3] Baker, *Albert N'yanza*, p. 196.
[4] Kingsley, *Travels in West Africa*, p. 65.
[5] *Last Journals*, Vol. I, p. 59.
[6] Moret, *Culte Divin*, p. 170.
[7] Junker, *Travels*, Vol. I, p. 245.

thousand , ten thousand 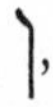, hundred thousand , million , and ten million ; thus it is clear that they could count up to very large numbers. The modern Baganda are also skilled arithmeticians, for before the Europeans entered their country they had developed the expressions for numerals, and used a decimal system of calculation. They have words for every multiple of ten up to twenty millions.[1] Among the Egyptians the number seven appears to have represented completeness, for we have the Seven Hathors, the Seven Ārits, the Seven Cows and their Bull, the Seven Spirits, the Seven Uraei, the Seven-headed Serpent, etc. The number nine also seems to represent finality and completeness, and the Companies of the Gods each contained nine members. And we have Nine Mourners, Nine Watchers, Nine Smeriu, Nine Task-masters, Nine Followers of Osiris, Nine Holders of the Rope for measuring land, etc. Among modern African peoples the number nine is regarded as sacred. When a man is killed by lightning in Uganda nine witches are sent for, who surround the body.[2] When Lukedi became king, he killed nine fowls, nine cows, nine old women and nine young women, and he made nine loads of beads into a head-dress, which he wore.[3] A magician works magic by means of nine kauri shells sewn on to a strip of leather, with which he makes the sign of the Cross.[4] In the Okijun country a fair is held every ninth day.[5] A woman does not work in the fields for nine days after the birth of her child.[6] Gelele was, according to his reckoning, the ninth king of the Dahoman dynasty, and at the Sin Kwain Custom he made nine stools, nine hammocks, nine flags, and nine swords to march in procession.[7] The number 110 seems to have possessed some special significance, and the Egyptians regarded it as the utmost limit of a man's

[1] Johnston, *Uganda*, Vol. II, p. 695. Compare Cunningham *Uganda*, p. 298.
[2] Johnston, *Uganda*, Vol. II, p. 589.
[3] *Ibid.*, p. 600.
[4] *Ibid.*, p. 678.
[5] Kingsley, *Travels in West Africa*, p. 475.
[6] *Ibid.*, p. 793.
[7] Skertchley, *Dahomey as It is*, p. 402.

life.[1] Thus in a papyrus[2] mention is made of some person who lived upon earth 110 years, and Nefer-Renpet, in a prayer cut on a libation tank in the British Museum, entreats the gods to allow him to live 110 years 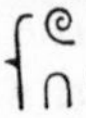, provided that they give him health and strength to enjoy them.[3] In connection with this number may be mentioned the custom in West Africa of giving a man who has committed some serious offence 110 lashes with a whip. Thus Du Chaillu commuted the punishment of death to a flogging of 110 lashes in the case of one Boulay who had tried to poison him.[4] Whether the Egyptians believed in certain numbers being lucky and others unlucky cannot be said, but it is probable that they did, and that they used numbers in divining. Among modern diviners by means of numbers may be mentioned the Nandi, who regard 2, 3, 5, 8, and 10 as lucky, especially 3 and 5, and 1, 4, 6, 7, and 9 as unlucky ;[5] the most unlucky number is 1 and the least so is 4.

21. Time, the Year, Seasons, etc.

The Egyptians divided the year into three seasons, each containing four months ; each month contained thirty days, or three weeks of ten days each.[6] Five intercalary days were added to make up a year of 365 days. They conceived of very long periods of time, *e.g.*,

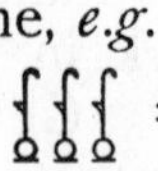 = tens of millions of years.

 = one million of millions of millions of years.

[1] Egyptians sometimes attained to a great age, perhaps actually to 110 years, for Ānkh-p-Khart tells us that he ministered in a temple for 80 years, and when he died he must have been 100 years old, or more. See his statue in the British Museum, No. 820.

[2] *Anastasi*, IV, p. 6, l. 14.

[3] Central Saloon, No. 605 (*Guide*, p. 167).

[4] *Adventures in Equatorial Africa*, p. 245.

[5] Hollis, *Nandi*, p. 89.

[6] In late times the year consisted of 12 months, each month containing 29 days, or 4 weeks of $7\frac{1}{4}$ days each, and a supplementary month of $17\frac{1}{4}$ days (equal 1 decade and 1 week). See Daressy, *La Semaine des Égyptiens* in *Annales du Service*, Vol. X, pp. 21–23, 180, 182.

In early Dynastic times each year was named by the most important event which took place in it. The Mandingoes in Mungo Park's day also distinguished each year by a particular name, founded on some remarkable occurrence which happened in that year. Thus they say, "the year of the Farbanna war," and the "year of the Kaarta war," the "year in which Gadou was plundered," etc. They calculate their years by the rainy seasons, of which there is one in each year.[1] Among many modern African peoples the year is divided into three seasons. Thus the Yorubas have Ewo-erun, "dry season"; Ewo-oye, "season of the Harmathan wind"; and Ewo-ojo, "rainy season"; and each of their months contains six weeks of five days each, from which, however, they deduct twelve hours.[2] The Bavili year is divided into three parts, which contain one month, four months, and eight months respectively[3]; they are called Mawalala, Xicifu, and Mvula. These three parts contain six seasons, each of two months, which are called Mwici (smoke), Bunji (mist), Mvumvumvu (drizzle), Waw Waw Waw (rains), Nvula Nxentu (female rains), Nvula Mbakala (male rains).[4] In Speke's time the Baganda reckoned only five months to the year,[5] and only recently has time been divided into years in Uganda.[6] The Egyptians gave names to each month, to each day of the month, and to each hour of the day and night, and some modern African peoples do likewise.[7] Our information about the divisions of time in use among modern Sûdânî folk is scanty, for the older travellers paid no attention to the matter.

In the Calendar of Lucky and Unlucky Days the Egyptians divided the day into three parts, but it is not clear whether each part contained four or eight hours, *i.e.*, whether they included the night in the day or not. Many African peoples divide the day into three parts,[8]

[1] *Travels in the Interior of Africa*, Dent's reprint, p. 210.
[2] Ellis, *Yoruba-speaking Peoples*, pp. 144, 151.
[3] Dennett, *At the Back of the Black Man's Mind*, p. 64.
[4] *Ibid.*, p. 107.
[5] *Journal*, p. 355.
[6] Cunningham, *Uganda*, p. 234.
[7] See Dennett, *op. cit.*, p. 106, and Hollis, *Nandi*, p. 94 ff.
[8] *E.g.*, the Mandingoes.—Mungo Park, *Travels*, p. 208.

i.e., into morning, mid-day, and evening, and, like the Egyptians, further subdivide it, when necessary, into parts which are distinguished by the sun's place in the heavens.[1]

22. Astronomy.

Under the Ancient Empire the Egyptians had very little knowledge of astronomy in the true sense of the word, and the stars were regarded by them as divine spirits round which the souls of the blessed collected. In the Pyramid Texts two classes of stars are clearly distinguished, the *Ȧkhemu seku*, or "imperishable stars," and the *Ȧkhemu urtchu*, the "stars which never rest." The heavens were divided into four parts, and the stars were classed as "northern" and "southern." Among the former they placed the constellation Mesekhti, the Great Bear, and among the latter the constellation of Orion and Sirius, or Sothis. The northern stars were associated in a certain degree with Set, Orion held the soul of Horus, and Sirius was identified with Isis. Venus as an evening and morning star was well known, and one at least of the planets, and some of the stars mentioned in the Pyramid Texts were afterwards included among the Thirty-six Dekans. The moon was the great "Runner," *khens* 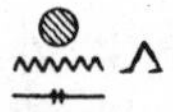, of the night-sky, and was in early times associated with Thoth; in later times it was regarded as the abode of Osiris.[2] The Sun and the Moon were the two great eyes of the Sky-god, the former being his right eye and the latter his left. Under the New Empire the Egyptians knew the five planets Mercury, Venus, Mars, Saturn, and Jupiter,[3] and drew up lists of the Thirty-six Dekans, and made star-maps of a limited character. On monuments of the

[1] Compare the pictures of the sun at each hour of the day and his names in Brugsch, *Thesaurus*, p. 57.

[2] Osiris entered the moon on the day when it was full, . See Brugsch, *Thesaurus*, pp. 30, 271; and Plutarch, *De Iside*, Chapter XLIII.

[3] Brugsch, *Thesaurus*, p. 66.

Ptolemaïc Period we find lists of the Signs of the Zodiac and pictures of their gods.

Modern African peoples pay little attention to the heavenly bodies in general, and travellers have, as a rule, surprisingly little to tell us of their views concerning them. Sir Harry Johnston says that beyond a slight interest in the sun or moon the Negro race, as contrasted with the Asiatic or European, takes little notice of the heavenly bodies. The average native of Uganda takes little or no interest in the stars. The Baganda know the Great Bear, and their name for it means "six stars"; Orion they call the three stars. Sirius is simply "Munyenye," or "*the* star."[1] The Bakongo regard Venus and Jupiter as the spouses of the moon.[2] Rŭmanika asked Speke "if the same sun we "saw one day appeared again, or whether fresh suns "came every day, and whether or not the moon made "different faces, to laugh at us mortals on earth."[3] Pingiro, chief of Nindo, asked Decle if there were two suns, one which went to bed one evening, and another which got up next day.[4] When Mungo Park asked the Mandingoes what they thought became of the sun during the night, they considered the question childish, for they had never thought out the matter, and the subject seemed to them to be beyond human investigation. The Nandi think that the sun retires into his scabbard at night time, and returns by a different road to his home in the east; and when the moon disappears she is supposed to fall, and to go home by a different road. When there is no moon the people say that the sun has killed his wife.[5]

The moon has attracted the notice of the natives of Africa more than any other heavenly body, and most of their religion and religious ceremonies are grouped about it. The new moon to them is a newly created thing, or a resurrection of its old body, and a new embodiment of the moon's spirit. To the African everywhere it has

[1] *Uganda*, Vol. II, p. 697.
[2] *George Grenfell*, Vol. II, p. 815.
[3] *Journal*, p. 193, Dent's reprint.
[4] Decle, *Three Years*, p. 370.
[5] Hollis, *Nandi*, p. 98.

always been the symbol of new birth, new life, growth development, and power. Many peoples in West, South, and Central Africa salute its appearance reverently, and Pagans as well as Muslims say a short prayer when they see its crescent in the sky at sunset for the first time each month. The prayer said, they spit upon their hands and rub them over their faces. Work of all kinds, especially that connected with agriculture, and journeys are undertaken during the waxing moon, and marriages are performed, and circumcision festivals are celebrated during this period. No work of any importance is begun during the moon's last quarter,[1] when mourning festivals are celebrated.[2] The institution of a general day of rest among the Yorubas and many other peoples in Africa and elsewhere is probably to be referred to moon-worship. Originally the first day of the new moon was observed as a day of rest, a holy day sacred to the moon. When the month was divided into weeks, the first day of each week, *i.e.*, of each phase of the moon, was also regarded as holy. As the Mendis do no work on the first day of the month, saying that if they did the rice and corn would grow red, the day of the new moon being "a day of blood," Colonel Ellis thinks that they at one time offered human sacrifices to the new moon.[3] As the African developed anthropomorphic conceptions of gods moon-worship decayed, but the new moon is still treated with reverence in most parts of Africa, and its appearance is celebrated with festivals, dancing, music, and joyful entertainments of all kinds.

23. The Pillow or Head-rest, .

The Egyptians often placed in their tombs head-rests, or "pillows," on which the heads of the dead rested, and they often attached to mummies small models of the pillow, made of haematite and other substances, which were supposed to possess the power of "lifting up" their heads. A large collection of pillows in wood, ivory, etc.,

[1] Mungo Park, *Travels*, pp. 208, 209; Hollis, *Nandi*, pp. 19, 52, 60, 79.
[2] Hollis, *Nandi*, p. 71.
[3] *Yoruba-speaking Peoples*, p. 146.

is exhibited in the Third Egyptian Room, and there are many pillow-amulets in the Fourth Egyptian Room, of the British Museum. In the Papyrus of Ani the pillow appears as one of the three chief amulets, the other two being the backbone of Osiris, , and a portion of the body of Isis, . It forms the vignette of Chapter CLXVI of the Book of the Dead, and the text suggests that it not only raised up the head, but prevented it from being carried off. The modern African peoples also use head-rests made of wood, etc., which closely resemble those of the Egyptians; for illustrations of these see Bentley, *Pioneering on the Congo*, Vol. I, p. 309, and Johnston, *George Grenfell*, Vol. II, pp. 745–748.

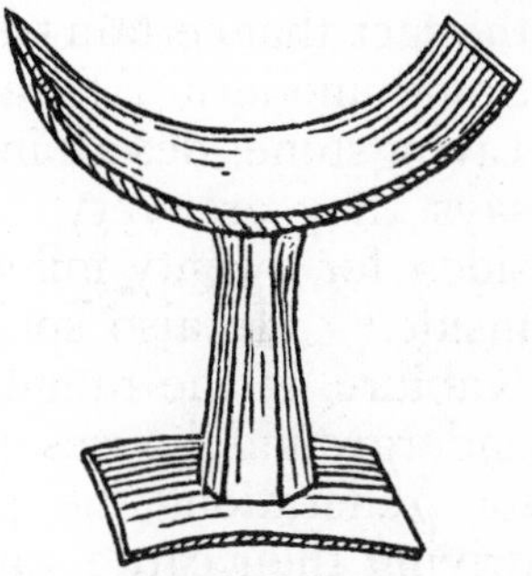
Egyptian Pillow.

24. The Dance of the God.

In the chapter on Osiris and dancing it has already been stated that most of the chief African peoples regard ceremonial dancing before a god as an act of worship. Allusion has already been made to the pygmy who was brought from the Sûdân to Egypt, and who knew how to dance the "dance of the god," the "god" being, presumably, Osiris, and we are justified in assuming that this "god" had his own special dance, which was not generally known in Egypt. There is certainly some good reason for the statement that the pygmy knew the dance of the "god." With this we may compare a remark of Colonel Ellis, who says: "On the Gold and Slave Coasts, every god of note has his own dance, which is sacred to him, and is known only to the initiated."[1]

25. Under-world.

The Egyptian Book of Gates and the Book Åm-Ṭuat suggest that some parts of the Other World were supposed

[1] *Yoruba-speaking Peoples*, p. 296.

to be underground, and the entrances to these, with the Porters or Doorkeepers, seem to indicate that the artists who drew the pictures of them were well acquainted with the fact that certain tribes lived in underground dwellings. Some modern African peoples live underground, and Livingstone, describing the underground houses in Rua, says they are very extensive, ranging along mountain sides for twenty miles, and in one part a rivulet flows inside.[1] He also speaks of underground store-houses in Kabiuré, in the range called Kakoma.[2] There are also underground houses in the Oasis of Khârgah, to which for generations the people have been in the habit of driving their cattle, and in which the people themselves have taken refuge, when attacked by the desert Arabs. I visited them in 1909 and found them well stocked with grain, and women, goats, and children living in them contentedly. The light of lamps and fires added a weirdness to the scene, which might well serve as a base for an imaginary Under-world, like the Ipo-oku of the Yorubas,[3] where the spirits of the dead lived and continued their existence which they had begun in the flesh on earth.

26. Magical Figures in Steatite.

In connection with what has been said about magical figures and figures of ancestors, it may be noted that small steatite figures are sometimes dug up in various parts of the Sherbro Hinterland, and that the people ascribe magical powers to them. They make offerings of flour to them, and then consult them about expeditions, wars, the crops, and the acquisition of wealth. Each figure, or devil, is in command of many spirits, who carry out his orders. If a figure is set on a small bamboo stool, within a little palm leaf shrine, in a secret place near a crop, it is believed that the crop will be doubled. If such a figure is acquired by theft its powers are supposed to be increased.[4]

1 *Last Journals*, Vol. I, p. 274.
2 *Ibid.*, p. 281.
3 Ellis, *op. cit.*, p. 127.
4 Alldridge, *Sherbro and Its Hinterland*, p. 163.

27. Incense.

Among the Egyptians of all periods one of the most important ceremonies was the burning of incense. Each substance used in the composition of incense was supposed to possess magical properties, and the smell produced by burning them together was believed to be much liked by the gods. The smoke was thought to form a material vehicle on which the words of the prayers recited by the worshipper would mount up to heaven, and when they reached the divine being to whom they were addressed, the odour of the incense which accompanied them caused him to receive them graciously, and to grant the suppliant his petition. And this was not all, for a passage in the Pyramid Text of Pepi II shows that the soul of the dead man ascended into heaven by means of the incense which was burnt on his behalf. The passage reads :—

> " The father of Pepi Nefer-ka-Rā is Shu.
> " The mother of Pepi Nefer-ka-Rā is Tefnut.
> " They draw up Pepi Nefer-ka-Rā to heaven, to heaven,
> " On the flame of the incense.[1]
> " Pepi Nefer-ka-Rā is pure.
> " Pepi Nefer-ka-Rā liveth.
> " Pepi Nefer-ka-Rā maketh his seat, behold, Osiris."

An interesting modern parallel to this old idea is given by Livingstone. A fire broke out at Hara, the night after he left that place, and destroyed the village, including the goods, beads, guns, powder, cloth, etc., of one Hamês. The news reached Livingstone's camp the next morning, and prayers were at once offered up for Hamês, and some incense burnt. The Muslims held their prayer book (Kur'ân ?) in the smoke of the incense whilst the responses were being said.[2] Thus all the

1 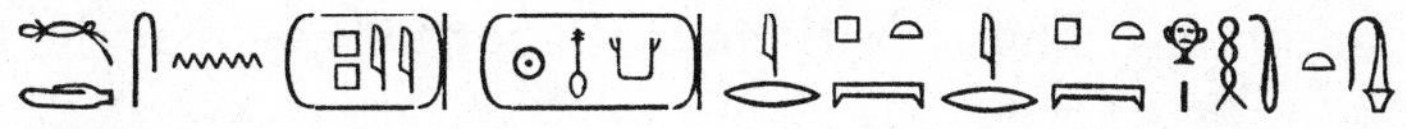
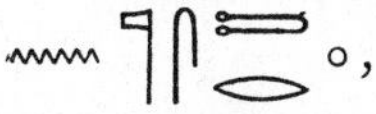 , l. 958.

2 *Last Journals*, Vol. I, p. 233.

prayers of the book were despatched to heaven on the wings of the burning incense, and the suppliants believed that they must be heard by God.

28. Sitting on the Shoulders.

In the Pyramid Text of Pepi I we read :

> Pepi cometh forth into heaven.
> He findeth Rā. Standing upright,[1] he meeteth him.
> He seateth himself on his shoulders.
> Rā will not permit him to descend to the ground,
> For behold, he knoweth that Pepi is greater than he.
> Pepi is more spirit than the spirits (*khu* ),
> More perfect than the perfect (*āqeru*  ),
> More stable than the stable ones (*tcheṭu* ).[2]

And in the Pyramid Text of Pepi II it is said, "Pepi Nefer-ka-Rā hath seated himself on thy shoulder, Osiris."[3] Thus we see that the kings of Egypt when they arrived in heaven were supposed to mount on the shoulders of both Rā and Osiris. The wording of the texts makes it clear that no allusion to the embracing of the king by these gods is meant, and it is quite clear that we are intended to understand that he seated himself on their shoulders. The idea seems strange until we remember that among many peoples in Africa chiefs and their wives are in the habit of travelling on the shoulders of their attendants from one place to another. Thus Sir Samuel Baker tells us that the chief

[1] *I.e.*, Pepi meets Rā as an equal, he does not bow before him.
[2] Pepi I, l. 91 = Meri-Rā, l. 120 = Pepi II, l. 698.
[3] , l. 958.

Katchiba was in the habit of travelling upon the back of a very strong subject, "precisely as children are wont "to ride pick-a-back. He generally had two or three "spare men, who alternately acted as guides and ponies, "while one of his wives invariably accompanied him, "bearing a large jar of beer."[1] When Livingstone was at Hara, "a daughter of Nsama came this afternoon to "be a wife and cementer of the peace! She came "riding 'pick-a-back' on a man's shoulders; a nice, "modest, good-looking young woman, her hair rubbed all "over with *nkola*, a red pigment, made from camwood, "and much used as an ornament."[2]

29. Red Body Colouring.

The wall paintings in Egyptian tombs, etc., often contain representations of men whose bodies are coloured red, and in papyri containing vignettes of the Book of the Dead the body of Osiris is frequently given this colour. From these it is clear that the Egyptians were in the habit of painting their bodies with red pigment, and many modern Africans follow their example at the present day. Thus among the Shilluks the poor anoint themselves with unguents with which wood-ashes are mixed, and their colour becomes grey; the landowners, or men of position, mix the ashes of cow-dung with their unguents, and when smeared with them their bodies have a dusky-red tint, like the "hue of red devils."[3] The Mañbattu use a "beauty-paint" made of the red powder of camwood, which is mixed with fat, and is rubbed over the whole body. The Niam-Niam also use a similar paint, which they apply to their bodies in spots and stripes; they stain red all their faces and breasts to increase the ferocity of their appearance.[4] The Acholi smear their whole bodies with red paint and fat.[5] The Baris paint their bodies with a pigment made of oxide of iron and grease, and give "themselves the

[1] *Albert N'yanza*, p. 210. See the illustration on p. 209.
[2] *Last Journals*, Vol. I, p. 231. See the illustration facing p. 232.
[3] Schweinfurth, *Heart of Africa*, Vol. I, p. 88.
[4] *Ibid.*, Vol. II, p. 106.
[5] Cunningham, *Uganda*, p. 354.

appearance of new red bricks."[1] The Baris pulled down the house built by the devoted Austrian missionaries, and having pounded and ground the bright red bricks of which it was built into powder, they mixed it with grease, and smeared their bodies with the mixture, and so "the house of God was turned into 'pommade divine.'"[2] The Nuers also stain their bodies red,[3] and the Mbichos rub their bodies all over with oils and red earth.[4] The people of Makalumbi use large quantities of red powder and oil in dressing their hair,[5] and the Taveta maidens smear themselves with red earth and fat.[6]

30. The Tortoise.

Among the Egyptians the tortoise was regarded as one of the personifications of evil, and the creature itself was classed with crocodiles, serpents, and other noxious creatures. In the Book of the Dead the death of the tortoise is followed by the living of Rā, and in Chapter CLXI the deceased says, "Rā liveth, the tortoise dieth." How the tortoise came to be associated with Thoth and the four winds of heaven, which are referred to in this Chapter, cannot be explained. In another place (Chapter LXXXIII) the deceased says, "I have dressed myself like the tortoise." The tortoise has an evil reputation among the Baganda, for they believe that the monster python Bemba, one of their mythical kings, was slain by the guile of Enfudu, the tortoise.[7] One of the ways of celebrating the making of peace after a war is to kill a tortoise with blows of a club.[8] Among the Fjort the tortoise is associated with the fire which came from heaven.[9]

[1] Baker, *Albert N'yanza*, p. 59.
[2] Baker, *Ismailia*, Vol. I, p. 237; *Albert N'yanza*, p. 59.
[3] Baker, *Albert N'yanza*, p. 39.
[4] Du Chaillu, *Adventures*, p. 109.
[5] Thomson, *To the Central African Lakes*, Vol. II, p. 111.
[6] Höhnel, *Discovery of Lakes Rudolf and Stephanie*, p. 102.
[7] Cunningham, *Uganda*, p. 154.
[8] Hollis, *Nandi*, p. 84.
[9] Dennett, *Notes on the Folklore of the Fiort*, p. 76.

31. The Primitive Village.

The Egyptian determinative for village, or town, or any inhabited district, is ⊗, *i.e.*, a circular enclosure surrounded by a wall, with two main streets at right angles to each other. Many modern villages in West Africa have this shape and arrangement of streets, *e.g.*, the Usimbi villages, Wenya and others, at Stanley Falls.[1] The villages of the Kavirondo are circular, have fences all round, and the cattle are brought in each night and the gates are shut.[2]

32. Decoration of Bows of Boats.

In the vignette to Chapter CXXXIII of the Book of the Dead we see Rā, the Sun-god, seated in his boat, from the bows of which hangs a sort of rectangular mat, with a bird perched on the top. The mat appears to be fringed. What seems to be a parallel to this is furnished by Stanley, who describes an Aruwimi war-canoe, and tells us that from its bow streamed a thick fringe of the long white fibre of the Hyphene palm.[3]

33. Tree-worship.

The Egyptians believed that certain deities took up their abode in trees, and several trees were regarded by them as sacred. Thus, in Heliopolis, there was the famous Persea tree, near which lived the Great Cat which cut off the head of the serpent of darkness,[4] and the god Sepes lived in a tree.[5] The god Rā appeared each morning from between two sycamore trees of turquoise,[6] and there was also in Heliopolis an olive (?) tree which was closely associated with Horus.[7] The goddesses Nut and Hathor lived in trees, and a vignette shows us the former giving bread and water to the

[1] Stanley, *Through the Dark Continent*, Vol. II, p. 260.
[2] Cunningham, *Uganda*, p. 279.
[3] *Through the Dark Continent*, Vol. II, p. 271.
[4] Book of the Dead, Chapter XVII, l. 19.
[5] *Ibid.*, Chapter CLXXIX, l. 3.
[6] *Ibid.*, Chapter CIX, l. 4.
[7] *Ibid.*, Chapter CLXXVIII, l. 3.

deceased, as he kneels by the stream on which the tree is planted.[1] In the celestial Heliopolis stood the sacred tree on the leaves of which Thoth and Sesheta wrote the names of kings and of the blessed dead.[2] This is, of course, the original of the Sidr, or Lote tree of Paradise, which the Muslims say contains as many leaves as there are human beings in the world, and that on each leaf the name of one human being is written. The cult of trees is common among many modern African peoples, some of whom regard tree-spirits as very powerful beings. Thus the Masai worship the spirits of the Subugo tree, and of the Retete tree, which is a species of parasitic fig. They propitiate these by killing a goat, and by bringing blood in a calabash and pouring it over the base of the tree trunk.[3] The cult of trees by the Masai is associated with the reverence which is paid to grass as a sacred symbol, and the "Laibanok," or sorcerers, pluck grass before they perform any of their magical ceremonies.[4] Near the Karŭma Falls is a tree in which lives a spirit that is supposed to gratify the powers and pleasures of men and women who summon its presence in the form appropriate to each.[5] Among the Gallas the Woda is esteemed holy, and under its shadow sacrifices and prayers are offered up to the exalted spirit who dwells in it. Of the greatest sanctity is the tree Worka (*Ficus sycamorus*), at Woda Nabi, by the River Hawash, where each year the Gallas offer up a great sacrifice to their deity Waka, and pray, saying: "O Wak, give us children, tobacco, corn, cows, oxen and sheep. Preserve us from sickness, and help us to slay our enemies who make war upon us, the Sidama (Christians) and the Islama (Muslims). O Wak, take us to thee, lead us into the garden, lead us not to Setani, and not into the fire."[6] The priests of this tree are called "Lubas," as opposed to the medicine-men, or sorcerers, who are called "Kalijas." The Camante perform their

[1] *Ibid.*, Chapter LIX.
[2] Figured in Lepsius, *Denkmäler*, Band III, Plate 169.
[3] Johnston, *Uganda*, Vol. II, p. 832.
[4] *Ibid.*, p. 833.
[5] Speke, *Journal*, p. 446, Dent's reprint.
[6] Krapf, *Travels*, p. 76.

religious ceremonies in dense forests, where they are said to pay particular reverence to the Cactus tree, ascribing to it a reasonable soul, and believing that the human race are sprung from it.[1] In the Camma country the people venerate a mighty tree which they call "Oloumi." Its bark is said to possess healing properties, and if a man washes himself in a decoction of it it is thought that he will be lucky and shrewd in making bargains.[2] In every Ibo community sacred trees and tree deities and spirits are to be found. The Efik people sacrifice a goat and a fowl each year to the tree called "Parando," and they present to it yams, plantains, and nimbo-tree wine. At Ogbe-abri lives the Tree-god Ani; at Isiskme is a grove sacred to Ede-mili, the Crop-god; Ofo, the god of justice and truth on the Niger, lives in the tree Ofo; and Osisi, a form of Ofo, lives in a tree. In Brass, when the Liana creeper is cut down, the natives have to perform expiatory ceremonies. In Southern Nigeria the Blood-plum tree is venerated. The Yorubas venerate the Aluki, a sort of prickly pear, and Asorin, the "father of trees," and the Ayan tree, and the Apa tree.[3] An account of a remarkable ceremony given by an eye-witness is quoted by Sir Harry Johnston. During a period of hunger a number of the Basoga came in canoes to a very fine specimen of a tree of the Parinarium species, which rose to the height of a hundred feet above the ground before giving out branches. The tree was surrounded by small fetish huts, and curious arcades, and umbrellas of straw. When the Basoga arrived at the base of the tree, they removed all their clothing, and wrapped ropes made of creepers round their arms and necks, and began to dance whilst songs were sung. After a time a little girl ten years old was brought, and laid at the base of a tree, and every action connected with slaying a sacrifice was gone through; and a slight incision was made in her neck. She was then thrown into a lake close by, but was saved from drowning by a man who stood ready to rescue her.

[1] *Ibid.*, p. 466.

[2] Du Chaillu, *Adventures*, p. 264.

[3] Leonard, *The Lower Niger*, p. 298 ff.; Ellis, *Yoruba-speaking Peoples*, p. 115.

The child was afterwards dedicated to a life of virginity. All this took place near Luba in Western Busoga.[1]

34. The Throne.

Egyptian hymns to Osiris, and those which relate to him and his successor Horus, lay great stress upon the fact that Horus inherited his father's throne, and sitting on it ruled the world. Thus in the Book of the Dead we have: "Thy throne hath descended to thy son Horus" (Chapter CLXXV, l. 14). "Horus, his son, is seated upon the throne of the Dweller in the Lake of Fire as his heir. . . . Horus is stablished upon his throne" (*ibid.*, ll. 20, 21). "Thy son Horus is triumphant. . . . The throne of Ḳeb hath been adjudged to him, together with the rank which was established by Temu, and ordered by decree in the Library, and recorded on a tablet according to the command of Ptaḥ-Tanen." (Chapter CLXXXIII, l. 12, f.). The throne of Horus passed naturally to his representative on earth, *i.e.*, to the king of Egypt, and from time immemorial in Africa the possession of the royal or tribal-chief's throne has been regarded as synonymous with the possession of the sovereignty over a country or district. The original throne of Osiris, as we have seen, probably contained portions of his body, and as long as these were preserved in it, his son Horus enjoyed the protection and power which they transmitted to the mystic seat, *i.e.*, he was under the direct influence of the great ancestral spirit. When the first king of Egypt sat upon that throne the spirit of Horus, as well as that of Osiris, protected and inspired him, and the divine power which these gods conferred upon him, by virtue of his succession to their sovereignty, gave to his words and deeds an authority which was divine and absolute. At certain periods in Egyptian history the people, from the highest to the lowest, regarded the king as god as well as king, and as the master of their lives, and bodies, and souls, and property. No one could sit upon the throne of Horus as king without the god's permission, and out of this belief grew up in

[1] Johnston, *Uganda*, Vol. II, p. 719.

Africa the idea of the divine right of kings. The oldest throne of Osiris was probably made of wood, but in late times fine alabaster, costly stone and metal, bronze, gold, etc., which were sometimes inlaid, were also employed. In the kingdom of Nubia the royal throne was made of gold, and in the inscription of Nȧstasen we are told that, after sacrificing two bulls, this king "went up and sat on the Golden Throne in the Golden Chamber, under the shadow of the great royal fans."[1] This he did at Napata. He then went to the city of Per-Ḳem, and having paid homage to Ȧmen he went up and sat on the golden throne; this act conferred upon him the sovereignty of that part of Nubia of which Per-Ḳem was the capital. He also went to P-nubs, the capital of another province, and went up and sat on the golden throne which was preserved there. Mention is also made by Nȧstasen that he went into an underground chamber and lay there for four nights, and that, having made offerings of all kinds to Ȧmen and sacrificed two bulls, he went into the temple and took his seat upon the "seat of state" which was in the "Chamber of the Throne." From the Book of the Dead we learn that the beatified in the Other World also possessed throne chambers with seats in them, for the XLVIIth Chapter is a spell the recitation of which prevented the "throne chamber and the throne," 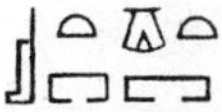, from being taken away from them.[2]

The importance of the tribal throne, which is one of the abodes of the ancestral spirit, is clearly recognized by modern African peoples. Thus the throne of Unyoro was very ancient, and had been in existence for many generations. It is quite a small object, and is made of copper and wood, and is regarded as a "cojoor," or talisman. The throne, and a very ancient drum, "which is considered with reverence as something uncanny," are always jealously guarded by special soldiers, and are

[1] For the text see Lepsius, *Denkmäler*, Band V, Plate 16.

[2] We may note, in passing, the "stark-naked people," the Wakidi, mentioned by Speke, who live up in trees, and have small stools fixed on behind, always ready for sitting upon. See *Journal of the Discovery of the Source of the Nile*, p. 81, Dent's reprint.

seldom used. Should the throne be lost or stolen, the authority of the king would disappear, together with the talisman, and disorder would reign throughout the country until the precious object should be restored.[1] Nothing can happen in Unyoro without the order of the king. The superstitious veneration for the possession of the magic throne produces a profound obedience.[2] It was on this throne that Kamrasi sat when Baker visited him, and on that occasion it rested upon a carpet of leopard skins.[3]

35. Dried Human Bodies.

Reference has already been made to the costliness of embalmment among the Egyptians. The remains of many bodies which have been found in large, common graves suggest that attempts were made to preserve them by drying them in the sun or by the help of fire; both methods were probably employed. Drying by fire has been commonly practised in many parts of Africa in recent years, and Miss Kingsley states that it was customary when a native of Benin died to dry his body over a gentle fire, and then to take it back for burial to his native city.[4] It may also be noted that when Livingstone died at Kataui on Lake Bemba, his faithful servants removed his internal organs and dried his body in the sun for twenty-two days; they then rolled it in blankets and put it in the bark shell of a small tree, and carried it to the coast. This information was given to Mr. H. Ward by Uledi Pagani.[5] In the late period the Egyptians preserved bodies in honey, and this custom is not unknown in West Africa, for when Sonni Ali, Emperor of Songhay, was drowned in 1492, his body was eviscerated by his sons, and filled with honey, and carried back and laid in the tombs of his fathers.[6]

[1] Baker, *Ismailia*, Vol. II, p. 206.

[2] *Ibid.*, p. 316.

[3] *Albert N'yanza*, p. 288.

[4] *West African Studies*, p. 455.

[5] Ward, H., *A Voice from the Congo*, p. 65. The names of the men who saved him from the lion were Wadi Mozera and Muini Hasali.

[6] Shaw, *Tropical Dependency*, p. 179.

36. Cannibalism, Human Sacrifice, etc.

In addition to the instances already given the following may be noted. The Gabun eat the dead, just as did the Gabun Fang and the Ogowe Fang,[1] and the Mañbattu,[2] Wasongora Meno, and Waregga are also cannibals.[3] The Gbalin tribe of Kpwesi fatten and eat prisoners and slaves.[4] In Ofurekpe, in Old Calabar, the people eat prisoners of war, otherwise the inhabitants "are everything to be desired."[5] It is on record that in 1668–9 four sailors were captured by some of them, and that three of the four were killed and eaten at once.[6] Among many secret societies in Africa the eating of human flesh forms one of their most sacred rites,[7] and many sorcerers are believed to eat portions of the bodies of the dead.[8] The Angicas were in the habit of eating human flesh,[9] and in the fifteenth century the Benins, the most civilized of all the coast tribes, lived upon it.[10] Queen Shinga before undertaking any new enterprise cut off the head of the handsomest man in her guard, and drank a deep draught of his blood.[11] In proof of the view that cannibalism is not a thing of the past, as some imagine, we may note Mr. H. Ward's remarks in his *Voice from the Congo*, London, 1910. Cannibalism is, he says, a regular practice, and the people eat human flesh as a standard article of diet because they have an innate love of it. They say: "It gives us a strong "heart for fighting, and we eat men because it is good "to eat meat that talked with us." Men are fattened

[1] Nassau, *Fetichism*, p. 235.

[2] Frobenius, *Heiden-Neger*, p. 420.

[3] Stanley, *Through the Dark Continent*, Vol. II, p. 106.

[4] Johnston, *Liberia*, Vol. II, p. 952.

[5] Kingsley, *West African Studies*, p. 564.

[6] *Ibid.*, p. 567.

[7] *Ibid.*, p. 538.

[8] Johnston, *Uganda*, Vol. II, p. 578. The Bakwains buried their dead hastily in their huts lest the witches (Baloi) should disinter them and use parts of their bodies in their fiendish arts.—Livingstone, *Travels*, p. 129. On eating the heart see *Last Journals*, Vol. II, p. 49.

[9] Battell, *Strange Adventures*, p. 101.

[10] Shaw, *Tropical Dependency*, p. 179.

[11] She had sixty male concubines who took the names of women and wore female dress.—Reade, *Savage Africa*, 1863 edit., p. 364.

and taken to the market at Mubangi, where they are hawked about alive. Mr. Ward saw four Lulungu captives soaked in water up to their chins, and then killed and eaten.[1]

With reference to human sacrifices at burial Mr. Ward describes the funeral of a chief of Bolobo. His body was painted white, black, red, and yellow, and he wore a feather headdress; as he lay in his grave, ten women and several young men were pushed into the grave with the body, and when earth had been poured in on them and they had been trampled down, a dance was held on the spot.[2] When a Bairo chief died his wives committed suicide as a matter of course,[3] and even at the death of a great African lady a slave was sacrificed.[4] The people of Senjero offer up human beings as sacrifices, and many families must slay their first-born sons, so that their blood may be poured out on the base of a certain pillar.[5] King Kwoffi Karri Kari sacrificed a human victim every Tuesday to his "fetish," which was kept in a gold box covered with plates.[6] On the terrible sacrifice of human life which went on at the "watering" of the skeletons and tombs of deceased kings in Dahomey, see a most interesting letter written by the Rev. P. W. Bernasko in 1860, and published by Burton.[7] In Ashanti many human victims were sacrificed yearly on the king's birthday, in addition to those which were offered up to the gods monthly, and to the spirits of the dead kings at the Annual Customs.[8]

37. THE SPIRIT-BURIAL, OR SECOND BURIAL.

Among the tribes of the Lower Niger the custom of Second Burial, or Spirit-Burial, is common. This burial is conducted on much the same lines as the first, except that a greater entertainment is provided, and the

[1] See pp. 231, 275, 277, 278, 283.
[2] *Ibid.*, p. 55. See also Junker, *Travels*, Vol. III, pp. 261, 262.
[3] Johnston, *Uganda*, Vol. II, p. 610.
[4] Kingsley, *West African Studies*, p. 453.
[5] Krapf, *Travels*, p. 69.
[6] Kingsley, *Travels in West Africa*, p. 512.
[7] Burton, *A Mission to Gelele*, Vol. II, p. 331, and see pp. 334, 335, and especially p. 354. Also Skertchley, *Dahomey*, pp. 340, 351, 416.
[8] Skertchley, *Dahomey*, p. 513.

expenses incurred are heavier. The second burial is, in a spiritual sense, of greater importance than the first, "because it is a special memorial service held over the deceased in order to release him from the thraldom of the region of the dead in which all souls are confined, . . . and to usher him triumphantly, as befits his birth, into the abode of his fathers in the world of spirits." No soul can attain to the peaceful ancestral habitations without the rite of second burial. Formerly human sacrifice accompanied this rite, one hundred slaves and a horse being sometimes killed on the death of an elder, but since the British Government has interfered in native customs, animals and gifts of food, etc., are contributed by friends instead of slaves. Among some sections of the Ibo peoples the Okuku ceremony, which is identical with the second burial or lamentation ceremony, was remarkable from the fact that during its performance a male or female slave was killed and eaten by those who belonged to the family of the deceased. The slave was beheaded by the eldest son. Without this sacrificial entertainment the soul, it was thought, would either remain for ever dormant, or, being in the power of the god of death, would be liable to be absorbed by him, or be used as a malignant force. The New Calabar people, prior to the introduction of Christianity, were in the habit of performing a still more elaborate set of ceremonies in connection with the "Duen-fubara," or image of the deceased.

The Duen-fubara was a painted wooden figure representing the head and shoulders of the deceased, which was intended to be the abode for his spirit. It was made by the Fucheans, who had the monopoly of making such things, and was brought to the house of the deceased, where living sacrifices were offered to it, and their blood poured over it. When this had been done, the sons of the dead man, with a number of followers, went to the house, and endeavoured to carry off the Duen-fubara by force. When the servants of the house resisted them, a sort of sham fight followed, and this was kept up for a time. At length the defenders of the Duen-fubara gave way, and the sons obtained possession of the figure, which they took to a small house that had been specially built to receive it. This was the house-chapel of the family, and a trusty man was appointed to guard the figure, and to keep the house swept and clean.[1] The wooden figure is identical with the KA figure of the Egyptians, the house is identical with the "KA chapel," and the ministrant is the equivalent of the "priest of the KA."

These ceremonies are identical with those of the memorial service for the dead which is common throughout Egypt and the Sûdân, and they closely resemble those which the ancient Egyptians performed for their dead, when their object was to secure the passage of their souls from the land of death to the land of the spirits. It cannot be too strongly insisted that spirits were believed to be alive in the land of death, and that death with them did not imply finality. The reason why the living were so anxious that the spirits of the dead should pass from the land of death to the land of spirits was that they might take up their position as spirit-fathers, and act as guardians and protectors of their families.

If we apply these considerations to the history of the burial of Osiris we shall see that the ideas which prompted the performance of the funerary ceremonies of Osiris are identical with those which cause the modern African to undertake the labour and expense of the second burial of his kinsfolk. The details of the murder and dismemberment of Osiris are given elsewhere, so we may pass on to consider his second burial. The Book of Opening the Mouth describes at considerable length the funerary ceremonies performed for Osiris at his first and second burials, but they have not been kept distinct in that work. The ceremonies connected with the slaughtering of the bulls, and with the presentation of the reeking hearts and the legs of the animals, represent those which were performed at the first burial, but we must note that, even at the early period when the Book of Opening the Mouth was reduced to writing, bulls had taken the place of the human victims which had been sacrificed at the actual burial of Osiris. Nearly all the other ceremonies, especially those which deal with the censing, anointing, dressing, and decoration

[1] See Leonard, *The Lower Niger*, p. 159 ff.

tion of the mummy, belong to the second burial, and their object was to give Osiris the power to pass from the land of death to the land of the spirits. In later times, when a KA figure, or statue, took the place of the mummy, the object was the same, but the figure was placed in a specially prepared chamber or shrine, like the Duen-fubara, in order that the spirit who used it as an abode from time to time might be consulted and appealed to for help in time of trouble, by those who lived on the earth. The second burial of Osiris thus not only freed his spirit from the land of death, but made him to become the great and powerful ancestral spirit and protector of the tribe which founded his cult in primitive times. At a later period, when his worship spread over all Egypt, he became the spirit-protector of all the country, and the ancestor-god, *par excellence*, of all its inhabitants.

Among modern African tribes the second burial may be deferred for several months after the death of an individual, and sometimes a whole year elapses before the spirit-burial takes place. Whether this was so in the case of Osiris cannot be said, but we know that the burial of this god was commemorated annually. In primitive times human beings were, no doubt, sacrificed before his statue, and their blood sprinkled on it and on the ground about his shrine, in much the same way as the skeletons of the kings of Dahomey are "watered," *i.e.*, bathed, with blood once a year. In course of time animals were substituted for men, and their flesh was eaten sacramentally by the priests and certain of the worshippers. It is possible that at some of the shrines one human being at least was eaten sacramentally, just as a human victim was eaten during the Okuku ceremonies of the Niger tribes. As time went on the slaughter of men ceased, and libations of wine took the place of "waterings" with blood, and in one of the vignettes in the Papyrus of Nebseni we see a series of bunches of grapes hanging from the roof of the shrine in which Osiris is seated. The offerings made to Osiris at the annual commemoration were very numerous, and their comprehensive character is well illustrated by the Great and Little Lists of Offerings which are included in the text of the Book of Opening the Mouth. They consisted of incense of different kinds, unguents of various sorts, wines from the South and the North, beer, the flesh of animals, geese and other birds, cosmetics, changes of raiment, fruit, vegetables, flowers, etc. The offerings at the tomb of Osiris much resembled those which are presented by relatives, friends, and neighbours in honour of a modern king or chief in Western Africa at his second burial. And the great feast which followed the conclusion of the solemn ceremonies was characterised by the same weepings, cries, shouts of joy, laughter, dancing, noise of pipes, drums, horns, etc., and acrobatic performances which accompany the second burial of a great king at the present day. Of course, they have nowadays, in addition, explosions of gunpowder, fusillades of rifles, and noises caused by instruments of music of European origin.

Under the New Empire the cult of Osiris developed with extraordinary rapidity, and temples were built in honour of the god at Abydos and at other great centres of his worship. In these his festivals were observed, and once a year commemorative ceremonies of a more or less elaborate character were performed. During such festivals priestesses assumed the characters of Isis and Nephthys, and recited before the shrine of the god addresses and hymns in which the sufferings and death, and the reconstitution and resurrection of Osiris, were described. Added to these were many expressions of great grief for the death of their lord, and invocations to him to return to them and to remove from their hearts the sorrow and pain which his departure had caused them. These addresses, which are commonly known as the "Lamentations of Isis and Nephthys," and the "Festival Songs of Isis and Nephthys," are equivalent to the words of mourning which are addressed to kings and chiefs of Africa at their second burials, and were sung with the same object, *i.e.*, to assist Osiris as the great ancestral spirit in his operations in the Spirit-world, to gratify him and to win his favour for deceased relatives and friends, to obtain his assistance for the Egyptians in their daily life, and to induce him to give them full and satisfactory inundations of the Nile, and good harvests.

CHAPTER XXV.

The Goddess Isis.

Of the exact position which Isis held among the gods of Egypt under the first four dynasties, and of the attributes which the Egyptians ascribed to her in the Archaic Period, we know nothing, but it is probable that she was generally regarded as the female counterpart of Osiris, and that she was believed to minister to his wants, and to guard and protect him with the devotion and fidelity of a truly loving wife. We find figures of a goddess who, as she appears with Osiris, must be Isis, on some of the cylinders which have been discovered at Abydos, and if this be the case, there is good reason for believing that Isis was known in the Predynastic Period. One thing seems to be quite certain: her fortunes were bound up with those of Osiris, and as his cult grew and developed throughout Egypt, so the fame and power of Isis increased in the land. It is impossible to arrive at a final conclusion on these points, for the evidence necessary is not forthcoming, but lack of evidence does not justify the statements made by those writers who assert that Isis had no place among the gods of the Ancient Empire. Until we know from hieroglyphic inscriptions what views were held about Osiris by the Egyptians of this period, it is futile to discuss the position of Isis. Those who took the view that Osiris was a mere tribal chief would regard Isis as a tribal chief's wife; those who worshipped Osiris under the form of a bull would naturally think of Isis as a cow; those who revered Osiris as a great, mighty, and terrible ancestral spirit would consider Isis as his spirit counterpart, and so on. The characteristics of Isis changed as Osiris absorbed little by little the attributes and powers of other gods, and from being in the earliest times a somewhat obscure, and probably local, goddess, she became the chief deity of all Egypt, and, in late times, her worship wholly eclipsed that of her male counterpart Osiris.

The oldest form of the name of the goddess in Egyptian is 𓊨𓏏, which is usually transcribed "Ȧst," but the true reading of the two hieroglyphic signs seems to be "S[e]t," or "S[a]t." The vowel which was prefixed to assist the pronunciation of the two consonants was probably *a* 𓄿 and not *ȧ* 𓇋, and in this case the name of the goddess is to be read "Ast." The classical form of the name suggests that a vowel to assist in pronouncing the two consonants was prefixed, and in modern times in Egypt we have *istîm* for "steam," and *exepress* for "express." The word *ast* means "seat, throne, chamber, house, abode, place," etc., but there seems to be no possibility of connecting any one of these with the attributes of the goddess in such a way as to give a rational explanation of her name, and none of the derivations hitherto proposed can be regarded as satisfactory. As the wife of Osiris she was her husband's throne, as the mother of Horus she was the house in which he came into being, as the great World-Mother she was the abode in which all life originated, and her womb was the source whence sprang gods and men, the harvest, and all living creatures. There is no doubt that at one time or another all these, and many other similar ideas, were associated by the Egyptians with her name, but she was dear to the Egyptians of all periods because they regarded her as the type of the faithful wife and loving mother, who bore pain and suffering, sorrow and solitude, and endured untold persecutions from Set, her husband's murderer, for the sake of her lord and his beloved son Horus.

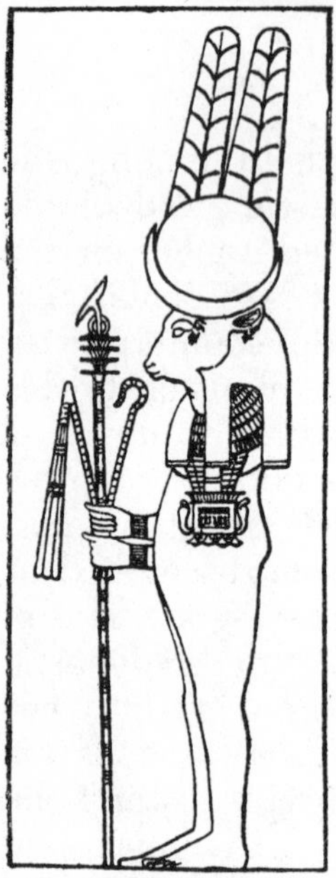

The Bull-god Ȧsȧr-Ḥep (Sarapis).

Numerous passages in the Pyramid Texts prove that, even so far back as the Vth dynasty, Osiris and Isis, Set and Nephthys, were regarded as the deified members of a family of human beings, and from this time onward, even down to and including the Roman Period, the conceptions of the Egyptians about this group of gods never changed. Set was detested as the murderer of his good and noble brother Osiris, and the persecutor of the forlorn widow Isis, his brother's wife, and the usurper of the throne and kingdom which belonged to the son of Osiris. The sympathy of all men went out to Isis, who, after her husband's murder, brought forth her son in the papyrus swamps of Lower Egypt, where Set, in the form of a scorpion, stung the child and killed him. Nephthys, her sister's constant and faithful companion, insisted that Isis should appeal to Rā in heaven, and as a result Thoth provided her with the knowledge of certain words of power which restored life to the body of Horus. Further, all men approved of the direct intervention of heaven at this juncture, and applauded Isis for training Horus to engage in mortal combat against his uncle Set, his father's murderer and the usurper of his throne. Throughout the history of Osiris Nephthys appears as her sister's most devoted helper in every trouble and difficulty, and as an affectionate ally of her murdered brother, and a gracious protector of her nephew, his son. Osiris was the type of the good god, king, and husband, Isis was the model of all that a goddess, queen, wife, and mother should be, and Horus exhibited the traits of filial love, which expressed themselves in constant care for his widowed mother and in killing his father's murderer, and which appealed to the heart of every father and mother in Egypt. Apart from these considerations the Egyptians throughout the Dynastic Period regarded their kings as the lineal descendants of that Horus, the son of Osiris, who was conceived and brought forth by Isis after her husband's death, and who became the first king of Egypt. Therefore Osiris and Isis were the ancestors of their kings, and the divine origin of their kings was the secret of their power, which at certain periods in the history of Egypt was absolute. In obeying the king the Egyptians believed they were obeying God, and in placing their souls, bodies, and possessions at the uncontrolled disposal of their king, they thought they were proving themselves to be loyal and religious servants of God. The sovereignty of this earth was inherited by the Horus, *i.e.*, king, not from Osiris, but from his grandfather Ḳeb, the god of the earth, and only his inheritance of heaven came to him from Osiris.

With the rise to power of the Theban princes of the XIth dynasty, and their successors of the XIIth, the cult of Osiris developed greatly, and about this time the fame and renown of Isis as the queen of Osiris, and the "mother of the god," *i.e.*, Horus, began to fill the land. The performances of the sacred Osiris-play at Abydos and elsewhere brought the loving care of Isis for her husband and son into great prominence, and as "queen of heaven" her protection was eagerly sought after throughout Upper and Lower Egypt. She became the great and beneficent goddess and mother, whose influence and love pervaded all heaven, and earth, and the Other World, and she became the personification of the great feminine, creative power which conceived and brought forth every living creature and thing, from the gods in heaven to man on the earth and the insect on the ground. What she brought forth she protected, and cared for, and fed, and nourished, and she employed her life in using her power graciously and successfully, not only in creating new beings, but in restoring to life those that were dead. Throughout the Book of the Dead Isis is spoken of as a giver of life and food to the dead, and she appears in the pictures of Osiris in his shrine in the Judgment Hall with the god, ready to assist in the judgment of the dead. Isis and Nephthys are often identified with the two goddesses of Truth (Maāti), and each may be regarded as a judge of the dead.

Of the sufferings of Isis we find no connected account until we come to the XXXth dynasty, when the famous stele, commonly known as the "Metternich Stele,"[1] was made. This valuable monument tells us that after Set had murdered Osiris, he placed Isis, who was with child, under restraint, but she, acting under the advice of

[1] It was given to Prince Metternich by Muḥammad 'Ali in 1828, and a facsimile of it, with texts and translations, was published by Golénischeff at Leipzig in 1877.

Thoth, who foretold the ultimate triumph of her son Horus, and his accession to his father's throne, succeeded in making her escape one evening. With her went the Seven Scorpion-goddesses—Tefen, Befen, Mestet, Mestetef, Petet, Thetet, and Maatet—and they led her to the village of Per-sui, near the Papyrus Swamps. When Isis arrived at Teb she wished to beg shelter from a woman of position, who lived there and was connected with the overlord of the district, but the woman, seeing her coming, shut the door in her face. Enraged at the treatment which Isis received from this woman, one of the Scorpion-goddesses, Tefen, made her way into the woman's house under the door, and stung her child to death, and set her house on fire. Isis, taking pity on the woman's grief for her child, laid her hands on him and restored him to life, and a flood of rain extinguished the flames of the burning house. Meanwhile a peasant woman had invited Isis to her house, and the goddess went in and stayed there, and the woman who had refused her admission suffered agonies of remorse for a whole night.

Soon after this Isis brought forth her child Horus on a bed of papyrus plants in the Swamps, and she rejoiced greatly in him, because she knew that he would avenge the murder of his father. She hid him carefully, and concealed him, fearing lest he should be stung by some venomous reptile, and one day set out to go to the city of Am, in order to obtain provisions and other necessaries for her son. When she returned she found him lying stiff and dead, with foam on his lips, and the ground round about him was soaked with water from his eyes. In a moment she realized what had happened; Set, in the form of a scorpion, had succeeded in discovering the child, and had stung him to death. The shrieks of Isis rent the air, and caused all her neighbours to run to the place where she was, but though they offered her sympathy, nothing which they could do brought Horus back to life. At length Nephthys came to her sister's help, and she counselled Isis to appeal to Rā in heaven for assistance. This she did, and having cried out to Rā, the sun stood still in heaven, the Boat of Millions of Years stopped, and

Thoth descended to earth to comfort Isis, and to repeat to her the spell which she was to use to restore Horus to life. Isis learned the words of power, and when she had uttered them the poison flowed forth from the body of Horus, air entered his lungs, sense and feeling returned to him, and he was restored to life. Thoth ascended into the sky and took his seat once more in the Boat of Millions of Years, and the sun resumed his course amid shouts of joy on the part of the denizens of heaven, who gloried greatly in the restoration of Horus to life. The temporary death of Horus turned out to be a blessing for mankind, for it was the immediate cause of Isis's obtaining from Thoth a potent spell against the bite of scorpions. This spell Isis transmitted to her priests, and by its use they were enabled to do away the effects of the reptile's poison in the human body, and so to preserve the lives of many Egyptians. The sorrows of Isis, the search for her husband's body, her weary wanderings, her loneliness when she brought forth Horus, the death of the child, etc., probably formed the subjects of scenes that were acted at the Osiris-play, which was performed annually at Mendes, Abydos, and other centres of the cult of Osiris. When Horus had grown up he fought a duel with Set, which lasted for three days and three nights. Towards the close of the fight Horus began to gain the upper hand, and at length he succeeded in fettering his adversary. When Isis saw this, pity for her brother Set moved her, and she uttered a spell which had the effect of causing the fetters of Set to fall away from him, and he escaped. Horus was filled with wrath at his mother's ill-timed clemency, and he raged at her like the savage leopard of the South, and as she fled from before his anger he pursued her and cut off her head. At this juncture Thoth intervened, and transforming the head of Isis into that of a cow, he attached it to her body straightway.

Under the New Empire Isis became, beyond all doubt, the greatest goddess in Egypt, and the following titles illustrate the estimation in which she was held throughout the land:[1] "She of many names. The

[1] See Brugsch, *Thesaurus*, pp. 102, 217–219.

"Great One who is from the beginning. The divine "one. The only one. The greatest of the gods and "goddesses. The Queen of all the gods. The best "beloved of all the gods. The prototype of all beings. "Queen of goddesses and women. The female Rā. "The female Horus. The Eye of Rā. The right eye "of Rā (as Sothis). The star-crown of Rā-Horus. The "Queen of the Dekan stars. Sothis, who openeth the "New Year. The lady of the beginning of the year. "Occupier of the chief place in the boat of heaven. "The maker of the sunrise. The lady of heaven. The "holy one of heaven. Light-giver in heaven with Rā. "She of the beams of gold. The golden one. The "most brilliant goddess. Lady of the north wind. The "Queen of earth. The mightiest of the mighty. The "mighty one on the earth of Ḳeb. The Queen of the "South and North. Queen of the South. Queen and "Lady of the lands of the South. Chieftainess in the "North. Lady of the solid earth. She who vomiteth "fire. Blazing flame. She who filleth the Ṭuat with "good things. She who is greatly feared in the Ṭuat. "The great goddess in the Ṭuat with Osiris in her name "'Tanit.' The mother of the god [Horus]. The "mother of the god Horus, the Mighty Bull. The "mother of the Golden Horus, who brought her son "into the world in the Birth-chamber so that he might "inherit the rank of his father. Giver of new birth to "the god of Panopolis (Ka Nekht). The nurse and "protector of her son Horus. The Lady of the Birth-"chamber. The Cow Ḥeru-sekha, who bringeth forth "all things. Who nourished the child Horus with her "milk. Bestower of life. Lady of life. Creatress of "green things. Bestower of life. Giver of her goods "to the gods, and giver of offerings to the spirits. "Green goddess, whose green colour is like unto the "greenness of the earth. Lady of bread. Lady of beer. "Lady of abundance. Lady of joy and gladness. Lady "of Love. Who delivereth to the king his rank, with-"out whom no king can exist. Lady of the temple. "Queen of the Great House and of the House of Fire. "Beautiful in appearance. Beloved in all lands. "Mighty one. Beautiful (or, majestic) one. Beautiful "of face in Thebes. Majestic one in Heliopolis. "Beneficent one in Memphis. Mistress of spells. "Weaver and fuller. Daughter of Ḳeb. Daughter "of the Universal Lord. Child of Nut. First royal "wife of Rā. Consort of her father. Whose son is the "lord of the earth. Whose husband is the lord of the "deep. Whose husband is the inundation of the Nile. "Who maketh the Nile to swell and overflow. Who "maketh the Nile to swell in his season." The last-mentioned titles of the goddess refer to Isis-Sothis, whose appearance in the sky indicated the immediate advent of the inundation of the Nile, and warned men to be ready to begin the agricultural labours of a new year. Though essentially the goddess, *par excellence*, of the South, Isis had control over the stars of the Great Bear and of the other constellations of the North who were supposed to be able to exercise an influence for evil over the sun in the season of spring. As Osiris was, in one of his aspects, the lord of grain, so Isis was the goddess of crops, and her benign influence made grain of all sorts to grow, garden produce to be abundant, and fruit to ripen. She was the personification of all tilled lands, the benevolent spirit of the fields, and the goddess of the harvest.

The association of Isis with the Other World is very ancient, and the history of the resurrection of Osiris proves that the powers of the goddess in this region were very great. An Egyptian legend asserts that Horus reconstituted his father's body with the help of his four sons, but it was the spells which Isis recited, having learned them from Thoth, which gave permanence to the work of Horus, and made the unguents, balsams, spices, and drugs used by the great physician Anubis, in the embalmment of the body of Osiris, to possess their marvellous properties. The Egyptians, believing that Isis gave to her lord a newly constituted body, spared no pains in invoking her help to attain new bodies in the Other World, and on her they relied for meat and drink. Under the form called Ȧmenit, 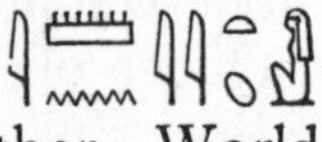, Isis was the personification of the Other World. Though Osiris was the absolute Lord of that region, and none entered therein except through him and by his consent, it was Isis who directed all matters connected with the maintenance of the Spirit-bodies of the blessed there, just as the first wife of a modern African chief directs the temporal affairs of her lord's household. Moreover, the righteous were re-born in Ȧmenit, or Isis, and the decision as to whether the dead should leave Ȧmentet, the "Hidden Land," or Hades, or Dead-land, and renew their lives in the region on the further side of the river, or sea, which ran through one portion of the Other World, rested entirely with her. Read in connection with what has already been said about the power of Osiris in the Other World, this statement may be thought to exaggerate the powers of Isis in the same region, but if we consider the part played by Isis in the history of Osiris, we shall find that without her help Osiris must have perished. It was Isis who searched out and collected the members of his mutilated body, and presided over its reconstitution. It was Isis who uttered the spells which revivified his body, and made him to have union with her after his death and beget their son Horus. Isis resisted the attacks made upon her by Set, and protected herself against his machinations. She hid herself in the Papyrus Swamps during the period of her pregnancy, and maintained herself until her child was born. Her spells raised Horus from the dead after he had been killed by the sting of a scorpion, and it was Isis who reared him and trained him until he was old enough to do battle with his uncle Set, the murderer of Osiris. Thus Isis revivified Osiris, gave him a son, revivified that son also, and, having made him avenge his father's death, seated him on his father's throne, and obtained for him the inheritance of her father Ḳeb.

Among the Egyptians of the Middle and New Empires Isis was regarded as a great magician, and the papyri contain several allusions to her magical powers. She knew how to weave spells and how to fashion magical figures, and she possessed the knowledge of all the secret or hidden names of all the gods and of all the spirits, both good and bad, and she used them in such a way that each of them was compelled to do her will. At her bidding the powers of nature ceased or modified their operations, and she could make everything, both animate and inanimate, to perform her will. There is a legend which states that at one time there existed one being whose secret name was unknown to her, viz., Rā the Sun-god. This name Isis determined to know, and to effect her purpose she took some of the spittle of the god and mixed it with dust from the ground, and, having formed a venomous serpent therewith, she endowed it with life, and set it on the path traversed by Rā when he went on his daily tour of inspection in heaven. As he passed the serpent, the reptile bit him, and the god became sick unto death. Then Isis went to him, and promised to destroy the effect of the poison and to restore him to health if he would tell her his secret name. This Rā hesitated to do, but as his sufferings increased, and he drew nigh to death, his agony forced him to reveal his name to the goddess Isis, who straightway uttered the spell which relieved his pain and healed him. One of the most powerful amulets known to the Egyptians was the object  *thet*, which carried with it the influence of her blood, and magical powers, and words of power. We have already seen that it is most probably a conventional representation of the uterus with its ligatures, and the vagina. The all-powerful symbol of Osiris is a portion of his backbone,  *teṭ*, or rather the *os sacrum* set on a stand, and analogy suggests that the amulet , the all-powerful symbol of Isis, represents some organ of her body. The greatness of the power of Isis is well illustrated by the fact that she did not suffer death like Osiris, and the Egyptian inscriptions do not mention any tomb of Isis.[1] Whether the Egyptians believed that she passed from this world to the Other World unchanged in respect of her body cannot be said, but there is little doubt that, at least in the latest days of her cult in Egypt, it was her immunity from death which most impressed the Egyptians and the nations around, and made them to

[1] Diodorus (I, 27) says that her tomb was at Nysa in Arabia.

exalt her powers over those of Osiris. When her cult finally broke down through the development and mighty spreading of Christianity in Egypt, Isis was to her votaries the type and symbol of all that is greatest and best in woman in her character of the unselfish, true, tender, loving, and eternal World Mother.

Isis is generally depicted on the monuments and papyri in the form of a woman who wears on her head a vulture-headdress, and holds in one hand 𓋹 and in the other 𓇅. The usual ornament or crown on her head consists of a pair of horns, between which is a solar or lunar disk; this is sometimes surmounted by 𓊨, the symbol of the sound of her name. Sometimes she wears the Crowns of the South and North, to the back of which is attached the feather of Maāt, and sometimes she wears with the pair of horns and the solar disk two plumes. Her horns are those of the Cow of Hathor 𓄋, but occasionally, as the female counterpart of the Ram of Mendes, she wears a pair of ram's horns under her double crown. Isis, as a woman, and not as a goddess, wears the ordinary head-dress of a woman, but even so she has an uraeus over her forehead, for the Egyptians never forgot her divine origin. As the goddess of the Island of Senemtet, near Philae, she wore a sort of flat cap, having a fillet decorated with uraei and fastened with cords or bands, the ends of which drop down behind her head.[1] By means of this head-dress Isis is identified with the local goddess of the Island. In her character of female counterpart of Osiris, Isis takes, naturally, the form of a cow, and she is often seen wearing the characteristic emblems of ancient Cow-goddesses, viz., Hathor, Meḥ-urt, etc. In the New Empire it became the fashion for women to wear attached to necklaces pendants made of porcelain[2] or metal, which represent the goddess seated among lotus

[1] Lanzone, *Dizionario*, tav. CCCIX.
[2] See the fine example in the British Museum, No. 26, 233.

plants with her newly born child Horus on her knees, and which were intended to commemorate the successful birth of her child. These pendants were, strictly speaking, amulets, which were supposed to give their wearers the power to conceive, and to give birth to children without difficulty, and to secure for them the help of Thoth, who acted as "medicine-man" at the confinement of Isis, and the protection of the goddesses of Upper and Lower Egypt, and of Rā, and of Isis herself. Similarly, the pictures of the bier of Osiris, with Isis standing or kneeling at the foot and Nephthys at the head, which are painted on coffins of the New Empire and of the Ptolemaïc and Roman Periods, are also amulets which brought to them the protection of Isis and Nephthys. In Chapter CLIA of the Book of the Dead Isis says that she has brought to the deceased "the north wind which cometh from Temu," and has strengthened his throat, and set all his enemies under his feet. Thus Isis presided over the conception and birth of human beings into this world and into the next.

CHAPTER XXVI.

The Worship of Osiris and Isis in Foreign Lands.

The raids made by the Egyptians into the Sûdân and the Sinaitic Peninsula under the Ancient and Middle Empires, and the military expeditions into Western Asia made by the great kings of the New Empire, must have carried among the conquered peoples and tribes a knowledge of the gods of Egypt. And the foreign sailors and merchants who traded with Egypt in the Red Sea and Mediterranean Sea must also have carried back with them to their coasts, or islands, and homes, accounts of the curious people whose gods were in the form of the bull, ram, cat, crocodile, jackal, hippopotamus, birds, reptiles, trees, stone pillars, etc. If any of them became acquainted with the strange legends of the gods which were current among the priesthoods of Heliopolis and Memphis, and reported them to their stay-at-home relatives and friends, it is easy to think that they would only be regarded, at first at least, as mere "travellers' tales." When the kings of Egypt ceased to raid countries, and began to occupy them effectively, and to work the mines in them by forced labour under military supervision, the vanquished peoples were brought face to face with men who worshipped these strange animal-gods and emblems, and built temples for them, and they were obliged to obey these foreign rulers. The gods of the indigenous Egyptians and the Sûdânî tribes were, I believe, in primitive times the same, and the worship of these formed a bond between Nubia and Egypt. The solar gods and the Nature gods and Phallic gods of Libya and the Eastern Desert which the later Egyptians adopted were strangers to the Nubians, and a considerable time must have elapsed before their cult became established in their country. We know from the bas-reliefs on tombs and temples and from the inscriptions in the Northern Sûdân that the tribes so far south as Wâd ben-Nagaa and Maṣawwarât adopted a great many of the Egyptian gods who were worshipped under the New Empire and in the Ptolemaïc and Roman Periods, but this was due to the effective occupation of the Northern Sûdân by the Egyptians, Ptolemies, and Roman Emperors, rather than to the deliberate choice of the people. The Northern Nubians as a whole can never have understood the mysteries and intricacies of the Egyptian religion, and there is good reason to believe that the Sûdânî tribes who lived in the country between Kom Ombo and the Equator always preferred the original African cult of ancestors to the modified form of it which became current in Egypt after the introduction of the cult of Rā under the IVth dynasty. The town of Meroë on the Island of Meroë and the Island of Philae were the great centres of the cult of Osiris and Isis for hundreds of years after the downfall of the native religion of Egypt. At the latter place Osiris, Isis, and a Phallic god (Menu) were worshipped in the reign of Diocletian, and the Blemmyes were in the habit of sacrificing men to the sun there.

The Edict of Theodosius I (378–395) against Paganism was disregarded at Philae, and when Olympiodorus visited Nubia between 407 and 425 the people were still pagans,[1] and the cult of Osiris and Isis flourished at Kalâbshah, Primis, and other places in Nubia. When Maximinus in the reign of Marcianus (450–457) went to punish the Nubians for a breach of their treaty obligations, they were still pagans. And in the new agreement which he made with them they stipulated that they should be allowed to visit Philae according to their ancient use and wont, and that they should be allowed to borrow the statue of Isis, and to take it to a certain place in their own country, so that they might make petitions to the goddess in their usual way. This custom was at least 250 years old when Priscus wrote.[2] In the reign of Justinian (527–565) it seems that the Nubian tribes became restless, and began to stir up trouble in Egypt. This brought down upon them the

[1] Ed. Bekker, p. 62.

[2] Priscus, Excerpt. legat., in Labbe, *Protrept.*, p. 40; Letronne, *Histoire du Christianisme*, p. 68.

wrath of Justinian, and partly for political reasons, and partly as the result of his hatred of paganism, he determined to put a stop to the worship of Isis and of the gods of her company at Philae. The Island, together with its immediate neighbourhood, formed a centre of religious fanaticism, and was, no doubt, a hotbed of conspiracy, unrest, and discontent. Effect was given to Justinian's decision by Narses the general, who went to Philae and closed the temple of Isis, and removed the statues of the gods from their shrines, and carried them off to Constantinople. He also confiscated the revenues of the sanctuary of the goddess, and threw her priests into prison. Thus the worship of Isis came to an end at Philae. Whether it survived on the Island of Meroë for any length of time there is no evidence to show.

Passing now from Nubia to the north, we find that many of the gods of Egypt were known in the countries near the Delta, *e.g.*, Syria and Palestine, under the XVIIIth and XIXth dynasties, but we find neither drawing nor representation of Isis in Phoenicia until about the sixth century B.C. About this time Adonis of Byblos (Gebêl), and the goddess of that city, whose characteristics resembled those of the Semitic goddess 'Ashtoreth and the Egyptian goddess Hathor, became confused with Osiris and Isis, and traces of this confusion appear in several places in Plutarch's story *De Iside*.[1] At a later period we find figures of Isis upon the coins of Tyre,[2] and figures of Sarapis on the coins of Gaza[3] and Bostra.[4] On the Stele of Teima we actually find the name of Pe-ṭā-Åsår,[5] *i.e.*, the "gift of Osiris," which proves that there was in and about Teima in Arabia a colony of worshippers as early as 500 B.C. From Egypt the cult of Sarapis and Isis passed to Asia Minor[6] and to the Islands of the Mediterranean, *e.g.*, Cyprus, Rhodes, Samos, Chios, Lesbos, Delos, Crete, etc. In the fourth century before Christ Athens

[1] See Movers, I, pp. 235–238; Scholz, *Götzendienst und Zauberwesen*, pp. 226–232.

[2] Imhoof, *M. Gr.*, p. 443.

[3] Reichardt, *Num. Chron.*, 1862, p. 122. [4] Leake, *N. H.*, p. 35.

[5] Nöldeke, *Sitzungsberichte*, 1884, pp. 813–820.

[6] See Drexler, *Der Isis und Sarapis-Kultus in Kleinasien* in *Num. Zeit.*, Band 21, pp. 1–234.

was a kind of centre of the Egyptian religion, and shrines to Isis, both public and private, seem to have been erected in many parts of Greece at this period,[1] and the bas-reliefs, coins, and other antiquities which have been found in Thessaly, Epirus, Megara, Corinth, Argos, and many other places prove that the worship of Isis was wide-spread, and that Osiris, or Sarapis, Anubis, Harpokrates, and even Nephthys, were associated with her in votive inscriptions. The coins of Malta of the second or first century before Christ show that the cult of Osiris and Isis was of importance in the island, and the monuments found in Catania in Sicily suggest that this city was a centre of the worship of Egyptian gods.[2] Southern Italy contained many temples of Isis, and the remains of statues, etc., found in Reggio,[3] Puteoli,[4] Pompeii,[5] and Herculaneum[6] suggest that the worship of Egyptian gods must have been as common as the worship of native gods in these cities. In Rome, in the first century before Christ, Isis was regarded as one of the principal goddesses of the city. Splendid buildings and temples were set up in her honour, filled with Egyptian objects, obelisks, altars, statues, lavers, etc., which were brought from Egypt with the view of making the shrines of the goddess to resemble those of her native country. Priestesses who professed to be well acquainted with the "mysteries" of Isis dwelt in or near these temples, and assisted in performing services and ceremonies in which large congregations participated.[7] From Rome, the capital, the cult of Isis naturally spread to the provinces, and thence, little by little, to Germany, Switzerland, Spain, Portugal, Gaul, and finally by way of Marseilles to Carthage[8] and the countries of North Africa.

[1] Köhler, *Hermes*, Vol. V, p. 351; *C. I. A.*, III, 896.

[2] Pistorio, *Lettera*, tom. XV, pp. 169–194; Zoega, *De Origine et Usu Obeliscorum*, pp. 86, 616, 647.

[3] Logoteta, *Il Tempio di Iside*, Naples, 1794.

[4] Lumbroso, *Recherches sur l'Économie*, pp. 126, 157.

[5] Nissen, *Pompei Stud.*, p. 671.

[6] See the works of Lafaye and Fiorelli, *passim*.

[7] For the literature see the article "Isis" in Roscher, *Ausführliches Lex.*, col. 400.

[8] See M. de Vogüé, *Rev. Arch.*, 3rd sér., tom. XIII, p. 167–176.

In the section on Isis it has been shown that this goddess during the course of her long history, and as a result of the development of her cult throughout Egypt and Nubia, was identified with many purely local spirits and goddesses, and the facts now available prove that the custom of identifying her with foreign goddesses went on in Greece and in Italy, and in nearly every place where her worship was introduced. Thus the Greeks and Romans identified her frequently with Selene,[1] and with Demeter, or Ceres, and with several goddesses of crops and of the harvest in general. She was also regarded as an Earth-goddess, and as such was the mother of all fertility and abundance. Some of her attributes caused her to be identified with Aphrodite, Juno, Nemesis, Fortuna, and Panthea, and among coast-dwellers she was regarded as a Sea-goddess and the patroness of sailors. Isis of "many names" was a mystery to many of her worshippers, among them being some who were wholly unable to satisfy their minds as to her true identity. Thus in the "Golden Ass" of Apuleius of Madaura,[2] Lucius prays to Isis in these words: "Queen of heaven, whether thou beest Ceres,—"the kindly mother from whom in the beginning spring "the fruits of earth, who, rejoicing to have found thy "daughter, didst take from men their bestial provender "of old-world acorns and show forth to them a sweeter "food, and now thou honourest exceedingly the soil of "Eleusis;—or beest thou Venus, the heavenly one, who "at the first beginning of things didst unite the diversity "of the sexes in the power of Love that is born of thee, "and, after thou hadst brought to birth the race of man "that shall endure from generation to generation, art "now honoured in thine island shrine of Paphos;—or "beest thou Phoebus's sister, who with gentle healing "dost bring relief to women in travail and hast reared "such multitudes, and art now worshipped in the most "glorious fanes of Ephesus;—or beest thou Proserpine, "to whom men render shuddering reverence with howls "by night, thou whose threefold visage awes the wild

[1] Wiedemann, *Herodots*, p. 192.

[2] Mr. H. E. Butler's translation, published at Oxford, 1910 (Book XI, 2 ff.).

"rages of the goblin-dead and holds fast the gates of "hell, who wanderest in many a diverse grove and art "propitiated with varied rite; thou that with thy tender "feminine light dost illumine the walls of all cities and "with thy moist fires dost nurture the springing seeds, "and dispensest thy beams that shift and change with "the changes of the sun;—by whatever name, by "whatever rite, in whatever semblance man may invoke "thee," etc.

To this prayer Isis made answer: "Lo, Lucius, I "am come . . . . I, nature's mother, mistress of all "the elements, the first-begotten offspring of all the "ages, of deities mightiest, queen of the dead, first of "heaven's denizens, in whose aspect are blent the "aspects of all gods and goddesses. With my rod I "rule the shining heights of heaven, the health-giving "breezes of the sea, the mournful silence of the Under-"world. The whole earth worships my godhead, one "and individual, under many a changing shape, with "varied rites and by many diverse names. There the "Phrygians, first-born of men, call me the mother of the "gods that dwell at Pessinus; there the Athenians, "sprung from the soil they till, know me as Cecropian "Minerva; there the wave-beaten Cyprians style me "Venus of Paphos; the archer Cretans, Diana of the "hunter's net; the Sicilians, with their threefold speech, "Stygian Proserpine; the Eleusinians, the ancient "goddess Ceres. Others call me Juno, others Bellona, "others Hecate, others the Rhamnusian, but those on "whom shine the first rays of the Sungod as each day "he springs to new birth, the Arii and the Ethiopians "and the Egyptians mighty in ancient lore, honour me "with my peculiar rites, and call me by my true name "Isis the Queen."[1]

The above extracts are important as illustrating the views which the pious devotees of Isis held concerning the goddess, and as enumerating the various foreign goddesses with whom the Egyptian Isis was pleased to identify herself. It is easy to see that the writer of them had no true knowledge of the actual position which

[1] Apuleius, *Metamorphoses*, XI, 5 (Butler's translation).

Isis held in early Egyptian mythology, and that he ascribed to her the attributes which belonged, strictly speaking, to Neb-er-tcher, Temu, and Kheperȧ in very early times, and to Rā, and Ȧten, and Osiris in later times. In short, he turned the Almighty God of the ancient Egyptians into a goddess with two natures, the one human and the other divine. Still more important, however, for the study of the history of Isis are two Greek inscriptions, one of which was found on the Island of Ios, and the other on the Island of Andros. The former is, unfortunately, incomplete, but the greater part of the missing portion of the text is supplied by the latter, and thus it is tolerably clear what a complete copy of the inscription contained. Both texts are edited by F. Hiller de Gaertringen in *Inscriptiones Graecae*,[1] and the following copy of the Ios text is taken from Herr A. Schiff's transcript which is printed, with an exact copy in uncials, in Vol. XII (Fasc. V, Part I, p. 217) of that work:—

[Ὁ δεῖνα ἀνέθηκεν Εἴ]σι[δι Σεράπ]ι[δ]ι [Ἀνούβιδι κ' Ἁ[ρποκρά]τῃ.

Εἶσις ἐγώ εἰμι ἡ τ[ύρανν]ος πάσης χόρας καὶ ἐπαιδ[εύ]θην ὑπὸ Ἑρμοῦ καὶ γράμματα εὗρον μετὰ Ἑρμοῦ τὰ δημόσια, ἵνα μὴ τοῖς αὐτοῖς πάντα γράφηται.

Ἐγὼ νόμους ἀνθρώποις ἐθέμην καὶ ἐνόμοθέτησα, ἃ οὐδεὶς δύναται μεταθεῖναι.

Ἐγώ εἰμι Κρόνου θυγάτηρ πρεσβυτάτη.

Ἐγώ εἰμι γυνὴ καὶ ἀδελφὴ Ὀσείρεος Βασιλέος.

Ἐγώ εἰμι θεοῦ Κυνὸς ἄστρῳ ἐπιτέλ(λ)ουσα.

Ἐγώ εἰμι ἡ παρὰ γυναιξὶ θεὸς καλουμένη.

Ἐ[μ]οὶ Βούβαστις πόλις οἰκοδομήθη.

Ἐγὼ ἐχώρισα γῆν ἀπ' οὐρανοῦ.

Ἐγὼ ἀστ[ρ]ων ὁδοὺς ἔδειξα.

Ἐγὼ ἡλίου καὶ σελήνης πορείαν συνέταξα.

Ἐγὼ θαλάσσια ἔργα εὗρα.

Ἐγὼ τὸ δίκαιον ἰσχυρὸν ἐποίησα.

Ἐγὼ γυναῖκα καὶ ἄνδρα συνήγαγα.

Ἐγὼ γυναιξὶ δεκάμηνον βρέφος ἐνέταξα.

Ἐγὼ ὑπὸ τέκνων γονεῖς φιλοστοργεῖσθαι ἐνομοθέτησα.

[1] See Vol. XII, Fasc. V, Part I, Berlin, 1903, No. 14, p. 7; No. 739, p. 213.

Ἐγὼ τοῖς ἀστόργοις γονεῖσι διακειμένοις τειμωρίαν ἐπέθηκα.

Ἐγὼ μετὰ τοῦ ἀδελφοῦ Ὀσείρεος τὰς ἀνθρωποφαγίας ἔπαυσα.

Ἐγὼ μυήσεις ἀνθρώποις ἀνέδειξα.

Ἐγὼ ἀγάλματα θεῶν τειμᾶν ἐδίδαξα.

Ἐγὼ τεμένη θεῶν εἱδρυσάμην.

Ἐγὼ τυράννω[ν ἀ]ρχὰς κατέλυσα.

Ἐγὼ στέργεσθαι γυναῖκας ὑπ' ἀνδρῶν ἠνάνκασα.

Ἐγὼ τὸ δίκαιον εἰσχυρότερον χρυσίου καὶ ἀργυρίου ἐποίησα.

Ἐγὼ τὸ ἀληθὲς καλὸν ἐνομοθέτησα νομίζ[εσ]θαι.

Ἐγὼ συνγραφὰς γαμικὰ[ς] εὗρα.

Ἐγὼ [δ]ιαλέκτους Ἕλλησι καὶ Βαρβάροις διεταξαμὴν.

Ἐγὼ τὸ καλὸν καὶ τὸ αἰσχρὸν διαγεινώσκεσθαι ὑπὸ τῆς φύ[σ]ε[ω]ς ἐποί[ησ]α.

Ἐγὼ ὅρκου φόρον [ἐπέβαλο]ν ἐπ[ὶ . . . .]ν ἀδίκως ε⌈ . . .

TRANSLATION.

[SO-AND-SO DEDICATED THIS] TO ISIS, TO SARAPIS, TO ANUBIS, AND TO HARPOKRATES.

"I am Isis, the mistress of every land, and I was "taught by Hermes,[1] and by aid of Hermes I found out "demotic letters, so that all things should not be written "with the same letters.

"I laid down laws for mankind,[2] and ordained things "that no one has power to change.

"I am the eldest daughter of Kronos.[3]

"I am wife and sister of Osiris the king.[4]

1 The Egyptian Ṭeḥuti,  (Thoth), who composed the spells which Isis learned from him; he was the inventor of 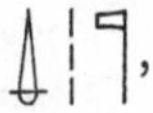, or "hieroglyphics." The use of demotic writing became general in Egypt after the XXVIth dynasty.

2 Here Isis assumes the attributes of Sesheta, the female counterpart of Thoth.

3 The Egyptian Ḳeb, .

4 , King of the South and North, Osiris.

"I am she who governs the star of Kuon the god.[1]
"I am she who is called Divine among women.[2]
"For me was built the city of Bubastis.[3]
"I divided the earth from the heaven.[4]
"I made manifest the paths of the stars.
"I prescribed the course of the sun and of the moon.[5]
"I found out the labours of the sea.[6]
"I made justice mighty.[7]
"I brought together woman and man.[8]
"I burdened woman with the new-born babe in the "tenth month.[9]
"I ordained that parents should be beloved by their "children.
"I inflicted retribution on those that feel no love for "their parents.[10]

[1] Sepṭ 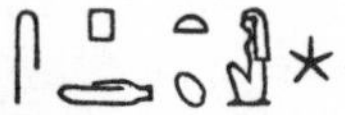, Sothis, or the Dog-star.

[2]  "great goddess."

[3] Isis as Bast, Lady of Bubastis.

[4] Here Isis assumes the *rôle* of the female counterpart of Shu, who lifted up the sky from the Earth-god Ḳeb; thus she is a goddess of light.

[5] Here Isis assumes the character of a female Thoth, or Maāt, who marked out the courses of the sun, moon, and stars in the heavens. Osiris was the soul of the sun, and Isis the spirit of the moon.

[6] Isis as Maāt directed the course of the two boats of the Sun-god, and so became a goddess of navigation. As a goddess of the winds she gave or withheld fair weather, and so, in later times, became the patroness of all seafaring folk, and delivered shipwrecked mariners from their peril.

[7] Isis and her twin-sister Nephthys were the two goddesses of truth and righteousness, Maāti, 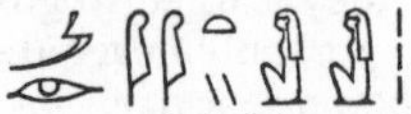, and they were always present in the Hall of Judgment of Osiris at the weighing of the hearts of the dead.

[8] Isis here assumes the character of the goddess Hathor.

[9] I know of no Egyptian parallel for this statement. It seems to mean that Isis decreed that the period of utero-gestation should be fully nine months, and that the perfect child was born in the tenth month.

[10] Love of parents and the devotion of children, especially to their mothers, are well-known characteristics of the ancient Egyptians. Numerous statues are inscribed with words which show that they were set up by pious sons to "make to live" their fathers' names, and the famous moralist Ani warns his son not to ill-treat or neglect his mother, for if she appeals to heaven God will certainly hear her and punish him.

"I, by aid of Osiris my brother, put an end to "anthropophagy.[1]

"I revealed initiations to mankind.[2]

"I taught mankind to honour the statues of the "gods.

"I founded sanctuaries of the gods.[3]

"I overthrew the sovereignties of tyrants.

"I compelled women to be beloved by men.[4]

"I made justice more mighty than gold and silver.

"I ordained that truth should be accounted beautiful.[5]

"I found out marriage contracts for women.

"I appointed separate languages for Greeks and for "foreigners.

"I made virtue and vice to be distinguished by "instinct.

"I imposed the tribute of an oath on those . . . "unjustly."

The exact form of the cult of Osiris and Isis as it obtained in the countries where Greek culture had penetrated, and especially in Italy, was based upon the religion which the early Ptolemies organized for their Greek and Egyptian subjects in Egypt. The first Ptolemy is said to have taken counsel with Manetho, the famous priest of Sebennytus, and with Timotheus, a Greek, who was skilled in the knowledge of the Eleusinian Mysteries. In it the Egyptian characteristics of Isis were retained, but to these were added attributes

[1] See the chapter on Osiris and Cannibalism. There seems to be no doubt that the primitive Egyptians were cannibals, and that men only ceased to be so after they learned to grow wheat, barley, and dhura. Sacramental cannibalism probably never died out, and it is common in some parts of Africa at the present day.

[2] *I.e.*, Isis established regulations which prescribed purity of mind and body for all who wished to become her priests. Fasting from meat and fish and abstention from the use of women were common among the Egyptians, as we see from the Rubrics to the Book of the Dead.

[3] The allusion here is probably to the fourteen, or sixteen, temples of Osiris which Isis built over her husband's scattered limbs.

[4] Isis here assumes the character of the goddess Hathor.

[5] Isis and her twin-sister Nephthys were the two goddesses of truth and righteousness, Maāti, , and they were always present in the Hall of Judgment of Osiris at the weighing of the hearts of the dead.

which were essentially the products of a non-African mind. The character of Osiris was changed in some respects, and his name was changed to Sarapis. The ancient legends of Osiris and Isis were mixed with legends of non-Egyptian Nature-spirits, and the rapidity with which the new form of the cult of Osiris and Isis spread proves that it offered to peoples of many climes and tongues a form of worship of God which satisfied their religious needs and was highly acceptable to them. In the first place the new cult came from Egypt, the land of mystery *par excellence*, and the home of a civilization which had lasted for thousands of years. The ascetic practices of the priests and priestesses, their abstention from meats, their fastings and habits of self-denial, and their continence, appealed to all men. The ceremonies connected with the worship of Isis impressed the imagination of all beholders, and the acting of the Isis-play, in which her search for the body of Osiris, her finding it, her union with her dead husband, the conception and birth of Horus, her sorrows, and her ultimate triumph, all represented by skilled actors, convinced men against their will that the cult of Osiris and Isis was based upon irrefutable facts. Moreover, it revived and increased the faith in God and in the reality of spiritual things, which the teachings of the philosophers had well-nigh destroyed in their hearts. Above all, it gave men the hope of a resurrection, and preached the doctrine of a second birth, and of a new and pure existence in heaven, in the kingdom of Osiris and Isis, the passport to which was the forsaking of sin, purity in word and deed, and reverent worship of these gods.

The progress of the cult of Osiris and Isis had made such strides in Italy at the beginning of the first century B.C. that it was possible for its votaries to found a College of the Servants of Isis, or Pastophori, in Rome in the time of Sulla, about 80 B.C., and to build a temple in the city. These proceedings were not regarded with favour by the authorities or by the local priesthoods, and as a result the temple of Isis was thrice destroyed by the Consuls, in 58, 50, and 48 B.C. In Campania the worship of Osiris and Isis was established at a still earlier period, for an inscription found at Puteoli, dated in the year equivalent to 105 B.C., proves that a temple of Sarapis existed in the city at that date.[1] In 44 B.C. the triumvirs built a temple in Rome in honour of Isis and Osiris, and a "few decades later" the festival of these gods was recognized in the public calendar. Somewhere about the beginning of the first century a temple of Isis was built at Pompeii. This appears to have been destroyed by an earthquake in the year 65, but it was rebuilt from its foundation by Numerius Popidius Ampliatus and his wife Corelia Celsa in the name of their son Celsinus, who was then a child only six years old. As a reward the City Fathers, the decurions, admitted the nominal rebuilder of the temple to their own rank, remitting the usual fees. According to Mau,[2] this temple consisted of an oblong cella, the east side of which was treated as a front, with a portico borne by six columns. A pit for the refuse of the sacrifices was made in the corner of the court near the entrance from the street, and in the opposite corner was an enclosure like a small temple. Near this were two altars, a third stood close to the temple, and there were five others between the columns. The temple possessed no specially Egyptian characteristics, and the ornaments were made of stucco. A broad flight of steps was built in front of the temple, and on the left side was a narrow stairway leading to a door opening in the cella. Across the rear of the cella was a base of masonry six feet high, on which were pedestals for statues of Isis and Osiris. In the two large niches outside were perhaps statues of Anubis and Harpokrates. The walls of the colonnade were painted in bright colours on a deep red ground. The upper parts of the columns were white, the lower were red, and the temple was white. In the colonnade was a yellow base, and above it were large red panels, alternated with light, fantastic, architectural designs in yellow on a red ground. The frieze was black, with garlands in strong contrast—green, blue, and yellow—enlivened with all sorts of animal forms. In the middle of each of the large panels was a priest of Isis, and in the lower parts of the intervening architectural designs

[1] *Pompeii: Its Life and Art*, London, 1899, p. 163.
[2] *Op. cit.*, p. 165 ff.

were marine pictures, galley manoeuvring, and sea fights. The principal altar was near the foot of the steps in front. At the back of the courtyard stood a cylindrical leaden vessel, adorned with Egyptian figures in relief; this was kept filled with water from a pipe connected with the city aqueduct, and here the devout made their ablutions, which formed a very important part of the worship of the goddess. In the south-east corner of the court was the Purgatorium, below which was an underground chamber, with a tank which held the holy Nile water. On the south side of the temple, at the back of the colonnade, were rooms which were used as a kitchen, a dining room, and a bed room. One of these rooms was richly decorated, in the last Pompeian style, with seven large paintings representing Egyptian landscapes, and Io watched by Argus, and Io being received by Isis in Egypt. In this room the Mysteries of Isis were probably acted. In an adjoining room, entered from the colonnade by a narrow door which could be securely fastened, the walls were decorated with large, sketchy pictures of Isis, Osiris, Typhon (Set), and sacred animals and symbols. This room was probably used for performing the most secret ceremonies connected with the worship of Isis; they were most likely phallic in character. In this room was an alcove in which temple property seems to have been stored.

Two services were held in the temple of Isis daily. Long before dawn the votaries of the goddess assembled outside the door of the courtyard of the temple, and the chief priest entered the temple through the small side door, and unbolted the great doors and threw them back, and hung up white linen curtains across the doorway, which hid the sanctuary from view. At dawn the door of the courtyard was opened, and the public streamed in, and people took their places in front of the temple. Then the linen curtains were drawn aside, and in the growing light the form and features of the goddess became visible to her worshippers. Whilst the priest went round performing the appointed rites at the various altars, and reciting prayers, the crowd continued to gaze on Isis, and prayed and rattled sistra at intervals. The priest then fetched water from the underground tank and poured out a libation from a holy vessel, and as the sun rose all present saluted him, and with loud cries announced the first hour of the day.[1] The second service was held early in the afternoon, and consisted in the adoration of the holy water of the Nile. A priest stood on the steps before the temple holding a vessel containing Nile water, whilst two priests, who stood on the top of the steps, one on each side of the temple door, rattled sistra; a fourth priest fanned a fire at an altar placed at the foot of the steps, and a player made music on his flute. A priestess of Isis stood on the top of the steps in the doorway. The worshippers assembled on each side of the altar and sang and rattled sistra. Details of the service are wanting.

The chief festivals of Isis were two. The first commemorated the murder of Osiris and the finding of his body by Isis. It opened on November 10 with the singing of dirges and loud and bitter lamentations for the death of Osiris, which were, no doubt, based upon the compositions which were sung in Egypt about the same time. Then, on the second day, scenes were enacted which represented the frantic grief and anxiety of those who went about searching for the body of Osiris. On the third day Isis found the body of her husband, and there was great rejoicing in the temple. Grief gave place to gladness and tears to laughter, musicians of all kinds assembled and played their instruments, and men and women danced, and the festival frequently ended with lascivious rompings and orgies.

The second great festival was celebrated in the spring, when Isis had "laid to rest the storms of winter and stilled the tempestuous waves of the sea," and the most important ceremony performed in connection with it was the dedication to the goddess of "a barque that had never sailed the waves." A good description of this festival, as it was celebrated at Cenchieae of Corinth, on the Aegean and Saronic seas, is given by Apuleius,[2] and from this the following summary is made. At the head of the great procession came men who were dressed to represent a soldier, a huntsman, a woman, and a

[1] See Apuleius, XI, 20.
[2] *Ibid.*, XI, 8 ff.

gladiator. These were followed by men dressed as magistrates, philosophers, fowlers, and fishermen. Then came a tame bear clad like a matron and borne in a litter; a monkey wearing a Phrygian plaited hat and saffron robe, and carrying a golden cup to represent Ganymede; and an ass with false wings glued to his back walking by the side of an old man. These were supposed to represent Pegasus and Bellerophon. Then came women wearing white raiment and garlands of spring flowers, scattering blossoms as they went; women with mirrors held reversed behind their backs, for the use of the goddess as she moved on her way; women with combs of ivory imitating actions connected with the combing and dressing of the hair of the goddess; and women who sprinkled the ground with scent and balsam as they walked. After these came a mixed multitude bearing in their hands lanterns, tapers, torches, and all kinds of lights, which represented the stars of heaven over which the goddess presided. These were followed by the musicians and a choir of youths, magnificently dressed in festal apparel, and singing to the sound of the pipe and flute a beautiful hymn to the goddess. With these came the flute-players of Sarapis, who "through a reed held slantwise toward the right ear, repeated the hymn that the god and his temple claim for their own."

Next followed a crowd of men and women of every rank and age clad in white linen apparel, the men with shaved heads, and the women with their scented hair covered with translucent gauze. These represented those who had been initiated in the divine rites. Among them were the priests who bore the "glorious emblems of the most potent gods," which consisted of a golden bowl of fire, an altar, a golden palm tree, the herald's staff of Mercury, a deformed left hand with open palm, a golden vessel, in the form of a woman's breast, from which libations of milk were poured, a golden winnowing fan, and a pitcher. After these came the gods who deigned to walk with feet upon the earth. First came Anubis, the dread envoy who goes between the lords of heaven and of the Nether World. He was lofty of stature, and his face appeared to be black at one time and golden bright at another; in his left hand he bore a herald's wand, and in his right a palm branch. Next came a priest supporting on his shoulders a heifer which held itself erect in human fashion, and symbolized the fruitful mother of all things. Another priest bore an ark full of objects of mysterious significations which symbolized the mysteries of the glorious faith. Another carried the awful image of the mighty deity, the emblem of whose meaning no man may speak, it was "the "symbol of the loftiest of faiths, whose mysteries must "be shrouded in deep silence." It was neither like cattle, nor wild beast, nor bird, nor man. This object was a small gold urn hollowed out with wondrous skill; its bottom was perfectly round, and its exterior was adorned with strange Egyptian figures. "Its mouth "projected into a long low spout with outstretched tube. "On the other side, with ample arch, extended a long "retreating handle, on which was set an asp with twisted "coils, holding erect the streaked scales of its swelling "neck."

When the procession reached shore,[1] the high priest arranged the images in order, and made solemn supplications, and then dedicated to the goddess, having first purified it with a torch, and sulphur, and the breaking of eggs, a beautifully made ship decorated with marvellous Egyptian paintings. On the sail was worked in thread of gold the inaugural prayer for prosperous seafaring in the new year's commerce. Its mast was of rounded pine, all the hull was made of polished sandalwood, and the stern was plated with gold. Then one vied with the other in loading the ship with winnowing fans heaped high with spice and other offerings of supplication. A libation of paste mixed with milk was poured over the waves, and when the ship was loaded, it was loosed from its moorings, and launched on the sea with the help of a favouring breeze; and all the people, having watched it till it was out of sight, returned to the temple in the order in which they had come. When they arrived there the priests, and the image-bearers, and the initiated arranged the "breathing effigies" each in its appointed place. Then the "scribe" summoned all the Pasto-

[1] Apuleius, XI, 16.

phori, or members of the College of Isis, and mounting a lofty tribunal recited from a book prayers for the prosperity of the Emperor, the senate, the knights, the Roman people, the sailors and the ships, and everything which was under the command and governance of the Roman world. Then in the Greek language, and after he had recited the Greek ritual, he proclaimed the "Launching of the Ships." A shout rose from the people, who kissed the feet of the silver statue of Isis which stood on the steps of the temple, and then departed to their homes in ecstasies of joy, bearing green branches and sacred wands and wreaths.

The above description of the "Launching of the Ships" is based on the account of the great festival of Isis written by one Lucius, who was a loyal servant of the goddess. It will be remembered that he had been transformed into an ass, and that having suffered many troubles in this form, he prayed to Isis to restore to him his human shape during the spring festival of the goddess. Having made to her the prayer already quoted, he lay down to sleep, and, he says:

"Yet scarce had I closed my eyes in sleep, when lo! "from the mid deep there rose a face divine that lifted "towards me a countenance to which even the gods "must do reverence. And then slowly, methought, "appeared a shining semblance, that rose till all its body "was in view and shook the brine from its limbs and "stood before me. I will strive to tell you all the "wonder of the sight, if but the poverty of human "speech give me power to tell, or the godhead itself that "dwelt within that form supply rich store of speaking "eloquence. First, the tresses of its hair were thick "and long and streamed softly down, now tangled, now "straying wide about that neck divine. About its lofty "brow was bound a crown of many shapes and varied "flowers, and in the midst thereof above the forehead "there shone white and glowing a round disc like a "mirror or after the semblance of the moon; to right "and left it was bound about with the furrowed coils of "climbing vipers; above, it stretched forth ears of corn. "The tunic was of many colours, woven of fine linen, "now gleaming with a snowy brightness, now yellow

" with hue of saffron, now blushing with roseate flame. " But the cloak it was that dazzled my gaze far beyond " all else, for it was of deep black glistering with sable " sheen; it was cast round and about the body, and " passing under the right side was brought back to the " left shoulder. Part of it hung shieldwise down and " drooped in many a fold, and the whole streamed " seemly to its utmost edge with tasselled fringe. Along " its broidered border, and on its surface also, were " scattered sparkling stars, and in their midst the full " moon breathed forth her flaming fire. But whereso- " ever streamed the embracing folds of that wondrous " cloak, there clung a garland's endless wreath, wrought " of all manner of flowers, all manner of fruit.

" In its hands the apparition held emblems of " different aspect. The right hand carried a bronze " rattle made of a slender sheet of metal curved like a " belt, through the midst of which were thrust a few " small wands, that gave forth a tinkling sound when the " arm that bore them shook thrice with quivering pulsa- " tion. From the left hand hung a golden cup, from " whose slender handle's most conspicuous part there " rose an asp towering with head erect and neck that " swelled to this side and to that. The ambrosial feet " were shod with sandals woven of the leaves of " victorious palm. Such was the vision, and of such " mighty aspect, that, breathing forth all the blest " fragrance of African balms, thus deigned to honour me " with utterance divine."[1]

In her answer the goddess promised to grant the request of Lucius, and told him how his transformation into human shape once more was to be effected. Everything happened as Isis said, and Lucius was filled with the deepest gratitude to the goddess, and determined to devote his life to her service. He frequented the worship of Isis, with all its exacting service, more zealously than ever, and his desire for admission to the Mysteries increased daily, and he visited the high priest frequently, and urged him to initiate him into the secrets of the night that is holy to the goddess. The priest entreated him to be patient, and told him that the day

[1] Butler's translation, p. 128 f.

of initiation was fixed by the goddess, who also chose the priest destined to perform the service, and fixed the sum to be expended on the ceremony. No one, he added, dares to venture rashly and sacrilegiously to undertake the service of the goddess without her express command and thus to contract mortal guilt. "For the gates of hell "and the power of life are in the hands of the goddess, "and the very act of dedication is regarded as a voluntary "death and an imperilling of life, inasmuch as the goddess "is wont to select those whose term of life is near its "close and who stand on the threshold of the night, and "are, moreover, men to whom the mighty mysteries of the "goddess may safely be committed. These men the "goddess by her providence brings to new birth and "places once more at the start of a new race of life.[1] The high priest then warned him to abstain from "impious and unlawful foods," so as to win his way to the purest of faiths.

Lucius took his advice, was patient, and with quiet, and gentleness, and silence zealously attended the daily performance of the rites of the goddess. Night by night he was cheered by the clear commands of Isis who told him that the day of his initiation was come, and what sums he must expend at the supplications, and that Mithras himself, the high priest, should reveal the Mysteries to him. Fortified by such revelations Lucius one night rose from sleep, and set out for the priest's house, intending to press him to appoint him at once to the service of the Mysteries. The priest met him on his way, and before Lucius could speak, told him that the day for the initiation into the most holy secrets of the Mysteries had arrived. Then he led him to the doors of the great shrine, and after celebrating with solemn rite the service of the opening of the gates and performing the morning sacrifice, he brought forth from the hidden places of the shrine certain books with titles written in undecipherable letters. Some of these were in the shape of animals of all kinds, and the extremities of others were knotted, or curved like wheels, or closely interwoven like the tendrils of the vine. The priest, having told Lucius what things he had to buy, escorted

[1] *Ibid.*, p. 146.

him to the nearest baths, and as he entered, the priest prayed the gods to be gracious to Lucius and sprinkled him with water. He then led him back to the temple and set him at the feet of the goddess, and having confided to him certain holy secrets bade him to abstain from all pleasures of the table, to eat no living thing, and to drink no wine. At the end of this time a new linen robe was placed on Lucius and he was taken by the priest into the very heart of the holy place. What was said to him there Lucius dared not divulge, but he says: "I drew nigh "to the confines of death, I trod the threshold of "Proserpine, I was borne through all the elements and "returned to earth again. I saw the sun gleaming with "bright splendour at dead of night, I approached the "gods above, and the gods below, and worshipped them "face to face." When the morning came, after the performance of the rites, Lucius appeared in the twelve cloaks that are worn by the initiate. He then, wearing an embroidered linen cloak called the "Cloak of Olympus," ascended a daïs, bearing a flaming torch in his right hand, and wearing a palm leaf crown, and the curtains were suddenly withdrawn, and the people thronged in to gaze upon him. After dwelling with the image of the goddess for some days, he at length entered into the presence of Isis herself, and having wiped her feet with his face, he addressed her with tears in his eyes and sobs in his voice, saying:—

"Holy and eternal protectress of the human race, that dost alway cherish mortals and bless them, thou tendest the mischances of miserable men with a sweet mother's love. Nor ever doth day nor restful night, nor even the least moment of time, pass uncrowned by thy blessings, but always by land and sea thou guardest men, thou drivest from them the storms of life and stretchest out to them thy saving hand, wherewith thou unbindest even the inextricable weft of Fate; thou assuagest the tempests of Fortune, and restrainest the baleful orbits of the stars. Thee do the gods of heaven adore, thee the lords of the world below do worship. It is thou that whirlest the sphere of heaven, thou that givest light to the sun, guidest the universe, and tramplest underfoot the powers of hell. For thee the stars shine, for thee the seasons return, in thee the gods rejoice and the elements are thy slaves. At thy nod the winds blow, the clouds give increase, the seeds spring to birth, and the buds burgeon. Before thy majesty tremble the birds that go to and fro in the sky, the beasts that roam the mountain, the serpents lurking underground, the monsters that swim the deep. But my wit is all too weak to tell of thy praise, my wealth too slender to make thee due offering of sacrifice. My voice is too poor in utterance to tell what I feel concerning thy majesty. Nay, had I a thousand mouths, a thousand tongues, and everlasting continuance of unwearied speech, it would be all too little. Therefore will I strive to do all that a poor yet faithful servant may. I will guard the memory of thy divine countenance and of thy most holy godhead deep hidden within my heart's inmost shrine, and their image shall be with me for ever."[1]

A few days later Lucius bade the priest farewell and departed from Cenchieae for Rome, and when he arrived there he became a continual worshipper in the temple of Queen Isis who, from the situation of her temple, was called "Goddess of the Field of Mars." When Lucius had spent a year in worshipping Isis in this way, the goddess began to warn him in his slumbers to prepare for a new initiation. Pondering what the warnings of the goddess might mean Lucius consulted some of the initiate, and at length he learned that he had still to be initiated into the Mysteries of the mighty god, "unconquered Osiris, supreme father of the gods"; for though the faith of Isis was identical with that of Osiris, the methods of initiation into the two faiths were different. On the very next night Lucius saw in a vision one of the initiate wearing a linen garment and bearing wands, and ivy, and mystic emblems, which he might not describe; having placed these before Lucius's household gods, he seated himself in his chair, and told him to give a banquet in honour of the great faith. This being walked with a halting step, and his left heel was bent slightly upwards. In the morning he saw among the Pastophori a man with a foot shaped like that which he had seen in

[1] Butler's translation, p. 151.

his dream, and on speaking to him he learned that he was called Asinius Marcellus, and that he had been warned by Osiris himself to admit Lucius into his Mysteries. Lucius was anxious for his initiation to take place at once, but lack of funds prevented this ; at length in obedience to the express command of Osiris, he sold his wardrobe, and with the money which it fetched purchased the things necessary for his initiation. When he had done this, he prepared himself by abstinence from animal food for ten days, and shaved his head, and frequented the service of Osiris, and was "illuminated by the nocturnal rites of the lord of all the gods." Meanwhile, he lived on the gains which his mastery of Roman eloquence won for him in the Forum.

After a short time the gods told him that he must prepare for a third initiation, but he was troubled in his mind about this matter, and began to doubt the good faith of the priests. Whilst thus tormented and stirred almost to madness by his doubts and fears, he saw a gracious midnight vision, and he was assured that this third initiation into the Mysteries was above all things needful for him. Comforted by this vision, Lucius put aside his doubts, and began a fresh course of abstinence, and spared neither toil nor expense in preparing for his initiation. After a few days Osiris appeared to him in the slumber of night, and welcomed him face to face with his own awful voice. He encouraged him to continue his profession in the Forum, to fear no ill-wishers, and chose him to be one of the chief elders among his Pastophori. Once more Lucius shaved his head, and joyfully performed the duties of that most ancient company of priests that was established in the great days of Sulla.

Lucius, it is clear, was a devoted priest of the cult of Osiris and Isis, and it is not difficult to think that his belief in the reality and greatness of these gods was equal to his professions of faith in them. But the Mysteries to which he refers so often must have possessed very little significance to the minds of the lower classes, who were attracted by the singing and dancing, and opportunities for rough play, which accompanied the celebrations of the festivals of the goddess, and there must have been large numbers of people who scoffed at the animal forms of the Egyptian gods, and at the extraordinary symbols and ceremonies which appertained to their cult. The feelings of such are voiced by Lucian in his short work, *The Council of the Gods*, in which he describes a meeting of the three gods, Zeus, Hermes, and Momus, to discuss the complaints made by the last named to the effect that the banquet of the gods had been thrown open to a number of undesirable persons. Momus, the "Accuser General," complained that many persons, in spite of their mixed origin, had been admitted to the feasts and councils of the gods upon terms of equality, that such had brought with them their servants and satellites and enrolled them among the gods; and that these menials shared in their rations and sacrifices without even so much as paying the customary tax.[1] Momus went so far as to point out to Zeus that the mixed state of society among the gods was due to him and his terrestrial gallantries, and that heaven was simply swarming with the demi-gods whom Zeus had introduced. It was all the result of the attentions paid by him to the daughters of Earth, and the goddesses were just as bad as the gods. Momus then went on to comment unfavourably on Dionysus, Attis, Corybas, Sabazius and Mithras, and then went on to attack the gods of Egypt. He said: "I shall just like to ask that Egyptian there—the dog-faced gentleman in the linen suit (Anubis)—who *he* is, and whether he proposes to establish his divinity by barking? And will the piebald bull yonder (Apis), from Memphis, explain what *he* has for a temple, an oracle, or a priest? As for the ibises and monkeys and goats and worse absurdities that are bundled in upon us, goodness knows how, from Egypt, I am ashamed to speak of them; nor do I understand how you, gentlemen, can endure to see such creatures enjoying a prestige equal or greater than your

[1] In the Bill to amend these matters introduced by Sleep and read by Momus it was stated that, owing to heaven being filled with false gods who troubled the banquets with a tumultuous rout of miscellaneous polyglot humanity, there was a deficiency in the supplies of ambrosia and nectar; and that owing to the increased consumption the price of the latter commodity had increased to four pounds the half-pint.—H. W. and F. G. Fowler, *Works of Lucian*, Vol. IV, p. 171.

own. And you yourself, sir, must surely find ram's horns a great inconvenience"? To this Zeus replied that the way in which the Egyptians went on was disgraceful, but he reminded Momus that there was an occult significance in most of the things, and that it ill became him, who was not one of the initiate, to ridicule them. To this Momus tartly replied: "A god is one thing, and a person with a dog's head is another; I need no initiation to tell me that."[1]

In spite, however, of all jibes, and jeers, and ridicule, the cult of Osiris and Isis spread all over Southern Europe, and into many parts of North Africa, and it continued to be a religious power in them until the close of the fourth century A.D. At Philae, as we have already seen, the worship of Osiris and Isis continued until the reign of Justinian, and it only came to an end in Nubia then because the Emperor caused the temple to be closed by force, and confiscated the revenues of the shrine. The ideas and beliefs which were the foundations of the cult were not even then destroyed, for they survived in Christianity. And the bulk of the masses in Egypt and Nubia who professed Christianity transferred to Mary the Virgin the attributes of Isis the Everlasting Mother, and to the Babe Jesus those of Horus. About the middle of the Ptolemaïc Period the attributes of Osiris were changed, and after his identification with Sarapis, *i.e.*, Pluto, the god of death, his power and influence declined rapidly, for he was no longer the god of life. In the final state of the cult of Osiris and Isis, the former was the symbol of Death and the latter the symbol of Life.

[1] *Ibid.*, p. 165 ff.

APPENDIX

Translations from the Pyramid Texts of Pepi I, Mer-en-Rā, and Pepi II.

Heaven is solid (or firm), the earth is strong. Horus cometh, Thoth riseth, and they raise up Osiris upon his side,[1] and they make him to stand up among the gods of the Two Companies. Remember Set, keep in thy heart the word which Ḳeb spake, and the threats (?) which the gods made to thee in the Temple of the Prince in Heliopolis, when thou hadst set Osiris down on the earth. Thou dost suppress Set, but dost not do these things to him (?). Thou hast the mastery there, thou art delivered, Horus hath made thee master. Thou dost suppress Set. The flesh of his body (?) maketh entreaty, his name becometh Åku-ta. Thou dost suppress Set. The flesh of his body journeyeth,[2] his name becometh Saḥ (Orion), whose leg is long, and his stride extended, the President of the Land of the South. Osiris beareth thee up as Set bore him up [when] he heard the threats of the gods, which the Father-God spake.[3] Thine arm is to Isis, Osiris Pepi, [and] the palm of thy hand is to Nephthys, and thou goest forward between them. Heaven is to thee, the earth is to thee, Sekhet Åaru is to thee, the Åats (Domains) of Horus, the Åats of Set; the cities are to thee, and Tem hath gathered together for thee the Nomes. Ḳeb hath spoken concerning it. Thoth grindeth his knife, and sharpeneth [his] knife, and crusheth in heads, and cutteth open breasts, He crusheth in heads and cutteth

[1] 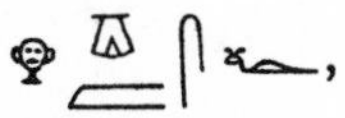, l. 186.

[2] There is a play on the words *seḥ* 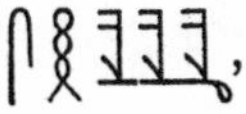, to travel, and *saḥ* 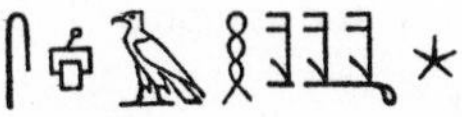, Orion.

[3] .

open the breasts of those who attack this Pepi, when he is journeying to thee, O Osiris, he breaketh the heads of those who would repel this Pepi when he is journeying to thee, O Osiris, that thou mayest give him life and serenity.

Pepi[1] hath come to thee, O Lord[2] of Heaven, Pepi hath come to thee, O Osiris. This Pepi hath cleansed (?) thy face, he hath arrayed thee in the apparel of the god, he hath purified thee in Tcheṭȧt.[3] The star Sepṭet (Sothis), thy beloved daughter, who maketh thine annual offerings to thee (*renput*) in her name of "Renpet," is the guide of this Pepi when he cometh unto thee. This Pepi cometh to thee, O Lord of Heaven. This Pepi cometh to thee, O Osiris. This Pepi hath cleansed thy face, he hath arrayed thee in the apparel of the god, he hath purified thee in Ȧaṭa,[4] he hath devoured the flesh of thine enemies,[5] he hath destroyed them, Osiris, and he hath placed them at the head of the Ḥenthi gods.[6] This Pepi cometh to thee, O Lord of Heaven, this Pepi cometh to thee, O Osiris. This Pepi hath cleansed thy face, he hath arrayed thee in the apparel of the god, and he hath done for thee what Ḳeb commanded him to do for thee. He hath stablished thy hand on life, he hath lifted up thy hand with serenity (?).[7] This Pepi cometh to thee, O Lord of Heaven, this Pepi cometh to thee, O Osiris. This Pepi hath cleansed thy face, he hath arrayed thee in the apparel of the god. This Pepi hath purified thee. Behold, Horus, thy son, whom thou hast brought forth, hath not put this Pepi at the head of the dead, but he hath set him among the gods who are divine. Their

1 Line 188. 2 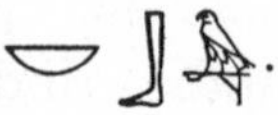. 3 , l. 189.

4 .

5 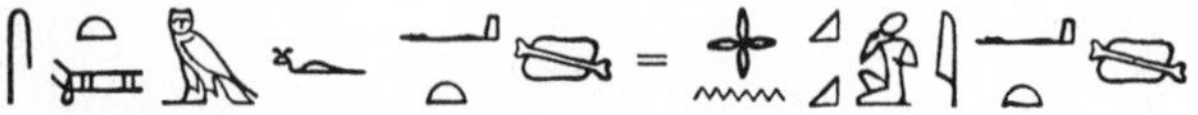, l. 189.

6 , l. 189.

7 . Perhaps the sceptre  is referred to.

water is the water of this Pepi, their bread is the bread of this Pepi, and their purifications are the purifications of this Pepi. What Horus hath done for Osiris he hath done for this Pepi (l. 191).

Homage to thee, O Ladder of the god! Homage to thee, O Ladder of Set. Stand up, Ladder of the god, stand up, Ladder of Set, stand up, Ladder of Horus, on which Osiris made his appearance in heaven, when he worked magical protection for Rā.[1] Thy brother Osiris cometh to thee seeking [thee], his brother Set welcometh him on his side (or, place) in his place in the Gazelle Land.[2] Horus cometh with his uraeus crown on him, he repulseth him like his father Ḳeb. This Pepi is thy son, this Pepi is Horus. Thou hast given birth to this Pepi as thou hast given birth to the god, the Lord of the Ladder. Thou hast given unto him the Ladder of the god, thou hast given unto him the Ladder of Set, whereon this Pepi made his appearance in heaven to work magical protection for Rā. Hail, god, behold their Doubles pass, [and] the Eye of Horus glideth on the wing of Thoth from the east side of the Ladder; men [have their] bodies in heaven. This Pepi is the Eye of Horus. When it journeyeth from wheresoever it is, this Pepi maketh the journey with the Eye of Horus. Be ye glad that this Pepi cometh among you, O gods, his brethren. Rejoice ye when ye meet this Pepi, O gods, his brethren, even as Horus rejoiced when he met his Eye. He hath set his Eye before his father Ḳeb, and every spirit, and every god reacheth out his hand to this Pepi when he appeareth in heaven on the Ladder. He hath not ploughed the earth, he hath not seized the offering, he hath not gone to the Chamber in Heliopolis, he hath not gone to the Chamber of Light in Heliopolis. He hath touch, he hath taste, he seeth, he heareth, he appeareth in heaven on the Ladder of the god.

Pepi riseth like the uraeus which is over the brow of Set, and every spirit and every god raiseth his hand for Pepi on the Ladder of the god. Pepi hath collected his bones, he hath gathered together his intestines, and this

1 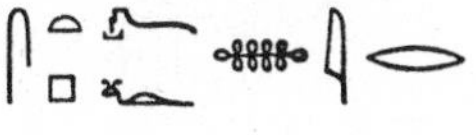 ⊙, l. 193.

2 .

Pepi hath ascended into heaven through the two fingers of the God, the Lord of the Ladder (l. 196).

Open the doors of heaven, throw open the doors of the sky[1] to Horus of the gods, on his appearance at dawn, having purified himself in Sekhet-Åaru.

Open the doors of heaven, throw open the doors of the sky to Horus of the East, on his appearance at dawn, having purified himself in Sekhet-Åaru.

Open the doors of heaven, throw open the doors of the sky to Horus of Shest,[2] on his appearance at dawn, having purified himself in Sekhet-Åaru.

Open the doors of heaven, throw open the doors of the sky to Osiris, on his appearance at dawn, having purified himself in Sekhet-Åaru.

Open the doors of heaven, throw open the doors of the sky to this Pepi, on his appearance at dawn, having purified himself in Sekhet-Åaru.

Therefore let appear him that appeareth at dawn, having purified himself in Sekhet-Åaru; let Horus of the gods appear at dawn, having purified himself in Sekhet-Åaru. Therefore let appear him that appeareth at dawn, having purified himself in Sekhet-Åaru; let Horus of Shest appear at dawn, having purified himself in Sekhet-Åaru. Therefore let appear him that appeareth at dawn, having purified himself in Sekhet-Åaru; let Osiris appear at dawn, having purified himself in Sekhet-Åaru. Therefore let appear him that appeareth at dawn, having purified himself in Sekhet-Åaru; let this Pepi appear at dawn, having purified himself in Sekhet-Åaru.

O Rā, the womb of Nut is filled with the seed of the Spirit which is in her. The earth bendeth under the feet of this Pepi. Tefnut stretcheth out her hand to Pepi. Seker purifieth this Pepi, Rā giveth his hand to Pepi, so that he may promote Pepi [to be] the head of the gods, Pepi hath taken his seat in the sky. O ye who sing and rejoice carry ye this Pepi with you; let him live for ever! (l. 199.)

Happy are those who see, fortunate (?) are those who see the appearance of this god in heaven, which is like

1 , l. 196.

2 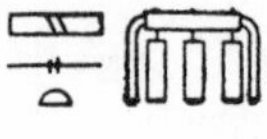, l. 196.

unto the appearance of Tem in heaven. His soul is on him. His spells[1] are on both sides of him, his book (?) (or knife) is at his feet. Pepi hath brought the towns, he hath embraced the nomes, and he hath gathered together the lands; Ḳeb the Erpā of the gods spake concerning this. The Domains of Horus, the Domains of Set, and Sekhet-Ȧaru praise this Pepi. And lo, Khensu,[2] and Ȧaḥes, the Governor of the Land of the South, Ṭeṭun, the Governor of the Land of the Bow (Ta-Sti = Nubia), and Sepṭ, under his trees, carry the ladder of this Pepi, they set upright the ladder of this Pepi, they lift up the ladder of this Pepi. Come, ladder; come, ladder, come [in] thy name spoken by the gods. Come ye who come! Come ye who come! Come ye who rest! Come ye who rest! Come ye who lack! Come ye who lack! Pepi appeareth on the two thighs of Isis, Pepi reposeth on the two thighs of Nephthys. Tem the father of Pepi hath stretched out his hand to Pepi, and thrust Pepi at the head of these gods, wise, understanding, imperishable. Consider, O gods, that which Tem speaketh unto you: This Pepi is at your head, and lo, he is established at your head like the bull which is sacrificed daily (l. 202).

Au-qau (?) and Ḥer-f-ḥa-f, Pepi setteth out in his boat. Make [him] to embrace the two horizons of the sky; this Pepi saileth therein with Rā to the horizon. Make Rā to embrace the two horizons of the sky; this Pepi saileth therein with Horus of the gods to the horizon. Make this Pepi to embrace the two horizons of the sky when he saileth therein with Rā to the horizon. Having sailed he standeth up on the east side of heaven, in the northern part thereof, among the imperishable stars, which stand up on their *tchām* sceptres, and support themselves on their staves, and this Pepi standeth among them. This Pepi is a brother of the Moon,

1 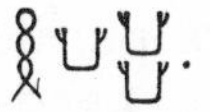. Pepi, l. 199.

2 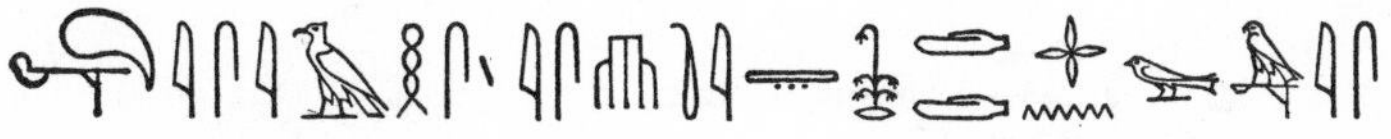

. Pepi, l. 200.

the Morning Star giveth birth to him; give thou thy hand to Pepi, [and] he shall live (l. 203).

Hail, Osiris this Pepi! Raise thyself up on thy left side, and place thou thyself on thy right side, by this water of rejuvenation which I have given to thee. Hail, Osiris this Pepi. Raise thyself up on thy left side, and place thou thyself on thy right side, by the warm bread which I have made for thee. Hail, Osiris this Pepi! The doors of heaven were opened to thee, and the doors of the Petchet[1] were thrown open to thee by the body (?) of the gods who dwell in Pe, when they came to Osiris by reason of the sound of the lamentation of Isis and Nephthys. The Souls of Pe smite for thee, they smite for thee their flesh, they grasp thee with their hands so tightly that they are to thee like their tresses. They make a speech to Horus, saying: Thou departest, thou comest, thou risest up, thou liest down, thou art stablished in life. Standing up thou seest these things, standing up thou hearest these things which Horus hath done for thee. He smiteth thee and thou art smitten. He fetters thee and thou art fettered. He placeth himself with his (or thy) eldest daughter in Qeṭem,[2] thy great sister, who collected thy flesh, and warmed thy hands, and embraced thee when she found thee on thy side on the place Neṭȧt,[3] and there is no grief in the Two Halves of Egypt. The gods say to him: "Hast thou brought him?" Appear thou, therefore, in Heaven; become thou like Ȧp-uat. Thy son Horus shall guide thee on the roads of heaven. Heaven is given to thee. Earth is given to thee. Sekhet-Ȧaru is given to thee, and these Two Great Gods who come forth from Ȧnu (Pepi II, l. 872).

Pour a libation. Pour a libation. Ȧqa and Ȧp-uat! Watch, O ye who are lying down! Wake up, O ye who are guardians. Horus watcheth. Osiris Pepi is raised up by the eldest son of Ḳeb, and the Great Company of the Gods quake [before] him. Thou art purified at [each] month, the dead rise before thee, heads are

1 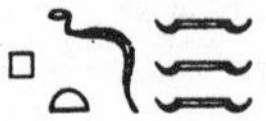. Pepi, l. 204.

2 .

3 .

offered to thee, Ment-urt[1] . . . . thee, even as " He who resteth not,"[2] dweller in Abydos, stood up. Earth, hear the things which Ḳeb spake; behold, he hath by his magical ceremonies made Osiris a god. The Watchers of the city of Pe make offerings to him. The Watchers of the city of Nekhen pay reverence to him. Behold Seker, at the head of the Petchṭu Lake, and Aḥa, and Ḥemen,[3] speak to the earth, and open the gates of Aker (or, the Ṭuat), and throw open the gates of Ḳeb. . . . Thy speech cometh forth before Ȧnpu, thy rank cometh forth from the mouth of Ȧnpu Ḥeru-khentȧ-menȧt-f; the Lord of Saut bindeth thee, the Jackal of the South, the Great Chief of the Great Company of the Gods. Thou art marvellous in heaven on thy throne of iron (or, alabaster). Thou sailest over the Lake, thy face is directed to the north of heaven, Rā invoketh thee as Ȧsken of the sky.[4] Thou approachest the god, Set maketh friends with thee, and the odour of Ṭeṭun, the Youth of the South, is on thee, he giveth to thee his purifying incense the gods poured forth for him at the birth of the two firstborn daughters of the King of the North [and] of the Great Lady. Thou art watered abundantly in the Green Field, and the water flood cometh to the Children of Ḳeb who are there. Raise up thy knives, have the mastery over [thy] bows, Ȧnpu giveth one offering, the palm tree followeth thee, the mulberry tree boweth its head to thee, thou goest round about heaven like the god Sunthu[5] (Pepi II, l. 854).

Every god draweth this Pepi to heaven [in] life and stability, cattle are slaughtered for him, and the thighs

1 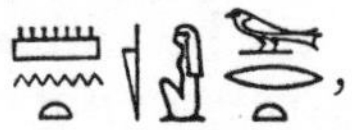, or . M., l. 330; Nu, l. 848.

2 . Nefer-ka-Rā, l. 848.

3 . Pepi I, l. 208.

4 . Pepi II, l. 851.

5 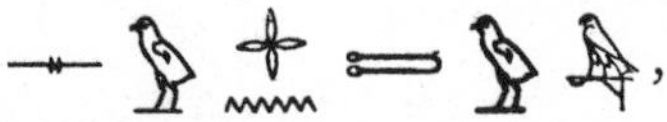, . M., l. 336; Pepi II, l. 854.

(or, fore-legs) have been selected for him. He cometh forth to Hathor of Heaven. . . . This Pepi cometh to thee, O Rā, a calf of gold brought forth by the sky, a being of gold made by the goddess Ḥesat. O Horus, carry thou with thee this Pepi [in] life and stability, and reject thou him not. Pepi cometh to thee, O Father, Pepi cometh to thee, O Ḳeb. Give thou thy hand to this Pepi. This Pepi cometh forth to heaven before his mother Nut. . . . Ḳeb cometh, with his *at* crown on his head, and his *qenȧt* garment on him. He smiteth you. He adjudged the lands[1] to the embrace of Osiris [when] he found him placed on his side in the town of Ḳeḥset.[2] Osiris, thy father Ḳeb stood up, he delivered thee from the hand of Set. . . . I am he who fettered his feet, fettered his hands, [when] he set himself on his side in the Land of Ru. O Horus on the womb of heaven,[3] give thy hand to this Pepi. This Pepi cometh forth to the heaven of Nut, give thou thy hand to Pepi with life and serenity. Collect his bones, group together the intestines of his body. . . . His light appeareth in the sky like that of a great star in the East.

Homage to you, O Waters brought by Shu, and lifted up by Menṭeftȧ,[4] wherein Ḳeb hath purified his members, the hearts after fear, and the breasts after the knife (?) Pepi was brought forth by Nu when there was no heaven, when there was no earth, when there was no established thing, when there was no fighting (or, disturbance), and when there was not the fear which arose through the Eye of Horus. This Pepi is one of the Great Offspring who were brought forth in Ȧnu, who have never been conquered by a king or ruled by chiefs, who are irresistible, whose words cannot be gainsaid. Therefore this Pepi is irresistible; he can neither be conquered by a king nor ruled by chiefs. The enemies of Pepi do not triumph. Pepi lacketh nothing. His nails do not grow long [for want of prey]. No debt is reckoned to Pepi. If Pepi falleth into the water Osiris

1 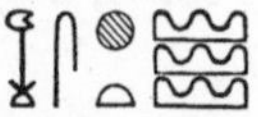.

2 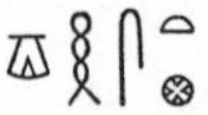.

3 .

4 .

will lift him out, and the Two Companies of the Gods[1] will bear him up on their shoulders, and Rā will give Pepi his hand, wheresoever the god may be. If Pepi falleth on to the earth, Ḳeb will lift him up, and the Two Companies of the Gods will bear him up on their shoulders, and Rā will give him his hand, wheresoever the god may be (Pepi II, l. 1235).

Adoration be to thee, O thou Osiris Pepi, thou Shining one in the horizon, thou Stable one in the Place of stability[2] who dost make decrees at the head of the living for ever! Stand up on thy left side, set thyself on thy right side, and receive thou this bread which I give unto thee. I am thy son, thine heir.

Hail, this Pepi, thy son Horus payeth thee homage. Thy diadem is like that of the Morning and Evening[3] Star in Nut. Thy feet and thy wings are like those of a hawk with a large body, that is, [like] the *ḳenḥesu* bird, the splendour of which is seen [as he passes] in the sky. Thou sailest over the firmament as Rā-Ḥeru-Khuti saileth over the waters [thereof], Nut layeth her hands upon thee. . . .

236. Heaven is open! Earth is open! The shrines[4] of Peter are opened! The strides of Nu are opened! The strides of the god (?) Åakhu[5] are opened. Behold, [he] is one, stable each day. These [things] his ancestors say unto him, [and] thereupon he cometh forth to heaven, anointed with unguents, and arrayed in the finest apparel of those who sit to give life to Maāt. His side is to the sides of the gods who are in the north of heaven. They are imperishable, he is imperishable; they are incorruptible, he is incorruptible; they cannot decay, he cannot decay. When the god Menthu riseth, he riseth with him; when Menthu maketh a progress, he maketh a progress with him.

243. Heaven is pregnant with wine, Nut maketh herself to give birth to her daughter, the Morning Star.

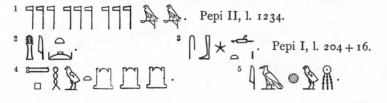

1 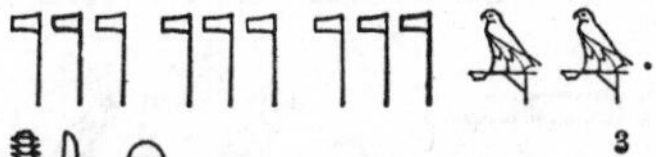. Pepi II, l. 1234.

2 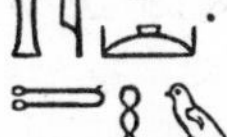.

3 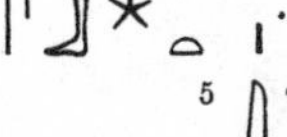. Pepi I, l. 204 + 16.

4 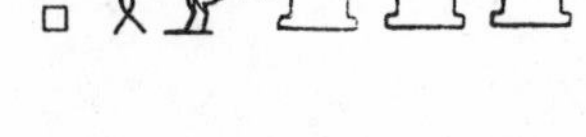.

5 .

Rise thou up, then, O Pepi, thou third Sepṭet[1] (Sothis), whose seats are purified. He hath been purified in the Lakes of the Ṭuat, he hath undressed in the Lakes of the Jackals.[2] O Baḳes[3] plant, remove thyself from his path, for he hath taken the Southern Portion of Sekhet-Åaru, and hath made a way into the blooming meadow of Kha. Grant that Horus may be embraced by the doors of the sky [when] he saileth before Rā to the horizon. Grant that Ḥeru-Khuti may be embraced by the doors of heaven [when] he saileth before Rā to the horizon. Grant that Ḥeru-Shesti may be embraced by the doors of the sky [when] he saileth before Rā to the horizon. Grant that Ḥeru-Åbti may be embraced by the doors of the sky [when] he saileth before Rā to the horizon. Grant that this Pepi, who is Horus of the gods, may be embraced by the doors of the sky [when] he saileth before Rā to the horizon. He hath received his throne in Sekhet-Åaru. He hath gone to the Southern Portion of Sekhet-Ḥetep. He is a great god, the son of a great god. He appeareth between the two thighs of the Two Companies of the Gods. Pepi giveth praise to Rā. Pepi giveth praise to Ḥeru-Åbti. Pepi giveth praise to Ḥeru-Khuti. He travelleth over the circuit. This Pepi resteth and Horus resteth with him on his throne; Horus resteth on his throne, and this Pepi joineth him thereon.

255. Pepi appeareth from Pe before the Souls of Pe, Pepi hath put on the *sheth* garment of Horus, and hath arrayed himself in the apparel of Thoth. Isis is before him, Nephthys is behind him. Åp-uat openeth for him a way. Shu beareth him up, and the Souls of Ånu draw him up the steps to set him before the face of Nut, who giveth to him her hand just as they did for Osiris, on that day when he came into port (*i.e.*, died). O Ḥer-f-ḥa-f, Pepi saileth to Sekhet-Åaru! Whether goest thou? He hath appeared in Auuaurt. To him is the body which proceedeth from the god,

1 

2

3

the uraeus proceeding from Rā, he himsel saileth, he placeth himself in Sekhet-Åaru. The Four Spirits who are with Pepi are Ḥep, Ṭuamutef, Åmset, and Qebḥsenuf, two on one side and two on the other. Pepi is steersman, and he findeth the Two Companies of the Gods who give their hands to him, and he taketh his seat among them to decide cases, and he issueth orders to those whom he findeth there.

265. This Pepi is Sethtȧ,[1] this Pepi is Sethtȧ, this Pepi is Susu,[2] this Pepi is Sunth,[3] who circleth about heaven. This Pepi is Arek, the spirit of the Kings of the North. This Pepi is Åmennu,[4] the Åmen of this earth. Pepi is the Unifier of the Two Lands.[5] Pepi is the Revolver, the god who revolveth.[6] Pepi is Ḥest,[7] Pepi is the Terrible one.[8] Pepi is Bat[9] of the two faces. Pepi is Neḥemu,[10] he delivereth himself from every evil thing. Pepi is Unshet.[11] Pepi is Unshtȧ.[12] Pepi is Ḥep. Pepi is Ṭuamutef. Pepi is Åmset. Pepi is Qebḥsenuf. Pepi is Ṭuaānuu.[13] Pepi is these great gods who are at the head of the Lake. Pepi is the Living Soul, with the face of Sepa. He rescueth his head, delivereth his body, carrieth off his body. In trouble he doeth what must be done, lying in death he doeth what must be done, decreeing what must be decreed. Pepi doeth the deeds of beneficence. Pepi decreeth a good decree. The two lips of Pepi are the

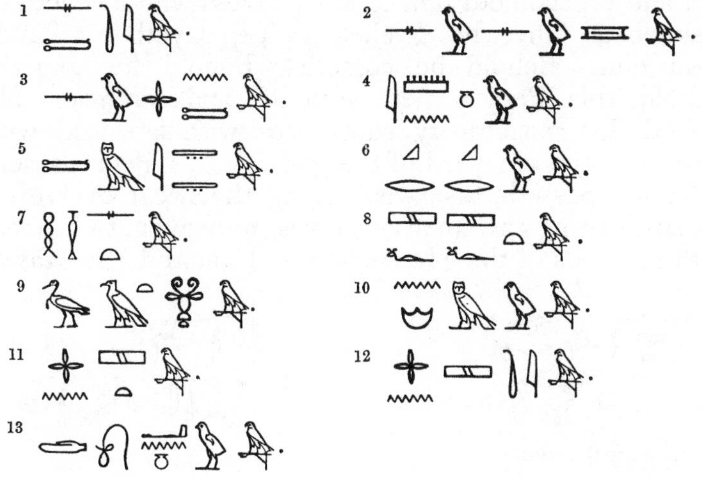

Two Companies of the Gods, Pepi is the Great Word.[1] Pepi is Senȧ.[2] Pepi is the unfetterer, and he is loosed from every evil thing. O men and gods, let your hands be under Pepi! Lift ye up Pepi, and raise him up to heaven (even as the two hands of Shu, which are under the sky, bear it up), to heaven, to heaven, to the Great Place among the gods . . . .

279. Pepi giveth commands to his father, the Moon, Pepi giveth birth to the Morning Star, Pepi giveth commands to those Four Rejoicing Ones[3] who sit on the eastern side of the sky, and to those Four Rejoicing Ones with shining hair who sit in the shade of the dwelling of the god Qatȧ.[4] Great of father, great of father, Pepi is great of father.

283. The Comer! The Comer! This Pepi cometh! The Lady of Ṭep is agitated, and the heart of the goddess dwelling in Nekheb fluttereth on that day wherein Pepi cometh in the place of Rā. Pepi hath carried away for himself thy light under his feet. Pepi cometh forth above it before his mother, the living uraeus of the head of Rā, and her heart is grieved for him. She giveth him her breast, he sucketh thereat. Son of the father, this breast is presented to thee, thou suckest thereat, therefore, behold, shall it happen that thy days shall be numberless. The sky speaketh,[5] the earth quaketh, and the gods of Ȧnu tremble at the voice, and the offering is before Pepi. His mother Bastet taketh him and proclaimeth him to the goddess who dwelleth in Nekhebet, She who dwelleth in Ṭep layeth her hands upon him. Behold he cometh! Behold he cometh! Behold, this Pepi cometh with life and serenity. He maketh his purificatory substances with figs and with wine from the vineyard of the god . . . . Pepi passeth as Horus passeth, his sweat being the sweat of Horus, his smell being the smell of Horus, to heaven, to heaven, with the gods of the House of the Lion and the Hawk.

1 

2 

3 

4 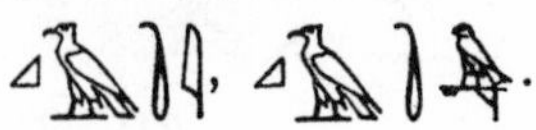

5 *I.e.*, it thunders.

Pepi is in heaven with the gods of the House of the Lion and the Hawk, and he is by their side in friendly converse. Behold, Ḳeb taketh Pepi by the hand, and he guideth him in through the doors of heaven, like a god into his place; beautiful is the god in his place. The goddess Sethȧt purifieth him with the four vessels of purification which are in Abu (Elephantine). Hail, where goest thou then, O son of the father? He cometh to the gods of heaven, and behold, he maketh Peq to be at peace. Hail, where comest thou then, O son of the father? He goeth to the gods of earth, and behold, he maketh Peq to be at peace. Hail, where comest thou then, O son of the father? He cometh to Tchenṭtchenṭer.[1] Hail, where comest though then, O son of the father? He cometh to his two mothers, these two vultures, with the long hair (or feathers) and the hanging breasts, which are on the Mountain of Seḥseḥ (?), and they put their nipples into the mouth of Pepi straightway, and they are with him for ever!

304. The sky speaketh, the earth quaketh. Ḳeb tottereth, the nomes of the god roar, the earth is ploughed up, the offering is taken before this Pepi, the living one, the stable one. Therefore he cometh forth to heaven, he saileth over the firmament with life and serenity, he passeth over the Milky Way (?),[2] overthrowing the walls of Shu. Now he appeareth in heaven on his wings like a great gander which hath escaped from his toils . . . . Now he appeareth in heaven among the imperishable stars. His sister the star Sepṭet (Sothis), his guide the Morning Star, take him by the hand to Sekhet-Ḥetep. He taketh his seat there on the crystal (?) throne, which hath faces of fierce lions and feet in the form of the hoofs of the Bull Sma-ur. He standeth up in his place which is between the Two Great Gods, with his *āba* sceptre and his *menḥ* staff in his hands. He lifteth up his hand to the Ḥenmemet spirits, and the gods come to him with bowings. The Two Great Gods watch in their places, and they find him among the gods deciding cases. The word of every noble is to him, and they make offerings to Pepi among the Two Companies of the Gods.

[1]  .

[2]  .

315. Behold, it is not Pepi who maketh entreaty to see thee in thy form in which thou art, O Osiris, who maketh entreaty to see thee in thy form in which thou art, it is thy Son who maketh entreaty to see thee in thy form in which thou art, it is Horus who maketh entreaty to see thee in thy form in which thou art. Thus say the beings who are inert (?) and are like the Great Males under Åkhemut (?)[1] to thee, thus say they to thee: "Come, beloved son, in the form of the Sa-mer-f," and they ferry Horus, they ferry Horus at the appearance of Horus among the Meḥt-urt goddesses. Open, O ye doors of heaven, be thrown open, O ye doors of the sky, to Horus of the East, who at dawn descendeth and purifieth himself in Sekhet-Åaru.[2] Open, O ye doors of heaven, be thrown open, O ye doors of the sky, to Pepi, who at dawn descendeth and purifieth himself in Sekhet-Åaru.

331. This Pepi hath ploughed the earth, he hath presented the offering. He riseth on the throne like a king, and occupieth it with honour. He saileth over the Lake of Petertå, and he traverseth the Lake of Kha. Neskestet[3] stretcheth out the hand to Pepi from her shrine, from her secret place, and she maketh him a god. Behold, Pepi is a pure being, the son of a pure being, and he is purified by [the contents of] the Four Nemast vases, which are emptied (?) [over him] in the Lake of Nether in the city of Nethru,[4] under the wind of Isis the Great Lady, and behold the Great Lady made Horus dry, and caused him to come with flesh purified. Is Rā more pure than Pepi [or] the doorkeeper of Qebḥu (the sky)? He taketh Pepi along to those Four Gods who are on the Lake of Kenstå, and they give gifts to Osiris Pepi, and they give gifts to Rā. No boundaries are fixed for him, and [he] findeth no limits [set for him]. Behold, one arm of Ḳeb is to heaven, and his [other] is to the earth, and he taketh Pepi along to Rā. Pepi

1 .

2 This formula is repeated for Horus of the Ṭuat and Horus of Shestå.

3 .

4 .

directeth the gods, he is master of the Boat of God. he conquereth heaven and its pillars and its stars.[1] The gods come to him with bowings, the Spirits follow Pepi because of his soul, they reckon up their war-clubs, they brandish their spears and wave their swords, for behold Pepi is a Great One, the Son of a Great One, and is born of Nut. The might of Pepi is the might of Set of Nubt (Ombos). Pepi is the Bull-god Sma-ur, coming forth from Khenti-Åmenti. Pepi is the efflux of the celestial water, and he appeared when Nu (?) came into being. Pepi is the serpent Neḥebkau, of manifold windings. Pepi is the Scribe of the Book of God,[2] who spake and what is came into being, and maketh to exist that which did not exist. Pepi is the band of the written rolls which came forth from the Great Trial. This Pepi is the Eye of Horus, which is stronger than men and mightier than the gods. Horus raiseth him, Set lifteth him up. Pepi maketh offerings of bread and beer and the libation offering at the door, he pacifieth the Two Gods who are to be pacified, he pacifieth the Two Gods who consume (?).

349. Ḳeb . . . . and Nut . . . . on the hands of Pepi, and he cometh forth to heaven. Heaven saluteth him joyfully, the earth trembleth before him, for he hath broken the power of the raging rainstorm, and he hath roared like Set. The keepers of the body of heaven and of the doors of heaven have opened unto him, he standeth up on Shu, and the stars supply him with an abode in the shade of the walls of the god. He strideth over the sky like the god Sunth, he is the third of the star Sepṭ (Sothis), whose seats are pure. He is purified in the Lakes of the Ṭuat. The goddess Nemt[3] maketh good roads for him, and she guideth him to the Great Place, which the gods made, and Horus made, and Thoth stablished (?). Isis receiveth him, Nephthys stablisheth him, and he taketh his seat on the Great Throne which the gods have made. The morning stars[4] come to him with rejoicing, and

1 

2 

3 

4 

the gods with gladness, and the gods of the horizon[1] having fallen on their faces, and the imperishable stars with homage. He taketh in hand the Sceptre, he directeth the mouth of the gods, he beareth up the sky on his shoulders with life, he supporteth the earth with gladness, his right arm beareth up the sky with power, his left arm supporteth the earth with gladness. He findeth Shetth, he addresseth the doorkeeper of Osiris, and an abomination to him it is to travel without . . . . He receiveth the breezes of life, he inhaleth joy of heart, the offerings of the god are laid before him in abundance, he snuffeth the air, he hath the air of the north wind in abundance, and he is happy among the gods. He is better equipped than Sepṭ-ur, and he is advanced more than Khent-Ȧtert. He striketh with his Sceptre, he ruleth with his *Ȧaat* staff; he setteth his remembrance before men, and his love before the gods. Speak the thing which is; speak not that which is not; an abomination unto God is the shifty word. This Pepi is thy son, this Pepi is thy flesh and blood.

369. I have made a heart for father Pepi, another hath prepared for him his . . .[2] Now when he cometh forth into heaven, and when he journeyeth through the pools of the Lake of Kha, Anubis cometh and meeteth thee, O Pepi, Ḳeb giveth to thee his hand, O father Pepi; the guardian of the earth, the director of the Spirits weepeth tears, O father Pepi. Hail, rise up, father Pepi! Thou hast received thy Four Nemast Vases, and the vases of offerings; thou hast been purified in the Lake of the Jackal, thou hast been censed in the Lake of Ṭat. Thou hast been made pure by thy Shabt flower[3] in Sekhet-Ȧaru. Thou sailest over the heavens, thou stoppest in Sekhet-ḥetep among the gods who pass to their Doubles. Thou sittest on thy throne of alabaster, thou takest in thine hand thy club and thy Ames staff, thou art the leader of the dwellers in Nu,

1 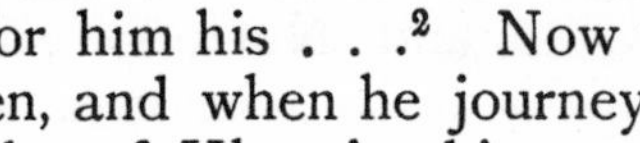

2 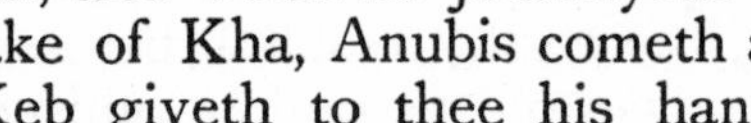

3 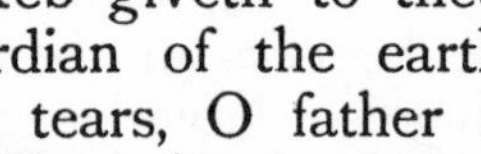

thou announcest decrees to the gods, thou placest a Spirit in his Spirit, thou takest thy course and thou sailest over thy lake as doth Rā over the domains of heaven. Pepi, thou art raised up, pass thou into thy Spirit.

377. Then Pepi cometh forth into heaven among the gods who are in heaven. He standeth then at the Great Uārt, he heareth the words of the Ḥenmemet beings. Rā is found in the domains of heaven by the double lake in Nut, whither the gods have journeyed and arrived. He (*i.e.*, Rā) giveth thee his hand in the Lake Åsken of the sky; the gods come to his throne. Pure is the coffer of thy throne in the Boat of Rā, thou sailest over the upper regions, thou approachest the roads, thou sailest with the imperishable stars, thou steerest thy way with the stars that never rest. Thou receivest thy tribute in the Semketet Boat, thou becomest a Spirit of the Ṭuat. Thou livest sweet life, all the life of the horizon is in thee.

390. The two spurs of Horus and the two wings of Thoth make Pepi to sail without shipwreck. Give thou bread to this Pepi, give thou beer to this Pepi, of thy bread of eternity and of thy beer of everlastingness. Pepi is the keeper of the Two Obelisks which are on earth; Pepi is the guardian of the Two Pillars which are in heaven. Pepi goeth to embrace the two doors which are in heaven before Rā. His flesh is under the libation (?) of the Firmament of Rā. The Land of the South is made pure before Rā, and he appeareth in his horizon. This Pepi is in the Field of Life, in the Birth-chamber of Rā in the Firmament. The goddest Qebḥut,[1] the daughter of Ånpu, findeth this Pepi, and she goeth to meet him with the Four Nemset Vases. She refreshed the breast of the Great God on the day of his watch, and she refresheth the breast of this Pepi with life. She washeth this Pepi, she censeth this Pepi. This Pepi receiveth his place of offerings in the Granary of the Great God. This Pepi arrayeth himself with the imperishable stars, the place of Pepi is more advanced than that of Khent-Återt, and he taketh his seat with those who have been equipped with their characteristics (?).

[1] .

396. Hail, Nuru, thou Ferry-god[1] of Sekhet-Pāt[2]! Pepi is thy herdsman, the chief of thy breeding ground (?). Pepi is thy fashioner on earth, the offspring of Tem to whom Nut gave birth. He cometh, he bringeth to thee this thy house, he builded it for thee on the night wherein thou wast brought forth, on the day of thy birth (?). This vessel . . . unknown is thy father, unknown is thy mother . . . Make thou him to sail with speed to the Earth, and arrive at the Field made by the gods, the Field wherein they enjoy abundance on the New Year's Days.

400. Hail, Ferryman, thou Boatman of Maāt, who dost transport [souls] to Sekhet-Åaru, this Pepi is true before heaven and before earth. This Pepi is true before the Island of the earth. Pepi swam and arrived at that which was between the thighs of Nut. Pepi is the pygmy, the dancer [before] the god, who rejoiceth the heart of the god, when he danceth before his Great Throne. This is what shall be heard of thee in the houses, and what shall be heard of thee on the roads. This is the day whereon this Pepi shall be proclaimed for life, and to hear the utterance of commands. Behold, the chiefs of the throne of the Great God shall proclaim this Pepi for life and serenity for ever. He is Strength and he is Health. This Pepi saileth to the Field, to the beautiful place of the Great God, and he shall do what hath to be done therein among the servants. He shall assign to them food, and tell out for them birds. Pepi is Horus, who assigneth food to Pepi, and telleth out to him birds.

405. Hail, Ferryman of Sekhet-ḥetep! Bring this to this Pepi; it is Pepi who passeth, it is Pepi who cometh, the son of the Māntchet Boat, which brought forth Kheft-Ta; Āntchet brought him forth. Ānkhet-taui is there, on the right side of Osiris. Pepi is the green-laden envoy of the year, O Osiris. Behold, he cometh with the message of thy father Ḳeb with the offerings of the year, the offerings of the year. Beautiful

1 

2

is that which belongeth to the year, beautiful things belong to the year. Pepi descended with the Two Companies of the Gods into Qebḥu, Pepi was the moulder of the Two Companies of the Gods, and he laid the foundation of Sekhet-ḥetep. This Pepi findeth the gods standing up, arrayed in their apparel, with white sandals on their feet. But they hurl their white sandals down on the earth, and they strip off their apparel, for their hearts are not happy because of thy coming to them. Ye speak, ye remain. "Sekhem-utcha" is the name of this weapon, the . . . of Sekhet-ḥetep. Stand up now, Osiris, and decree this Pepi to the chiefs of "Sekhem-utcha," the . . . . of Sekhet-ḥetep, as thou didst decree Horus to Isis on the day when thou didst beget him in her, so that they may give him food to eat in the fields, and water to drink from the wells in Sekhet-ḥetep.

411. Hail, Ḥer-f-ḥa-f, thou doorkeeper of Osiris! Osiris saith: Make thou to come to this Pepi thy boat wherein thou makest to sail thy purified [souls].[1] And when thou hast received thy cool water at that Uārt of the imperishable stars, make him to make his journey therein, by means of the rope of green and red which towed along the Eye of Horus. Now the finger of Osiris there passeth along, in pain (?). This Pepi journeyeth along with great speed (?), guarding himself in the Great Lake. Be opened, O doors of Peter, be opened wide the doors of the Lower Ȧat! O ye Two Companies of the Gods, make ye this Pepi to travel with you to the Sekhet-ḥetep, and make him to become a lord of fealty. This Pepi smiteth with his *Āba* sceptre, he ruleth with the *Ȧaata* staff. He guideth the revolutions of Rā, the watering of the earth, the dew of Ḳeb, and the . . . of the Two Companies of the Gods. Pepi is the Divine Soul who maketh his way among you, O ye gods, who forceth a way through Pāt Lake, who filleth Pāt Lake with water, who maketh Sekhet-Ȧaru to blossom, and filleth Sekhet-ḥetep with water. Behold, as those Four Tchanu,[2] who stand on the East side

1 .

2 .

of heaven, travelled on and transported Rā in their boat through the two defiles (?) so that he might journey to his horizon, so shall they transport this Pepi through the defiles (?) so that he may journey to the horizon with Rā, and give thanks to Horus of the Ṭuat, the Divine Hawk, yellowish-green in colour, who produced the heavens.

420. Homage to thee with thy Four Faces which are at rest and gaze at what is in the Land of Kenset, and change the storms into calms (?). Give thou to this Pepi thy two fingers which thou didst give to Nefert, the daughter of the Great God, when she was the messenger from heaven to earth, when the gods made their appearance in heaven. O Soul-god, who risest at the head of thy Boat of seven hundred and seventy cubits, thou hast transported the gods of Pu, thou hast completed the gods of the East, and thou hast made this Pepi to travel with thee in the cabin of thy boat.[1] This Pepi is the son of KhepRer (the Beetle-god),[2] who was born in Ḥetepet-ḥemt (?), under the hair of Iusāas,[3] to the north of Ȧnu, and came forth from the brow of Ḳeb. This Pepi is he who was between the thighs of Khent-Merti, on the night of the grinding (?) of the weapon (?), and on the day of sharpening (?) the tips of the weapons. Thou hast received thy spear (or, harpoon)[4] and thy fighting weapon wherewith thou layest waste the lands —now its hooks (or, barbs) are the fiery darts of Rā, and its two staves are the claws of the Lynx-goddess[5] (or, Leopard-goddess). Pepi smasheth in the heads of the enemies of Horus who are in Sekhet-ḥetep. Pepi descendeth (*i.e.*, embarketh) on the Great Green,[6] and, O Great Green, thou hast bowed thy head and bent thy knees [before him]. And these Children of Nut have embarked on thee, and they have put their crowns on their heads, and chains of *ȧb* flowers round their necks.

[1] 

[2] 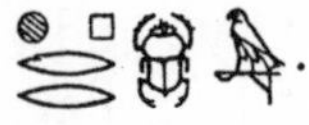

[3] 

[4] 

[5] 

[6] The Mediterranean Sea.

And they decorate themselves with Crowns of the North [made of flowers] of the Lakes of Sekhet-ḥetep for Isis, the Great Lady, bearer of the diadem (?) in Akh-khebit. And behold, she bringeth them and placeth them before her son Horus the Child, the Babe. He journeyeth over the earth in his white sandals, and he goeth to see his father Osiris. This Pepi openeth his way among the feathered fowl (?), he goeth along with the Lords of Doubles, he travelleth to the Great Lake in Sekhet-ḥetep, by which the Great Gods alight, and these great ones of the imperishable stars give unto Pepi the tree of life whereon they themselves do live, so that he also may live thereon. Make thou this Pepi to journey with thee into thy Great Field which hath been put under thy authority by the gods, wherein thou eatest from night to dawn, being in possession of the god Ḥu, and let this Pepi eat of what thou eatest there, and let this Pepi drink of what thou drinkest there. Grant thou that this Pepi may be satisfied there . . . Grant thou that this Pepi may sit in his truth (?), and that he may stand up in his loyal service. Let this Pepi stand up and take possession of his service before thee, even as Horus took possession of his father's house from Set, his father's brother, before Ḳeb. Proclaim thou in truth that this Pepi is a Chief among the Spirits, the imperishable ones of heaven, who are Governors of offerings and Guardians of oblations, and who make to descend those who are at the head of their Doubles in heaven.

436. Hail, ye Four Gods who are in front of the flowing hair of Horus, whose hair is in front of you, whose hair is above your temples, whose hair is in your caps on the middle of your heads! Hail, ye Smiters, bring ye the Mekhent Boat to this Pepi, bring ye the Ȧntu (?) Boat to this Pepi. Behold, Ḥeqrer,[1] they transport this Pepi with Maa-ḥa-f and he ferrieth him to that region of the imperishable stars so that he may be among them. Whensoever he giveth the order, take ye over the Mekhent Boat to this Pepi, so that this Pepi may declare your names to the men whom he knoweth,

[1] 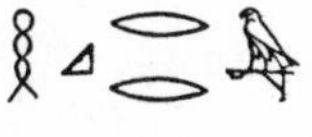.

and to mortals, and so that he may pluck out these Smiters which are in (?) your heads like lilies from the pools.

440. O Lake of gifts! O Lake of gifts! Behold, this Ser goose is brought, behold, this Set goose is brought, behold, this Neḳ Bull is brought. This Pepi darteth like the *Āḥāu* bird, and he rusheth on his prey like the *Bennu* (?) bird. Pepi journeyeth on with his fathers who are in the Lake of Petchu. The bread which cannot go mouldy is brought to Pepi, and his wine which cannot go sour. This Pepi eateth his bread alone by himself, this Pepi doth not cast it behind his back, and he is delivered from the *Kenmut* bird.

Hail, Maa-ḥa-f! Hail, Ḥer-f-ḥa-f! Behold, this Pepi cometh as a living being! He bringeth to thee the Eye of Horus, the fettered (?) one which is in Sekhet-Khennu, and it is in the Eye-of-Khnem Boat that Pepi hath brought it. Hail, Ḥep, Åmset, Ṭua-mut-f, and Qebḥsenuf. Pepi bringeth this Eye-of-Khnemu Boat, which is in the Lake of Kha (or, Lake of Ḥetem). Hail, thou god Ām,[1] open thou a way for Pepi. Hail, thou god Qererȧ, open thou a way for this Pepi. Hail, thou goddess Nekhebet, open thou a way for Pepi. Homage to thee, O goddess Nefert, in peace! Love ye this Pepi. Love ye this Pepi. Do ye no harm to him. Carry him not away. Carry not ye him away.

447. The splendour of Pepi maketh strong the heavens when this Pepi maketh to take flight to heaven the Eye of Rā. Stand thou up, O this Pepi, by that left Eye of Horus whereby thou shalt hear the words of the gods. Stand thou up, O Pepi, at the head of the Spirits, even as Horus standeth up at the head of the Living. Stand thou up, O Pepi, at the head of the imperishable Spirits, as Osiris standeth up at the head of the Spirits.

449. Pepi hath been made pure with the purifications which Horus performed for his Eye; Pepi is Thoth, your avenger, and not Set who stole it (*i.e.*, the Eye). The gods make supplication, and the Two Companies of the Gods rejoice when they meet this Pepi. Pepi raiseth up the White Crown wherein the Eye of Horus is

1 .

mighty; the gods rejoice in his appearance. The face of Pepi is the face of a jackal. The arms of Pepi are the arms of a hawk. The tips of the wings of Pepi are those of Thoth. Ḳeb maketh this Pepi to fly to heaven. Pepi draweth the Eye of Horus to him. Pepi judgeth the dead (?). A wall to Pepi are the tablets which are between the legs and under the hands of Osiris. Pepi obstructeth the ways of Set, and continueth on his way with the messengers of Osiris. No god can lay a hand on Pepi, and no mariner can foul the way of this Pepi. Pepi is Thoth, the strength of the gods. Tem calleth this Pepi to heaven to life. Pepi draweth the Eye of Horus to him. Pepi is the son of Khnemu. No evil thing hath Pepi wrought. These words reach to thy face, O Rā, the Bull of the Company of the Nine hearkeneth to them. Open thou the way of this Pepi, make thou spacious the seat of this Pepi at the head of the gods. Pepi draweth the Eye of Horus to him, he exalteth it, and it appeareth on his head. Grant to Pepi that he may see with his two eyes completely, and to destroy his enemies therewith. Horus hath taken his Eye, he hath given it to this Pepi. His odour is the odour of the god, the odour of the Eye of Horus appertaineth to the flesh of this Pepi, Pepi advanceth with it. This Pepi sitteth on the Great Throne of the gods, he supporteth himself on Tem, between the Two Powers (?). O Pepi, ... the gods, in the embraces of the Eye of Horus. It seeketh this Pepi in Pe, it findeth [him] in Ȧnu, it draweth him on to the head of Set in that place wherein they fought. Horus, give thy hand to this Pepi. Horus, thine Eye hath been presented to thee, it cometh forth to thee, it cometh forth to thee. This Pepi cometh to thee a living being. The Eye of Horus cometh to thee with this Pepi, on Pepi for ever.

461. Thou hast purified Rā, thou hast decorated Horus, ... on the hands of the god Un,[1] the son of the god, the messenger of the god. This Pepi journeyeth in the Lake of Kenset. This Pepi is purified in Sekhet-Ȧaru, the Shesu-Ḥeru (Body-guard of Horus) have purified him. They recite for this Pepi

[1]

the "Chapter of those who come forth," they recite for this Pepi the "Chapter of those who travel." This Pepi embarketh in thy Boat, O Rā, the gods are the sailors, this Pepi saileth on and they rejoice to meet him even as they rejoice at meeting Rā, when he cometh forth from the East, mounting up, mounting up. This Pepi hath bathed in the Lake of Reeds wherein Rā bathed, Horus hath dried (?) him; the back of this Pepi is the back of Thoth, the legs of Pepi are the legs of Shu, Shu draweth him to heaven, [O gods], give ye your hand to this Pepi.

465. The god Temu once in Heliopolis took the form of a man who masturbated.[1] He thrust his phallus into his hand and worked it about in it, and two children, a brother and a sister, were produced,[2] Shu and Tefnut. May they place this Pepi between them, may they place this Pepi among the gods at the head of Sekhet-ḥetep. *Recite four times.* This Pepi cometh forth to heaven, this Pepi descendeth to earth, living for ever. Hail, Sunth, who dost traverse the heavens nine times during the night, stretch out a hand to this Pepi—of life, and ferry thou him to this Lake. This Pepi embarketh in the Boat of the God, and the company of the gods in it act as the sailors thereof, and this Pepi also becometh a sailor in it. Thou recitest the "Chapter of Beṭu incense," thou recitest the "Chapter of Natron incense." The Natron standeth up at the head of the Great Company of the Gods. The Beṭu sitteth down at the head of the great Ȧtert. Hail, thou Doorkeeper of heaven! Act thou thus in respect of the Messenger of the God when he cometh forth. If he cometh forth by the West Gate of heaven, bring to him the South Gate of heaven; if he cometh forth by the East Gate of heaven, bring to him the North Gate of heaven.

471. Homage to thee, O Ladder, which beareth up the abode of the souls of Pe and the souls of Nekhen, give thou thy hands to this Pepi, and let Pepi sit between the Two Great Gods. Advance the seats of this Pepi, take [him by] the hand to Sekhet-ḥetep, and let him sit among the stars in heaven. The Two

1 

2 

Tchert birds (*i.e.*, Isis and Nephthys) on the wings of Thoth swoop down and alight, and they bring this Pepi and set him upon his place. This Pepi of life is a messenger (?) of Horus. . . . The Ṭeṭ setteth free the Māntchet Boat for its Lord, the Ṭeṭ setteth free the Māntchet Boat for its chief Isis cometh, Nephthys cometh, one on the right, one on the left, one of them as a *Ḥat* bird—Nephthys cometh—one of them as a *Tchert* bird. They find Osiris, his brother Set hath cast him down to the ground in Neṭȧt.[1] . . . They remove thy foulness—now thy name is Ȧnpu. They remove the efflux of thy filth to the earth—now thy name is "Jackal of the South." They remove the evil odour of thy body—now thy name is "Ḥeru-shati." They remove the filth of Ḥeru-ȧbti. They remove the filth of Ḥeru-neb-pāt. They remove the filth of Ḥeru-Ṭatti. They remove the filth of Ḥeru-neb-taui. . . . Watch, O Horus, stand up upon Set. Thou art raised up, O Osiris Pepi, the firstborn son of Ḳeb. The Two Companies of the Gods tremble [before] him. . . . Advance thou to the Lake, sail thou to the Great Green Sea. Behold, thou art he who standeth up, he who never resteth, dweller in Abydos. Thou art endowed as a spirit in the horizon, thou art made stable in Tcheṭet. The Souls of Ȧn take thy hand, Rā taketh thy hand, the Two Companies of the Gods raise up thy head, and they make thee, O Osiris Pepi, to be at the head of the Ȧterti of the Souls of Ȧn. Live thou, live thou, thou art raised up . . . O thou Pepi, [thy] marking cometh forth from Rā, thy sweat cometh forth from Isis. . . .

531. Lo Isis and Nephthys! The *Ḥat* bird cometh, the *Tchert* bird cometh, Isis and Nephthys. They come with embraces for their brother Osiris, with embraces for their brother, this Pepi. Thou hast being (?) Thou hast being (?). Thy sister Isis weepeth for thee. Thy sister Nephthys weepeth for thee. Isis, sitting down with her hands upon her head, and Nephthys give the nipple of their breasts to their brother Pepi. Ȧnpu is on his belly. Osiris is on his seat (?) Ȧp-uat is at the head of

1 .

his fist (?) Thy humours are not, O Pepi. Thy sweat-drops are not, O Pepi. Thy efflux is not, O Pepi. Thy emission is not, O Pepi. . . . Horus covereth thee with his garment, he seizeth those who are in the following of Set. He seizeth them, he breaketh their heads, he cutteth off their haunches, he teareth out their intestines, he diggeth out their hearts, he drinketh copiously of their blood! Count thou up their hearts in thy name of Ȧnpu, counter of hearts. Thine eyes are made for thee like those of two uraei. Thou art Ȧp-uat upon his standard, Ȧnpu of the Divine House. Hail, thou Pepi, thou art at the head of the Great Houses in Ȧnu. The Spirits fear thee, the imperishable one. Thou castest the dead on their faces before thee, thou seizest with thy hand the *Ḥenmemet*. The Souls of Ȧnu pay thee loyal homage, and they fill thee with life and well-being (or, serenity). He liveth among the living, Seker liveth among the living. He liveth among the living, this Pepi liveth among the living. Hail, thou Pepi! Come, live this thy life in thy season, in thy season, in these years of peace. Warm is the love of thee.

548. Thy water is to thee. Thy flood is to thee. Thy humours are to thee, coming forth from Osiris. The doors of heaven are open to thee, the doors of Nut are open to thee; the doors of heaven are open to thee, the doors of the firmament are open to thee. Isis and Nephthys cry in content over thee [when] they see their brother raised up. Thy fetters are untied, thou layest aside thy humours, thou sittest on thy throne of alabaster (?), thou art purified by thy Four Nemset vessels and thy Four Ābt vessels. Thou comest from the God-house, the god is with thee, thou hast abundance in the God-lake. Horus of Nekhen is given to thee, he giveth to thee his Spirits, the Jackals. Behold, by the will of Horus, thou art advanced to the head of the Powers.[1] Abiding is that which thou hast done. Ȧnpu Khenti-neter-seḥ hath decreed that thou shalt descend like a star, the Morning-star. Thou rushest on

[1] .

the Domain of Horus of the South, thou rushest on the Domain of Horus of the North. Thou seizest captives (?), their hands are at the feet of thy throne. Thy father cometh to thee, Ḳeb cometh to thee, he doeth that which thou didst for thy father Osiris, on the day of thy perfect festival in the waters, counting up the lists, establishing the sandals, decorating his nails, upper and lower. The Ȧtert of the South and the Ȧtert of the North come to him with bowings. . . .

559. Hail, thou Pepi! Stand up, and sit thou upon the throne of Osiris. Thy flesh (body) is complete like [that of] Tem. Thy face is that of a jackal. Rā hath given to thee thy mouth ; he hath removed the impediments in thy speech, he hath made thy words to flow. Stand up, then, thou shalt not come to an end, thou shalt never perish. Live, thou Pepi! Thy mother Nut layeth hold upon thee, she joineth herself to thee, and Ḳeb taketh thy hand ; come in peace before thy fathers. Thou art master of thy body, thou dressest thy body. Thou comest forth like Horus of Ṭat at the head of the imperishable stars. Seat thyself on thy throne of alabaster, on thy lake Qebḥu. Live thou, as liveth the Beetle, be stablished, like the Ṭeṭ, for ever and ever.

Get thee back, Ḳen Ȧḳa! Thy head is in the hand of Horus, thy tail in the hand of Isis, and the fingers of Tem are on thy brow.

565. The head of this Pepi is that of a hawk; he cometh forth, he flieth up into heaven.[1] The skull of this Pepi is that of the beard (?) of the god; he cometh, etc. The brow of this Pepi is that of . . . and Nu. The face of this Pepi is that of Ȧp-uat. The eyes of this Pepi are those of Urt-Khentet-baiu-Ȧnu. The nose of this Pepi is that of Thoth. The mouth of this Pepi is that of Khens-ur (?) The tongue of this Pepi is the Maāȧ portion of the Maāt Boat. The teeth of this Pepi are those of the Souls [of Ȧnu?]. The lips of this Pepi are those of . . . The chin of this Pepi is that of Khert-Khent-Sekhem. The backbone of this Pepi is that of [the Bull] Sma. The shoulders of this Pepi are those

[1] "He cometh forth," etc., is repeated after the identification of each member.

of Set. . . . The . . . of this Pepi is that of Baȧbu.[1] The breast of this Pepi is that of Bast. The belly of this Pepi is that of Nut. . . . The . . . of this Pepi is that of the Two Companies of the Gods. The haunches of this Pepi are those of Ḥeqet. The buttocks of this Pepi are those of the Semktet and Māntchet Boats. The phallus of this Pepi is that of Ḥep. The thighs of this Pepi are those of Net and Serqet. The legs of this Pepi are those of the Twin Souls in Sekhet-Tcher. The soles of the feet of this Pepi are those of the Two Maāti goddesses. The toe-nails of this Pepi are those of the Souls of Ȧnu.

Now this Pepi is a god, the son of a god.[2] Pepi is the son of Rā, who loveth him.[2] Rā sendeth forth Pepi,[2] Rā hath conceived Pepi.[2] Rā hath brought forth Pepi.[2] This word of power is the intestines of Pepi.[2] Pepi is the Great Sekhem among the Great Taskmasters in Ȧnu.[2] [He] worketh the Boat of [of Rā].[2] [He is] Horus the Babe, the Child.[2] Nut hath not united [with him], she hath not given her arms.[2] Ḳeb hath not travelled on his path (?)[2] No god hath drawn aside the feet of this Pepi.[2] He hath no fruit (?), he hath no shade, he hath not washed himself in the laver, he hath not smelled the haunch, he hath not carried the flesh and bone, he hath not ploughed the earth, he hath not carried the offering.[2] Behold, it is not this Pepi who saith these things to you, O ye gods, but it is Ḥeka who saith them to you. Pepi is the warden of the stand which is under Ḥeka.[2] Ho, let every god draw his feet to Pepi.[2] Ho, let every god prepare his throne in his Boat.[2] Let him plough the earth, let him carry the offering, let him make ready the *nemtet* vessel, let him smell the haunch, let him carry the offering.[2] Ho, let every god take the hand of this Pepi in heaven, let him make him journey to the House of Horus in the firmament,[3] let his KA be triumphant before Ḳeb.

1 .

2 Here comes the refrain "He cometh forth," etc.

3 .

587. This Pepi cometh before thee, his father, he cometh before thee, O Osiris. He bringeth to thee thy KA, it existeth endowed with soul (?). His mother Nut raiseth him up upon her brow (?) Thou art raised up. Thou art made complete. Shesa-Khent-Shenāt hath opened thy mouth. Tua-ur in the House of Gold hath opened thy mouth. The two Statues in Ḥet-Ḥesmen have opened thy mouth. Horus hath opened thy mouth with his little finger wherewith he opened the mouth of his father, opened the mouth of his father Osiris. This Pepi is thy son, this Pepi is Horus. This Pepi is the son loving his father, in his name of Sa-mer-f. Thou art pure in thy collar (or, breastplate), apparel is given to thee, Thy thousand suits of byssus, thy thousand suits of fine linen, doth this Pepi bring to thee, and he stablisheth thee therewith.

593. O sons of Horus, Ḥep, Ṭuamutef, Ȧmset, and Qebḥsenuf, make the motions which transfer the fluid of life to your father Osiris Pepi, since it is that which shall give him being before the gods. Set striketh. Defend this Osiris Pepi from him until the dawn. Horus hath the mastery. He himself delivereth his father this Osiris Pepi. The father hath worked, praise him! It is Horus who hath come, he judgeth his father Osiris Pepi. . . . . . This Osiris Pepi maketh his way. Osiris Pepi, is brought to thee the Sma Bull, he escapeth not from thee. Osiris Pepi, is brought to thee the Sma Bull, he maketh his march. Osiris Pepi, is brought to thee the Sma Bull cut in pieces. O sons of Horus, this Osiris Pepi marcheth. O ye sons of Horus, when your son passeth under this Osiris Pepi, do not ye remove yourselves from under him, but bear ye him up. O Osiris Pepi, the Sma Bull is brought to thee cut in pieces; he maketh his march. O sons of Horus, Ḥep, Ṭuamutef, Ȧmset, Qebḥsenuf, bear ye up your father Osiris, guide ye him along. O Osiris Pepi, he giveth thee sustenance, he openeth thy mouth, stand thou up. I am Nut, I make to approach this Osiris Pepi, I set him [in his place], taking him in my arms. Hail, father Osiris Pepi, I have made thee to approach. Hail, Osiris Pepi, I have brought thee forth . . . .

601. The earth hath opened her mouth to this Osiris

Pepi, and Ḳeb hath spoken to him. This Pepi is as great as a king, and as glorious as Rā. The Two Companies of the Gods have travelled in peace to Pepi. Ȧmen-Kau hath opened to him the eastern door of heaven. Nut, the great goddess with the long . . . . and the pendent breasts, hath given to him her hands, and she suckleth him, and he lacketh nothing from her. She draweth him to heaven, and droppeth him not on the earth, she maketh him to be stable as Khent Ȧtert. He saileth in the Boat like Rā over the regions of Kha, he saileth in the Ḥenbu Boat, and worketh an oar therein to Sekhet-Nentȧ,[1] at the head of the land of Sekhet-Ȧaru. Rā taketh him by the hand, Tem raiseth up his head, Isis graspeth the rope of his prow, and Nephthys holdeth fast the rope from his stern. Qebḥet placeth him upon her verdure, and maketh him one of her husbandmen and one of those who tend the young cattle. Get thee back, Babuȧ, thou of the red ear and the striped rump! Thou transportest the joint . . . . thy statue and thy utterance. Get thee back, Kam-ur! Retreat into Kher-Āḥa, into the place wherein they (*i.e.*, the fiends) retreat there.

605. Thou livest, O Pepi, for ever. Ḳeb raiseth thee up . . . . Behold, thou art a spirit, Nephthys suckleth thee with her left breast. Osiris hath given thee spirits. Horus hath reared thee. Thy steps are before the Ḥat of Horus, whither hath gone, hath gone the god from the time of Rā. He hath grasped thee by thy hand, Seker-Khent-Petchu hath purified thee. Thy throne is in the firmament. Thou art raised up a spirit, O thou Pepi. Thou sittest down, thou eatest. Thy Ka sitteth, and it eateth and drinketh with thee, lacking nothing for ever. Behold, Isis and Osiris[2] they rub thy feet with their hands. They bring thee thy things of festival. Thy teeth are white (?), and thy nails are those of Ȧnpu (?). Thou sailest, the Mighty Bull, to the Field of Verdure (Sekhet-uatchet), to the places of Rā which are pure. Thou art raised up, this Pepi is a spirit. Thy water is to thee, thy flood is to thee, thy effluxes

[1]

[2]

are to thee, coming forth from the emissions of Osiris. The doors of heaven are open to thee, the doors of the firmament are thrown open to thee, the doors of the Ḥat-house are open to thee, and the doors of Nut are unclosed to thee. Isis crieth welcome to the Father, Nephthys maketh the Father to advance in peace . . . . Thy Spirit-soul is behind thee, thy Sekhem is within thee . . . . Heaven weepeth for thee, the earth trembleth at thee, Smentet crieth out to thee, Menȧnt imploreth thee, rubbing for thee the feet, chafing for thee the two hands. Thou comest forth to heaven like a star, like the Morning Star Pepi cometh to thee, his father, he cometh to thee, O Ḳeb . . . . This Pepi is the son of the Cow, Smat, the great wife, who conceived him and brought him forth, and set him inside her wing. She saileth over the Lake with thee, she goeth along the canal with thee . . . . Thy sceptre is firm in thy hand. Thou smitest [therewith], thou directest, thou leviest tax on the lords of service. Behold, thou revolvest about Rā, near the Morning Star; there is no evil to thee, there is no evil attached to thy name on the earth.

614. Pepi cometh forth from Pe. His garment is like that of Horus, his apparel is like that of the Two Companies of the Gods. Pepi hath made himself to rise on his throne like a king, he hath exalted himself like Ȧp-uat. He hath received the White Crown and the Green Crown. His mace is in his hand, his Ames sceptre resteth in the palm of his hand. The mother of Pepi is Isis, his nurse is Nephthys, the goddess Sekhat-Ḥeru suckleth him, Net (Neith) followeth him, Serqet-ḥet goeth before him, his tackle is tightened, his boats are grouped together. Behold, the son of Tem hungereth [and] thirsteth, [and] thirsteth [and] hungereth on this southern side of the Lake of Kha. O Thoth, who art in the shade of thy grove, give thou to Pepi the tip of the feather of thy wing on this northern side of the Lake of Kha. Pepi is protected, his flesh is protected; Pepi is protected, his apparel is protected. He cometh forth to heaven like Menthu, he descendeth like a Ba bird into his net, like the Soul of Āshem . . . . Exalted is father Osiris Pepi like Ȧp-uat . . . . Thy

feet are like those of a jackal; stand up then. Thy hands are like those of a jackal; stand up then . . . . Father Osiris Pepi crieth out to the Steersman,[1] father Osiris Pepi crieth out to the captain,[2] and they transport father Osiris Pepi in their boat, to the eastern side of heaven, to the place where the gods were born . . . . father Osiris Pepi is brought forth there in the place where the gods are born. This star cometh on the morrow, and on the third day (?). Behold, father Osiris Pepi standeth up at the door under the belly of heaven . . . .

This Pepi hath taken his apparel (?),[3] this Pepi cometh forth to heaven, stablished like the earth, the male (?) in thy body, O Nut, under the seed of the god in thy mother. Pepi is Horus, the seed of the god in thy mother Nut. Thou hast received[4] this Pepi as thou hast received the son of the god. O Hapath, O Hapath, O Henenȧ, O Henenȧ, make ye Pepi to travel with you, and establish ye him among you. O Ḥeftnet,[5] Mother of the Gods, give thou thy hand to this Pepi, give thou his hand for life, draw him to heaven, even as thou hast drawn Osiris to heaven. O Henenȧ, O Henenȧ, O Hapath, O Hapath, make ye Pepi to travel with you, and establish ye him among you.

637. Pure, pure is the Lake of Ȧaru. Pure is Rā in the Lake of Ȧaru, and Pepi himself is pure in the Lake of Ȧaru. Pure is Shu in the Lake of Ȧaru, and Pepi himself is pure in the Lake of Ȧaru. O Shu, Shu, lift up this Pepi to heaven, O Nut, give thou thy two hands to him. Hepaf, Hepaf, Henen-henen-henen, Hepaf, Hepaf. Pepi is pure and is conveyed to heaven. This Pepi is stablished with men. This Pepi riseth to the gods. This Pepi riseth with Rā in his rising. Those who are with him are four; one followeth him,

1 .

2 .

3 .

4 Or, swallowed.

5 .

one goeth before him, one giveth him water, and one giveth him sand (?). This Pepi riseth on thy hands, O Shu, even as Rā riseth on thy hands, and they find seated to meet him the Two Spirits, who are mistresses of this earth. Nut rejoiceth to meet this Pepi. Pepi taketh the *nepenpet* garment which is in her . . . . of life and serenity, and which is under her . . . . and they sit down together with Pepi. He hath removed from himself the evil which appertained to him. The goddess Serqet giveth her two hands to this Pepi, she conveyeth her breast to the mouth of Pepi, the great Morning Star[1] shaveth him, and the goddess Sepṭ poureth water on his hands. Pepi is born this day [among] the gods. His first mother knoweth him not, but Nut who bringeth him forth with Osiris knoweth him.

643. This Pepi setteth forth with thee, O Horus. O Thoth, bear him on the tip of thy wing. Behold, it is Seker at the head of the Maāt Boat . . . . He who passeth passeth with his Ka. Em-khent-merti passeth with his Ka, and this Pepi passeth with his Ka to heaven. He hath taken the Ladder, and hath ascended it in its name of "Āq-er-pet." He saileth in its boat to the sceptres of the imperishable stars. The Bull of Heaven inclineth his horn and maketh him to pass on his way to the Lakes of Ṭat. Hail, Pepi, thou shalt not fall to the earth. This Pepi hath grasped the Two Sycamore Trees which are in the midst of that side of the sky, he saileth on, and they place him in that eastern side of heaven. Know thou thy name, be not ignorant of thy name. Thy name is "Ȧn-tcher-f," and "Urrt" is the name of thy father, and the mother who bore thee is "Ḥetep." If thou repulsest the offspring of Ȧn-tcher-f in the horizon, thou wilt repulse this Pepi when he cometh to the place where thou art. If thou repulsest the offspring of Serqet, thou wilt repulse this Pepi when he cometh to the place where thou art. If thou repulsest the Two Lands[2] of Horus, thou wilt repulse this Pepi when he cometh to the place where

1 

2 

thou art. If thou repulsest the offspring of Saḥ (Orion), thou wilt repulse this Pepi when he cometh to the place where thou art. If thou repulsest the offspring of Sepṭ (Sothis), thou wilt repulse this Pepi when he cometh to the place where thou art. If thou repulsest the Two Bentu[1] of Rā, his two sons who love him, thou wilt repulse this Pepi when he cometh to the place where thou art. If thou repulsest the offspring of Ȧp-uat in Per-Khen, thou wilt repulse this Pepi when he cometh to the place where thou art. If thou repulsest the men of the king, the son of God, thou wilt repulse this Pepi when he cometh to the place where thou art. If thou repulsest thy sailors of the imperishable stars of thy boat, thou wilt prevent them from allowing Pepi to embark in thy boat. If thou repulsest the men belonging to the dead (or, death), thou wilt prevent this Pepi from embarking in thy boat. If thou repulsest the men belonging to earth, thou wilt prevent this Pepi from embarking in thy boat. Behold, thou art Seksen,[2] the messenger of Rā. This Pepi is not driven away from heaven, and the goddess Mathet[3] giveth her hands to this Pepi, the Doorkeeper of heaven. Ḥer-f-ḥa-f uniteth him to his boat of the Lake of Kha, he doth not repulse this Pepi, he maketh no obstacles for him, [saying]: "He is one of you, O ye gods." This Pepi cometh to thee, O Rā, this Pepi cometh to thee, O Ȧn-tcher-f. He worketh the boat for thee, he maketh passes over thee [with his hands], he loveth thee with his body, he loveth thee with his heart.

652. Water on the sky, O Baq-tree of the firmament! The sky hath produced a god on the hand of Shu and Tefnut, on the hands of Pepi. The gods say: O Uben-ur (*i.e.*, Great Light), hearken to this word which Pepi uttereth to thee. Be gracious to this Pepi, for he is a Chief, the son of a Chief. This Pepi is with thee, rear thou this Pepi for everlasting life and serenity with thyself. O Khepṛer, hear thou this word which he shall say unto thee. Be gracious to this Pepi,

1 

2 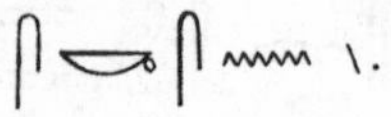

3 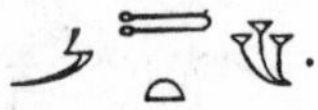

for he is a Chief, the son of a Chief. This Pepi is with thee, rear thou this Pepi with thee. O Nu, hear thou this word which he shall say unto thee. Be gracious unto him, for he is a Chief, the son of a Chief. This Pepi is with thee, rear thou him with thee. O Tem, hear thou this word which he shall say unto thee. Be gracious to this Pepi, for he is a Chief, the son of a Chief. He is with thee, rear thou him with thee. O Uash,[1] son of Keb, Power, son of Osiris, hear thou this word which he shall say unto thee. Be gracious unto him, for he is a Chief, the son of a Chief. This Pepi is with thee, rear thou him with thee. Come (?) thou to this Pepi in thy name of "Rā destroyed of the covering of the sky." Let Ḥeru-khuti cause him to hear his souls praised in the mouth of the Two Companies of the Gods. "Beneficent one," saith his mother; "Heir," saith Osiris. This Pepi hath not eaten the Eye of Horus; men say: "He will die because of this." Pepi hath not eaten the flesh of Osiris; the gods say: "He will die because of it." This Pepi liveth as the equal (?) of his father Tem. Protect (?) thou him, O goddess Nekhebet, thou hast protected this Pepi, O Nekhebet, dweller in the House of the Prince which is in Ȧnu (Heliopolis).

. . . 657. Pepi hath passed his day under death, even as Set hath passed his day under death. Pepi hath passed his half-months under death, even as Set hath passed his half-months under death. Pepi hath passed his months under death, even as Set hath passed his months under death. Pepi hath passed his year under death, even as Set hath passed his year under death.

The hands of Pepi have not ploughed the earth. Behold it is Shu who beareth up Nut. The bones of Pepi are of alabaster (?), and his flesh is imperishable. Pepi is the star Ȧp-shep-pet (Jupiter ?). This Pepi approacheth the God and is protected. Heaven shall not be empty of this Pepi, and earth shall not be empty of this Pepi for ever. This Pepi liveth life more than your sceptres *āu*. O ye gods of the Sky, ye imperishable

[1] , l. 654.

ones, who sail over the Land of Tehenu in your boats, and direct them with your sceptres, this Pepi directeth his boat with you by means of the *Uas* sceptre and the *Tchām* sceptre, and he is the fourth (or, third) with you. O ye gods of heaven, ye imperishable ones, who sail over the Land of Taḥennu, who transport yourselves by means of your sceptres, this Pepi transporteth himself with you by means of the *Uas* and *Tchām*, and he is the fourth with you. O ye gods of heaven, ye imperishable ones, who sail over the Land of Taḥennu, who transport yourselves by means of your sceptres, this Pepi transporteth himself with you by means of the *Uas* and *Tchām*, according to the decree of Horus, the Erpāt, the King of the gods. This Pepi hath seized the White Crown which is bound to the Green Crown. Pepi is the uraeus which cometh forth from Set, which carrieth off that which is brought, and Pepi beareth it away and giveth himself life. Pepi is the written roll which cometh forth from Nunu. Pepi is the Eye of Horus which is uninjured and watereth; he is uninjured and watereth. Hearken, O Rā, unto this word which Pepi uttereth to thee; thy body is Pepi, O Rā, make to live thy body in him, O Rā. Kenmut slaughtereth the apes, and the apes slaughter Kenmut. O thou Fowler, O thou Male, be there agreement between you. For that first body, Pepi, of the swathings, and of the triumph, was born when Tchenṭ did not exist, was born when the Word did not exist, was born when Shentet did not exist, was born when Khennu did not exist, was born when the Eye of Horus was not stabbed and when the testicles of Set were not eradicated.

This Pepi is the *ȧnes* matter which cometh forth from Isis, and the red essence which cometh forth from Nephthys. Pepi is strong . . . the gods do nothing against him. Pepi is the seat[1] of Rā, and he dieth not. Ḳeb, the Erpāt of the gods, beareth him, Tem provideth him with his Eye, Thoth beareth what is among the offerings of the gods, Horus openeth for him, and Set protecteth him. This Pepi shineth in the eastern

[1] .

part of heaven, just as Rā shineth in the eastern part of heaven.

663. O Guardian, mother in whom is Pepi, he being in Nut, this Pepi was brought forth by father Tem when there was no heaven, when there was no earth, when there were no men, when the gods were not brought forth, when there was no death. This Pepi hath shortened [his] day under death as Set shortened his day under death. Pepi is at your vases, O gods of Nut,[1] who smite not your enemies, whom their enemies smite not. This Pepi is not smitten, his enemies are not. Ye do not die like a king, and Pepi dieth not like a king ; ye do not die like every one who dieth, and Pepi doth not die like every one who dieth. Pepi is imperishable, the king (?) of the great heaven, who dwelleth in Ḥet-Serqet. Rā hath drawn Pepi to the sky, this Pepi liveth, just as he who entereth on the right side of heaven and cometh forth from the left side, liveth. Pepi commandeth Åm-ḥent-f, and Åm-Sep-f . . . Pepi is a star. The magical power of Rā is on this Pepi, Rā weigheth not his magical power on this Pepi. Horus throweth this Pepi on his shoulders, he accounteth him as Shu, directing [his] hands under Nut. O Rā, give thy hand to this Pepi! O Great God, give thy staff to Pepi and let him live for ever!

667. " Happy are those who see, those who rest in Petet," saith Isis. This god cometh forth to heaven, his soul is on him, his knife is with him, words of power are his speech, and Tem doeth for him what he did for himself. The gods who belong to heaven bring this Pepi, and the gods who belong to earth embrace him. They place their hands under him, they form a ladder for him, and he entereth into heaven thereby. The doors of heaven are open to him, the firmament is thrown wide open before him. Tem hath gathered together the nomes to him, and Ḳeb hath given him towns which are called " Åats," the Åats of Horus, the Åats of Set, and Sekhet-Åaru. Pepi is Raḥes,[2] Governor of the South-land. Pepi is Ṭeṭun, Governor of Ta-sti

1 .

2 , var. .

(Nubia). Pepi is Sepṭ, under his Sebt trees. If ye were to slay him, if ye were to order his death, he would not die, for this Pepi shall most certainly live for ever . . . .

669. Thou watchest in peace, Ḥesmenu, in peace. Thou watchest in peace, Ḥeru-ȧbt, in peace. Thou watchest in peace, Ba-ȧbt, in peace. Thou watchest in peace, Ḥeru-khuti, in peace. Thou sleepest in the Semktet Boat, thou wakest up in the Māntchet Boat, behold, thou seest the Chief of the gods, but no god seeth thy chief. O Rā, Father of Pepi, thou drawest him with thee to life with thy mother Nut. Open the doors of heaven to him, unfold the doors of the firmament to him, and let him be thy porter, and vivify thou him. Command thou that he is to sit by thee, on the shoulders of the Morning Star on the horizon. O Rā, Father of Pepi, command the Great Bear which is near thee to yield up its place to him on the Uārt-ur under the firmament, and command Ānkh, the son of Sepṭet, to speak over (?) Pepi. Make him to establish a throne for him in heaven. Pepi giveth orders to Ur-shepsef, the beloved of Ptaḥ, the son of Ptaḥ. His words are on Pepi, he maketh to grow the *tchefa* food (or, offering) in his abode on the earth. Pepi is one of those four gods Ȧmset, Ḥep, Ṭuamutef, and Qebḥsenuf, who live on Maāt, who are exalted by reason of their sceptres, and watch over (?) the Land of the South. He flieth, he flieth from you, O men, like the geese, he delivereth his hands from you like a hawk, he removeth his body from you like a *tchert* bird. Deliver this Pepi from Ȧm-uārt on the earth, remove him from Ȧm-āȧ.

682. Homage to thee, O Sycamore, companion of the god, whereunder stand the gods of Nut! Flame blazeth about it, fire burneth inside it, Maāt extinguisheth it (?). Those who are in Nu embrace thee, those who are in the canals put their arms about thee. Thy breast is on the shoulder of Osiris, ... the Great Ṭeṭ . . . . Thou standest up, Osiris, thy shadow (?) is on thee, O Osiris. Thy diadem repulseth Set . . . . The terror of thee is on the wardens of the sky, the fear of thee is on the wardens of the earth. Thou layest thy knife (?) on

the hearts of the Kings of the North who are in the town of Pe. This Pepi cometh to thee, O Horus, the Heir of Ḳeb, the Word of Tem. To thee is Tem and the Two Companies of the Gods speak ; to thee is Tem and thou speakest. Behold, this Pepi is the counterpart of the gods who dwell in the sky. Those who are in the canals embrace thee, those who are in the imperishable stars encompass thee . . . .

685. Behold him who cometh. Behold him who cometh, saith Seḥpu.

Behold, the son of Rā cometh, the beloved of Rā cometh, saith Seḥpu.

Let him come, let him come, saith Horus.

Behold him who cometh. Behold him who cometh, saith Seḥpu.

Behold, the son of Rā cometh, the beloved of Rā cometh, saith Seḥpu.

Let him come, let him come, saith Set.

Behold him who cometh. Behold him who cometh, saith Seḥpu.

Behold, the son of Rā cometh, the beloved of Rā cometh, saith Seḥpu.

Let him come, let him come, saith Ḳeb.

Behold him who cometh. Behold him who cometh, saith Seḥpu.

Behold, the son of Rā cometh, the beloved of Rā cometh, saith Seḥpu.

Let him come, let him come, say the Souls of Ȧnu and the Souls of Pe.

Praise be to Rā, is what men say when they stand by the side of Pepi on the earth. Behold, thou risest in the East of the sky. Give thy hand to Pepi, and draw thou him with thee to the eastern side of the sky. Praise be to Rā, is what men say when they stand by the side of Pepi on the earth. Behold, thou risest in the South of the sky. Give thy hand to Pepi, and draw thou him with thee to the Southern side of the sky. Praise be to Rā, is what men say when they stand by the side of Pepi on the earth. Behold, thou risest in the heart of the sky. Give thou thy hand to Pepi, and draw thou him with thee to the heart of the sky. Thine offerings are brought unto thee, and gifts for thee are brought before thee.

Saith Set, the brother of Osiris: "Place Osiris on his side." Saith Rā: "Let the dweller in Neṭȧt move, and "raise up his head. The thing which he abominateth is "sleep, what he hateth is weakness; he shall not rot, he "shall not become corruption, this Pepi shall not "perish." Saith your . . . . O gods: "Thou watchest "in peace. Osiris watcheth in peace. He who is in "Neṭȧt watcheth in peace." "Raise his head," saith Rā. "His odour is that of the Uraeus." "Raise the head of "Pepi," saith Rā. "The odour of Pepi is that of the "Uraeus. He shall not rot, he shall not become corrup-"tion, this Pepi shall not perish," saith your Tchenṭ, O gods. "This Pepi is of thy seed, O Osiris [and "Sepṭet] in thy name of 'Am-Uatch-ur Ḥeru-khent-"khu.' He shall not rot, he shall not become corrup-"tion, this Pepi shall not perish," saith your Tchenṭ, O gods. He cometh forth from his house clothed like Horus, arrayed like Thoth. The mother of Pepi is thy Ȧnt, O God, the father of Pepi is Ȧnu, and Pepi himself is thy Ȧnu, O God. Rā hath conceived Pepi, Rā hath brought him forth, Pepi is of thy seed, of Rā and Sepṭet, in thy name of "Ḥeru-khent-khu," the star which saileth over the Great Green Sea. "He shall not rot, he shall not become corruption, he shall not perish," saith your Tchenṭ, O gods. He is one of the Four Gods, children of Ḳeb, who travel over the South and North, and stand by their sceptres, who are anointed with *ḥātet* unguent, and arrayed in *ȧṭmȧ* apparel, who live on figs, and drink wine, and are anointed with that same substance wherewith ye are anointed. Pepi is dressed as ye are dressed, he liveth upon what ye live upon, he drinketh that which ye drink, he journeyeth with you, he liveth upon what ye yourselves live on. Give ye to him his allotted portion from that which your father Ḳeb gave unto you so that, having it, ye might not hunger or perish. Stretch ye out your hands to this Pepi of life, the sweetest smelling being of those who smell sweet. Collect the bones of this Pepi, knit together his limbs. He sitteth on his throne, he shall not rot, he shall not suffer corruption, he shall not perish, saith your Tchenṭ, O gods.

694. Pepi cometh to you, O mother of Pepi, he cometh to Nut. Thou makest him enter the sky, thou makest the stars to withdraw before him, his odour is like the odour of thy son who cometh forth from thee, his odour is like the odour of Osiris thy son, who cometh forth from thee. O Nu, Pepi hath raised his arm to the sky, he ruleth the earth, and he giveth [it] to thee. He cometh forth, he ascendeth to heaven. He worketh magic for Rā, [he is] Ḥeru-khent-khu, the sweetest smelling of those who smell sweet. Thou watchest in peace. Rā watcheth in peace. Thou watchest in peace. Meṭȧ watcheth in peace. He giveth a writing to this Pepi, into his hand, the sweetest smelling of those who smell sweet. Osiris riseth, pure of Sekhem, exalted, Lord of Maāt at the New Year, Lord of the Year. Tem, the father of the gods, is at peace. Shu and Tefnut are at peace. Ḳeb and Nut are at peace. Osiris and Isis are at peace. Set and Neith are at peace. All the gods in heaven are at peace, all the gods who are in the earth and in the water are at peace, all the gods of the South and North are at peace, all the gods of the West and East are at peace, all the gods of the nomes are at peace, and all the gods of the cities are at peace by reason of this great and mighty word which cometh forth from the mouth of Thoth to Osiris, the seal-bearer of life, the seal of the gods.

697. Anubis, the judge of hearts, judgeth Osiris Pepi with the gods who belong to the earth and the gods who belong to heaven, the lord of wine in Uakh, counting for him his year, remembering for him his hours. Pepi counteth his year with him, he remembereth his hours with him. Nu cometh, saith Tem. Come to us, say they, say the gods to thee, Osiris. The brother of the Eldest One cometh, the first of his father, the image of his mother. Heaven conceived him, the Ṭuat brought him forth. Heaven conceived this Pepi with him. The Ṭuat brought this Pepi forth with him. Heaven beareth thee up on thy right side with life, and thou livest, by the command of the gods thou livest. Heaven beareth up this Pepi on his right side with life, and he liveth, he liveth, by the command of the gods he

liveth. Thou rulest the earth on thy left side with the sceptre, thou livest, thou livest, by the command of the gods thou livest. Pepi ruleth heaven on his left side with life, and he liveth, he liveth, by the command [of the gods] he liveth. Pepi appeareth on the east side of heaven, he descendeth like a green goose, he descendeth to the Lakes of the Ṭuat. Pepi hath been purified in the Lakes of the Smen Goose.

Osiris Pepi, pass thou not through the Lands of the East, but pass thou through the Lands of the West, by the path of the Followers of Rā. Thy tribute cometh to thee, thy messengers bear unto thee thy dues; thy ancestors march to thee, and they bear thee to Rā, supporting the East on [their] sceptre[s]. Thou knowest them, thou art gracious to them, thou settest them in thy hands, they pasture for thee thy calves. Behold, thou art their conqueror, they come into thy hands. Thou goest forth to them, endowed with soul, provided . . . in thy name of "Smeṭu." Thy Nekhakha whip is in thy hand, thy Mekes sceptre is near thee, those who bow their faces make obeisance unto thee, and the imperishable stars adore thee. Behold, thou art their conqueror, and they make their way into thy hands. Thou bindest their faces in thy name of "Meḥit." They count thee up complete in thy name of "Ȧnpu." The gods do not come down to thee in thy name of 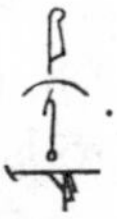. Thou standest upright at the head of the gods, thou eldest son; behold thou art the heir on the throne of Ḳeb.

702. This coming forth of thine, O thou Osiris Pepi, is in thine house. Horus cometh forth embracing thee, O thou Osiris Pepi. Thy tribute cometh to thee, thy messengers bear unto thee thy dues, thy servitors surround thee, they say to Rā: "Behold, Pepi cometh to "thee, the son of Ḳeb, [he who is seated] on the throne "of Ȧmen." Thou sailest over the Lake of Kha, thou traversest the Lake of Kenset. Thou bowest at the east side of heaven, thou takest thy seat in the two Halls of the Horizon. Thou stretchest out thy hand to them, thou stretchest out thine hand to the gods; they give unto thee praises, they come unto thee with bowings of their backs in homage. They praise thee as they

praise Rā, they come with bowings to thee as they do to Rā.

704. Smite, Father, the Bull Sma-ur. Thou smitest, Father, thou slayest the Great Bull. O Father, Osiris Pepi, the Bull is smitten, smitten for thee, smitten for thee, smitten by the Smiter (or, Slaughterer). The Neḳ Bull is smitten for thee, smitten. Thou art upon his back, upon the back of the Bull. Thou openest the Bull with thy weapon. Thou drivest thy lance into the Bull. Thou takest him by the ear. His head is cut off. His tail is cut off. His forelegs are cut off. His haunches are cut off. His haunch is to serve as a haunch before Tem, the father of the gods. His two cheeks (?) are for Shu and Tefnut. His two jaw-bones are for Ḳeb and Nut. His two flanks are for Isis and Nephthys. His two *khentchui* are for Khent-merti and Nest (?). His backbone (?) is for Neith and Serqet. His heart is for Sekhmet-urt. His intestines are for the Four Gods whom Horus brought forth, and who are beloved by him, Ḥep, Åmḳest (?), Ṭuamutef, and Qebhsenuf. His head, his tail, his forelegs, his hind legs, are for Ånpu-ṭep-ṭu and Osiris-Khent-ment-f. The character (?) of the gods is in him, of the Souls of Nekhen, of the Souls of Pe. [He] eateth the red bull, [he] journeyeth on the Lake. Horus hath done [this] for his father Osiris, this Pepi.

Behold, this is thy habitation, Ḥent-ḥet (?), O Osiris Pepi. The winds are brought to it, the north wind is collected therein, and it raiseth thee up in the form of Osiris Pepi. The god Shesmu cometh to thee with water and wine; Khent-ment-f [cometh] with vessels of drink for the Chief of the two Återt-gods. Thou standest up, thou sittest like Ånpu, Chief of Ta-Tchesert. The god Aker standeth up before thee, Shu riseth to meet thee. Ḥep (the Nile) trembleth at the sight [of thee] . . . The pools are full of fragrant flowers, the banks of the canals are covered with blossoms. The offerings of the gods come. Men are glad, and the hearts of the gods rejoice.

709. Pepi cometh to thee, Horus, and thou declarest unto him that great and beautiful word which thou didst utter to Osiris. Pepi becometh great by means of it.

and he becometh mighty thereby. He hath gained possession of his viscera, his BA (heart-soul) is with him, he is prepared with his head, which Horus gave unto Osiris. He is established in heaven as firmly as a mountain [is established in the earth], and is like the support of heaven. He swoopeth down upon heaven like the great crane *āḥāu*, which pursueth his way through the tresses of heaven. The feathers upon his pinions are like unto sharp knives of flint, he giveth to Pepi the nails of his claws. The star Septet (Sothis) graspeth the hand of Pepi. Pepi plougheth the earth, he slaughtereth the captive victim for an offering. The two Nomes of the god roar at Pepi when he advanceth to become the Chief of the gods. He taketh his seat on his crystal (?) throne, and the Āb sceptre which is in his hand [is] crystal. He lifteth up his hand to the children of their fathers, they stand up before him, he layeth his hand upon them, they sit down. His face is like that of the jackal, his interior is like the Nome of Aphroditopolis. He passeth judgment like Sebek, the dweller in Sheṭet, and like Ȧnpu (?), the dweller in Tabet. Pepi crieth out to a thousand (?), and the Ḥenmemet Spirits come to him bowing their backs in homage, and they say unto him: "Who hath done this for thee?" Behold, the Mother of Pepi is the goddess Smat-urt, she who hath long hair, and a headdress of flowing hair, and long, pendent breasts.[1] She beareth Pepi up to heaven, not allowing him to touch the ground, among the glorious gods. Pepi looketh upon their splendour, and himself becometh splendid likewise, Pepi [resembleth] his father Osiris, and the Ḥenmemet Spirits glorify him (or, make him glorious).

Homage to thee, Tem! Homage to thee, Khepher, thou self-created one! Thou art exalted in thy name of "Qa," thou comest into being in thy name of Khepher. Homage to thee, O Eye of Horus! He is equipped with his arms and hands completely. He will not allow thee to be heard by those in the west, he will

1 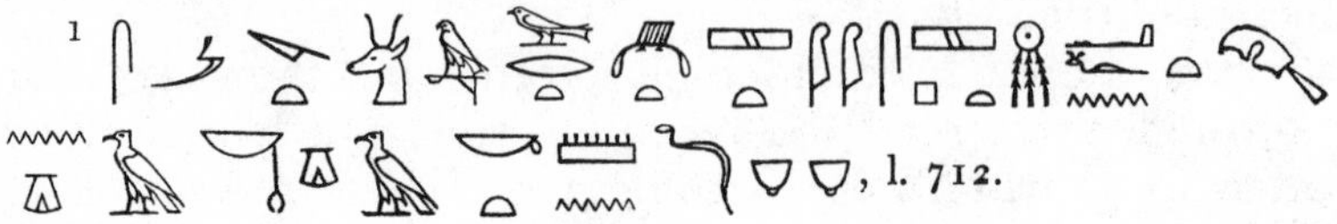, l. 712.

not permit thee to be heard by those in the east, he will not permit thee to be heard by those in the south, he will not permit thee to be heard by those in the north, he will not permit thee to be heard by those in the middle of the earth, [but] thou shalt be heard by Horus. There shall be performed for him everything which he speaketh in every place whither he shall go. Water (?) shall be raised up for him there, water (?) shall be raised up for him when it is there. Thy staff shall be lifted up for him there, thy staff shall be lifted up for him when he is there. Food-offerings shall be raised up for him there, food-offerings shall be raised up for him when he is there. The ḥenket-offerings shall be raised up for him there, they shall be raised up for him when they are there. Everything shall be raised up for him there, and it shall be raised when it is there. He shall be transported to every place wherein he desireth to be. The celestial doors stand [closed] for thee through Ȧnmutf.[1] They shall not open to those in the west, they shall not open to those in the east, they shall not open to those in the north, they shall not open to those in the south, they shall not open to those in the middle of the earth. They shall open to Horus, he worketh them, he maketh them to stand [closed]. He delivereth them from every deadly thing which Set doeth unto them. He holdeth thee fast[2] in thy name of "Ḳer[ḳ]-shet." He conducteth and followeth after thee in thy name of "Nut." He delivereth thee from every deadly thing which Set doeth unto thee. Nut welcometh (?), welcometh (?) thee, Ḳeb hath decreed thee to be welcomed (?) in thy name of "Nut." . . .

Osiris [Pepi], thy mother Nut spreadeth herself over thee in her name of "Shet-pet," she causeth thee to exist as god; no enemy is to thee in thy name of "god"; she protecteth thee against every evil thing in her name of "Khnemet-urt." Thou art the greatest of her children. Osiris [Pepi], thou art the double of all the gods. Horus toucheth thee, and thou becomest his double.

Hail, Ḳeb, this Osiris [Pepi][3] is the son of Shu. Thy

1 . 2 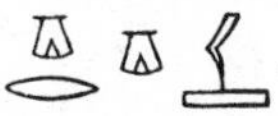. 3 See Mer-en-Rā, l. 126.

mother overfloweth [with love] for thee in thy name of "Ḳeb." Thou art the first-born son of Shu, his image. Hail, Ḳeb, this is the Osiris [Pepi], present thou to him everything which belongeth to him. Thou art the great God, the One alone. Tem hath given unto thee his heirship. The Company of the gods hath given unto thee offerings, and, behold, it is Tem himself who presenteth them to thee, and so maketh an offering to his grandson thyself! He looketh at thee; thou art splendid, thy heart is great. Thou art glorious in thy name of "Re-pān," the hereditary Chief of the gods. Thou standest upon the earth. Thou dost issue thy decrees of doom before the gods. Thy fathers and thy mothers are before them. Thou art the strongest of all the gods. This Osiris cometh to thee, defend thou him against his enemies. Hail, Ḳeb Re-pān, Chief of the gods, the Osiris [Pepi] is thy son. Make thou to live thy son in him. Make thou strong thy son in him. Thou art the Lord of the earth to its uttermost limit. Thou art as strong as the Company of the gods, behold, thou art as every god. Thou art strong, remove thou every evil thing from this Osiris. Delay not, come thou to him in thy name of "Horus, whose work delayeth not." Thou art the Ka of all the gods. Thou bringest them, thou rearest them, thou vivifiest them; vivify thou this Osiris. Thou art God, strong as all the gods. The Eye appeareth from thy head as Urt-ḥekau of the South, the Eye appeareth from thy head as Urt-ḥekau of the North.[1] Horus followeth thee, he loveth thee. Thou art crowned King of the South and North, strong as all the gods and their Doubles also.

Stand up. Give thou thy hand to Horus, he maketh thee to stand up, Ḳeb smiteth for thee thy mouth, the Great Company of the gods "touch" thee. They place Set under thee, his offerings are under thee; they protect thee from him when he spitteth at thee. Nut boweth down over her son in thee, she protecteth thee, she uniteth herself to thee, she embraceth thee, she raiseth thee up, thou art the greatest among her children. Thy two sisters come to thee—Isis and Nephthys—

[1] , l. 129.

they retreat from the place where thou art. Thy sister Isis stretcheth out her hand to thee, she consoleth (?) thee —Kamt-urt—through thy name of Kamt-urt. Thou encirclest everything with thy hand in thy name of "Ṭeben Ḥa-nebu."[1] Thou art mighty through thy name of "Āa-sek."[2] Horus bringeth Set to thee, he giveth him to thee, he (Set) boweth his back before thee, thy strength (or, valour) is greater than his. Horus maketh thee to encircle with thy hand all the gods (*i.e.*, all the gods are in the hollow of thy hand). Horus loveth his father in thee, he permitteth not thee to be injured. Horus is not more wonderful than thou, he avengeth his father in thee. Thou livest with the life of the Beetle (Kheperȧ?), thou art firmly established in Ṭeṭet (Busiris). Isis and Nephthys work protection by magic for thee in the city of Saut,[3] they recognize thee as their lord in thy name of "Neb-Saut," and as their god in thy name of "She-neter." They adore thee; depart not thou from them. Isis cometh to thee rejoicing at thy love. Thy seed entereth her, she becometh heavy with childlike Sepṭ (Sothis). Ḥeru-Sepṭ cometh forth from thee in his name of "Horus in Sepṭet." Thou shinest in him in his name of Khu-ȧm-tchenṭeru.[4] Horus avengeth thee through his name "Horus the son who avengeth his father."

The Father standeth up, and this Osiris [Pepi] standeth up.[5] I am he, thy son. I am Horus. I have come to thee to wash thee, to purify thee, to vivify thee, to knit together thy bones, to collect thy humours, to unite thy hacked flesh. Behold, I am Horus the avenger of his father. I have smitten thee, smitten; I have saved thee, O father Osiris, from the hand of him that would do thee harm. I have come unto thee as the

1 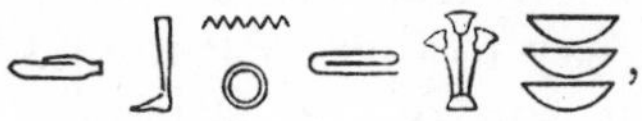, *i.e.*, "Circuit of the Lords of the North," (l. 142).

2 , l. 143.

3 , or .

4 .

5 Mer-en-Rā, l. 446 = Pepi II, l. 1257.

Envoy of Horus, who set thee, O father Osiris, upon the throne of Rā-Tem. Thou guidest the Ḥenmemet Spirits. Thou embarkest in the Boat of Rā, the approach of which the gods love, and they love to embark therein. In it Rā saileth to the horizon, [Pepi] embarketh therein as doth Rā. Thou sittest on the throne of Rā, thou makest decrees for the gods. Thou art Rā appearing on the horizon; Rā is born every day, and [Pepi] is born every day like Rā. Thou hast taken possession of the inheritance of thy father Ḳeb before the gods in Ȧnu (Heliopolis), the Company of the gods consenting, the great and mighty Company of the gods, in the presence of the Souls of Ȧnu. And those two great and mighty gods who are over Sekhet Ȧru set thee upon the throne of Horus, and behold it is they who place Shu on thine east side, Tefnut on thy west side, Nu on thy south side, and Nenet[1] on thy north side. And they lead thee to their beautiful and pure seats (or, places) which they made [ready] for Rā when they set him upon their thrones. They make thee to live more years than those of Ḥeru-khuti, when they made for him the name of "Ḥer-ȧr-neteru" (*i.e.*, "higher than the gods"). They recite for thee this chapter as they do for Rā-Tem as he shineth each day. They set thee upon their thrones at the head of all the gods, even as they do Rā [when] making him to take his seat.[2] They make this [Pepi] to be like Rā, through his name of "KhepVer."[3] Thou advancest towards them as doth Rā through his name of Rā, and thou retreatest from them as doth Rā through his name of "Tem." The Two Companies of the gods rejoice, Father, at their meeting thee, O father Osiris [Pepi], and they say, "Come to us; this is our brother." The Two Companies of the gods say to Osiris [Pepi], "Father Osiris [Pepi], come to us, [thou art] one of us." The Two Companies of the gods say to thee, "Father Osiris [Pepi], come to us, O eldest son of his father." The Two Companies of the gods say to thee, "Father Osiris [Pepi] is the begetter of his mother." The Two Companies of the gods say to thee, "Father Osiris [Pepi], "come thou to us, O thou to whom thy brother Set

1 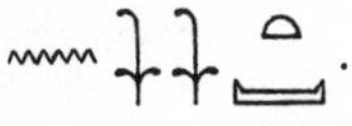 2  3 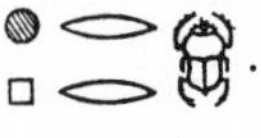

"caused death." The Two Companies of the gods say, "Most assuredly Set cannot make to be a vain thing our exalting of thee for ever, O father Osiris [Pepi]." The Two Companies of the gods say to thee, "Father "Osiris [Pepi], thou art exalted; Father Osiris [Pepi], "thou livest!"

The Eye of Horus is set on the pinion of his brother Set [when] the son of Tem worketh the tackle and maketh the boats to sail together. The son of Tem shall not suffer shipwreck. This [Pepi] belongeth to the son of Tem, the son of Tem shall not suffer shipwreck (Mer-en-Rā, l. 785).

Hail, thou god Ubnenȧ, who revolvest,[1] Kheprer, Khepre, thou art for Pepi, and Pepi is for thee. Thy life is for Pepi, and the life of Pepi is for thee. Hail, Green One, proceeding from the Green Goddess (Uatchet), thou hast proceeded from Pepi, and Pepi hath proceeded from thee. Pepi is strong through thy strength. The god Ḥu[2] is at noon the meat and drink of Pepi, Aḳeb[3] is [his] food in the evening, the food of Pepi. The Heṭṭut apes cannot gain the mastery over the life of Pepi. The town of Sensent[4] is remote from Pepi. Pepi liveth on thine overflow, Pepi is overwhelmed with the great abundance of thy food, O Rā, each day. O Father of Pepi, stand up! Thou hast received thy libations, of the best of the water which cometh forth from Akh-khebit. Those who are in their sepulchres stand up, and turn over your . . . . and measure the grain before thy face (?). Thou risest on thy left side, thou art strong on thy right side. Lift up thy face and see what I have done for thee. I, thy son, thine heir, have trodden (?) the barley, and ploughed the wheat, grain for the Uaḳ festivals, barley for thy offerings of spring plants. The Eye of Horus is presented unto thee, it groweth old before thee, it departeth before thee. O Lord of the House,[5] thy hand is on thy possessions.

1  Pepi II, l. 705.

2 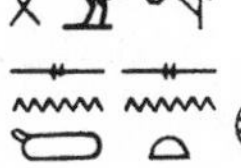

3 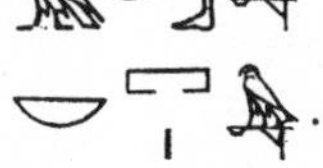

4

5

The[1] doors of heaven open, the doors of the waterways of heaven are unclosed before the gods who dwell in Pe, [when] they come to Osiris Pepi, at the sound of the weeping of Isis, at the noise of the cry of Nephthys, at the wailing of these two Spirits for this great one, which cometh forth from Ṭat (Neṭȧt ?). Get ye gone, O Souls of Pe. They beat their bodies for thee, they smite their hands together for thee, they pluck out their hairs for thee, they beat their thighs for thee, and they say to thee, O Osiris Pepi: "Advance, come, lie down, awake thou, come into port, thou livest. Stand up and behold what thy son hath done for thee. Awake, and hearken thou to what thy son Horus hath done for thee. He hath smitten for thee, smitten the Ox (or, Bull). He hath slain for thee, slain the Sma Bull. He hath bound him with cords for thee, he hath placed him under thy great daughter dwelling in Ḳeṭem. Lamentation is ended (?) at the Ȧterti (temples) of the gods." Osiris saith to Horus: "The evil which appertaineth to Pepi shall exude on the fourth day, he shall not know what hath been done to him on the eighth day." Thou appearest from the Lake of Life, being purified in the Lake of Qebḥ. Thou hast become like Ȧp-uat. Thy son Horus maketh thee advance. He hath given to thee the gods who are thine enemies, Thoth bringeth them to thee. Happy are those who see. Content are those who behold, who see Horus. He giveth life to his divine Father, he maketh great the serenity of Osiris, as Chief of the gods of Ȧmenti. Isis poureth holy water over thee, Nephthys purifieth thee. Thy two great and mighty sisters gather together thy flesh, they raise up thy members, they make thine eyes to appear like crowns in thy head, the Semktet Boat and the Māntchet Boat. Tem is given to thee, the Two Companies of the gods work for thee. The children of thy children[2] lift thee up, viz., Ḥep, Ȧmset, Ṭuamutef, and Qebḥsenuf, and they also make for thee their names. They wash thy face, they collect (?) thy tears, they open thy mouth with their fingers of iron (?). Thou appearest coming forth into the Hall of Tem, thou journeyest to

[1] Pepi II, l. 759 ff.
[2] *I.e.*, grand-children.

the Sekhet-Ȧaru, thou sailest over the seats of the great god. Heaven is given unto thee, earth is given unto thee, Sekhet-Ȧaru is given unto thee. And lo! the two great gods transport thee, Shu and Tefnut, the two great gods of Ȧnu. Awake, stand up! This Spirit came forth from Ṭat, Osiris Pepi cometh forth from Ḳeb. Hail, Pepi! Thou art the son of the great god. Thou hast been purified in the Lake of Tattȧ, thou hast received thy throne in Sekhet-Ȧaru.

805. Thy water is to thee, thine abundance is to thee, thy effluxes are to thee, coming forth from Osiris. Thou collectest thy bones, thou settest in place thy members, thou puttest in order the fluids in thee, thou workest thy cords. The *ḥat* chamber (tomb) is open for thee, the doors of the sarcophagus are drawn asunder, and the gates of heaven are thrown wide open. Isis welcometh thee, Nephthys said, "In Peace" (*i.e.*, welcome). They see their brother at the festival of Tem. These libations, O Osiris, protect thy flesh in Ḳerḳubaf. Thy soul is within thee. Thy Power (sekhem) is nigh thee, thou art stablished as the Chief of thy Powers. Thou art lifted up, Osiris Pepi! Thou rushest upon the Domains of the South, thou rushest upon the Domains of the North. Thou hast the mastery of the Powers which are in thee. Thou makest thy spirits jackals, which are given to thee by Horus of Nekhen. Thou art raised up, O Pepi, sit thou upon thy crystal (?) throne, by the decree of Ȧnpu, Chief of the Divine Hall. Thou art purified with thy eight libations, [and] eight *nemset* vases, and *ȧābet* vases, which came forth from the God-house. God therefore art thou, bearing up heaven on thy shoulders, and supporting the earth. Smentet[1] supplicateth thee, Ment-urt[2] addresseth thee. Hands are turned aside for thee, removed (?) for thee are feet. This appearance of thine is like that of a star, the Morning Star.[3] He cometh to thee, his Father, he cometh to thee, Ḳeb. Take his hand, make his seat to be on the Great Throne. He uniteth with the two Channels (?) of Qebḥu (the

1 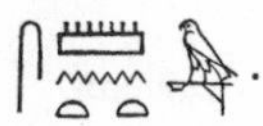

2 

3 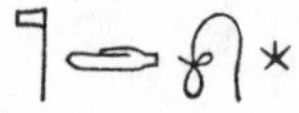

Sky). His mouth is purified with incense and natron on the thighs of Khent-Merti.[1] His nails, upper and lower, are made clean. There hath been done for him that which thou didst do for his brother Osiris on the day of counting up the bones, of making firm sandals, and of sailing over Uārt-urt.[2]

814. The great one boweth over his side, the god standeth up; his power is with him, his Ureret Crown is on him. Pepi boweth over his side, the god Pepi standeth up; his power is with him, his Ureret Crown is on him, as the Ureret Crown is [on] Rā. He cometh forth from the horizon, and . . . in the horizon avengeth him. Hail, Pepi! Thou art raised up. Thou hast received thy seal which the Two Companies of the gods made for thee. Thou art on the throne, in the seat of Khenti Åmenti. Thou hast received his power, thou hast received his Ureret Crown. Hail, Pepi, beautiful and great are these things which thy father Osiris hath done for thee. He hath given thee his throne. Thou makest decrees for those whose places are hidden, thou guidest their noble ones, and all the Spirits follow thee according to their names.

Hail, Pepi, thy heart is glad, great is thy breast, thou shalt never cease to be thus. Rā calleth thee by thy name; all the Spirits fear him. Thou slayest their hearts as doth Rā when he cometh forth from the horizon. Hail, thou Pepi! He whose form is hidden, that is Anubis, [croucheth] on his belly. Thou hast received thy face of a jackal; thou art raised up, stand upright! Sit for thy thousand cakes, thy thousand vessels of beer, thy thousand oxen, thy thousand geese, and thy thousand things whereon the god liveth there. Hail, Pepi, thou art pure. Rā findeth thee, thou standest with my mother Nut, she guideth thee over the roads of the horizon. Thou passest thy day happily with thy Ka for ever and ever.

872. Hail, Åḥmet! Hail, Setemȧ![3] Harm not Pepi,

1 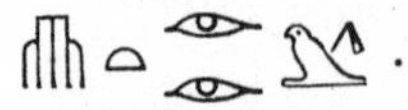

2 A portion of the celestial river or ocean.

3 

injure not Pepi. Strike not the word of power from the hand of Pepi, snatch not away the word of Pepi from the hand of Pepi. Thy word of power is to Pepi, the word of power of Pepi is to him.

950. O Mighty Heaven, give the hand to Pepi. O Great Sky, give the hand to Pepi. Pepi is thy divine hawk. Pepi cometh, he appeareth in heaven, he cleaveth Qebḥu (*i.e.*, the sky). Pepi doeth homage to his father Rā, he ministereth to him like Horus, Pepi cometh to him. Rā maketh Pepi to rise a new being. He establisheth for Pepi his two eyes.[1] Pepi cometh before him, great like Horus of Nu, with the lock of hair, he smiteth the Crowns of the North,[2] he issueth decrees to the Utennu.[3] The Āfa gods[4] follow in the train of Pepi, and those who are at the head of heaven and earth come to him with bowings of homage, and the Two Uraei, and the Jackals and the Spirits, and the Set-gods, upper and lower,[5] act as guides to him. Anointed with perfume, arrayed in *pat*, and living on offerings, Pepi issueth decrees, putteth the Doubles under a yoke, and occupieth the thrones. Pepi giveth offerings, Pepi conducteth ceremonies of offerings, Pepi himself is the ONE of heaven, the master of what he doeth, Chief of Nent.[6]

953. Homage to thee, Pepi, saith Seker. Wash thy face, saith the Great Morning Star (?).[7] Pepi swoopeth down like the divine hawk. Pepi entereth the water like the great crane. Pepi maketh a noise like the Smen goose. The pinions of Pepi are like those of the divine hawk, and the tips of the pinions of Pepi are like those of the divine hawk. The bones of Pepi are lifted up; he is pure. The loin-cloth of Pepi is about his loins. The *qenȧ* garment is on his shoulders, and his girdle is attached to his tunic (?). Pepi embarketh with Rā in

1 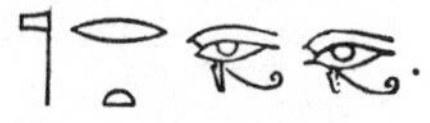

2 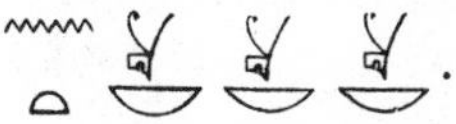

3 

4 

5  , l. 951.

6 

7 

his Great Boat, and he worketh it on with him to the horizon to issue decrees to the gods therein. Horus roweth with him in the Great Boat to the horizon. Pepi issueth decrees to the gods therein with him in the horizon, Pepi is one of them.

955. Behold the things which they say concerning Pepi, what the gods say concerning Pepi, the words which the gods speak concerning Pepi: "This is Horus coming out of Ḥep (the Nile). This is the Neḳa bull coming forth from the walled camp. This is the serpent which cometh forth from Rā. This is the uraeus which cometh forth from Set. Everything happeneth for Pepi even as it happeneth for the goddess Metcheṭet-ȧt,[1] the daughter of Rā, who is on the knees of Rā. Everything happeneth for Pepi even as it happeneth for the goddess Metcha,[2] the daughter of Rā, on the knees of Rā. Behold, Pepi is the god Utcha,[3] the son of Utcha, the issue of Utchat.[4] Strong is Pepi, strong is Pepi, strong is the Eye of Horus in Ȧnu. Pepi liveth, Pepi liveth, the Eye of Horus liveth in Ȧnu. Pepi cometh forth as thou comest forth, Osiris. Pepi speaketh to his Double in heaven. The bones of Pepi are crystal, the flesh of Pepi is like the imperishable stars.[5] If Pepi be set there the Great Goddess boweth herself over the arms of Pepi. The mother of Pepi is Nut. The father or Pepi is Shu, the mother of Pepi is Tefnut, they raise Pepi to heaven on the flame of incense. Purified is Pepi, living is Pepi; moreover, he maketh his seat to be Osiris. Pepi sitteth on thy arm, Osiris, Pepi spitteth on thy hair.

959. Pepi is one of those four [gods] who are the children of Tem, the children of Nut. They do not suffer corruption, Pepi doth not suffer corruption. They decay not, Pepi decayeth not. They do not fall to the earth from heaven, Pepi doth not fall to the earth from heaven. They embrace Pepi, they find Pepi with them,

1 

2 

3 

4 

5 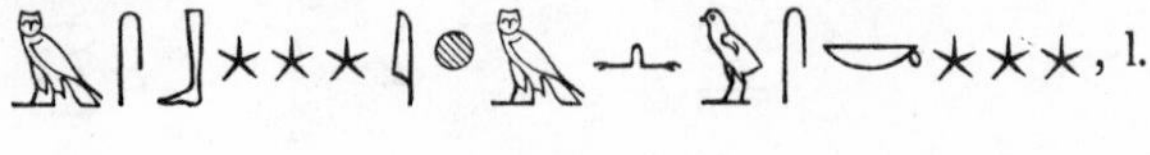, l. 957.

Pepi is one of them, a favoured one of the Bull of Heaven, Pepi raiseth up his Ka, maketh [it] turn back, maketh [it] stay [with him]. O beautiful warder, raise up the Ka, make [it] turn back, make [it] stay [with him]. Therefore is Pepi stable under the constellation [called] the "Belly of the Sky"[1] in the form of a beautiful star [shining] over the bends of the Lake of Kha. Pepi cometh forth into the sky, thou givest to Pepi this Chapter, he is happy with Rā every day. Pepi setteth himself on thy way, O Ḥeru-shest,[2] along which thou guidest the gods to the beautiful ways of the sky [and] of Sekhet-ḥetep.

968. The water of life cometh into heaven, the water of life cometh on the earth. The sky catcheth fire before thee, the earth quaketh before thee, at the hands of the Children of God. The two mountains are cleft, the god appeareth, and the god hath the mastery over his own body. The two mountains are cleft, Pepi appeareth, and Pepi hath the mastery over his own body. Behold, Pepi breatheth the air. His feet stand by the pure water which is with Tem, and which hath been produced by the phallus of Shu and the body of Tefnut,[3] for they have come and brought to thee the pure water which is with their father [Tem]. They purify thee [therewith]. They cense thee, Pepi. Thou liftest up the sky on the palm of thy hand, thou placest the earth under thy sandal. There is a laver of the water of heaven at the door of this Pepi, [wherein] each god washeth [his] face. Thou washest thy hands therein, O Osiris, thou washest thy hands therein, O Pepi, and thou renewest thy youth, the third god (?),

[1] Compare 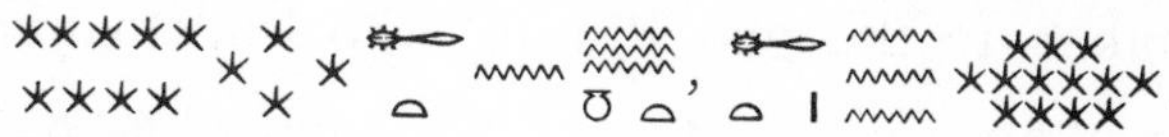, and , *i.e.*, the "House of the Thirteen Stars," or the "House of the Eight Stars," which are the names given to the 29th Dekan in one of the Lists published by Brugsch, *Thes.*, p. 146.

[2] 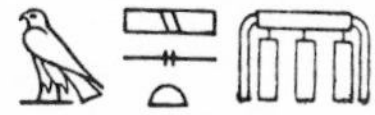, l. 961.

[3] , l. 970.

Utchu-ḥetep.[1] The smell of the things of the uraeus cometh to Pepi, as do the pyramidal loaf in Ḥet-Seker and the thigh in the House of Ȧnpu. Pepi is strong, the shrine standeth ready, the month is born, the nome is alive, and the towing cords are worked; thou ploughest for wheat, thou ploughest for barley. Gifts are made to Pepi there for ever.

971. Unguent of Horus! Unguent of Set! Horus taketh possession of his Eye, and delivereth it from his enemies; Set hath not been able to keep it [from him]. When Horus hath filled his Eye with the unguent he is content with (or, resteth on) his Eye; he is provided with his . . . ., he joineth himself to it, its odour is with him. Its violent wrath falleth upon his enemies. This unguent is to Pepi, he hath filled himself therewith, he hath united himself thereto, and its odour is on him; its violent wrath shall fall on the enemies of Pepi.

974. These four Divine Kinsmen[2] of Pepi, Amḳest, Ḥep, Ṭuamutef, and Qebḥsenuf, children of Horus of Sekhem (Letopolis), stand up, and they bind with bands the Ladder of Pepi, and they make permanent the Ladder of Pepi, and they make Pepi to approach the god Khepre,[3] when he cometh into being in the eastern sky. The god Ȧshsamer (?)[4] hath shaped with an adze the wood. The god Ḳas...ut,[5] the Bull of Heaven, hath fastened firmly with knots the leathers (?) belonging to it. The rungs have been firmly fixed in the sides by means of the [leather made of] the skin of the god . . . .[6] born of the goddess Ḥesat.[7] The goddess Sepeḥ-urt[8] maketh it to be set up by a band under it. The Ka of Pepi is raised up [by this Ladder] to the god, and he is taken to the god Rurutȧ[9] who leadeth him forward to

[1] 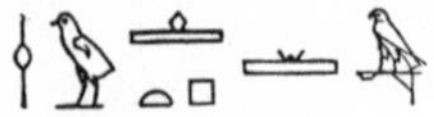, l. 971.

[2] 

[3] 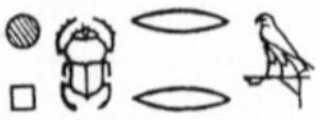

[4] 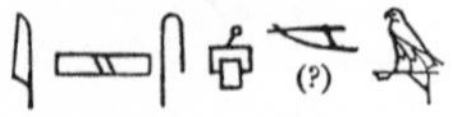

[5] , l. 975.

[6] , l. 976.

[7] 

[8] 

[9] 

Tem. Tem hath done what he said he would do for Pepi ; he hath tied bands for him about the Ladder, and he hath made it strong for Pepi. This Pepi is remote from that which is an abomination to men, and he shall not handle that which is an abomination to the gods, he shall not eat that which is . . . ., he shall not lie down [in death ?] in the night, he shall not keep vigil. He is not without his body like one of the two growths (?) of Kheprer. The bodies of those who are in Ṭat are reckoned up, and their ears are open to the voice of Pepi. He goeth down among them, reciting the decree of Sekhmef (?). The existence of Pepi is like that of one who is among them. The staff (?) of Pepi is among them like the god of the Great Staff,[1] making his advance to Åm-urt. The seal of Pepi is in the House of Rurutȧ. The god who obliterateth sin, Åṭer-ȧsfet,[2] obliterateth the transgressions which belong to Pepi in the presence of Khenti-merti in Sekhem.[3]

1 .

2 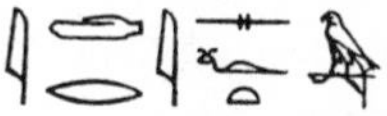.

3 , l. 980.

ADDITIONAL NOTES

1. The Creation.—The Bushongo legend is as follows :—In the beginning there was nothing but darkness, and on the earth there was nothing but water ; in this chaos Bumba, the Chembe (God, = the Egyptian Tem), reigned alone. Bumba had the form of a huge man, and his colour was white. One day, owing to pains in his stomach, he vomited, and the sun, moon, and stars were the result. The water ran off the sand and left it dry, but there was neither vegetation nor animal life upon it. Bumba again vomited and brought up : 1. The leopard, Koy Bumba ; 2. The crested eagle, Ponga Bumba ; 3. The crocodile, Ganda Bumba ; 4. A little fish, Yo Bumba ; 5. The tortoise, Kono Bumba ; 6. The thunderbolt (a black animal like a leopard), Tsetse Bumba ; 7. A white heron, Nyanyi Bumba ; 8. A scarab ; 9. A goat. He afterwards vomited men, but there was only one of them white like himself, and he called him Loko Yima. The creatures mentioned above produced all the other creatures which filled the world. Nyonye Ngana, a son of Bumba, vomited the white ants, and died. Another son, Chonganda, vomited a plant which was the parent of all vegetation, and a third son vomited kites, but nothing else. King Bumba made Loko Yima "god upon earth" (Chembe Kunji), and then ascended into heaven. Torday and Joyce, *Notes Ethnographiques*, p. 21.

2. The Soul.—The Bambala think that man is composed of four elements : Lo, the body ; Ilo, the double (Ka) ; N'shanga, the soul ; and Lume-Lume, the shadow. The Bushongo also think that man is composed of four elements : Modyo, the body ; Mophuphu, the soul ; Ido, the double (Ka) ; and Edidingi, the shadow. Torday and Joyce, *Notes Ethnographiques*, p. 124.

3. The Amulet of "Life," ☥.—It has already been shown in this book that two of the most important

amulets of the Egyptians, 𓊽 and 𓎬, represent the *os sacrum* of Osiris, and the uterus and its ligatures and vagina of Isis. They symbolized the vital power of Osiris and Isis, procreation, new birth, fecundity, and resurrection. Hence we find them, with appropriate formulae, in the Book of the Dead, and on coffins we see frequently one hand grasping 𓊽 and the other 𓎬, *i.e.*, the fetishes which held the spirits of life-power of Osiris and Isis. There is, however, another amulet, *i.e.*, 𓋹, which has, up to the present, defied all explanation. That it was of vital importance to the living and the dead is proved by its frequent occurrence on the monuments and in papyri. About its meaning "life" there is no doubt, but the identity of the object is difficult to discover. Now as the Ṭeṭ, 𓊽, represents the *os sacrum* of Osiris, and the *thet*, 𓎬, represents the uterus and vagina of Isis, it is only natural to think that the sign 𓋹 also represents some part or organ of the body either of Osiris or Isis, and preferably some member of the body of Isis. As 𓋹 is intimately connected in the vignette of Chapter XVI of the Book of the Dead with the rising sun, and was presented to Isis by Åmen-Rā (see Vol. I, p. 301), when she was giving birth to Horus, it is clearly associated with new life and childbirth and, one would think, with the womb of Isis, or with something in it which was connected closely with the growth of the foetus. Reference has already been made to the importance attached to the umbilical cord by modern Sûdânî peoples (for the passages, see the Index), and to the disposal of the placenta, and analogy suggests that the primitive Egyptians attached as much importance to these objects as to the uterus itself. I discussed the matter with Dr. W. L. Nash, and he informs me that the sign 𓋹 may well be a conventional representation of the placenta and umbilical cord as they appear after they have left the body, the oval loop of the sign being intended for the placenta, the projections at the side for ligatures, and the straight line below for the umbilical cord. The placenta and the umbilical cord taken together would make a very powerful fetish, of the same character as 𓊽 and 𓎬, and I believe them to be the objects represented by the sign ☥, or "life." If this be so, 𓊽, 𓎬 and ☥ were fetishes, in the truest sense of the word, of the same class. Since writing the above, Messrs. Seligmann and Murray have published a paper in *Man*, Vol. XI, No. 8, p. 113 ff., in which they attempt to show that the sign 𓄹 also represents the uterus of Isis, and hence was associated with childbirth. If this be so, the ancient Egyptian ideas connected with 𓎬, ☥ and 𓄹 were all transferred by the Christian Egyptians to the Cross.

INDEX

Åaat, Åaata, a staff, II, 322, 325.
Aābet vases, II, 357.
Åāḥ, Moon-god, I, 389; II, 62.
Åaḥes, god, I, 76; II, 311.
Åakhu (Spirit-soul), II, 132, 315.
Aal (see also Åar), field of, I, 97.
Āamu, II, 163.
Åār, I, 71.
Åar, Åaru, field of, I, 97, 126; II, 338.
Aaru, lake of, I, 129.
Åaru, marshes of, I, 103.
Āa-sek, II, 353.
Aasu, I, 145.
Åat (domain) of Horus, I, 98; of Kheper-Rā, I, 44; of Osiris and Set, I, 98.
Åats (domains) of Horus and Set, II, 160, 307.
Åats, the Fourteen, II, 160.
Åats, the Fifteen, I, 99.
Åaṭa, II, 308.
Aaṭi, I, 341.
Åat-tcha-Mut, II, 54.
Āb, I, 58.
Åb flowers, II, 326.
Åb (heart), II, 130, 137.
Āb, Āba, sceptre, II, 319, 325, 350.
Åbå, an official, I, 307.
Āba-åner, II, 178, 214.
Ababua, I, 375; II, 89, 110, 242.
Ababua Babati, I, 326.
Abâka, I, 226.
Abambo, I, 298, 365; II, 152.
Abarambo, I, 179; II, 88.
'Abd al-Laṭîf, quoted, I, 177, 195; II, 93.
Abiala, goddess, I, 295.
Abôk, I, 375.
Abomey, I, 227; II, 243.
Abonsŭm, I, 371.
Absolutism of king, II, 161.
Abstinence, II, 176.
Ābt vessels, the four, II, 332.
Åbṭu (Abydos), I, 53, 67, 149, 153; II, 66.
Abtu (victims), I, 220.
Abu (Elephantine), II, 319.
Abû Beshr, I, 286.
Abû Dọm, I, 247.
Abû Tamara, I, 285.
Abukaya, I, 226.
Ābut sceptres, I, 166.
Abydos, town of, I, 31, 34, 37, 39, 46, 53, 66, 67, 81, 149, 153, 159, 197, 212, 214, 254, 279, 290, 354, 379; II, 1–4, 8, 18, 44, 57, 69, 75, 83, 156, 157, 270, 313, 331.
Abydos, canal of, II, 12.
Abydos, ceremonies of Osiris at, I, 289.
Abydos, relic chamber of, II, 13.
Abydos, Ṭeṭ of, I, 6.
Abydos, well of, II, 12.
Abyssinia, I, 30, 362; II, 68, 223, 270.
Abyssinian burial, II, 114.
Acaju plant, II, 104.
Acanthus, grove of, II, 13.
Accra, II, 223.

Apollodorus, I, 210.
Apostles, I, 354.
Apparel of Osiris, II, 5.
Apron, II, 208.
Āpshait, II, 171.
Åp-shet-pet, II, 341.
Åptet (Ombos), II, 55.
Åpts, II, 74.
Åpt-uat, I, 139.
Åpu (Panopolis), II, 55.
Åp-uat, I, 77, 103, 123, 166, 197, 247, 288, 289; II, 5, 6, 159, 312, 316, 331, 333, 337, 340, 356.
Åp-uat gods, II, 2.
Apuleius quoted, II, 287.
Åqa, I, 103; II, 312.
Āq-er-pet (ladder), II, 339.
Åqert, I, 43, 142; II, 56.
Åqeru, I, 142; II, 256.
Ara = thunderclap, I, 373.
Arab, Arabs, I, 192, 298, 391; II, 159, 209.
Arab burial, II, 113.
Arabia, I, 11, 321; II, 222, 280, 285.
Arabia Felix, I, 10.
Archangels, I, 368.
Arek, II, 317.
Argos, II, 286.
Argus, II, 295.
Åri-em-åb-f, I, 342.
Arii, II, 288.
Arithmetic invented, I, 10.
Aristocracy of Ṭuat, II, 160.
Aristotle, II, 237.
Ari Umker, I, 376.
Armant, II, 239.
Arms of Horus destroyed, I, 62.
Army of Osiris, I, 11.
Arnold, Mr. C., II, 159.
Arnot, Dr., II, 187.
Aro sacrifice, I, 227.
Arrogance, I, 342.
Arrows of death, II, 37; poisoned, I, 180; shot at funeral, II, 86.
Arsinoë, Crocodilopolis, II, 239.
Åru country, I, 146.
Aruwimi, I, 292; II, 141, 191, 257; burial, II, 109.
A-Sande, II, 222.
Åsår (Osiris), I, 24, 27, 67.
Åsår-Åāh, I, 21.
Åsår-Ānkhti, II, 16.
Åsår-bati-Erpit, II, 16.
Åsår-Ḥep (Sarapis), I, 60, 61; II, 272.
Åsår-Ḥepi, I, 398.
Åsår-ḥer-åb-Set, II, 16.
Åsår-Khenti-Amenti, II, 15.
Åsår Khenti Peḳu, II, 16.
Åsår Khenti peru, II, 16.
Åsår Khenti Restau, II, 16.
Åsår Khenti Un, II, 16.
Åsår neb-ānkh, II, 16.
Åsår Neb-er-tcher, II, 16.
Åsår nub-ḥeḥ, II, 16.
Åsår Ptaḥ-neb-ānkh, II, 16.
Åsår-Saa, II, 16.
Åsår-Saḥ, II, 16.
Åsår Taiti, II, 17.
Åsår Un-nefer, II, 16.
Ås-åri, I, 24, 27.
Asen, I, 300.
Åsert-tree, 1, 103.
Ashanti, I, 181, 222, 227, 228, 229, 372; II, 92, 266.
Āshem, I, 121.
Ashiga (net hunting), II, 242.
Ashsamer, god, II, 362.
Ashtoreth, I, 5; II, 285.
Asia Minor, II, 285.
Asinius Marcellus, II, 304.
Asista, I, 382; II, 186.
Asken, II, 313, 323.
Aso, Queen, I, 3.